Cognitive Technologies

Titles in this series now included in the Thomson Reuters Book Citation Index and Scopus!

The Cognitive Technologies (CT) series is committed to the timely publishing of high-quality manuscripts that promote the development of cognitive technologies and systems on the basis of artificial intelligence, image processing and understanding, natural language processing, machine learning and human-computer interaction.

It brings together the latest developments in all areas of this multidisciplinary topic, ranging from theories and algorithms to various important applications. The intended readership includes research students and researchers in computer science, computer engineering, cognitive science, electrical engineering, data science and related fields seeking a convenient way to track the latest findings on the foundations, methodologies and key applications of cognitive technologies.

The series provides a publishing and communication platform for all cognitive technologies topics, including but not limited to these most recent examples:

- Interactive machine learning, interactive deep learning, machine teaching
- Explainability (XAI), transparency, robustness of AI and trustworthy AI
- Knowledge representation, automated reasoning, multiagent systems
- Common sense modelling, context-based interpretation, hybrid cognitive technologies
- Human-centered design, socio-technical systems, human-robot interaction, cognitive robotics
- Learning with small datasets, never-ending learning, metacognition and introspection
- Intelligent decision support systems, prediction systems and warning systems
- Special transfer topics such as CT for computational sustainability, CT in business applications and CT in mobile robotic systems

The series includes monographs, introductory and advanced textbooks, state-of-the-art collections, and handbooks. In addition, it supports publishing in Open Access mode.

Alejandro Peña-Ayala
Editor

Self-Regulated Learning

Development, Advances and Future Trends—Empowering Learners to Accomplish Better Academic Results

Springer

Editor
Alejandro Peña-Ayala
WOLNM and IPN, ESIME-Z,
SEPI, Z-4, 2 piso
Unidad Profesional Adolfo López Mateos
Zacatenco, Gustavo A. Madero
Ciudad de México, Mexico

ISSN 1611-2482 ISSN 2197-6635 (electronic)
Cognitive Technologies
ISBN 978-981-92-0657-5 ISBN 978-981-92-0658-2 (eBook)
https://doi.org/10.1007/978-981-92-0658-2

This Springer imprint is published by the registered company Springer Nature Singapore Pte Ltd.
The registered company address is: 152 Beach Road, #21-01/04 Gateway East, Singapore 189721, Singapore

Preface

The advent of *4th Industrial Revolution* represents the global emergence of disruptive scientific and technological advances that transform the human sceneries and activities at home, school, market, industry, and services. In consequence, people as visionaries, pioneers, developers, manufactures, marketers, consumers, and users must engage with this trend to fully benefit from it; otherwise, they risk falling behind in the evolution of contemporary society.

At present, 21st Century Education across K-12, Higher Education (HE), and Lifelong learning should rise to the challenge of instilling in students relevant and up-to-date knowledge from all disciplines (particularly science, technology, engineering, arts, and mathematics "STEAM"), equipping educators with technology enhanced learning (TEL) literacy to master personalized pedagogies and digital resources to transform teaching practices in classroom and distance settings, and cultivating and refining students' psychomotor skills to easily assimilate knowledge, achieve meaningful learning, and reach the expertise demanded by the labor market for professional success.

To attain the last purpose, 21st Century Skills emerge as the paradigm that fosters students' mental and behavioral attitudes and faculties to facilitate formal, informal, and non-formal learning. This paradigm encompasses various soft skills and dispositions, including communication, social and cross-cultural competences, collaboration, creativity and innovation, critical thinking, problem-solving, metacognition, and self-regulation. Although there is a general consensus that these skills are essential for all learners, concerns exist regarding how teachers can help students learn these skills, and how to embed such skills into the academic knowledge being taught in schools and online environments.

In this context, *self-regulated learning* (SRL) represents a 21st Century Skill in vogue that is conceptualized as: the cognitive and behavioral paradigm that empowers students to consciously direct their mental processes, comportment, and interactions in educational settings. SRL relies on various branches of psychology primarily cognitive and educational psychology, whose kernel is self-regulation that involves goal-directed behavior and exercising control over oneself in line with preferred standards. SRL's early works date back to the 1980s; since then, researchers have focused on defining its foundations, models, methods, and approaches to support new theoretical developments and practical applications.

With this in mind, Springer Book Series in Cognitive Technologies presents this edited volume to contribute to the expansion of the SRL field by encouraging novel research, presenting recent advancements, highlighting outcomes, broadening the scope of practices, and identifying future trends, thereby enabling learners to achieve enhanced academic performance. Consequently, the literature is intended for education management professionals, educators, pedagogues, cognitive and behavioral scientists, and postgraduate students seeking to acquire a conceptual, formal, and practical perspective on how to use, develop, and deploy SRL to personalize education, enhance teaching, and improve learning.

To meet these expectations, this volume compiles a sample of the work recently completed by eight research groups from three continents, who are committed to contributing to the expansion of the SRL domain, by proposing sound constructs, describing relevant frameworks, and sharing valuable experiences that encourage to guide future projects and practices. The quality of the publication is assured by the editorial process, which involved an extensive "call for chapters", the submission of abstract proposals and their subsequent assessment. Those approved were expanded into full chapters, which were then rigorously evaluated by experts to recommend enhancements and determine their inclusion in the volume. As a result, this book comprises eight chapters, whose summaries are outlined as follows:

Chapter 1: Aiming to enable students to apply strategies, achieve goals, match their learning pace to individual's learning needs, *personalization* acts as the driver for instilling SRL through artificial intelligence and digital tools, creating adaptive academic settings tailored to student preferences;

Chapter 2: In pursuit of the *universality of SRL in TEL scenarios*, this study uses a person-centered approach to examine whether relationships hold across diverse learner profiles, where latent profile analysis is used to identify SRL disposition profiles and explores their links to epistemic learning dispositions;

Chapter 3: The description of basic learners' attitudes, cognitive skills, behaviors, social interactions, and use of resources to learn across diverse domains, is made through a *learner SRL model* designed as a three-tier architecture depicting soulful, leading, and scenery functionalities, agents, and features;

Chapter 4: With the goal of assessing the effect of role models on the learners' SRL progress during direct and indirect learning experiences, four studies were conducted to identify their impact on the SRL skills of middle school, high school, and HE students by comparing the results with existing literature;

Chapter 5: The development of SRL in secondary education, as a student-centered pedagogy, is fostered through peer observation guides and group discussions, which provide feedback and identify strengths and improvements that support the forethought, performance and self-reflection phases of SRL;

Chapter 6: As some undergraduates present specific learning disabilities (SLD), this work examines SRL dimensions to find that working memory and processing speed act as proximal constraints on SRL; specifically, the former predicts SRL for all students, and the latter predicts SRL within the SLD group;

Chapter 7: From the view of SRL in TEL settings, it is applied the Technology Acceptance Model and the Attitude and Motivation Test Battery to assess the influence of personal perceptions and affections on dual-focus engagement of the semantic content and linguistic input to predict learning outcomes; and

Chapter 8: This work explores the use of SRL strategies by HE learners for collaborative academic writing, gathering and examining empirical evidence through semi-structured interviews, learning artifacts, and thematic analysis to find students optimized forethought, performance, and self-reflection phases.

As Guest-Editor of this volume, I express my gratitude to authors, reviewers, and the Springer Editorial board and team, where participate: Series Editor *Prof. Dr.-Ing. Daniel Sonntag*; as well as *Nick Zhu*, Senior Editor and *Rachel Zhang*, Editorial Assistant. All of them developed a valuable collaboration to accomplish the edition of this book.

Furthermore, I recognize that the idea to develop this edited book emerged when I was a visiting scholar at Stanford University (2023–2024), where James L. McClelland—Lucie Stern Professor in the Social Sciences—hosted me and facilitated useful discussions about the SRL domain in the Department of Psychology and the Center for the Neural Basis of Cognition.

Moreover, I also recognize the support given by the Secretaría de Ciencia, Humanidades, Tecnología e Innovación (SECIHTI) and the Instituto Politécnico Nacional (IPN), both institutions pertain to the Mexican Federal Government, which provided the following grants: SECIHTI-SNII-CVU-201000-36453, IPN-COFAA-SIBE-2025-2026, IPN-SIP-EDI-2026-2028, and the research projects IPN DG24 2023-342-1-8 Sabbatical Year, IPN-SIP-2026-0613.

Last but not least, I express a testimony of the unction and strength given by my *Father*, *Brother Jesus*, and *Helper*, as part of the research projects performed by World Outreach Light to the Nations Ministries (WOLNM), and dedicate this work to the cherished memory of my mother, *María Teresa Ayala-Tinoco.*

Ciudad de México, Mexico
April 2026

Alejandro Peña-Ayala

Contributors (Reviewers)

Amr Adel AbdElRehim ElSayed Lecturer, Arab Academy for Science, Technology and Maritime Transport, College of Management and Technology, Business Information Systems Department, Arab Academy for Science

Sonja Berger Research Associate, Chair of Educational Psychology, LMU Munich, Germany

Jung Ah Choi Associate Professor, School of General Education, Kumoh National Institute of Technology, South Korea

Penny Van Deur Full Academic Status, Flinders University, Australia

Lorraine Graham Professor of Learning Intervention, The University of Melbourne, Australia

Lyn Corno Herbert Education and Psychology (Retired) Teachers College, Columbia University, Dartmouth, MA, USA

Nida Husna Lecturer, State Islamic University, Jakarta, Indonesia

Michael J. Lawson Researcher, Flinders University of South Australia, Australia

Donatella Persico Associated researcher and Emeritus Professor, University, Institute for Educational Technology, National Research Council of Italy, Italy

Uaiana Prates Invited Professor at the Univeridade Aberta, Researcher at the Distance Education and E-Learning Laboratory, Universidade Aberta, Portugal

Chee Wei Tan Associate Professor, Nanyang Technological University, Singapore

Quincy Q. Wang Research Intelligence and Knowledge Mobilization Officer, Faculty of Education. Simon Fraser University, Canada

Jianhua Zhang Professor. Sichuan University of Arts and Science, New Zealand

Contributors (Authors)

Karla Marlen Álvarez-Olvera ESIME-Zacatenco, Instituto Politécnico Nacional, Unidad Profesional Adolfo López Mateos, Gustavo A. Madero, CDMX, México

Oktay Bektaş Education Faculty, Mathematics and Science Education, Erciyes University, Kayseri, Türkiye

Ana Eloisa Carvalho Centre for Research and Intervention in Education (CIIE), University of Porto, Porto, Portugal

Thiago Freires Centre for Research and Intervention in Education (CIIE), University of Porto, Porto, Portugal

Bas Giesbers Department of Educational Research and Development, School of Business and Economics, Maastricht University, Maastricht, The Netherlands

Mingyue Michelle Gu Graduate School, The Education University of Hong Kong, Tai Po, Hong Kong

Lihang Guan School of Foreign Languages, Ludong University, Zhifu District, Yantai, Shandong, China

Kevin Kien Hoa Chung Department of Early Childhood Education, The Education University of Hong Kong, Hong Kong; Centre for Child and Family Science, The Education University of Hong Kong, Hong Kong

Melek Karaca Independent Researcher, Izmir, Türkiye

Abílio Lourenço Institute of Education, University of Minho, Braga, Portugal

James L. McClelland Department of Psychology and Center for the Neural Basis of Cognition, 450 Jane Stanford Way, Bldg. 420, Stanford University, 94305, CA, USA

Alejandro Peña-Ayala Artificial Intelligence on Education Lab, WOLNM; ESIME-Zacatenco, Instituto Politécnico Nacional, Unidad Profesional Adolfo López Mateos, Gustavo A. Madero, CDMX, México; Department of Psychology and Center for the Neural Basis of Cognition, 450 Jane Stanford Way, Bldg. 420, Stanford University, 94305, CA, USA

Daniela Pinto Centre for Research and Intervention in Education (CIIE), University of Porto, Porto, Portugal

Bart Rienties Institute of Educational Technology, The Open University, Milton Keynes, UK

Antonio Romero-Hernández ESIME-Zacatenco, Instituto Politécnico Nacional, Unidad Profesional Adolfo López Mateos, Gustavo A. Madero, CDMX, México; UPIICSA, Instituto Politécnico Nacional, Te 950, Granjas México, Iztacalco, CDMX, México

Dirk Tempelaar Department of Quantitative Economics, School of Business and Economics, Maastricht University, Maastricht, The Netherlands

Ana Cristina Torres Centre for Research and Intervention in Education (CIIE), University of Porto, Porto, Portugal

Sabina Valente CARE—Research Centre in Health and Social Sciences, Portalegre Polytechnic University, Portalegre, Portugal; Research Centre in Education and Psychology (CIEP), University of Évora, Évora, Portugal

Candradewi Wahyu Anggraeni English Education Department, Universitas Tidar, Magelang, Indonesia

Li-Chih Wang Department of Special Education and Counselling, The Education University of Hong Kong, Hong Kong; Integrated Centre for Wellbeing at The Education University of Hong Kong, Hong Kong

Contents

Part I
Personalization in Self-Regulated Learning

Chapter 1
Personalization in Self-Regulated Learning: Educational Technologies and Artificial Intelligence as Key Facilitators

Abílio Lourenço and Sabina Valente

Abstract Personalized learning is fundamental for strengthening self-regulated learning, enabling students to adapt strategies, goals, and pace to individual needs. This chapter highlights digital tools and artificial intelligence as key facilitators of personalized, self-regulated learning, emphasizing their role in developing adaptive environments tailored to students. It examines the challenge of implementing personalized and self-regulated pedagogies across diverse contexts, from traditional to digitally limited environments, focusing on inclusive and flexible approaches that optimize engagement and success. Drawing on empirical evidence and theoretical frameworks, the chapter explores how AI-based adaptive systems and learning analytics support personalization, promoting autonomy, motivation, and self-regulatory skills. The results demonstrate the benefits of technology-mediated self-regulated learning, such as enhanced academic performance and metacognitive skills development. Relevant ethical considerations and the necessity of teacher training are discussed to ensure the effective, equitable use of educational technologies, fostering accessibility and reducing digital inequalities. Integrating personalization with technology-supported self-regulated learning leads to more effective and sustainable academic outcomes, reinforcing the pivotal role of ICT and artificial intelligence in educational innovation. This chapter proposes an innovative conceptual framework in which the articulation between personalization, educational data analytics, and self-regulatory processes is understood as a catalyst for inclusive, technology-driven, and ethically-informed teaching practices.

A. Lourenço (✉)
Institute of Education, University of Minho, Braga, Portugal

S. Valente
CARE – Research Centre in Health and Social Sciences, Portalegre Polytechnic University, Portalegre, Portugal

Research Centre in Education and Psychology (CIEP), University of Évora, Évora, Portugal

S. Valente
e-mail: svalente@ipportalegre.pt

A. Peña-Ayala (ed.), *Self-Regulated Learning*, Cognitive Technologies,
https://doi.org/10.1007/978-981-92-0658-2_1

Keywords Adaptive teaching · Artificial intelligence · Educational technology · Learning strategies · Metacognition · Motivation · Personalisation · Self-regulated learning

Abbreviations

AI	Artificial intelligence
ICT	Information and communication technologies
SRL	Self-regulated learning

1.1 Introduction

In contemporary educational landscapes, self-regulated learning (SRL) is indispensable due to the shifting demands of knowledge acquisition and student diversity. Digital platforms have transformed how students learn, elevating SRL from a useful skill to a central pillar for academic autonomy and lifelong competence (Hassan et al., 2022; Lämsä et al., 2025). SRL involves the systematic activation, monitoring, and regulation of thoughts, behaviors, and emotions to reach learning goals (Wang et al., 2025; Zimmerman, 2023).

Personalization in education means adapting learning strategies, resources, and environments to each learner's needs, interests, and cognitive styles, fostering student ownership and engagement (Viberg et al., 2020). Students plan, monitor, and evaluate their learning, adjusting as challenges arise, increasing resilience and motivation.

Educational systems must systematize personalized SRL to help students flourish in complex, dynamic world. This chapter explores strategies and future directions by integrating learning sciences, psychology, and technology-enhanced pedagogy.

The intersection of personalization and SRL fosters autonomy, motivation, and emotional regulation (Elias & Vosgerau, 2024; Ismail et al., 2023). Flexible frameworks accommodate individual differences while supporting collective goals, crucial in digital transformation.

SRL-driven personalization leads to dynamic, responsive environments: students set goals, choose strategies, and monitor progress (Lourenço & Paiva, 2024; Passos et al., 2024), improving performance, engagement, and lifelong skills (Júnior et al., 2023), with regular reflection and adaptability.

Empirical research supports these insights. Lisbôa and Guimarães (2024) found that first-year university students who use SRL strategies report better academic performance, suggesting higher education can benefit from personalized approaches.

Implementing personalized SRL faces barriers, especially in low-digital contexts, where resources and teacher training impede effective adoption (Tur et al., 2022). Questions arise about which strategies, tools, and pedagogies best support personalization across varied settings.

Recent empirical studies and theoretical models highlight active methodologies and digital technologies like real-time feedback and adaptive scaffolding (Ferreira et al., 2020; Järvelá & Hadwin, 2024), encouraging metacognitive awareness and guided adaptation.

A socio-cognitive perspective frames personalization as a catalyst for agency and autonomy (Deshmukh & Mehta, 2025; Ingkavara et al., 2022; Miao & Ma, 2023). Culturally relevant interventions, such as the storytelling-based program described by Azevedo et al. (2022), demonstrate effectiveness in promoting SRL strategies and achievement, even in disadvantaged contexts.

The rationale of this chapter is to offer flexible, inclusive, SRL-oriented experiences that respond to contemporary classroom heterogeneity (Alliprandini et al., 2023; Fischer et al., 2020). Key contributions include systematizing the SRL-personalization relationship, identifying adaptive strategies, analyzing technology's role, and suggesting future directions for student-centered practices. This review intends to inform teachers, researchers, and policymakers about methods that foster autonomy and adaptability in diverse, digitally mediated settings.

Contemporary research highlights adaptive pedagogical models, project-based learning, flexible pacing, and learner-centred assessment (Viberg et al., 2020; Zimmerman, 2023). AI, analytics, and adaptive feedback are expanding the possibilities for scalable personalization (Ferreira et al., 2020; Holmes et al., 2019; Ifenthaler & Yau, 2020).

Despite these advances, integrating such innovations in traditional settings remains challenging due to infrastructure and training gaps. This chapter critically examines how to combine SRL foundations with technology-enhanced personalization and considers ethical concerns and professional development for inclusive, equitable implementation.

This introduction outlines the theoretical and practical framework of personalization in SRL, emphasizing digital technologies and AI. The chapter is organized around core concepts, the SRL-personalization relationship, adaptive strategies, active methodologies, technology's impact on motivation and performance, ethical challenges, teacher training, and implications for future practice.

Distinguishing itself from previous literature, this chapter proposes an integrative conceptual framework operationalizing personalization through data analysis and adaptive modeling, linking technology, autonomy, and ethical-pedagogical considerations. By focusing on the teacher's role as architect of data-driven personalization, new pathways for inclusive practices in digital and traditional educational environments are set forth.

1.2 The Concept of Personalization in Self-Regulated Learning

Personalization in SRL has been increasingly recognized as a key educational paradigm that connects autonomy, adaptability, and individual diversity in the learning process (Viberg et al., 2020; Zimmerman, 2023). It seeks to align teaching methods, content, and assessment with each student's needs, goals, and learning pace, enhancing motivation, self-efficacy, and engagement.

Within the SRL framework, personalization supports the development of metacognitive, cognitive, and emotional competencies that enable learners to manage their own progress effectively. This section explores the theoretical foundations, principles, and strategies of personalization, its applications and challenges in SRL contexts, and the ways in which educational technologies contribute to creating more adaptive and inclusive learning environments.

Fundamentals, Principles and Strategies of Personalization in Self-Regulated Learning

Personalization in learning consists of an educational approach that adjusts teaching to the needs, competences, interests and individual styles of each student, promoting personalized environments capable of fostering progress at each student's own pace (Zhang et al., 2024). This pedagogical orientation is based on valuing diversity, respecting individuality, and promoting inclusive and motivating contexts—focusing design on student autonomy and engagement, factors fundamental to quality and academic success at any educational level.

Different strategies operationalize this vision, such as project-based learning that integrates students' personal interests and motivations, the use of digital technologies for personalized content and feedback, continuous assessment dedicated to the needs and skills of each student, and curricular and organizational flexibility (Dutta et al., 2024; Holmes et al., 2019; Ingkavara et al., 2022). Added to this is the importance of constant communication and collaboration between teachers and students, allowing for dynamic adjustment of objectives, resources and strategies and creating a responsive and empowering learning context. Educational personalization thus gives relevance and adaptability to the formative experience, responding to the challenges of an accelerating world.

In the context of SRL, personalization emerges as a robust solution to the challenges of the twenty-first century, especially considering the increasing heterogeneity of profiles, democratization of access to knowledge, and exponential integration of digital technologies. Under these conditions, systematic adaptation of teaching and learning processes to the specificities of students (Viberg et al., 2020) becomes particularly important, fostering experiences that are not only reactive but also proactive, promoting social and educational equity.

Applications, Dimensions and Challenges of Personalization in SRL

SRL is defined as an iterative process of planning, monitoring and regulating thoughts, behaviors and emotions aimed at achieving academic goals (Lourenço et al., 2025; Zimmerman, 2023). Personalization reinforces autonomy, intrinsic motivation and cognitive engagement, placing the student in the position of active agent of his learning decisions (Nascimento-Fragoso & Coutinho, 2025), promoting continuous reflection, adaptability and metacognition. The challenges of the new paradigm demand integration of self-assessment and feedback strategies, preparing the student to adjust methodologies and attitudes in varied formative contexts, skills that are fundamental to effective self-regulated learning.

Recent advances in cognitive science and educational technologies make personalization more feasible. Luckin et al. (2016) highlight the potential of AI to create adaptive pathways, real-time supports and personalized experiences, adjusting pace and support to each profile. Zhang et al. (2024) underline the distinction between differentiation (homogeneous groups), individualization (adjustment of pace) and personalization (emphasizing the active role of the student in goal setting, strategies and progress evaluation). This emphasis reinforces the student's ability to develop agency, self-efficacy (Bandura, 1997) and to take control of their trajectory, essential conditions for resilience, lifelong learning and building transferable skills.

The operationalization of personalization occurs in different dimensions: at the curricular level, by offering flexible pathways and thematic options; at the methodological level, with projects, flipped learning, gamification (Sajja et al., 2024); and in assessment, with multiple formats for demonstration and tailored feedback. Digital platforms with AI algorithms enable monitoring of progress, adapting difficulties and supporting informed pedagogical decisions, making large-scale personalization possible (Dutta et al., 2024; Ismail et al., 2023; Miao & Ma, 2023).

However, the inclusion of technology brings challenges. Notable obstacles include reconciliation with standardized curricula, institutional resistance to change, specific teacher training requirements, infrastructure limitations, and ethical issues related to data privacy, algorithmic transparency and the risk of "learning bubbles" (Faza & Lestari, 2025; Fischer et al., 2020; Selwyn, 2019; Tur et al., 2022). Overcoming these barriers requires innovative educational policies, structured professional development and the construction of robust ethical frameworks, as well as attention to accessibility and digital literacy to ensure equity.

Impacts, Empirical Evidence and Future Perspectives for Personalized SRL

Empirical research provides support for the effectiveness of personalization in SRL. Studies with higher education students show that the use of personalized self-regulated strategies is positively correlated with perception of academic success

(Lisbôa & Guimarães, 2024). In addition, innovative interventions such as personalized narrative programs developed in socially disadvantaged contexts demonstrate significant potential in promoting self-regulation skills and school performance (Azevedo et al., 2022). Such results attest that personalization, when carefully integrated and supported by inclusive practices, is strategic for promoting equity and reducing disparities in success, respecting contextual, social and cultural differences.

Technology, through adaptive platforms and digital self-regulation tools, becomes central. Tools such as electronic planners, reflective journals or mindfulness apps foster the development of metacognitive and socioemotional skills. However, the effective integration of these solutions requires attention to equity of access and continued teacher training (Faza & Lestari, 2025). The teacher's role assumes the dimension of architect of personalized experience, mediator of self-regulation and promoter of motivating and inclusive environments (Tur et al., 2022; Valente et al., 2024), which implies pedagogical, digital, reflective and ethical skills.

The future of personalization in SRL points to convergence between adaptive pedagogical practices, intelligent technologies and metacognitive strategies, strengthening flexible, fair and autonomy-promoting learning environments (Elmabaredy & Gencel, 2024; Steinert et al., 2024). However, as Fan et al. (2025) warn, it is vital to balance technological innovation with intentional development of metacognitive skills, as uncritical use of AI may result in "metacognitive laziness", devaluing essential self-regulated engagement.

In short, personalization in self-regulated learning should be seen as a lever for school environments oriented towards autonomy, equity and innovation, in which intentional teacher action and a critical integration of technology come together to build resilient, meaningful and lasting learning trajectories.

1.3 Strategies of Personalization in Self-Regulated Learning

Within the scope of SRL, personalization emerges as a central element that permeates multiple dimensions of the educational process. Beyond promoting active student engagement, personalization requires the intentional and systematic adaptation of practices, materials, and pedagogical supports to the individual characteristics of learners.

In addition to personalization, recent literature distinguishes and highlights the concept of adaptation as a central approach in educational technologies. While personalization involves choices and individualized pathways based on the learner's preferences or decisions, adaptation refers to the systems' ability to automatically adjust resources, levels of difficulty, and pedagogical sequences based on data from performance, interaction, and progress (Dutta et al., 2024; Zhang et al., 2024). Adaptive learning platforms, learning analytics, and intelligent tutoring systems exemplify adaptation strategies which, together with personalization, enhance self-regulated learning environments, promoting greater flexibility, equity, and efficiency (Chen et al., 2020; Ifenthaler & Yau, 2020). Studies confirm that the integration of these approaches leads to improvements in performance, motivation, and self-regulation (Elmabaredy & Gencel, 2024; Gomes et al., 2024).

Furthermore, the successful implementation of adaptive and personalized systems depends on the continuous professional development of teachers and collaborative efforts among educators, developers, and policymakers (Bell & Cooper, 2013; Tur et al., 2022). Ongoing training and communities of practice equip educators to interpret learning data, fine-tune adaptive pathways, and integrate these technologies meaningfully into diverse classroom settings. This comprehensive and dynamic approach is essential for maximizing the pedagogical benefits of new technologies while ensuring responsible and inclusive innovation (Fischer et al., 2020).

Additionally, regular evaluation of adaptive practices and stakeholder feedback is crucial for refining technological solutions and maintaining alignment with educational goals (Ifenthaler & Yau, 2020). Such reflective processes foster resilience and adaptability in schools, supporting the long-term sustainability and success of personalized learning initiatives (Chen et al., 2020).

Moreover, engaging students as active participants in the development and adaptation of these systems further enhances their relevance and effectiveness (Holmes et al., 2019). This shared responsibility cultivates a culture of innovation and shared ownership, fundamental to the continuous advancement of adaptive educational environments (Viberg et al., 2020).

This section explores various strategies and approaches that facilitate personalization, ranging from the flexibility of learning environments and teaching materials to the identification and consideration of students' learning styles. It also examines technological support, adapted feedback, and the growing role of digital technologies in promoting personalized learning. The integrated analysis aims to provide a detailed overview of the possibilities and challenges of personalization for fostering self-regulation and educational success, emphasizing how these strategies must be carefully designed and contextualized to meet the evolving and diverse needs of contemporary learners in various educational settings.

Personalization of Teaching and Learning Practices

Personalization of teaching and learning practices is fundamental to fostering student autonomy and engagement. Flexible learning environments allow multiple learning paths and paces tailored to individual needs, supported by adaptive pedagogical materials that cater to diverse learning styles and preferences. The integration of active methodologies further stimulates strategic planning, self-assessment, and social interaction, creating inclusive and responsive educational experiences (Li et al., 2022; Tur et al., 2022).

In this framework, flexibility, material adaptation, and the integration of active methodologies converge synergistically to foster meaningful and responsive learning experiences that address each learner's unique needs and contexts.

Flexibility of Learning Environments

Flexible environments promote multiple learning paths and paces, adapting to the individual characteristics of students. The organization of time, space, and resources should facilitate choice and autonomy, contributing to greater intrinsic motivation and the development of self-regulatory skills (Turan et al., 2022). Hybrid or fully online environments, when well structured, can offer such flexibility, provided they are accompanied by intentional pedagogical support and the provision of appropriate assistance.

These environments also require continuous evaluation to ensure that they effectively meet the diverse needs of learners and foster meaningful engagement across various contexts. Consequently, teachers must be prepared to design and implement supports that address potential challenges arising from varying levels of student independence and access to technology.

Adaptation of Pedagogical Materials

Personalization also takes shape through the modulation of content, forms of presentation, and levels of complexity, according to students' learning styles, interests, and specific needs. Multimodal resources (videos, infographics, podcasts, simulations), as well as adaptive platforms based on AI, such as DreamBox or Knewton, allow for a more tailored response to each student's profile, promoting both cognitive and affective engagement with the task (Dutta et al., 2024). These technologies are capable of collecting real-time data on student performance and preferences, continuously adjusting the learning path to maximize educational effectiveness.

Furthermore, they enhance student autonomy by providing experiences that respect their individual pace and motivation, thereby contributing to a more inclusive and dynamic learning environment. This ongoing adaptation fosters deeper learner involvement and supports the development of personalized strategies, ultimately leading to more meaningful and sustained educational outcomes across diverse learner populations.

Implementation of Active Methodologies

The use of methodologies such as project-based learning, problem-based learning, or game-based learning (gamification) fosters the construction of knowledge in a more meaningful and contextualized way. These approaches stimulate goal setting, strategic planning, self-assessment, and critical reflection—core processes of self-regulation (Ismail et al., 2023). By allowing students to choose topics, work formats, and forms of assessment, these methodologies reinforce the sense of agency and personalization of the educational experience. Furthermore, they encourage collaboration and communication among learners, enhancing social interaction as a key component of the learning process.

The peer observation methodology is a valuable tool for professional teacher development, involving the reciprocal process of observation between colleagues in a classroom setting aimed at improving teaching practice (Hendry & Oliver, 2012). This process enables the exchange of constructive feedback and joint reflection, promoting the continuous improvement of active teaching strategies. Peer observation is grounded in the foundations of social cognitive theory, enabling teachers to learn from one another by observing effective practices and adapting them to their own contexts (Burgess et al., 2021). Moreover, this methodology helps increase teacher confidence in experimenting with new approaches while fostering a collaborative and supportive culture.

In the context of implementing personalized and self-regulated active methodologies, peer observation plays a crucial role in facilitating the exchange of experiences on strategies that promote student autonomy and engagement. The practice enables the identification of effective aspects and challenges of active education, supporting the adaptation and improvement of these practices in different educational settings (Bell & Cooper, 2013). Thus, including peer observation reinforces the commitment to ongoing teacher training and the effective implementation of active methodologies.

Together, these strategies contribute to the creation of a learning ecosystem that recognizes student diversity and promotes a pedagogy centered on integral, equitable, and self-regulated development. Building on the foundations of adaptive teaching, it is equally critical to address the personalization of learning styles, which caters to individual perceptual and cognitive preferences.

Personalization of Learning Styles

The personalization of learning styles begins with the identification of students' individual preferences (visual, auditory, or kinesthetic), as highlighted by Teixeira (2023). Recognizing these differences is fundamental for adapting pedagogical strategies, optimizing the effectiveness of teaching, and promoting a more engaging learning experience tailored to each student's needs. Moreover, adaptation enables educational resources to be selected and presented in a way that maximizes understanding and content retention, respecting the individual's pace and learning style.

Recent studies suggest that the use of digital technologies facilitates the implementation of these adaptations, providing interactive tools that cater to various sensory preferences (e.g., Dutta et al., 2024; Elmabaredy & Gencel, 2024; Ingkavara et al., 2022). Promoting self-assessment and critical reflection in the learning process strengthens students' autonomy, encouraging them to recognize their style and seek strategies that enhance their cognitive development (Tunçeli et al., 2022).

In this regard, both Pizarro (2021) and Fleming (2001) emphasize the importance of utilizing materials and activities that consider students' sensory preferences, as outlined in the VARK model (Visual, Auditory, Reading/Writing, and Kinesthetic). According to the author, visual learners benefit from resources such as videos, infographics, and mind maps; auditory learners prefer audio content, podcasts, and lectures; while kinesthetic learners perform better with practical activities such as drawing, fixing, or creating something manually. The author emphasizes that adapting the virtual environment to different learning styles can significantly improve academic performance. Despite being digital natives, both students and teachers had to adjust to the transition to virtual learning to maintain the effectiveness of the educational process. Therefore, strategies compatible with each learning style are essential to enhance content retention and comprehension.

Beyond adapting materials and methods, it is essential to promote students' self-reflection on their learning styles. According to Zimmerman (2023), encouraging metacognition and awareness of personal cognitive processes contributes to the development of autonomy and self-adjustment, optimizing the learning process. Students who reflect on their learning strategies tend to be more resilient, engaged, and capable of adapting their approaches according to task demands. This reflective practice fosters a deeper understanding of one's strengths and areas for improvement, empowering learners to take ownership of their educational progress.

Personalization based on learning styles not only makes teaching more effective but also creates an inclusive and motivating environment where students feel valued and supported in their educational journey (Pizarro, 2021). In this way, education becomes a more meaningful experience, one that is aligned with the needs and potential of each student. Such an approach ultimately cultivates lifelong learners equipped with the skills necessary to navigate diverse learning contexts and challenges. Complementing the focus on learning preferences, the next dimension involves personalized learning support, integral to fostering autonomy and academic success.

Personalization of Learning Support

Personalized learning support encompasses continuous monitoring, adaptive interventions, individualized formative feedback, and customized tutoring. These interconnected elements utilize data analytics and AI-based tools to deliver timely, personalized support that enhances cognitive and affective learner engagement, promoting effective self-regulation (Holmes et al., 2019; Ifenthaler & Yau, 2020). The main personalization strategies and their expected outcomes in SRL are summarized in Table 1.1, providing an overview before the detailed discussion in the following subsections.

Integration of Educational Data Analytics and Adaptive Modeling in Personalized SRL

Advances in educational technologies, including learning analytics, artificial intelligence, and intelligent tutoring systems, have created new opportunities to enhance

Table 1.1 Personalization strategies and expected outcomes in SRL

Personalization strategy	Objective	Expected SRL outcome
Continuous formative feedback	Adapt interventions to individual learning pace	Increased self-regulation and intrinsic motivation
Intelligent tutoring systems (ITS)	Identify knowledge gaps and suggest activities	Improved academic performance and engagement
Educational data analytics (learning analytics)	Monitor progress and anticipate difficulties	Support for pedagogical decision-making and learner autonomy
Personalized mentoring	Provide emotional and strategic support	Higher motivation, resilience, and socio-emotional engagement
Adaptive platforms (e.g., Knewton, DreamBox)	Dynamically adjust content to student progress	Personalized learning, strengthened cognitive and affective skills

Source Developed by the authors based on the reviewed literature

personalized SRL through continuous data collection and adaptive modeling of learner behavior (Holmes et al., 2019; Ifenthaler & Yau, 2020). These tools provide real-time feedback and tailored interventions, enabling teachers to monitor progress accurately and support goal-oriented, adaptive learning (Papamitsiou & Economides, 2014; Viberg et al., 2020).

Moreover, they facilitate the identification of individual learning trajectories and behavioral patterns, allowing for timely adjustments to instruction and the early detection of learning difficulties. By integrating predictive analytics, these systems can anticipate students' needs and suggest personalized strategies to enhance motivation, persistence, and self-regulation. Such dynamic and data-informed approaches not only promote deeper engagement but also empower learners to take a more active role in managing their learning processes, thereby strengthening their autonomy and metacognitive awareness (Azevedo & Gašević, 2019; Zawacki-Richter et al., 2019).

Adaptive platforms analyze engagement, performance, and preferences to adjust content and scaffolding, optimizing motivation and cognitive challenge (Chen et al., 2020; Dutta et al., 2024). Such dynamic adaptation strengthens learner autonomy by promoting planning, monitoring, and self-evaluation, central SRL processes (Lourenço & Paiva, 2024; Zimmerman, 2023).

In addition, these systems can personalize learning pathways based on learners' progress and responsiveness, ensuring that each student receives the right level of support and challenge at every stage. By providing continuous formative feedback and adaptive prompts, they encourage students to reflect on their strategies and make informed decisions about how to regulate effort and time allocation. This iterative process of feedback and adjustment nurtures metacognitive awareness and fosters a sense of ownership over learning. Furthermore, the integration of gamified elements and data-driven insights can enhance persistence and engagement, creating learning experiences that are both individualized and intrinsically motivating (Fischer et al., 2020; Viberg et al., 2020).

Teachers, therefore, evolve into reflective mediators who integrate these technologies ethically and inclusively, requiring digital literacy and analytical competence (Luckin et al., 2016; Selwyn, 2019; Tur et al., 2022; Valente et al., 2024). Ensuring data privacy, algorithmic transparency, and equitable access remains essential to maintaining trust and fairness in personalized learning (Fischer et al., 2020; Holmes et al., 2019).

The integration of data-driven personalization and adaptive modeling offers an evidence-based framework that enhances metacognitive awareness, strategic regulation, academic engagement, intrinsic motivation, and sustained performance (Azevedo et al., 2022; Elmabaredy & Gencel, 2024). Applicable across varied educational contexts—including low-digital environments—its effectiveness depends on teachers' thoughtful mediation to ensure contextual relevance and accessibility (Lobo, 2023; Tur et al., 2022).

In essence, the convergence of educational data analytics, adaptive technologies, and reflective pedagogy forms a dynamic ecosystem that promotes personalized SRL. Continuous teacher training and the establishment of ethical guidelines should remain priorities to ensure equitable and effective educational innovation (Fischer et al., 2020; Zawacki-Richter et al., 2019).

To successfully implement these strategies, it is essential to foster collaborative partnerships among educators, technology designers, and policymakers, ensuring that adaptive solutions are shaped by diverse perspectives and contextual realities (Bell & Cooper, 2013; Holmes et al., 2019). Periodic evaluation and stakeholder feedback play critical roles in refining systems and tailoring interventions to evolving learner needs (Ifenthaler & Yau, 2020). To facilitate understanding of the integrated data-driven model of personalisation in SRL, Table 1.2 presents a synthesis of its core elements.

It outlines a dynamic and interdependent cycle that involves the collection and analysis of educational data, adaptive modeling, and pedagogical personalization mediated by the teacher, as well as the strengthening of students' self-regulatory processes. This visual representation highlights the crucial role of ethical and inclusive pedagogical mediation, demonstrating how integrating these components fosters learner autonomy, motivation, and sustainable academic achievement.

Grasping this cycle is essential for developing educational practices that effectively respond to needs, leveraging technological and pedagogical resources in a coherent and reflective manner.

Educational Technologies for Performance Monitoring and Adaptive Interventions

With the advancement of learning analytics, educational AI, and intelligent tutoring systems, teachers now have tools at their disposal that can capture and interpret learning data in real-time, enabling more accurate diagnoses, anticipation of difficulties, and personalized interventions tailored to each student's cognitive profile and

Table 1.2 Integrated model of data-driven personalization for self-regulated learning

Element	Description	Examples/sources
Educational data	Continuous and systematic collection of data on student performance, engagement, and preferences	Papamitsiou and Economides (2014), Ifenthaler and Yau (2020)
Adaptive analysis and modelling	Processing of data by systems with algorithms that diagnose individual needs and suggest interventions	Chen et al. (2020), Dutta et al. (2024)
Personalisation	Tailored adjustments in content, strategies, formats, and feedback based on the learner's profile	Zimmerman (2023), Viberg et al. (2020)
Pedagogical mediation	The teacher's role as an ethical and pedagogical mediator, interpreting data and promoting equity and inclusion	Luckin et al. (2016), Valente et al. (2024), Tur et al. (2022)
Self-regulated learning	Development of learners' self-regulatory capacities including planning, monitoring and self-assessment	Azevedo et al. (2022), Elmabaredy and Gencel (2024), Zimmerman (2023)

Source Developed by the authors based on the reviewed literature

pace (Long & Siemens, 2014; Papamitsiou & Economides, 2014). These technologies enable more accurate diagnoses, anticipation of difficulties, and personalized interventions tailored to each student's cognitive profile and pace.

Holmes et al. (2019) highlight that AI applied to education enables the automation of these processes, adapting content, pedagogical mediation, and activity sequencing according to the student's progress, thereby contributing to more relevant learning experiences. Furthermore, these technologies facilitate scalable and continuous adaptation, allowing institutions to respond dynamically to evolving learner needs while supporting individualized educational pathways.

Ifenthaler and Yau (2020) reinforce the role of personalized dashboards as instruments that enable monitoring of progress for both teachers and learners. These dashboards integrate data such as participation, performance, and engagement, presenting intuitive visualizations that guide pedagogical decision-making. For teachers, they facilitate continuous adjustment of teaching strategies; for students, they promote self-regulation and greater awareness of their learning process. By providing immediate and contextualized feedback, these systems also strengthen educational communication, fostering a more collaborative learning environment between teachers and learners.

Van Leeuwen (2015) argues that integrating learning analytics with virtual environments enhances pedagogical responsiveness and equity. His study on synchronous collaborative learning demonstrates how learning analytics support teachers through filtering information, directing attention, and increasing confidence in diagnosis.

This allows pedagogical interventions based on concrete evidence, promoting more agile and needs-oriented teaching for students. Moreover, this integration helps identify equity gaps in real-time, enabling targeted support that addresses individual differences and fosters inclusive learning conditions across diverse student populations.

Concrete examples of educational technologies include Learning Management System (LMS) platforms, such as Moodle Analytics and Canvas Learning Analytics, which allow the real-time collection of data on students' participation, performance, and engagement (Ifenthaler & Yau, 2020; Van Leeuwen, 2015; Viberg et al., 2020). Complementarily, intelligent tutoring systems, such as Carnegie Learning (MATHia) and ALEKS, use adaptive algorithms capable of identifying knowledge gaps and automatically adjusting the proposed activities, promoting personalized learning (Chen et al., 2020; Dutta et al., 2024; Walkington, 2013). Adaptive platforms, such as Knewton Alta and DreamBox Learning, further exemplify the capacity for continuous analysis of student performance, offering individualized recommendations in real-time, which reinforces the personalization of the educational process (Gomes et al., 2024; Sajja et al., 2024).

In addition, tools such as ClassDojo and Edmodo Insights enable the monitoring of socioemotional and engagement aspects, providing immediate indicators that assist teachers in implementing more effective pedagogical interventions (Allman et al., 2023; Elmabaredy & Gencel, 2024). These examples illustrate how the integration of various technologies can facilitate rapid diagnostics and personalized interventions, thereby strengthening students' self-regulation and promoting greater equity in the learning process (Alliprandini et al., 2023; Azevedo & Gašević, 2019; Schunk & Zimmerman, 2023).

Formative Feedback Adapted to Each Student's Pace

Formative feedback is more effective when it is continuous, relevant, and adapted to individual progress. Instead of a standardized model, the use of digital platforms allows personalized feedback that respects the individual learning pace and specific gaps of each student. Carless and Boud (2018) argue that personalized feedback promotes metacognition and SRL by actively involving the student in the learning process. They introduce the concept of "student feedback literacy", which encompasses the capacities necessary to understand and utilize feedback effectively. The authors propose a model with four interconnected dimensions: appreciation of feedback, capacity to make judgements, management of emotions, and action. They emphasize that effective feedback is also formative, strengthening self-regulation and contributing to educational equity.

Nicol (2021) updates the understanding of feedback by describing it as an essentially internal and comparative process, in which the student interprets the information received in light of previous standards and experiences. This approach reinforces the conception of feedback as dialogical engagement, underlining the importance of contextualizing this process to individual performance to favor active and SRL.

Furthermore, the author highlights that effective feedback should stimulate critical reflection and continuous adjustment of study strategies, becoming a dynamic development tool. This view aligns with the potential of educational technologies, which offer immediate and personalized responses, expanding opportunities for adaptive intervention and strengthening student autonomy.

Shute et al. (2021) demonstrate that intelligent and personalized feedback, based on AI, is effective in improving retention, motivation, and the development of complex skills such as problem-solving, especially in hybrid teaching environments. The authors explore the concept of "stealth assessment" integrated into adaptive educational games, demonstrating how these systems provide continuous, contextual, and non-intrusive feedback that is dynamically adjusted to student performance. The implications extend beyond the gaming context, highlighting the potential of adaptive supports to promote engaging and personalized learning. Moreover, such feedback mechanisms enable learners to identify their strengths and areas for improvement in real-time, empowering them to take proactive steps toward their educational goals and fostering sustained motivation throughout the learning process.

Personalized Tutoring and Mentoring

Personalized tutoring and mentoring have emerged as essential for a more humane, affective, and responsive education, offering emotional, motivational, and strategic guidance, particularly in contexts of vulnerability or online learning (Ingkavara et al., 2022). This approach integrates self-regulation in digital environments by utilizing intelligent tutoring systems based on AI, which provide adaptive feedback and suggestions tailored to students' preferences, thereby promoting autonomy and engagement. Thus, these strategic and motivational elements form a personalized mentoring approach, supporting learning in contexts that require greater autonomy. Additionally, the personal connection established through tutoring fosters trust and a sense of belonging, both of which are crucial for sustaining students' motivation and resilience over time.

Zawacki-Richter et al. (2019) argue that individualized tutoring is essential in distance and hybrid education, as it offers active listening, individual monitoring, and relationship building. They highlight that AI-based tools have great potential to support students, teachers, and administrators throughout the student lifecycle, promoting intelligent systems that favor adaptive and personalized environments. Furthermore, the application of AI must consider pedagogical, ethical, social, cultural, and economic dimensions, reinforcing the need for approaches that integrate active listening, individual monitoring, and relationships, central characteristics of individualized tutoring. Thus, the importance of personalized support is increasingly recognized, particularly in remote and hybrid work contexts. These elements contribute to a holistic educational experience that empowers students to overcome challenges and thrive in diverse learning settings.

In this regard, Lobo (2023) emphasizes the importance of personalizing emotional and academic support in online learning during the COVID-19 pandemic. The study underlines that personalized emotional tutoring is crucial for promoting academic resilience and school engagement, taking into account the student's full context, including socio-emotional aspects, rather than just academic content. It warns that such personalized support is essential to mitigate learning losses, such as the "summer slide," and to renew students' interest and participation, highlighting the urgency of strategies for post-pandemic recovery. Such personalized mentoring thus plays a vital role in re-engaging learners and fostering long-term academic success and well-being.

Personalization of learning support, anchored in emerging educational technologies and student-centered pedagogical practices, represents a powerful strategy for addressing the diversity of rhythms, styles, and trajectories. The use of AI, data analytics, individualized feedback, and caring mentoring converges towards a more responsive, equitable, and effective educational model (Allman et al., 2023). Recent literature confirms that such approaches not only improve academic outcomes but also strengthen students' connection with knowledge and school. Ultimately, this comprehensive support framework promotes learner empowerment, motivation, and sustained engagement across educational contexts.

Personalized Learning and Digital Technologies

The personalization of learning through digital technologies has proven to be a fundamental strategy for meeting the individual needs of students, enhancing the effectiveness of teaching, and promoting greater autonomy in the educational process (Dutta et al., 2024; Nascimento-Fragoso & Coutinho, 2025; Sajja et al., 2024). In this context, AI plays a central role by enabling the recommendation of personalized content based on each student's profile, history, and performance. According to Zawacki-Richter et al. (2019), intelligent recommendation systems utilize advanced algorithms to select materials that match students' preferences and knowledge levels, thereby increasing engagement and learning relevance. The authors identify "adaptive systems and personalization" as one of the primary application areas of AI in higher education, highlighting that these technologies tailor content to individual needs, thereby promoting a more engaging educational experience.

Moreover, adaptive platforms that operate with real-time data analysis allow the adjustment of the learning pathway according to the student's progress. Examples of such platforms include Knewton Alta, DreamBox Learning, ALEKS, and Carnegie Learning (MATHia), which dynamically modify the difficulty of activities, propose suitable challenges, and suggest targeted reviews, promoting personalized and efficient learning (Chen et al., 2020; Gomes et al., 2024; Mei et al., 2024; Sajja et al., 2024).

Studies emphasize that AI platforms in education can dynamically modify the difficulty of activities, propose suitable challenges, and suggest specific reviews, promoting personalized and efficient learning.

By analyzing students' learning patterns, strengths, and weaknesses, these platforms adapt educational content to meet individual needs, adjusting the learning path according to each student's progress. In this way, the application of AI in teaching favors flexible and personalized learning environments, optimizing the educational process (Chen et al., 2020; Mei et al., 2024). This data-driven approach helps to overcome the rigidity of traditional models, promoting flexibility, continuous support, and more informed pedagogical decision-making.

Another relevant aspect addressed by Ferreira and Pedrosa (2024) is the use of interactive technological tools that promote self-assessment and knowledge management. The authors highlight that digital environment integrating adaptive quizzes, concept maps, and personalized dashboards contribute to students monitoring their progress, reflecting on their learning strategies, and better organizing acquired content. Furthermore, they stress the role of AI in creating adaptive systems that support these processes, strengthening metacognition and promoting the development of learning self-regulation.

Additionally, the integration of these technologies fosters more responsive learning, where the student ceases to be a passive receiver and becomes an active agent of their educational journey (Gomes et al., 2024). The combination of AI, adaptive platforms, and self-regulation tools not only enriches the academic experience but also contributes to equity in access to knowledge by enabling more tailored interventions for different learning contexts and profiles. These technological advances encourage continuous and personalized engagement, ultimately enhancing learner motivation and facilitating educational success across diverse populations.

Thus, the convergence of AI, data analytics, and interactive digital resources redefines teaching, making it more student-centered, responsive, and capable of promoting deep, meaningful, and sustained learning.

1.4 Benefits of Personalization in Self-Regulated Learning

Personalization in SRL offers multiple, interrelated advantages for students and educators. By adapting instruction, materials, and support to individual learner profiles, personalization can enhance motivation, engagement, and autonomy, while promoting the development of self-regulation skills. It also contributes to improved academic performance and greater efficiency in teaching and learning processes.

This section provides an overview of these benefits, which are further explored in the subsequent subsections: increased motivation and engagement, development of autonomy and responsibility, improvement of academic performance and self-regulation skills, and greater efficiency in teaching and learning. Figure 1.1 illustrates the hierarchical organization of these benefits within the context of personalization, highlighting how personalized practices support deeper cognitive, emotional, and behavioral engagement in learning.

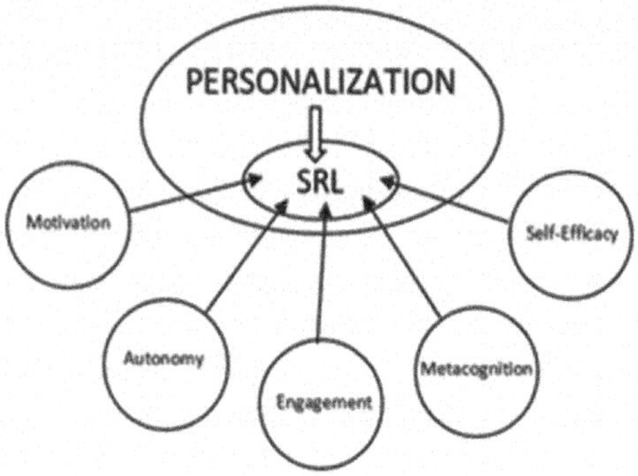

Fig. 1.1 Components of SRL within the context of personalization. *Source* Developed by the authors based on the reviewed literature

Introductory Overview

This section outlines the main and interrelated benefits of personalization for SRL. Personalization can significantly enhance student motivation and engagement, support the development of autonomy and responsibility, improve academic performance, and strengthen self-regulation skills. It also increases the overall efficiency of teaching and learning by enabling more targeted and timely pedagogical actions.

The following paragraphs discuss these benefits in detail, drawing on empirical studies and theoretical frameworks (e.g., Self-Determination Theory) to explain how personalized practices foster sustained engagement and deeper learning. Figure 1.1 illustrates this hierarchical relationship, showing how the core components of SRL are organized within the context of personalization.

When instruction adapts to individual student needs, preferences, learning styles, and rhythms, it is possible to enhance competencies associated with SRL. This section examines the primary benefits of personalization in SRL, categorized into four key areas: motivation and engagement, autonomy and responsibility, academic performance and self-regulation skills, and efficiency in the teaching and learning process.

Furthermore, personalization fosters a more inclusive educational environment by addressing diverse learner profiles and promotes sustained interest and commitment through relevant, meaningful learning experiences tailored to each student's unique context and goals.

Such dynamic adaptation ultimately supports deeper cognitive, emotional, and behavioral engagement in learning, enabling students to develop self-regulation skills more effectively and enhancing the overall quality of the learning process.

The results presented in this study corroborate several pieces of evidence found in recent literature (e.g., Elmabaredy & Gencel, 2024; Viberg et al., 2020), revealing the positive impact of personalization on the development of self-regulation. However, differences are observed regarding the mediating role of certain contextual factors, such as technological infrastructure in traditional educational settings, which may differ from conditions in prior studies. These variations highlight the complexity of operationalizing personalization in diverse educational contexts and indicate the need for further research to explore them in depth.

Increased Motivation and Engagement of Students

One of the most evident effects of personalization in teaching is the increase in students' motivation and engagement in the learning process. This relationship is widely supported by educational literature, particularly in the context of Ryan and Deci's (2020) Self-Determination Theory, which posits that students become more motivated when their basic psychological needs for autonomy, competence, and relatedness are met.

Personalization acts directly on these three fundamental dimensions. By offering students the possibility to choose study topics, content formats, and even types of assessment, a sense of control and relevance over their learning is promoted. This feeling of autonomy transforms the educational process into a more meaningful experience, one that is aligned with each student's interests. Consequently, there is an increase in cognitive effort, persistence in the face of difficulties, and enjoyment in completing educational tasks (Sajja et al., 2024).

Moreover, personalization contributes to the development of a sense of competence, since content can be adjusted to the individual student's level, avoiding both boredom caused by overly easy activities and frustration generated by excessively complex challenges (Nascimento-Fragoso & Coutinho, 2025). When students perceive that they can overcome obstacles that are appropriate to their skills, their self-confidence grows, further strengthening their intrinsic motivation.

Studies such as Walkington (2013) exemplify this dynamic, demonstrating that personalizing mathematical problems based on students' interests, particularly through adaptive technologies, significantly enhances engagement and academic performance. This is particularly relevant for students with average or low academic results, who tend to benefit more from approaches that respect their learning preferences and rhythms. Beyond academic gains, personalization helps create more inclusive and emotionally safe educational environments where students feel valued in their differences and uniqueness.

By adapting problems to reflect everyday contexts and personal interests, such as sport, music, or video games, students demonstrate greater motivation and a more positive attitude towards the proposed activities. This recognition of individuality through contextualized content reinforces the sense of belonging and relevance, crucial factors for maintaining engagement over time (Gomes et al., 2024).

Another fundamental aspect is the role of adaptive technologies, which adjust content in real-time based on students' individual profiles and responses, thereby enhancing the positive effects of personalization. These technologies enable dynamic, flexible, and student-centered learning that quickly responds to their needs and preferences.

According to Alliprandini et al. (2023), this individualized recognition significantly contributes to a stronger affective connection of students with learning, reducing demotivation phenomena frequently observed in uniform and standardized educational environments. By promoting personalization, a context is created where the student is seen and heard in their uniqueness, making the educational process more human, engaging, and effective. This holistic connection fosters sustained interest and a greater willingness to invest effort, ultimately supporting long-term academic success and personal growth.

Development of Autonomy and Responsibility in Learning

Personalization also contributes to the development of core SRL competencies, such as autonomy and self-responsibility. When students actively participate in setting goals, selecting strategies, and self-assessing their progress, they develop a clearer awareness of their learning processes (Zimmerman, 2023). This process is particularly evident in contexts where students have access to personalized feedback and tools that promote metacognitive reflection. For example, adaptive digital platforms can provide individualized study suggestions based on previous performance, encouraging students to make informed decisions about how and when to study. This contributes to the development of self-regulated habits and the acquisition of the competence of learning how to learn (Elmabaredy & Gencel, 2024).

At the same time, the student's accountability for their progress, which personalization reinforces, allows for the development of a sense of agency. When students recognize that their decisions have a direct impact on their academic success, they become more committed to their learning journey and are better equipped to proactively deal with obstacles (Miao & Ma, 2023). Moreover, the development of autonomy and responsibility in learning fosters academic resilience, as students who are more aware of their role and impact on outcomes are better equipped to adjust their strategies in the face of difficulties, thereby maintaining motivation and a long-term focus (Bandura, 1997; Ryan & Deci, 2020).

Another important aspect related to the development of autonomy and responsibility in learning is the influence of the social and collaborative environment. Support from peers, teachers, and family members can enhance self-regulation by offering models, encouragement, and feedback that strengthen students' intrinsic motivation (Júnior et al., 2023; Tunçeli et al., 2022). Environments that promote collaboration and the exchange of experiences encourage students to reflect on their strategies and take an active role in constructing knowledge, thereby reinforcing autonomy and a sense of responsibility in the educational process (Järvelä & Hadwin, 2024; Ryan & Deci, 2020).

Social interaction enables students to better manage their own cognitive and emotional processes through dialogue and the negotiation of meaning, facilitating the internalization of self-regulatory strategies. Furthermore, collaborative environments provide opportunities for the development of metacognitive skills, as the confrontation of ideas and peer feedback help students to perceive different perspectives and adjust their study plans (Tur et al., 2022). These social processes create dynamic spaces in which learners continuously refine their understanding and regulatory strategies, fostering deeper engagement and adaptability.

Social contexts stimulate student engagement by transforming learning into a collective activity, in which each participant is responsible for their progress and supporting the group. This creates a network of mutual accountability that favors perseverance in the face of challenges and strengthens the sense of belonging and engagement (Järvelä & Hadwin, 2024). The same authors highlight the role of these contexts in SRL, especially in collaborative environments, through the "triggers of regulation framework", which identifies events that require regulatory responses at both the individual and collective levels. They also emphasize socially shared regulation of learning, in which group members collaborate in goal setting, strategy selection, and progress monitoring, promoting collective responsibility and engagement.

Thus, students' autonomy and responsibility are developed not only individually but also strengthened through social interactions and the collaborative environment—essential elements for the construction of meaningful and lasting learning (Elias & Vosgerau, 2024). This dual process, integrating personal and social dimensions, forms a robust foundation for lifelong learning and adaptive expertise, preparing students to navigate complex and evolving educational and professional landscapes.

Improvement of Academic Performance and Self-Regulation Skills

The personalization of learning has been proven to contribute to improved academic performance and enhanced self-regulation. By adapting content and challenges to the students' level of competence, learning is promoted within their zone of proximal development, fostering knowledge consolidation and sustained progress (Zhang et al., 2024). These practices have proven effective in diverse contexts, including populations with specific needs. Personalized environments frequently incorporate formative feedback and specific guidance that help students monitor and adjust their performance, promoting essential SRL skills such as planning, monitoring, and evaluation (Viberg et al., 2020). Moreover, intelligent tutoring systems and platforms based on learning analytics can identify behavioral patterns and suggest effective strategies to improve outcomes, such as allocating more time to specific tasks or revisiting previously misunderstood content.

Recent studies confirm that educational interventions combining personalization and SRL training result in significant gains in academic performance, especially when compared with more directive traditional teaching models (e.g., Elmabaredy & Gencel, 2024; Faza & Lestari, 2025; Zhang et al., 2024). In addition to performance gains, personalized learning has proven effective in promoting students' active engagement and intrinsic motivation, decisive factors for more autonomous and lasting learning (Schunk & Zimmerman, 2023). The possibility of individualized pathways enables students to take greater control over their learning process, thereby strengthening their sense of self-efficacy and commitment to setting goals.

Additionally, adaptive environments support the development of transferable skills, such as decision-making, time management, and problem-solving, which are fundamental abilities for facing the complex challenges of today's society (Azevedo & Gašević, 2019). These enhanced competencies not only contribute to immediate academic success but also prepare learners for lifelong learning in diverse and evolving contexts, thereby extending the impact of personalized education beyond formal schooling.

Greater Efficiency in Teaching and Learning

Ultimately, personalization enhances the efficiency of teaching and learning processes. For teachers, access to data on individual student progress enables more informed, focused, and timely pedagogical decisions. Instead of applying generic interventions, teachers can adjust content, methods, and support based on the real needs of each student or group (Ifenthaler & Yau, 2020). This targeted approach enables teachers to allocate their time and resources more strategically, maximizing instructional impact while effectively addressing diverse learner needs.

For students, this efficiency translates into optimized study time. By receiving content tailored to their level and immediate feedback on their performance, they can avoid redundancies and focus on areas that need improvement. This type of dynamic differentiation reduces cognitive overload and enhances the effectiveness of the study strategies employed. Fischer et al. (2020) discuss how the use of big data and learning analytics can support personalized teaching through continuous analysis of student behavior. This includes adapting content to each student's level of competence, providing immediate and personalized feedback, identifying learning gaps to avoid unnecessary revisions, and focusing on areas of greater difficulty, as well as promoting learning efficiency by helping students better manage their time and cognitive resources. The study reinforces that these technologies contribute to more efficient learning, with less redundancy and greater focus on students' actual needs.

According to Viberg et al. (2020), personalized environments often utilize progress visualization tools (e.g., dashboards) that help students understand their current position on the learning path, identify the next steps, and identify the resources they can utilize. This clarity contributes to more efficient management of time and learning resources.

Despite the progress and benefits highlighted in the previous chapters, the effective implementation of personalization in SRL still requires further attention. Ensuring its sustainable adoption will depend on continued research and educational innovation aimed at consolidating these practices and enhancing their impact on diverse learning contexts.

1.5 Challenges and Future Perspectives

This section discusses the main challenges that hinder the effective implementation of personalization in SRL, as well as possible future directions to overcome them. Personalized learning, particularly within the framework of SRL, continues to gain prominence across educational systems and research. However, its widespread and effective adoption still faces substantial obstacles relating to technological infrastructure, teacher preparation, equity of access, data privacy, and ethical considerations. At the same time, rapid advances in artificial intelligence, adaptive technologies, and pedagogical innovation offer exciting opportunities to transform learning environments and support diverse learners. This section systematically examines the most significant challenges encountered in translating personalized learning theory into practice, as well as key future perspectives, including research gaps, promising developments, and policy implications likely to shape the evolution of SRL and personalized education in the coming years.

Challenges in Teacher Training and Pedagogical Integration

One of the most significant challenges concerns teacher training, as many educator's report feeling insufficiently prepared to integrate personalization practices and SRL strategies effectively within their pedagogical contexts. Effective implementation of adaptive systems requires teachers to possess technological, pedagogical, and analytical competencies (Luckin et al., 2016). Digital literacy, the ability to interpret learning data (learning analytics), and pedagogical expertise are necessary to integrate these tools effectively. Limited access to technological infrastructure and insufficient training can further exacerbate inequalities, particularly in less advantaged contexts (Selwyn, 2019).

Another key aspect involves the ongoing need for professional development opportunities that empower teachers to adapt to technological advancements and evolving pedagogical frameworks. Structured continuous training programs, mentorship, and collaborative communities of practice can support educators in acquiring and updating skills relevant to personalization and SRL. Such initiatives not only enhance teachers' confidence and competence but also foster innovation and the sustained integration of adaptive learning practices within diverse educational environments (Bell & Cooper, 2013; Tur et al., 2022).

Evaluating the Effectiveness of Personalized Learning

Assessing the real effectiveness of personalized approaches remains complex, as their impact depends on multiple contextual and motivational variables. Recent research highlights the need for robust, context-sensitive metrics capable of capturing not only academic performance but also self-regulatory and motivational dimensions (Fischer et al., 2020; Ifenthaler & Yau, 2020). Evaluating large-scale educational data and measuring impacts beyond grades, including engagement and self-regulation, requires sophisticated and contextually adjusted assessment tools.

Furthermore, longitudinal studies and mixed-methods approaches are increasingly recommended to better understand both the short- and long-term effects of personalized learning interventions. Combining quantitative analytics with qualitative insights, such as student reflections, teacher observations, and learning diaries, allows researchers and practitioners to capture the nuanced ways personalization influences learners' autonomy, motivation, and persistence. This holistic perspective is vital for informing effective educational policy, practice, and ongoing refinement of personalized learning environments (Ifenthaler & Yau, 2020; Viberg et al., 2020).

Ethical and Equity Considerations

Ethical and practical challenges, such as data privacy, equity in access to technology, and continuous teacher development, also represent critical areas that require sustained attention. The adoption of AI and other advanced technologies must follow strict ethical standards to ensure algorithm transparency, privacy protection, and equitable access. Without clear ethical frameworks, AI integration may deepen inequalities and undermine trust in educational systems (Holmes et al., 2019).

In addition, addressing equity requires ongoing efforts to identify and mitigate biases embedded in both technological systems and pedagogical practices. Strategies such as participatory design, inclusive policy making, and regular auditing of algorithms can help ensure that adaptive learning solutions serve all student groups fairly (Chen et al., 2020; Ifenthaler & Yau, 2020). Continuous dialogue between stakeholders—including educators, learners, and developers, is essential for promoting ethical reflexivity and greater social justice in personalized education contexts.

Moreover, fostering transparency in data collection and usage builds trust among all participants and supports informed consent, particularly when handling sensitive information from diverse populations (Holmes et al., 2019; Ifenthaler & Yau, 2020). It is also important to promote digital literacy and ethical awareness among teachers and students so they can actively identify and respond to potential ethical concerns (Chen et al., 2020). These collective measures strengthen the integrity of personalized learning environments and contribute to more equitable and ethical educational outcomes.

Future Directions and Opportunities

Artificial intelligence, learning analytics, and intelligent tutoring systems offer significant opportunities to advance personalization, enabling precise adaptations to learners' individual needs and fostering more efficient and motivating learning experiences (Fischer et al., 2020; Ifenthaler & Yau, 2020; Luckin et al., 2016; Viberg et al., 2020). Future research should prioritize the optimization of adaptive models, continuous professional development for teachers, collaborative policy-making, and alternative personalization methodologies that consider socio-economic and contextual factors. Longitudinal studies and qualitative approaches are recommended to evaluate the long-term impact of personalized learning on autonomous and self-regulated learning.

Additionally, the integration of student voices and stakeholder engagement in the design and implementation of personalized learning solutions is emerging as a critical factor for sustainable innovation. Co-design processes and participatory methodologies can help ensure that adaptive technologies are relevant, inclusive, and responsive to diverse learner needs (Chen et al., 2020; Holmes et al., 2019). By fostering strong partnerships among educators, policymakers, learners, and technology developers, future initiatives can better balance technological advances with pedagogical values, equity, and ethical considerations, laying the groundwork for educational environments that are both adaptive and socially responsible.

Summary of Challenges and Strategies

The challenges and strategies discussed throughout Sect. 1.5 highlight the multifaceted nature of implementing effective personalization in self-regulated learning. Table 1.3 provides a synthesized overview of the main obstacles identified, including teacher training, evaluation complexities, ethical and equity issues, and future directions, and summarizes the corresponding strategies proposed to address them. By bringing together these insights, the table facilitates a holistic understanding of current barriers and practical solutions, serving as a reference point for researchers, educators, and policymakers seeking to advance personalized learning in diverse educational contexts.

1.6 Contributions, Limitations and Implications

This study provides relevant contributions to the field of SRL by integrating personalization, educational data analytics, and adaptive technologies into a coherent conceptual framework. It advances theoretical understanding by demonstrating how personalized approaches can foster autonomy, metacognition, and intrinsic motivation, while also offering practical insights for technology-mediated pedagogies. The analysis highlights personalization as a pedagogical principle that values individual learning pathways, promoting inclusivity and deeper engagement.

By integrating strategies such as formative feedback, intelligent tutoring systems, and learning analytics, it is possible to foster academic achievement and transferable

Table 1.3 Challenges in implementing personalized learning and recommended solutions

Challenge	Impact	Recommended strategies/ solutions
Equity in access to technologies	Exclusion of students in less advantaged contexts	Provide adequate technological infrastructure, offline/hybrid resources
Ethical issues and data privacy	Risk of misuse of information	Establish ethical guidelines, algorithm transparency, and data protection
Insufficient teacher training	Difficulty in applying personalized strategies	Continuous professional development programs, training in educational technologies
Resistance to pedagogical change	Limited adoption of new practices	Awareness campaigns, pedagogical innovation workshops, gradual implementation
Evaluation of intervention effectiveness	Difficulty measuring real impact	Develop robust and contextually adapted metrics, use learning analytics

Source Developed by the authors based on the reviewed literature

skills (e.g., time management, decision-making, self-monitoring), strengthening both affective and cognitive dimensions of learning and the development of autonomous, self-regulated learners.

Looking ahead, artificial intelligence, learning analytics, and intelligent tutoring systems offer significant opportunities to advance personalization. However, successful adoption requires continuous professional development for teachers, data-driven policies, and robust ethical frameworks, as previously discussed in Sect. 1.5.

Some limitations should be noted, including limited generalizability of findings due to contextual factors (e.g., low-digitalization contexts, resistance in traditional settings), challenges in assessing the effectiveness of personalized interventions and impact metrics, and the need for qualitative and longitudinal research on personalization models that include socio-economic and cultural perspectives.

Future research should invest in adaptive learning models and evaluation metrics sensitive to context and diversity, support continuous teacher professional development for effective integration of technology, and foster collaborative networks between educators, researchers, and technology developers.

In summary, the framework presented in this chapter strengthens the relationship between theory and practice, highlighting the critical, ethical, and innovative role of teachers in mediating personalization. By embracing the complexity of educational ecosystems and focusing on the holistic development of learners, personalization in SRL is established as both an evidence-based and future-oriented pedagogical innovation.

1.7 Conclusion

Personalization plays a central and transformative role in fostering SRL. It enables educational pathways to be adapted to the unique characteristics, learning paces, and individual needs of students. The main outcomes identified in this study include increased motivation and engagement, the development of autonomy and self-regulation, improved academic performance, and the strengthening of affective and cognitive dimensions of learning.

The personalization of learning styles, discussed in Sect. 1.3.2, demonstrates how pedagogical strategies aligned with students' sensory preferences can enhance both engagement and cognitive development. Similarly, emerging technologies such as AI-based adaptive platforms, personalized feedback mechanisms, and intelligent tutoring systems, presented in Sect. 1.3.3, have proven effective in expanding learner autonomy and improving performance, thus promoting an educational dynamic centred on individuality and contextualization.

The benefits of personalization in SRL are broad and multidimensional. They encompass not only academic gains but also the development of metacognitive strategies and socio-emotional skills that support lifelong learning. The integration of personalization into SRL also reinforces the teacher's role as a designer of learning experiences and as a facilitator of reflective, participatory, and ethically aware learning processes.

At the same time, the challenges discussed in Sect. 1.5, such as digital literacy, teacher training, and the ethical use of AI, remind us that personalization is not an automatic or neutral process. Its success depends on sustained investment in teacher development, equitable access to technologies, and the creation of policies that ensure inclusion and transparency. Overcoming these barriers will be decisive for personalization to realize its full transformative potential.

Thus, investing in SRL personalization means committing to an educational model that is more adaptable, equitable, and future-oriented, one capable of training critical, autonomous, and resilient learners. Technology, when ethically and pedagogically integrated, becomes a mediator for human development rather than an end in itself.

Ultimately, embracing personalization within SRL entails recognizing education as a complex, evolving ecosystem where every learner is valued as a whole person, responsible, reflective, and empowered to construct their own learning trajectory. When these conditions are achieved, personalization transcends methodology and becomes a catalyst for meaningful and enduring educational transformation.

Funding This research was funded by the Fundação para a Ciência e a Tecnologia, I.P. (FCT, https://ror.org/00snfqn5816) under grant UID/06173/2025—CARE (https://doi.org/10.54499/UID/06173/2025).

References

Alliprandini, P. M. Z., Santos, D. A., & Rufini, S. É. (2023). *Autorregulação da aprendizagem e da motivação em diferentes contextos educativos: Teoria, aprendizagem e intervenção.* EDUEL.

Allman, B., Kimmons, R., Rosenberg, J., & Dash, M. (2023). Trends and topics in educational technology, 2023 edition. *TechTrends, 67*(3), 583–591. https://doi.org/10.1007/s11528-023-00840-2

Azevedo, R., & Gašević, D. (2019). Analyzing multimodal multichannel data about self-regulated learning with advanced learning technologies: Issues and challenges. *Computers in Human Behavior, 96*, 207–210. https://doi.org/10.1016/j.compedu.2019.103703

Azevedo, R., Rosário, P., Magalhães, P., Núñez, J. C., Pereira, B., & Pereira, A. (2022). A toolkit to help students from low socioeconomic status background: A school-based self-regulated learning intervention. *European Journal of Psychology of Education, 37*(4), 981–1005. https://doi.org/10.1007/s10212-022-00607-y

Bandura, A. (1997). *Self-efficacy: The exercise of control.* Macmillan.

Bell, M., & Cooper, P. (2013). Implementing departmental peer observation of teaching in universities. In D. Gosling & M. Parsell (Eds.), *Peer review of learning and teaching in higher education: International perspectives* (pp. 151–164). Springer. https://doi.org/10.1007/978-94-007-7639-5_10

Burgess, S., Rawal, S., & Taylor, E. S. (2021). Teacher peer observation and student Est scores: Evidence from a field experiment in English secondary schools. *Journal of Labor Economics, 39*(4), 1155–1186. https://doi.org/10.1086/712997

Carless, D., & Boud, D. (2018). The development of student feedback literacy: Enabling uptake of feedback. *Assessment and Evaluation in Higher Education, 43*(8), 1315–1325. https://doi.org/10.1080/02602938.2018.1463354

Chen, L., Chen, P., & Lin, Z. (2020). Artificial intelligence in education: A review. *IEEE Access, 8*, 75264–75278. https://doi.org/10.1109/ACCESS.2020.2988510

Deshmukh, S., & Mehta, M. (2025). AI-enabled self-regulated learning: Reinforcing a proactive workplace culture—a viewpoint. In *Development and learning in organizations.* Advance online publication. https://doi.org/10.1108/DLO-09-2024-0277.

Dutta, S., Ranjan, S., Mishra, S., Sharma, V., Hewage, P., & Iwendi, C. (2024). Enhancing educational adaptability: A review and analysis of AI-driven adaptive learning platforms. In *Proceedings of the 2024 4th international conference on innovative practices in technology and management (ICIPTM)* (pp. 1–5). IEEE. https://ieeexplore.ieee.org/abstract/document/10563448

Elias, A. P. A. J., & Vosgerau, D. S. A. R. (2024). Self-regulation for learning in the context of Brazilian education: An integrative review. *Revista Lusófona de Educação, 64*, 45–65.

Elmabaredy, A., & Gencel, N. (2024). Exploring the integration of self-regulated learning into digital platforms to improve students' achievement and performance. *Discover Education, 3*, 262. https://doi.org/10.1007/s44217-024-00233-4

Fan, Y., Tang, L., Le, H., Shen, K., Tan, S., Zhao, Y., et al. (2025). Beware of metacognitive laziness: Effects of generative artificial intelligence on learning motivation, processes, and performance. *British Journal of Educational Technology, 56*(2), 489–530. https://doi.org/10.1111/bjet.13544

Faza, A., & Lestari, I. A. (2025). Self-regulated learning in the digital age: A systematic review of strategies, technologies, benefits, and challenges. *The International Review of Research in Open and Distributed Learning, 26*(2), 23–58. https://doi.org/10.19173/irrodl.v26i2.8119

Ferreira, A., & Pedrosa, D. (2024). Uso da inteligência artificial para apoiar a autorregulação de aprendizagem: Uma revisão de literatura. *PRÁTICA Revista Multimédia de Investigação em Inovação Pedagógica e Práticas de e-Learning, 7*(2), 101–111.

Ferreira, P. C., Veiga Simão, A. M., & Silva, A. L. (2020). Promover a autorregulação da aprendizagem em ambientes apoiados pela tecnologia: O registo digital do processo de aprendizagem. In M. J. Alvarez, A. M. Veiga Simão, J. A. Ferreira, & E. Santos (Eds.), Psicologia educacional: Investigação e intervenção em Portugal (pp. 113–138). Coisas de Ler. https://repositorio.ulisboa.pt/bitstream/10451/62577/1/Ferreira_et_al_2020_cap_tese_dout.pdf

Fischer, C., Pardos, Z. A., Baker, R. S., Williams, J. J., Smyth, P., Yu, R., Slater, S., Baker, R., & Warschauer, M. (2020). Mining big data in education: Affordances and challenges. *Review of Research in Education, 44*(1), 130–160. https://doi.org/10.3102/0091732X20903304

Fleming, N. D. (2001). *Teaching and learning styles: VARK strategies*. Editorial Christchurch.

Gomes, A. J. F., Verçosa, B. F. M., Pinto, C. R. S., de Moura, C. C., dos Santos Silva, C., & dos Reis, O. B. (2024). Potencializando a aprendizagem ativa com tecnologia de IA. *Revista Ibero-Americana de Humanidades, Ciências e Educação, 10*(8), 3625–3631. https://doi.org/10.51891/rease.v10i8.15451

Hassan, M., Malik, A. S., Sang, G., Rizwan, M., Mushtaque, I., & Naveed, S. (2022). Examine the parenting style effect on the academic achievement orientation of secondary school students: The moderating role of digital literacy. *Frontiers in Psychology, 13*, 1063682. https://doi.org/10.3389/fpsyg.2022.1063682

Hendry, G. D., & Oliver, G. R. (2012). Seeing is believing: The benefits of peer observation. *Journal of University Teaching and Learning Practice, 9*(1), 1–9. https://doi.org/10.3316/informit.T2025021900013401621413338

Holmes, W., Bialik, M., & Fadel, C. (2019). *Artificial intelligence in education: Promises and implications for teaching and learning*. Center for Curriculum Redesign. https://discovery.ucl.ac.uk/id/eprint/10139722/

Ifenthaler, D., & Yau, J. Y. K. (2020). Utilising learning analytics to support study success in higher education: A systematic review. *Educational Technology Research and Development, 68*(4), 1961–1990. https://doi.org/10.1007/s11423-020-09788-z

Ingkavara, T., Panjaburee, P., Srisawasdi, N., & Sajjapanroj, S. (2022). The use of a personalized learning approach to implementing self-regulated online learning. *Computers and Education: Artificial Intelligence, 3*, 100086. https://doi.org/10.1016/j.caeai.2022.100086

Ismail, S. M., Nikpoo, I., & Prasad, K. D. V. (2023). Promoting self-regulated learning, autonomy, and self-efficacy of EFL learners through authentic assessment in EFL classrooms. *Language Testing in Asia, 13*, 27. https://doi.org/10.1186/s40468-023-00239-z

Järvelä, S., & Hadwin, A. (2024). Triggers for self-regulated learning: A conceptual framework for advancing multimodal research about SRL. *Learning and Individual Differences, 115*, 102526. https://doi.org/10.1016/j.lindif.2024.102625

Júnior, J. F. C., Moraes, L. S., de Souza, M. M. N., Lopes, L. C. L., Meneses, A. R., Pinto, A. R. D. A. P., et al. (2023). A importância de um ambiente de aprendizagem positivo e eficaz para os alunos. *Rebena Revista Brasileira de Ensino e Aprendizagem, 6*, 324–341.

Lämsä, J., de Mooij, S., Aksela, O., Athavale, S., Bistolfi, I., Azevedo, R., et al. (2025). Measuring secondary education students' self-regulated learning processes with digital trace data. *Learning and Individual Differences, 118*, 102625.

Li, K. C., Wong, B. T.-M., Kwan, R., & Cheung, S. K. S. (2022). Guest editorial: Personalization in open and flexible learning environments. *Interactive Technology and Smart Education, 19*(4), 393–395. https://doi.org/10.1108/ITSE-11-2022-250

Lisbôa, T. J., & Guimarães, S. B. (2024). Evolução do uso de estratégias de aprendizagem autorregulada em universitários ingressantes. *Educação Online, 19*(46), e24194604. https://doi.org/10.36556/eol.v19i46.1608

Lobo, J. (2023). Instructor emotional support, academic resiliency, and school engagement in an online learning setting during Covid-19 pandemic. *Journal of Learning for Development, 10*(2), 252–266. https://doi.org/10.56059/jl4d.v10i2.826

Long, P. D., & Siemens, G. (2014). Penetrating the fog: Analytics in learning and education. *TDTecnologie Didattiche, 22*(3), 132–137. https://doi.org/10.17471/2499-4324/195

Lourenço, A. A., & Paiva, M. O. A. (2024). Academic performance of excellence: The impact of self-regulated learning and academic time management planning. *Knowledge, 4*, 289–301. https://doi.org/10.3390/knowledge4020016

Lourenço, A. A., Paiva, M. O. A., & Valente, S. (2025). Strategies that transform: Self-regulation and volitional control as keys to academic achievement. *Social Sciences, 14*(5), 285. https://doi.org/10.3390/socsci14050285

Luckin, R., Holmes, W., Griffiths, M., & Forcier, L. B. (2016). Intelligence unleashed: An argument for AI in education. *Pearson*. https://discovery.ucl.ac.uk/id/eprint/1475756/
Mei, T., Yuan, L., & Li, C. (2024). Uma revisão da pesquisa sobre o impacto da inteligência artificial na aprendizagem. *Revista Científica de Pesquisa em Sistemas Inteligentes, 6*(7), 10–17. https://doi.org/10.54691/15yd7r45
Miao, J., & Ma, L. (2023). Teacher autonomy support influence on online learning engagement: The mediating roles of self-efficacy and self-regulated learning. *SAGE Open, 13*(4), 7737. https://doi.org/10.1177/21582440231217737
Nascimento-Fragoso, M. D. J., & Coutinho, D. J. G. (2025). Inteligência artificial no apoio à educação personalizada: Potencialidades e desafios. *Revista Ibero-Americana de Humanidades, Ciências e Educação, 11*(4), 2509–2523. https://doi.org/10.51891/rease.v11i4.18748
Nicol, D. (2021). The power of internal feedback: Exploiting natural comparison processes. *Assessment and Evaluation in Higher Education, 46*(5), 756–778. https://doi.org/10.1080/02602938.2020.1823314
Papamitsiou, Z., & Economides, A. A. (2014). Learning analytics and educational data mining in practice: A systematic literature review of empirical evidence. *Educational Technology and Society, 17*(4), 49–64.
Passos, T. S., Oliveira, L. C. F., Reis Neto, R. A., Meneses, A. R., Reis Soares, G., Sousa, M. A. D. M. A., et al. (2024). Além do convencional: Como a sala de aula invertida revoluciona o ensino tradicional. *Revista Educação, Humanidades e Ciências Sociais, 21*, e00132–e00132.
Pizarro, I. F. (2021). Estilos de aprendizagem VARK na sala de aula virtual da universidade: Uma ferramenta para melhorar o desempenho acadêmico. *RECEITA Revista Eletrônica Científica de Pesquisa Educacional, 5*(2), 221–234.
Ryan, R. M., & Deci, E. L. (2020). Intrinsic and extrinsic motivation from a self-determination theory perspective: Definitions, theory, practices, and future directions. *Contemporary Educational Psychology, 61*, 101860. https://doi.org/10.1016/j.cedpsych.2020.101860
Sajja, R., Sermet, Y., Cikmaz, M., Cwiertny, D., & Demir, I. (2024). Artificial intelligence-enabled intelligent assistant for personalized and adaptive learning in higher education. *Information, 15*(10), 596. https://doi.org/10.3390/info15100596
Schunk, D. H., & Zimmerman, B. J. (2023). *Self-regulation of learning and performance: Issues and educational applications*. Taylor & Francis. https://doi.org/10.4324/9780203763353
Selwyn, N. (2019). *Should robots replace teachers? AI and the future of education*. Polity Press.
Shute, V., Rahimi, S., Smith, G., Ke, F., Almond, R., Dai, C. P., Kuba, R., Liu, Z., Yang, X., & Sun, C. (2021). Maximizing learning without sacrificing the fun: Stealth assessment, adaptivity and learning supports in educational games. *Journal of Computer Assisted Learning, 37*(1), 127–141. https://doi.org/10.1111/jcal.12473
Steinert, S., Avila, K. E., Ruzika, S., Kuhn, J., & Küchemann, S. (2024). Harnessing large language models to develop research-based learning assistants for formative feedback. *Smart Learning Environments, 11*, 62. https://doi.org/10.1186/s40561-024-00354-1
Teixeira, A. D. A. O. M. (2023). *Uma metodologia baseada em estilos de aprendizagem para recomendação e adaptação de recursos educacionais* [Tese de doutoramento em Ciência da Computação, Universidade Federal do Maranhão]. https://tedebc.ufma.br/jspui/handle/tede/5149.
Tunçeli, H. İ., Yorulmaz, A., & Şahan Aktan, B. (2022). Teacher candidates' critical thinking and learning autonomy: The mediating role of self-regulation. *Journal for Educators, Teachers and Trainers, 13*(3), 100–110. http://194.27.153.46/xmlui/handle/20.500.12809/10284
Tur, G., Castañeda, L., Torres-Kompen, R., & Carpenter, J. P. (2022). A literature review on self-regulated learning and personal learning environments: Features of a close relationship. *Interactive Learning Environments, 32*(4), 1402–1421. https://doi.org/10.1080/10494820.2022.2121726
Turan, Z., Kucuk, S., & Cilligol Karabey, S. (2022). The university students' self-regulated effort, flexibility and satisfaction in distance education. *International Journal of Educational Technology in Higher Education, 19*, 35. https://doi.org/10.1186/s41239-022-00342-w

Valente, S., Dominguez-Lara, S., & Lourenço, A. (2024). Planning time management in school activities and relation to procrastination: A study for educational sustainability. *Sustainability, 16*, 6883. https://doi.org/10.3390/su16166883

Van Leeuwen, A. (2015). Learning analytics to support teachers during synchronous CSCL: Balancing between overview and overload. *Journal of Learning Analytics, 2*(2), 138–162.

Viberg, O., Khalil, M., & Baars, M. (2020). Self-regulated learning and learning analytics in online learning environments: A review of empirical research. In *Proceedings of the tenth international conference on learning analytics and knowledge* (pp. 524–533). ACM. https://doi.org/10.1145/3375462.3375483

Walkington, C. A. (2013). Using adaptive learning technologies to personalize instruction to student interests: The impact of relevant contexts on performance and learning outcomes. *Journal of Educational Psychology, 105*(4), 932–945. https://doi.org/10.1037/a0031882

Wang, C., Chen, X., Li, Y., Wang, P., Wang, H., & Li, Y. (2025). Meta classroom: A new paradigm and experience for programming education. *Journal of Educational Computing Research, 2*, 470. https://doi.org/10.1177/07356331251322470

Zawacki-Richter, O., Marín, V. I., Bond, M., & Gouverneur, F. (2019). Systematic review of research on artificial intelligence applications in higher education: Where are the teachers? *International Journal of Educational Technology in Higher Education, 16*(1), 1–27. https://doi.org/10.1186/s41239-019-0171-0.pdf

Zhang, L., Carter, R. A., Jr., Bernacki, M. L., & Greene, J. A. (2024). Personalization, individualization, and differentiation: What do they mean and how do they differ for students with disabilities. *Exceptionality, 16*, 1–22. https://doi.org/10.1080/09362835.2024.2446219

Zimmerman, B. J. (2023). Dimensions of academic self-regulation: A conceptual framework for education. In D. H. Schunk & B. J. Zimmerman (Eds.), *Self-regulation of learning and performance* (pp. 3–21). Routledge.

Chapter 2
Person-Centered Perspectives on the Universality of Self-Regulated Learning in Technology-Enhanced Learning Environments

Dirk Tempelaar, Bas Giesbers, and Bart Rienties

Abstract Empirical research often seeks universal relationships—laws presumed to apply to all students—typically by comparing natural groups such as gender or culture. We argue that such comparisons are insufficient and advocate for a person-centered approach to examine whether relationships hold across diverse learner profiles. Drawing on a self-regulated learning (SRL) framework, this study on student learning regulation applies latent profile analysis to identify self-regulation disposition profiles and explore their links to epistemic learning dispositions, including mindsets, effort beliefs, and academic motivation. While antecedent-consequence relationships appear broadly generalizable across gender and prior-knowledge subgroups, these patterns do not consistently extend to latent profile-based classes. In several profiles, maladaptive beliefs show stronger associations with learning regulation outcomes than adaptive ones, diverging from trends in the overall sample. This suggests that interventions for specific learner profiles should prioritize reducing maladaptive beliefs rather than merely strengthening adaptive ones. More broadly, our findings highlight the need to test the boundaries of relative universalism beyond natural groupings by employing person-centered SRL approaches to refine the design of targeted educational interventions. Data were drawn from 16 cohorts (N > 16,000) enrolled in an introductory mathematics and statistics course.

D. Tempelaar (✉)
Department of Quantitative Economics, School of Business and Economics, Maastricht University, Maastricht, The Netherlands
e-mail: d.tempelaar@maastrichtuniversity.nl

B. Giesbers
Department of Educational Research and Development, School of Business and Economics, Maastricht University, Maastricht, The Netherlands
e-mail: Bas.Giesbers@MaastrichtUniversity.nl

B. Rienties
Institute of Educational Technology, The Open University, Milton Keynes, UK
e-mail: Bart.Rienties@open.ac.uk

A. Peña-Ayala (ed.), *Self-Regulated Learning*, Cognitive Technologies,
https://doi.org/10.1007/978-981-92-0658-2_2

Keywords Self-regulated learning · Learning regulation · Dispositional learning analytics · Relative universalism · Student dispositions · Person-centered analysis · Technology-enhanced learning environment

Abbreviations

AIC	Akaike information criterion
AMOT	A-motivation
AMS	Academic motivation scale
AN	Anxiety
ANAL	Analyzing
AUTON	Autonomous motivation
BIC	Bayesian information criterion
CONC	Concrete processing
CONTROL	Controlled motivation
CRIT	Critical processing
DLA	Dispositional learning analytics
DS	Disengagement
EN	Effort negative
EP	Effort positive
ERLP	External regulation of learning processes
ERLR	External regulation of learning results
ET	Entity theory
FA	Failure avoidance
IB	International baccalaureate
ILS	Inventory of learning styles
IT	Incremental theory
LA	Learning analytics
LACK	Lack of regulation of learning
LF	Learning focus
LPA	Latent profile analysis
LPF	Learning patterns framework
MEMO	Memorizing
PBL	Problem-based learning
PL	Planning
PS	Persistence
REL	Relating and structuring
SB	Self-belief
SLQ	Study of learning questionnaire
SM	Study management
SRL	Self-regulation learning
SRLC	Self-regulation of learning content
SRLP	Self-regulation of learning processes
SS	Self-sabotage
TEL	Technology-enhanced learning

TELE	Technology-enhanced learning environment
UC	Uncertain control
VS	Value of school

2.1 Introduction

Educational psychology has long sought to understand how learners engage with and respond to the demands of formal learning environments. Central to this endeavor is the investigation of intra-individual psychological processes—such as self-regulation and motivation—that guide learners' behavior over time (Schunk et al., 2008). However, despite this theoretical focus on individual-level functioning, a considerable portion of empirical research in the field continues to rely on between-person analyses and cross-sectional group comparisons (Hamaker, 2012; Molenaar, 2004). This misalignment between theory and methodology raises a critical issue: the conclusions drawn from inter-individual differences may not translate to the intra-individual mechanisms they aim to explain (Fisher et al., 2018; Hamaker et al., 2015).

This discrepancy is not merely a philosophical concern but a statistical one. Full sample associations often mask—or even distort—within-person relationships, a phenomenon known as the ecological fallacy. For example, a correlation observed across individuals between motivation and academic performance may not hold within any single individual over time or within subgroups of the sample. Consequently, many researchers now advocate for analytic approaches that center the individual, such as within-person longitudinal modeling (Murayama et al., 2017; Voelkle et al., 2014). Yet these methods often demand intensive data collection protocols, limiting the scope of learning activities that can be studied and restricting the generalizability of findings to more authentic educational settings (Moeller et al., 2021).

A promising alternative lies in person-centered approaches, which emphasize identifying subgroups of learners with similar psychological profiles. Among these, latent profile analysis (LPA) has gained traction for its ability to uncover hidden heterogeneity in learner characteristics while maintaining ecological validity (Howard & Hoffman, 2018; Pastor et al., 2007). By grouping learners based on shared patterns of behavior, belief, or disposition, person-centered methods bridge the gap between the variable-centered assumptions of most psychological models and the reality of diverse, context-sensitive learner experiences (Marsh et al., 2009; Morin, 2016).

One domain where person-centered methods show particular promise is in testing the assumption of relative universality—the idea that the structure of psychological models may hold across subgroups of learners, even if the magnitude of relationships varies (Pekrun & Goetz, 2023; Voelkle et al., 2014). Relative universality provides a more flexible alternative to the strict universalism commonly sought in the natural sciences (Pekrun, 2024). While demographic comparisons (e.g., by gender, culture or academic field) have traditionally been used to test generalizability (Frenzel et al., 2007; Pekrun, 2018), recent research suggests that more psychologically meaningful groupings—such as those based on motivation or emotion profiles—may better reflect the true sources of variation in learning outcomes (Pekrun & Goetz, 2023).

This chapter explores the potential of person-centered analysis to evaluate the relative universalism of theoretical models in educational psychology, specifically in relation to antecedent-consequence relationships for self-regulated learning (SRL). SRL is widely acknowledged as a key determinant of academic success, especially in technology-enhanced learning (TEL) and technology-enhanced learning environments (TELEs), which place heightened demands on learners' autonomy and self-regulation. Both terms relate to the field or practice of using technology in support of education, where the field in itself is mostly characterized as TEL, and a specific application often is characterized as the use of technology in a learning environment of a specific educational unit like a course. In this contribution, both terms are used interchangeably. SRL involves a dynamic interplay of cognitive, metacognitive, behavioral, motivational, and contextual processes through which learners actively set goals, monitor progress, and adapt strategies and motivation accordingly (cf. Panadero, 2017; Puustinen & Pulkkinen, 2001). By distributing instructional control across learners, interfaces, and algorithms, TELEs increase the need for students to set goals, plan time, and monitor progress.

Reviews of SRL and digital supports argue that learning in for example online, blended, and mobile formats place greater demands on independent regulation than learning in traditional classrooms, making SRL a gatekeeper of learning success in TELEs (Prasse et al., 2024). A substantial body of research has examined both the antecedents and consequences of SRL, drawing on diverse theoretical frameworks such as motivation theory (Ryan & Deci, 2017) and mindset theory (Dweck & Master, 2008). Notable meta-analyses, including those by Broadbent and Poon (2015) and Hemmler and Ifenthaler (2024), provide evidence of these relationships. Assessing whether such models meet the criterion of relative universalism is crucial for informing the design of educational environments that effectively foster SRL.

In testing the relative universalism of SRL models, we adopt the perspective of students' self-perceptions of their learning regulation. This perspective is characterized by two key features. First, it approaches regulation from a dispositional standpoint—focusing on how students believe they apply learning regulation strategies—rather than from a behavioral perspective that measures actual use. Second, it conceptualizes learning regulation broadly, encompassing not only self-regulation strategies but also external regulation strategies. In this way, our analysis emphasizes the antecedent relationships underlying SRL.

We apply latent profile analysis to a large-scale dataset drawn from a dispositional learning analytics framework embedded in a first-year university mathematics and statistics course. With over 16,000 students across 16 cohorts, the dataset captures self-reported measures of learning-regulation (based on Vermunt's Inventory of Learning Styles; Vermunt & Donche, 2017), motivation and engagement (Martin, 2007), and epistemic beliefs (inspired by Dweck's meaning system; Dweck,

1999; Dweck & Master, 2008). Using mixture modeling in Mplus, we identify five distinct learner profiles that reflect both quantitative and qualitative differences in students' learning dispositions.

We then test whether key antecedent relationships for SRL—such as those between SRL skills and learning regulation perceptions—hold across the full sample, between natural groupings as gender and prior education, and within each latent profile. This allows us to evaluate not only whether models exhibit relative universality, but also whether certain relationships differ structurally between learner groups.

Following this introduction, the literature review section discusses research on SRL, with particular attention to its implementation in TELEs and the broader framework of learning regulation. This section also examines the skills essential for effective SRL and the antecedents of successful learning regulation. The method section then explains how these concepts were operationalized through a dispositional analysis approach. The results section first presents student profiles derived from a latent profile analysis, followed by findings on predictive relationships for learning regulation, emphasizing differences between profiles. Finally, the paper concludes with the discussion and conclusion sections.

2.2 Literature Review

Self-regulated learning (SRL) is a multidimensional construct encompassing the cognitive, metacognitive, motivational, and behavioral processes through which learners actively manage their own learning. This literature review examines SRL and its key antecedents through seven interconnected perspectives. Section 2.2.1 explores SRL within TELEs, emphasizing both the opportunities and regulatory demands that digital learning contexts impose. Section 2.2.2 introduces the Learning Pattern Framework to conceptualize SRL in relation to broader forms of learning regulation and processing strategies. Building on this, Sect. 2.2.3 identifies the core skills underlying SRL, such as goal setting, monitoring, and strategic task management, and their operationalization through Martin's Motivation and Engagement Wheel.

Sections 2.2.4 and 2.2.5 review two major antecedent domains: mindsets, reflecting implicit beliefs about intelligence and effort, and motivation, grounded in self-determination theory's distinction between autonomous and controlled forms. Section 2.2.6 then considers the moderating roles of gender and prior knowledge in shaping SRL behaviors. Finally, Sect. 2.2.7 discusses the concept of relative universalism and the application of person-centered methods—particularly latent profile analysis—to test whether SRL mechanisms operate consistently across diverse learner profiles. Together, these sections provide a comprehensive foundation for examining the universality and variability of SRL processes.

Self-Regulated Learning in Technology-Enhanced Learning

The foundational models of SRL underscore its multifaceted nature. Pintrich's framework, for example, conceptualizes SRL as a cyclical process comprising forethought (goal setting and planning), performance (strategy use and monitoring), and reflection (self-evaluation and adaptation), and extending across domains of cognition, motivation, behavior, and context (Schunk, 2005). Zimmerman and Winne's contributions further highlight SRL as inherently feedback-driven, where learners continuously monitor the outcomes of their actions and adjust approaches accordingly (Butler & Winne, 1995; Zimmerman, 2000; Zimmerman & Schunk, 2011). This monitoring process is central; students interpret feedback from the environment or self-generated sources, using it as a cue to maintain or modify their behaviors and strategies.

TELEs—ranging from MOOCs to intelligent tutoring systems—offer both opportunities and challenges for SRL. The shift to digital education increases learner autonomy but also necessitates higher proficiency in SRL skills due to reduced direct teacher scaffolding and elevated complexity in managing digital resources. For instance, the ability to set goals, plan strategically, monitor progress, and adjust strategies is crucial for managing the open-ended nature of many Technology Enhanced Learning (TEL) platforms (Winne & Hadwin, 1998; Azevedo & Hadwin, 2005). TELEs can support SRL, provided they are designed with explicit scaffolds and user adaptability, yet learners differ widely in their ability to benefit from these affordances (Tempelaar et al., 2024).

A significant finding in the online context is the variability in SRL profiles among learners (Tempelaar et al., 2024). Here, cluster analyses using the Study of Learning Questionnaire (SLQ; Rovers et al., 2018) have identified multiple distinct learner profiles of students' use of learning strategies when learning in a blended learning environment having problem-based learning as its face-to-face mode and intelligent tutoring systems as its online mode. Thus, SRL skills are not evenly distributed, and TELEs can inadvertently widen achievement gaps if not paired with appropriate supports. This becomes all the more important in the light of recent developments regarding the use of AI tools in education. The affordance of AI to (partially) take over learner regulation can benefit learning. However, by taking over it also limits learners in developing SRL skills themselves making transfer of learning to new contexts and the development of lifelong learning skills problematic (Molenaar, 2022).

TEL platforms as intelligent tutorials offer a wide range of learning scaffolds (Tempelaar et al., 2020). Some of these scaffolds have the aim to support students' self-regulation, whereas other types of scaffolds more or less take over learning regulation, in which case learning gets externally regulated. Because of this combination of different types of scaffolds, it is attractive to study self-regulation not in isolation, but in the context of alternative forms of learning regulation: external regulation, or even lack of any type of regulation. A theoretical framework that allows doing so is the learning patterns perspective on student learning developed by Vermunt (1998); see also Vermunt and Donche (2017). Vermunt's Learning Patterns Framework

(LPF) distinguishes between self-regulation (students orchestrate learning proactively), external regulation (teacher or environment driven), and lack of regulation (disorganization or confusion). To examine SRL in relation to these other forms of regulation, this study adopted the LPF framework.

Learning Regulation and Learning Processing

The Learning Pattern Framework (LPF), developed by Vermunt (1998) and further elaborated by Vermunt and Donche (2017) and Lonka et al. (2021), distinguishes various metacognitive learning regulation strategies and integrates them with cognitive processing strategies, aligning with the broader approaches-to-learning tradition. The framework identifies three main types of cognitive learning strategies:

- Deep learning: Involves meaning-making, critical thinking, and connecting new information to existing knowledge and conceptual frameworks. Students using this strategy tend to elaborate on content and strive for deep understanding.
- Stepwise or reproduction-oriented learning: A learning approach marked by memorizing facts, repeating information, and concentrating on superficial aspects of the content rather than deeper understanding.
- Concrete of application-oriented learning: Focuses on applying knowledge to practical, real-world situations, often through examples and authentic contexts.

Metacognitive regulation operates in conjunction with these cognitive approaches: deep learning typically involves self-regulation, whereas surface learning is often associated with external regulation. Within the LPF framework, learning regulation is examined through the combined lens of self-regulation and external regulation. While most empirical research emphasizes self-regulation, a few theoretical models adopt a broader perspective that incorporates both personal and contextual dimensions. Among these, the Theory of Self- versus Externally-Regulated Learning (de la Fuente et al., 2021, 2022; see also de la Fuente & Kauffman, 2025) highlights the interplay between individual and environmental regulation of learning processes.

The SRL component captures how students actively manage their motivation, cognition, and behavior to achieve learning goals, whereas the Externally-Regulated Learning (ERL) component addresses how features of the learning environment (e.g., teachers, tasks, feedback, structure) support or constrain students' efforts. Crucially, learning outcomes are shaped by the alignment between SRL and ERL. The LPF, as applied in the present study, builds on an analog principle by investigating the full spectrum of learning regulation, focusing on students' self-perceptions of their use of different regulatory strategies. In this project, cognitive learning strategies are considered as antecedents to learning regulation, serving as predictors of students' use of metacognitive regulation strategies.

Core Skills for Self-Regulated Learning

A crucial category amongst SRL antecedents are SRL skills: student learning dispositions that are not only predictive for the intensity students apply SRL, but are also instrumental in this application (Zimmerman, 2002). Effective SRL involves the integration of several interrelated skills, broadly categorized as cognitive, metacognitive, motivational, and behavioral:

- Goal Setting and Planning: Learners must formulate clear academic goals and devise strategic plans to navigate complex, often open-ended digital environments. Planning is the foundation upon which other regulatory activities are built and can enhance self-efficacy (Raković et al., 2022).
- Strategic Task Management: Selecting and applying appropriate cognitive strategies—such as note-taking, summarizing, or multi-modal engagement—is especially important with hypermedia and diversified digital content. Adaptive use of available tools distinguishes effective self-regulators (Tempelaar et al., 2024).
- Self-Monitoring and Metacognition: Continuous awareness of one's understanding and learning processes is essential for identifying misconceptions or ineffective strategies. Monitoring, in particular, serves as the hub of self-regulated cognitive engagement, integrating incoming feedback and scheduling adjustments (Raković et al., 2022).
- Time Management and Environment Structuring: The freedom and flexibility of TELEs demand robust skills in managing study schedules and personal learning environments (Wolters et al., 2025).
- Help Seeking and Resource Management: TELEs often provide myriad support mechanisms (e.g., forums, tutorials, automated help), but the onus is on learners to proactively seek and utilize these resources (Tempelaar et al., 2020).
- Motivation and the Regulation of Motivation: Regulation of motivation is increasingly recognized as a core SRL skill, distinct from but related to cognitive and metacognitive control (Wolters et al., 2025).
- Self-Evaluation and Reflection: Learners must assess the outcomes of their efforts, interpret feedback, and refine their approaches for future learning episodes (Raković et al., 2022).

In the current research project, we opted to operationalize SRL skills through concepts from Andrew Martin's (2007, 2011, 2023) Motivation and Engagement Wheel. The Motivation and Engagement Wheel, as conceptualized by, is a model that categorizes eleven facets of student motivation and engagement—each corresponding to empirical constructs widely recognized within the SRL literature. Three concepts from the wheel are motivations of adaptive, cognitive type: Self-Belief, Value of School and Learning Focus. Self-belief is congruent with academic self-efficacy, a cornerstone of SRL according to both social cognitive theory and the triadic model of self-regulation. The subjective value attributed to school reflects intrinsic and identified forms of motivation. The concept of Learning Focus is analogous to mastery goal orientation or deep learning orientation in SRL literature.

In the behavioral, adaptive area of the wheel, the positive engagement factors, we find Planning, Study Management, Persistence, Planning, or strategic goal setting, is a foundational process during the forethought phase of SRL. Analogous to time management and behavioral regulation, Study Management enables learners to create conducive environments for focus, minimize distractions, and structure learning activities. Persistence represents volitional control—the capacity to maintain effort in the face of setbacks. Persistent students leverage their motivational resources to sustain task focus and adapt strategies.

Negative motivation, the cognitive maladaptive, is represented by the concepts Anxiety, Failure Avoidance and Uncertain Control. Anxiety can disrupt SRL by depleting cognitive resources, impairing metacognitive monitoring, and lowering self-efficacy. Failure avoidance reflects maladaptive orientation toward achievement, often resulting in self-protective or avoidance-driven behaviors that inhibit adaptive strategy use. Experiences of uncertain control or learned helplessness thwart self-regulatory initiation—students who do not believe their actions affect outcomes are less likely to set goals, plan, or self-monitor.

The last area of the wheel is for negative engagement: the maladaptive, behavioral concepts of Self-Handicapping and Disengagement. Self-handicapping behaviors—such as procrastination or intentional impediments—can be seen as volitional failures within SRL models. Disengagement signifies withdrawal from both the motivational and behavioral aspects of self-regulation; it is often the result of repeated regulatory failures.

Mindsets as Antecedents of Self-Regulated Learning

Learning mindsets, as conceptualized by Dweck (1999), reflect individuals' implicit beliefs about the nature of intelligence—specifically, whether it is fixed or malleable. A growth mindset (or incremental theory of intelligence), which holds that intelligence can be developed through effort and learning, predisposes students to view challenges as opportunities for growth. This perspective fosters core SRL behaviors, including adaptive strategy use, self-monitoring, and persistence in the face of setbacks (Dweck & Master, 2008). Research grounded in social cognitive theory further supports the reciprocal relationship between personal beliefs—such as growth mindset—and the deployment of metacognitive strategies like planning, monitoring, and regulating cognition (Lodewyk et al., 2009).

In contrast, a fixed mindset (or entity theory of intelligence), which views intelligence as innate and unchangeable, often leads learners to avoid difficult tasks, respond maladaptively to failure, and engage less in metacognitive regulation, ultimately undermining effective self-regulation (Zimmerman, 2000).

Moreover, effort beliefs—students' interpretations of what their effort signifies—moderate the relationship between mindset and SRL. Students with positive effort beliefs (e.g., viewing effort as a means to learn and improve) are more likely to persist through difficulty and apply metacognitive strategies such as time management and self-monitoring (Blackwell et al., 2007). In contrast, negative effort beliefs (e.g., interpreting effort as a sign of low ability) can lead to learned helplessness, task avoidance, and shallow engagement, thereby undermining SRL at its core (Dweck, 1999; Blackwell et al., 2007).

Finally, insights from the motivational regulation literature emphasize that effective self-regulation extends beyond cognitive and metacognitive strategies to include the regulation of motivation itself. For instance, reappraising effort as purposeful and meaningful has been shown to enhance goal striving and cognitive engagement, further reinforcing the SRL process (Wolters et al., 2025).

An illustrative example is Hertel et al. (2024), who applied LPA to examine mindset antecedents of SRL facets. Their study identified three profiles of mindset dispositions and found that these profiles differed in levels of learning strategies. However, they did not estimate profile-specific antecedent relationships.

Autonomous and Controlled Motivation as Antecedents of Self-Regulated Learning

Self-determination theory (SDT; Ryan & Deci, 2017) positions motivation along a continuum from the highly self-determined, or autonomous, to the less self-determined, or controlled, and this distinction is foundational for understanding its impact on SRL. The nature of motivation—whether autonomous or controlled—shapes both the depth and quality of students' SRL processes.

Autonomous motivation encompasses intrinsic motivation (engaging in learning for inherent enjoyment or interest) and well-internalized forms of extrinsic motivation (acting out of personal endorsement or identified value). Empirical studies show that this form of motivation predicts higher engagement in SRL strategies at cognitive, metacognitive, and behavioral levels, as students with higher autonomous motivation report greater use of metacognitive strategies such as planning, monitoring, and evaluating learning, as well as more frequent use of deep processing approaches like critical thinking and elaboration (Zimmerman & Schunk, 2012).

Autonomous motivation also fosters persistence, adaptability, and resilience in the face of academic difficulties. Students who feel their motivations are congruent with their interests and values are more likely to persist after setbacks, reflecting the cyclical nature of SRL where feedback, self-monitoring, and readjustment drive continuous improvement (Wolters et al., 2025).

Controlled motivation, in contrast, involves external regulation (acting to obtain rewards or avoid punishments) and introjected regulation (acting out of internal pressures, such as guilt or self-worth contingencies). While controlled motivation can stimulate compliance or temporary diligence, it is associated with more surface-level and reactive learning regulation. Research indicates that students motivated primarily for controlled reasons are more likely to adopt performance goals geared toward proving ability or avoiding failure, which promotes less adaptive learning regulation (Ryan & Deci, 2017).

An illustrative example is Zhao and Ling (2022), who applied LPA to examine self-determination antecedents of SRL facets. Their study identified three profiles of SRL dispositions—self-management and self-monitoring—and found that these profiles differed in levels of autonomous and controlled motivation. However, they did not estimate profile-specific antecedent relationships.

The Role of Gender and Prior Knowledge in Self-Regulated Learning

Numerous studies have suggested that female students tend to report higher levels of SRL behaviors than their male counterparts. For example, research consistently shows that girls are more likely to engage in goal setting, time management, help seeking, and use of metacognitive strategies (Nota et al., 2004; Pajares, 2002). These findings are often interpreted through the lens of socialization theories, which suggest that girls are typically encouraged to be more organized, compliant, and reflective—traits aligned with SRL (Usher & Pajares, 2008).

In large-scale studies, such as PISA assessments, female students often outperform males in SRL-related variables, particularly in motivation and strategy use (OECD, 2015).

Prior knowledge refers to the information, concepts, and experiences that learners bring to new learning situations. It serves as a foundation for constructing new knowledge and plays a critical role in how learners engage in SRL (Alexander, 1996). SRL, which includes cognitive, metacognitive, motivational, and behavioral components (Zimmerman, 2000; Pintrich, 2004), is shaped by learners' pre-existing schemas, beliefs, and understandings. Prior knowledge influences SRL in at least two major ways: it affects how learners interpret tasks and goals, and it guides their selection and deployment of cognitive and metacognitive strategies (Winne & Hadwin, 1998).

Research has consistently shown that prior knowledge enables more effective regulation of learning processes. Learners with higher levels of domain-relevant knowledge are better able to plan, monitor, and evaluate their understanding (Moos & Azevedo, 2008). For example, studies have found that prior knowledge supports metacognitive monitoring accuracy—learners with more accurate schemas can more effectively judge what they know and don't know. Conversely, low prior knowledge may lead to overestimation of competence, miscalibration, and the ineffective use of strategies. Moreover, strategic behaviors such as goal setting, resource management, and the use of elaboration or organization strategies are more likely when learners have a well-developed knowledge base.

Beyond cognition, prior knowledge also interacts with motivational components of SRL. Learners with stronger prior knowledge often demonstrate higher self-efficacy, as past success in a domain builds confidence (Pajares, 1996). This in turn supports greater persistence and willingness to engage in self-regulated behavior (Schunk & Ertmer, 2000). Additionally, prior knowledge can influence attributions for success and failure. Learners who understand content well are more likely to attribute success to effort and strategy use, rather than luck or fixed ability—promoting a growth mindset (Dweck, 1999; Wolters et al., 2025).

Relative Universalism and Person-Centered Analysis

When exploring theoretical frameworks to understand how students learn, two central—yet sometimes competing—objectives often shape the direction of inquiry: parsimony and universalism. Parsimony favors simpler over more complex models when both explain a phenomenon equally well. Universalism, on the other hand, aims to identify models that apply broadly across all learning contexts, rather than relying on multiple, context-specific models (King & McInerney, 2014).

While universal theories are common in the natural sciences, the social sciences—especially educational psychology—rarely produce models that apply equally to all individuals. Instead, a more viable and context-sensitive alternative is the principle of relative universalism (Goetz et al., 2024; Pekrun, 2009, 2018, 2024; Pekrun & Goetz, 2023). This concept holds that although the functional structure of a psychological model may remain stable across diverse learner groups, the parameters (e.g., the strength or intensity of effects) can vary depending on the group in question.

Empirical research on relative universalism often compares natural groupings, such as gender, cultural background, or academic discipline. For instance, Pekrun (2018) observed notable differences in the intensity of math-related learning emotions between male and female students. However, the underlying relationships—such as how students' emotional experiences relate to their appraisals—were found to be structurally equivalent across groups, supporting the principle of relative universalism.

Yet, demonstrating relative universalism across broad demographic categories is insufficient. As Pekrun (2018) points out, within-group variability (e.g., differences among girls or among boys) may exceed the variability between groups. Thus, grouping students by gender, culture, or academic domain, while useful, is a necessary but not sufficient condition for testing relative universalism. A more rigorous approach requires identifying alternative groupings that reduce within-group variation while amplifying between-group differences.

One promising direction lies in the use of person-centered approaches, such as those explored by Tempelaar and Niculescu (2022, 2023), which cluster students based on dispositional profiles rather than demographic or academic characteristics. This method aligns closely with the core aim of relative universalism: to understand how psychological phenomena are actually experienced by different learners. A powerful tool within this paradigm is LPA, which allows researchers to identify subgroups of students who share distinct dispositional patterns. LPA not only captures both within- and between-group variation, but also enables more precise tests of whether key psychological mechanisms hold across these profiles.

Person-centered approaches can be situated midway on a methodological continuum that spans from inter-individual (between-person) to intra-individual (within-person) analyses (Howard & Hoffman, 2018). This continuum is particularly relevant to research on learning emotions, where the debate over the relative merits of each approach is well established. Intra-individual methods—such as experience sampling—have been used for over two decades to explore emotional dynamics as they unfold over time.

Calls for broader adoption of within-person designs in educational psychology can be traced to Molenaar's (2004) work on systems theory and ergodic theorems, which address whether results derived from between-person data can be generalized to individual-level processes. According to Molenaar and Campbell (2009), such generalization is only valid when two conditions are met: (1) homogeneity, meaning individuals conform to the same statistical model, and (2) stationarity, meaning the model remains consistent over time. The latter is especially relevant in the study of dynamic psychological processes, as emphasized by Murayama et al. (2017), who caution against interpreting between-person results as evidence for within-person change.

However, not all educational research focuses on dynamic processes. Some questions—such as what self-regulation skills best predict regulatory behavior—do not inherently involve developmental change. In such cases, stationarity is not required, and only homogeneity is necessary to justify generalization from group-level data (Tempelaar et al., 2020, 2023). In such cases, person-centered methods strike a balance between inter-individual (variable-centered) and intra-individual approaches by grouping individuals into homogeneous subpopulations, revealing hidden heterogeneity while maintaining analytic simplicity Howard and Hoffman (2018).

Despite their advantages and widespread use in fields such as organizational science (Masyn, 2013; Morin 2016; Morin et al., 2011, 2018), person-centered methods remain underutilized in educational psychology. Moreover, those studies that do employ person-centered models often do not combine them with variable-centered analyses to test theoretical relationships within identified profiles—a missed opportunity given that many educational questions require testing static models across diverse learner groups.

In the context of exploring the relative universality of antecedent models of SRL, applying person-centered methods to identify combined regulation and regulation skills profiles presents a more nuanced and empirically robust alternative to traditional demographic grouping. This approach offers stronger evidence for whether core self-regulatory mechanisms function consistently across meaningful learner subgroups, thereby advancing both theory and practice in the study of SRL.

2.3 Method

This section outlines the study's methodology across four components. Section 2.3.1 describes the participants and educational context, detailing sixteen cohorts of first-year business and economics students in a Dutch problem-based, blended learning environment. Section 2.3.2 presents the materials, including validated instruments measuring SRL dispositions, motivational beliefs, mindsets, and effort orientations. Section 2.3.3 outlines the procedures for data collection within the course structure and summarizes ethical considerations. Section 2.3.4 details the statistical analyses, including latent profile analysis and structural equation modeling, used to identify SRL-related learner profiles and examine antecedent relationships. Together, these subsections provide a concise and coherent overview of the study's design and analytic approach.

Participants and Educational Context

This study investigates 16 academic cohorts of first-year students enrolled at a Dutch business and economics school between 2008/2009 and 2023/2024. The institution is recognized for its student-centered, problem-based learning (PBL) approach, offering predominantly English-taught programs that attract a largely international student population. It also holds the prestigious Triple Crown accreditation, a distinction awarded to only a select group of business schools worldwide.

The dataset includes 16,641 first-year students, of whom 39% are female and 61% male; 21% are domestic students, while 79% come from international backgrounds. Most students enter the program directly after completing secondary education, typically between the ages of 18 and 20 (M age = 19.20, SD = 0.40). Data were collected during students' initial course, an introductory module in mathematics and statistics.

Given the diverse educational backgrounds of the international student body, assessing prior education presented notable challenges. Many European secondary school systems—and the International Baccalaureate (IB)—offer tiered mathematics curricula aligned with intended university disciplines (e.g., mathematics tracks for arts/humanities, social sciences, or sciences). While admission to the business and economics program generally requires a social sciences-level mathematics qualification, 34% of students in the sample had completed mathematics at the highest available level. As such, advanced mathematics coursework was used as a key indicator of students' academic preparedness. Importantly, national regulations mandate a standardized curriculum for all students, prohibiting educational streaming.

The institution's pedagogical model centers on PBL, implemented through small tutorial groups of approximately 14–15 students. To accommodate differences in prior knowledge—particularly in mathematics and statistics—a blended learning model is employed. This includes digital resources that complement traditional instruction, fostering a flipped classroom environment (Williams et al., 2016). Students engage in self-directed preparation using e-learning materials, followed by collaborative problem-solving during tutorials.

To further enhance student learning in this module, Dispositional Learning Analytics (DLA) is utilized. Learning Analytics (LA; Buckingham Shum & Deakin Crick, 2012) involves the analysis of digital trace data to provide students with actionable feedback on their learning behaviors. DLA extends this by incorporating data from self-report surveys that assess students' learning dispositions, grounded in social-cognitive theories of learning (Buckingham Shum & Deakin Crick, 2012; Tempelaar et al., 2015, 2018). These surveys serve dual purposes: they provide personalized feedback to students on their learning mindsets and behaviors, and they supply individualized data for hands-on statistical training, thereby supporting the development of data analysis skills. Accordingly, the survey instruments were selected primarily for their relevance to student learning and feedback, rather than being tailored specifically to this research design.

Materials

A comprehensive set of validated self-report instruments was used to assess students' dispositions, motivations, beliefs, and background characteristics relevant to SRL in STEM education. These measures capture multiple dimensions of learners' cognitive, metacognitive, motivational, and affective profiles, enabling a multidimensional examination of how students regulate their learning and engage with academic tasks. The following subsections describe each instrument in detail, including their theoretical foundations, subscale structures, and specific constructs assessed.

SRL Dispositions

Students' self-perceptions of their metacognitive regulation and cognitive processing strategies were assessed using Vermunt's (1998) Inventory of Learning Styles (ILS). For self-perceptions of learning regulation, the instrument comprises five subscales measuring metacognitive strategies: *Self-Regulation of Learning Processes* (*SRLP*) and *Self-Regulation Learning Content* (*SRLC*), *External Regulation of Learning Processes* (*ERLP*) and *External Regulation of Learning Results* (*ERLR*), and *Lack of Regulation of Learning* (*LACK*).

The self-perceived learning processing strategies component of the instrument includes five subscales for cognitive processing strategies, distinguishing between two subscales representing deep learning: *Critical Processing* (*CRIT*) and *Relating and Structuring* (*REL*), two subscales representing surface or stepwise learning: *Analyzing* (*ANAL*) and *Memorizing* (*MEMO*), and a strategic or organized approach, *Concrete Processing* (*CONC*).

The Motivation and Engagement Scale

The Motivation and Engagement Scale (Martin, 2008, 2011), grounded in Martin's (2007) Motivation and Engagement Wheel framework, classifies learning cognitions and behaviors into adaptive and maladaptive categories across cognitive and behavioral domains. Adaptive cognitive factors include *Self-Belief* (*SB*), *Value of School* (*VS*), and *Learning Focus* (*LF*), while adaptive behavioral factors involve *Planning* (*Pl*), *Study Management* (*SM*), and *Persistence* (*PS*).

Maladaptive cognitive factors, such as *Anxiety* (*AN*), *Failure Avoidance* (*FA*), and *Uncertain Control* (*UC*), may sometimes serve as activating cognitions, while maladaptive behaviors, such as *Self-Sabotage* (*SS*) and *Disengagement* (*DS*), consistently hinder engagement.

Mindsets

Mindsets, also referred to as Implicit Theories of Intelligence, were assessed using a two-dimensional model that captures individuals' beliefs about the malleability of intelligence. This framework distinguishes between fixed (entity) theories, which conceptualize intelligence as a stable and unchangeable trait, and growth (incremental) theories, which view intelligence as something that can be developed through effort, strategies, and learning. Assessing both dimensions provides a more nuanced understanding of participants' underlying beliefs, recognizing that individuals may hold varying degrees of each theory rather than aligning exclusively with one.

To measure these constructs, the Theories of Intelligence Scale—Self Form for Adults (Dweck, 1999) was administered. This scale includes eight items: four assessing *Entity Theory* (*ET*) and four assessing *Incremental Theory* (*IT*). Participants rated each item using a Likert-type scale, allowing for quantification of their endorsement of both facets of intelligence beliefs. This dual-scale structure enables researchers to examine mindsets as multidimensional constructs, rather than as a single continuum, thereby improving precision in interpreting participants' implicit theories.

Effort Beliefs

Effort beliefs were assessed using a set of items adapted from Dweck (1999) and Blackwell (2002), capturing individuals' interpretations of the role of effort in learning and achievement. This conceptualization differentiates between two contrasting perspectives: effort as an indicator of low ability, and effort as a productive pathway toward growth and improvement. The former reflects a maladaptive belief system in which needing to try hard is seen as evidence of incompetence, while the latter aligns with adaptive motivational patterns, emphasizing effort as a key driver of learning, skill development, and academic success.

The scale consisted of ten items in total, divided into five *Effort Positive* (*EP*) belief items and five *Effort Negative* (*EN*) belief items (Blackwell et al., 2007; Tempelaar et al., 2015).

Autonomous and Controlled Motivation

Motivation was assessed using the Academic Motivation Scale (AMS; Vallerand et al., 1992), a widely used instrument grounded in Self-Determination Theory (SDT). The AMS captures the full spectrum of motivational orientations by distinguishing between autonomous, controlled, and a-motivated forms of regulation. *Autonomous Motivation* (*AUTON*) was operationalized by combining scores from the three intrinsic motivation subscales—intrinsic motivation to know, to accomplish, and to experience stimulation—and the identified regulation subscale. Each of these subscales contains four items. Together, they reflect self-endorsed and volitional forms of motivation, in which learners engage in academic activities out of genuine interest, personal importance, or a sense of meaningful choice.

Controlled Motivation (*CONTROL*) was measured using items from the introjected and external regulation subscales, each comprising four items. These subscales capture more pressured forms of motivation, where behavior is regulated by internal contingencies (e.g., guilt, ego-involvement) or external demands (e.g., rewards, punishments). Finally, *Amotivation* (*AMOT*) was included as an indicator of a complete lack of motivation, characterized by feelings of incompetence, lack of intention, or an absence of perceived value in academic tasks.

Student Background Data

Gender (coded as Female) and prior mathematics education at an advanced level (Math-Major, indicating high school mathematics coursework designed to prepare students for science- and technology-oriented study rather than social sciences) were included as binary indicator variables.

These variables serve as important demographic controls, allowing the analyses to account for systematic differences in students' educational backgrounds and potential disparities related to gender. Sample items of students' dispositions toward learning regulation and their regulation skills are provided in Table 2.1.

Procedures

During the first 8 weeks of their initial academic semester, students completed two mandatory modules: one combining organizational theory and marketing, and another dedicated to introductory mathematics and statistics. Within the first 4 weeks, students engaged in a data analysis project, during which they completed self-report questionnaires on learning dispositions, both during class and independently.

Table 2.1 Sample items of students' dispositions toward learning regulation and their regulation skills

Scale	Sample item
SRLP	When I start a new chapter or article I first think about the best way to study it
SRLC	I add something to the material from other sources
ERLP	I learn everything exactly as I find it in the textbooks
ERLR	When doing assignments, I train myself thoroughly in applying the methods dealt with in a block
LACK	I realise that I miss someone to fall back on in case of difficulties
CRIT	I try to approach the interpretations of experts critically
REL	I compare conclusions from various chapters with each other
ANAL	I analyse the separate parts of a theory step by step
MEMO	I learn definitions by heart as literally as possible
CONC	I use what I learn during my activities in a course outside of my studies
SB	If I try hard, I believe I can do my university work well
VS	Learning at university is important
LF	I feel very pleased with myself when I really understand what I'm taught at university
PL	Before I start an assignment, I plan out how I am going to do it
SM	When I study, I usually study in places where I can concentrate
PS	If I can't understand my university work at first, I keep going over it until I do
AN	When exams and assignments are coming up, I worry a lot
FA	Often the main reason I work at university is because I don't want people to think that I'm dumb
UC	When I get a bad mark I'm often unsure how I'm going to avoid getting that mark again
SS	Sometimes I don't try hard at assignments so I have an excuse if I don't do so well
DS	I've pretty much given up being involved in things at university

Achievement emotions and value-attitude questionnaires were administered at the midpoint of the module (end of Week 4). This timing ensured that students had gained sufficient exposure to the course structure, learning environment, and assessment methods to provide meaningful reflections.

Given the naturalistic, student-centered context of the learning environment—characterized by independent problem-solving—it was not feasible to link emotional responses to specific, predefined tasks. As such, students completed the emotion survey retrospectively, reflecting on their individual learning experiences and problem-solving activities from the previous week.

Thanks to the structured nature of the project, missing data were minimal and occurred only in cases of student withdrawal from the module. These students were excluded from the analysis.

The study received ethical approval from the Ethics Review Committee of the Maastricht University Inner-City faculties (ERCIC_044_14_07). All participants provided informed consent for the use of their personal data for the dual purpose of generating personalized learning feedback and contributing to educational research aimed at improving teaching and learning.

Statistical Analysis

This study employed a person-centered approach, utilizing the three-step procedure for LPA (Asparouhov & Muthén, 2008) with distal outcomes as proposed by Asparouhov and Muthén (2014), implemented in Mplus version 8.10.

In the first step, the latent profile model was estimated using the default mixture modeling estimator—maximum likelihood with robust standard errors (MLR). The goal was to identify categorical latent variables that captured distinct subgroups of students based on shared patterns across five learning regulation scales (*SRLP*, *SRLC*, *ERLP*, *ERLR*, *LACK*), five learning processing scales (*CRIT*, *REL*, *ANAL*, *MEMO*, *CONC*), and eleven adaptive and maladaptive cognitions (adaptive: *SB*, *VS*, *LF*; maladaptive: *PL*, *SM*, *PS*) and behaviors (adaptive: *AN*, *FA*, *UC*; maladaptive: *SS*, *DS*) considered indicators of regulation skills.

In the second step, each participant was assigned to the most likely profile based on the posterior probabilities derived from the latent class distribution.

The third step involved estimating structural equation models (SEMs) to examine the relationships between class membership and potential antecedents by modeling the joint distribution of the latent class variable and relevant auxiliary variables, as outlined by Asparouhov and Muthén (2014).

To determine the optimal number of latent profiles in step one, models specifying between two and nine classes were estimated. Consistent with previous findings (e.g., Tempelaar & Niculescu, 2022, 2023) and broader trends in mixture modeling research—where model fit indices tend to improve with additional classes (Howard & Hoffman, 2018)—we anticipated that statistical criteria alone would be insufficient to guide model selection. While indicators such as AIC and BIC typically show monotonic improvement, our final model selection also incorporated substantive criteria.

A key practical constraint was the need to avoid small class sizes, given the demands of subsequent structural modeling. Substantively, we sought profiles that not only varied quantitatively (e.g., levels of positive versus negative emotions) but also differed qualitatively in terms of regulation patterns, to ensure theoretically meaningful distinctions among student groups.

In step three, SEMs were used to explore antecedent relationships across the identified profiles. Because mixture models rely on latent (unobserved) class membership, conducting traditional chi-square tests for parameter invariance presents methodological challenges. One common workaround involves treating the most likely class assignments as known and performing multiple-group analyses. However, the aim of this study was not to test strict universalism, but rather to explore relative universality—specifically, whether the functional form of SRL models holds across distinct student profiles. As such, formal chi-square testing of equality constraints was deemed unnecessary for addressing the core research objective.

2.4 Results

This section presents the empirical results in six sequential steps, moving from descriptive patterns to explanatory modeling. Section 2.4.1 reports the descriptive statistics of learning regulation constructs, learning strategies, and regulation skills, as well as subgroup comparisons by gender and prior education. Section 2.4.2 outlines the latent profile analysis and describes the resulting five-class solution. Building on these foundations, Sections 2.4.3–2.4.7 present a series of structural equation models testing how different antecedent domains predict learning regulation. Specifically, Section 2.4.3 examines learning strategies, Sect. 2.4.4 focuses on adaptive regulation skills, Sect. 2.4.5 investigates maladaptive regulation skills, Sect. 2.4.6 tests self-determination-based motivational antecedents, and Sect. 2.4.7 explores mindset-related beliefs. Across these analyses, both full-sample and subgroup models are compared to evaluate the robustness and potential boundaries of relative universalism in predicting SRL across diverse learner profiles.

Descriptive Statistics of Learning Regulation and Learning Skills

Table 2.2 presents the descriptive statistics for measures of learning regulation and its antecedents, including means, standard deviations, skewness, kurtosis, sample reliability (Omega), and intercorrelations—limited to those between learning regulation constructs and other variables. On average, both self- and external-regulation scores exceed the neutral midpoint of four, though the differences are modest. An exception is observed for *SRLC*, which aligns closely with the neutral anchor.

All cognitive learning strategy scales display mean scores above the neutral value, as do the adaptive motivation and engagement factors. In contrast, maladaptive motivation and engagement factors generally fall below the neutral point, with the exception of *AN*, which scores higher.

Strong positive correlations are found between all learning regulation scales and the five cognitive learning strategies. Notably, *ERLP* and *ERLC* exhibit their strongest associations with stepwise or reproduction-oriented strategies such as *MEMO* and *REL*. Conversely, self-regulation facets are correlated with both deep and stepwise learning strategies.

All variables meet standard criteria for univariate analysis (Kline, 2023), except for the a-motivation variable, which shows a highly skewed and leptokurtic distribution due to most responses clustering at the lower end of the scale. Applying a logarithmic transformation to this variable addresses the issue.

Table 2.3 reports the effects of gender and prior education on learning regulation and regulation skills, examined in the context of how student classifications influence learning regulation relationships. While all gender differences of the learning regulation constructs, as well as the prior education differences for *ERLR* and *LACK*, are statistically significant ($p < 0.001$), likely due to the large sample size, the associated effect sizes (η^2) are negligible.

Table 2.2 Descriptive statistics of students' dispositions toward learning regulation and their regulation skills

Scale	Mean	SD	Skewness	Kurtosis	Reliability	Correlations				
						SRLP	SRLC	ERLP	ERLC	LACK
SRLP	4.501	0.945	−0.228	−0.043	0.859	1.00				
SRLC	3.963	1.079	−0.083	−0.263	0.801	***0.520***	1.00			
ERLP	4.619	0.771	−0.120	−0.004	0.776	***0.199***	***0.117***	1.00		
ERLR	5.128	0.726	−0.308	0.438	0.814	***0.290***	***0.182***	***0.477***	1.00	
LACK	3.806	0.999	−0.015	−0.272	0.829	0.015	***0.032***	***0.064***	***−0.031***	1.00
CRIT	4.475	0.981	−0.248	0.185	0.806	***0.487***	***0.421***	***0.102***	***0.235***	***−0.023***
REL	4.902	0.799	−0.336	0.317	0.889	***0.569***	***0.408***	***0.206***	***0.360***	***−0.110***
ANAL	4.699	0.813	−0.193	0.161	0.844	***0.508***	***0.422***	***0.478***	***0.446***	***−0.043***
MEMO	4.400	0.979	−0.247	−0.056	0.817	***0.400***	***0.341***	***0.396***	***0.303***	***0.048***
CONC	4.780	0.901	−0.341	0.202	0.844	***0.516***	***0.414***	***0.142***	***0.290***	−0.005
SB	5.888	0.739	−0.658	0.612	0.771	***0.183***	***0.153***	***0.136***	***0.237***	***−0.178***
VS	5.879	0.682	−0.874	1.708	0.672	***0.238***	***0.195***	***0.190***	***0.251***	***−0.117***
LF	6.109	0.705	−0.907	1.160	0.796	***0.248***	***0.209***	***0.210***	***0.285***	***−0.035***
PL	4.814	1.028	−0.364	−0.010	0.768	***0.331***	***0.252***	***0.248***	***0.221***	***−0.132***
SM	5.601	0.904	−0.774	0.739	0.758	***0.269***	***0.201***	***0.219***	***0.220***	***−0.083***
PS	5.420	0.843	−0.530	0.431	0.792	***0.331***	***0.314***	***0.232***	***0.261***	***−0.153***
AN	4.585	1.257	−0.307	−0.367	0.831	***0.031***	***0.047***	***0.115***	***0.041***	***0.375***
FA	2.568	1.234	0.803	0.083	0.843	−0.016	0.000	−0.003	***−0.047***	***0.260***
UC	3.461	1.160	0.174	−0.515	0.808	***−0.064***	***−0.060***	0.010	***−0.078***	***0.417***
SS	2.347	1.090	0.929	0.514	0.826	***−0.124***	***−0.117***	***−0.161***	***−0.167***	***0.198***
DS	1.872	0.857	1.360	2.140	0.756	***−0.128***	***−0.121***	***−0.131***	***−0.187***	***0.191***

(continued)

Table 2.2 (continued)

Scale	Mean	SD	Skewness	Kurtosis	Reliability	Correlations				
						SRLP	SRLC	ERLP	ERLC	LACK
Auton	5.317	0.720	−0.591	0.674	0.898	***0.269***	***0.226***	***0.209***	***0.258***	***−0.085***
Control	5.200	0.957	−0.666	0.481	0.818	***0.072***	***0.021***	***0.174***	***0.174***	***0.053***
Amot	1.472	0.775	2.522	7.708	0.815	***−0.066***	***−0.048***	***−0.114***	***−0.163***	***0.201***
LnAmot	1.908	1.212	1.384	1.288	0.828	***−0.076***	***−0.061***	***−0.123***	***−0.170***	***0.224***
IT	4.694	1.137	−0.522	0.151	0.839	***0.158***	***0.128***	***0.128***	***0.126***	***−0.024***
ET	3.521	1.284	0.316	−0.481	0.852	***−0.096***	***−0.099***	***−0.043***	***−0.050***	***0.100***
EP	5.320	0.692	−0.341	0.359	0.631	***0.265***	***0.208***	***0.231***	***0.274***	***−0.130***
EN	2.820	0.821	0.496	0.422	0.684	***−0.129***	***−0.111***	***−0.042***	***−0.121***	***0.279***
OG	6.019	0.815	−1.032	1.691	0.833	***0.193***	***0.188***	***0.251***	***0.291***	***−0.068***
AG	4.744	1.101	−0.498	0.193	0.722	***0.140***	***0.112***	***0.172***	***0.197***	***−0.026***
NOG	4.224	1.231	−0.177	−0.319	0.768	***0.108***	***0.148***	***0.118***	***0.136***	−0.008
NAG	3.126	1.373	0.380	−0.495	0.903	***0.030***	***0.064***	***0.019***	***0.030***	**0.022**
LG	5.685	0.811	−0.548	0.521	0.762	***0.286***	***0.261***	***0.191***	***0.262***	***−0.140***
CMG	4.904	0.979	−0.262	0.151	0.763	***0.267***	***0.246***	***0.079***	***0.145***	***−0.158***

Note Scales based on Likert 1–7 type items; correlations: $p < 0.001$: bold and italic; $p < 0.01$: bold; $p < 0.05$: italic

Table 2.3 Means of learning regulation constructs, by gender and prior education

Scale	Female	Male	EtaSquare	Math−	Math+	EtaSquare
SRLP	4.604	4.442	0.007	4.499	4.516	0.000
SRLC	4.056	3.910	0.004	3.971	3.957	0.000
ERLP	4.733	4.551	0.013	4.633	4.604	0.000
ERLR	5.224	5.074	0.010	5.117	5.165	0.001
LACK	3.878	3.764	0.003	3.860	3.706	0.005
CRIT	4.378	4.541	0.007	4.458	4.511	0.001
REL	4.942	4.882	0.001	4.889	4.940	0.001
ANAL	4.801	4.640	0.009	4.701	4.709	0.000
MEMO	4.604	4.273	0.027	4.424	4.369	0.001
CONC	4.714	4.822	0.003	4.765	4.806	0.000
SB	5.866	5.901	0.001	5.859	5.947	0.003
VS	5.954	5.831	0.008	5.876	5.891	0.000
LF	6.258	6.013	0.029	6.106	6.118	0.000
PL	5.050	4.662	0.034	4.809	4.825	0.000
SM	5.805	5.471	0.033	5.614	5.577	0.000
PS	5.547	5.339	0.014	5.393	5.475	0.002
AN	5.049	4.286	0.088	4.650	4.457	0.005
FA	2.630	2.528	0.002	2.574	2.539	0.000
UC	3.628	3.354	0.013	3.515	3.354	0.004
SS	2.239	2.416	0.006	2.352	2.323	0.000
DS	1.786	1.928	0.007	1.858	1.880	0.000

Gender differences in regulation skills, while still small, are generally more pronounced than those observed for regulation types. Female students report more frequent use of the memorization strategy, higher scores on the adaptive motivational factors of *LF*, *PL*, and *SM*, as well as greater levels of anxiety. In contrast, the effects of prior education are negligible across all variables, with explained variance not exceeding 0.5%.

Latent Profile Analysis and the Description of the Five-Class Solution

Latent profile analyses were conducted using scores from the five learning regulation scales—*SRLP*, *SRLC*, *ERLP*, *ERLR*, and *LACK*—along with measures considered indicative of learning regulation skills: five learning strategy scales, six adaptive and five maladaptive motivation and engagement variables. Models with two to nine latent classes were tested, with the selection of the optimal number based on both statistical fit indices and substantive interpretability.

Although fit indices (AIC, BIC, and adjusted BIC) improved steadily with additional classes, none identified a clearly optimal solution. Notably, the rate of improvement tended to diminish after the five-class model. Substantively, the two- to four-class models primarily reflected quantitative differences in adaptivity, ranging from low to high. The most adaptive profile in these models featured high levels across all regulation and learning strategy measures, strong adaptive skills, and low maladaptive tendencies. Less adaptive profiles achieved lower scores across the board, with the exception, of course, of the maladaptive skills.

In contrast, the five-class and higher-order models introduced qualitative distinctions between profiles. However, models with six or more classes yielded diminishing interpretive value, often splitting into smaller, more extreme subgroups that lacked practical relevance. Therefore, the five-class solution was selected as the most meaningful and parsimonious representation. The defining characteristics of each profile are visualized in Fig. 2.1 and detailed in Table 2.4.

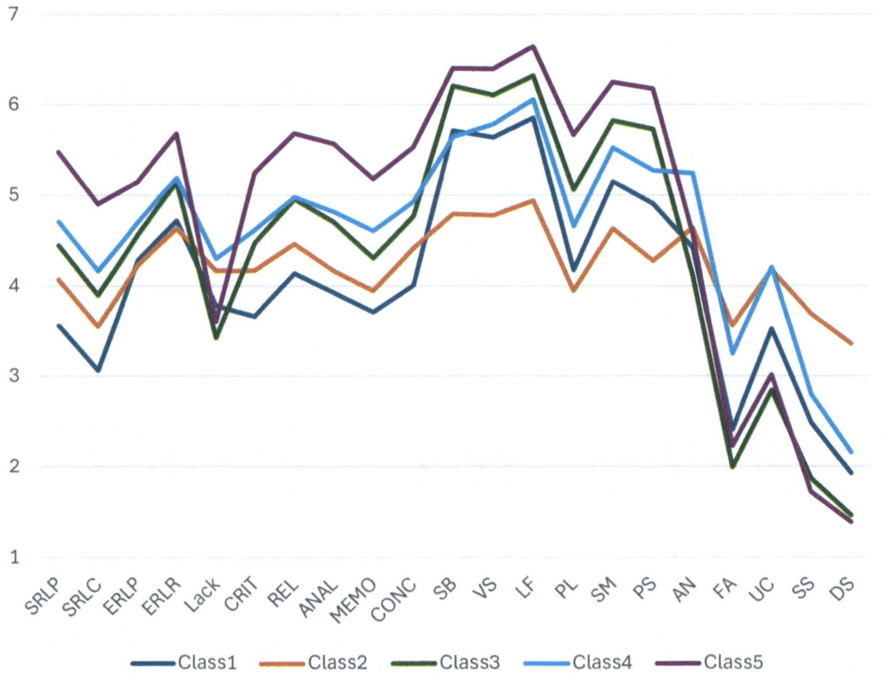

Fig. 2.1 Class means of learning regulation constructs and regulation skills

Table 2.4 Class size (N) and class means of learning regulation constructs and regulation skills

Scale	Class 1	Class 2	Class 3	Class 4	Class 5
N	2916	1356	4886	4265	2940
SRLP	3.556	4.069	4.445	4.704	5.476
SRLC	3.060	3.552	3.898	4.164	4.902
ERLP	4.275	4.226	4.557	4.702	5.146
ERLR	4.714	4.634	5.142	5.192	5.681
Lack	3.778	4.170	3.423	4.297	3.607
CRIT	3.664	4.171	4.471	4.617	5.246
REL	4.138	4.466	4.958	4.978	5.687
ANAL	3.922	4.170	4.701	4.816	5.573
MEMO	3.708	3.947	4.304	4.605	5.183
CONC	4.004	4.418	4.768	4.929	5.535
SB	5.710	4.793	6.204	5.646	6.401
VS	5.641	4.776	6.101	5.786	6.397
LF	5.851	4.939	6.316	6.055	6.646
PL	4.172	3.951	5.060	4.660	5.672
SM	5.151	4.630	5.822	5.525	6.249
PS	4.904	4.277	5.725	5.272	6.178
AN	4.416	4.643	4.104	5.243	4.576
FA	2.408	3.563	1.993	3.252	2.232
UC	3.523	4.180	2.845	4.204	3.015
SS	2.489	3.692	1.866	2.800	1.724
DS	1.926	3.362	1.463	2.159	1.387

Learning Regulation as Predicted by Learning Strategies

Table 2.5 presents the regression equations predicting various learning regulation constructs based on learning strategies and control variables for the full sample. Among the constructs, *SRLP* shows the highest level of explained variance. *SRLP* is positively predicted by all learning strategies, with the strongest contribution from the deep learning strategy Relating and Structuring.

SRLC is similarly predicted by a broad range of strategies, without a clear dominant one. In contrast, the two external regulation constructs are primarily predicted by the surface strategy *ANAL*. As expected, the maladaptive construct *LACK* shows the lowest level of explained variance, with no strong predictor emerging, by lack of any distinctly maladaptive strategy.

Control variables have a limited impact. Female students tend to score slightly higher on all regulation constructs compared to male students. Prior knowledge plays a minimal role, as indicated by the small beta coefficients and inconsistent signs of *MathMajor* (representing prior educational track) and *MathEntry* (entry test score),

Table 2.5 Standardized beta coefficients and explained variance in structural equation models predicting learning regulation from learning strategies

	SRLP	SRLC	ERLP	ERLR	Lack
CRIT	0.142***	0.185***	−0.073***	−0.020	0.017
REL	0.253***	0.088***	0.014	0.163***	−0.169***
ANAL	0.212***	0.177***	0.386***	0.289***	−0.077***
MEMO	0.131***	0.141***	0.217***	0.072***	0.080***
CONC	0.179***	0.134***	0.014	0.102***	0.064***
Female	0.056***	0.040***	0.035***	0.066***	0.075***
MathMajor	−0.019**	−0.035***	−0.009	0.034***	−0.040***
MathEntry	0.030***	0.038***	0.007	0.002	0.101***
R^2	0.481	0.286	0.280	0.250	0.049

Note ***$p < 0.001$; **$p < 0.01$; *$p < 0.05$

The predictive models demonstrate strong robustness across subgroups based on gender, prior education, and latent profiles identified through LPA. The amount of explained variance remains relatively stable, though slightly lower for profiles Class 1 and Class 3. While some variation in beta coefficients occurs, the consistency in their direction suggests that the predictive relationships between learning strategies and regulation constructs hold across different learner subgroups, supporting the notion of relative universalism.

Learning Regulation as Predicted by Adaptive Learning Regulation Skills

This subsection examines how students' adaptive regulation skills and selected control variables predict key learning regulation constructs. Table 2.6 summarizes the regression models estimated for the full sample, providing an overview of the relative contributions of cognitive, behavioral, and motivational factors to different forms of learning regulation.

Once again, *SRLP* exhibits the highest level of explained variance. Both self-regulation facets—*SRLP* and *SRLC*—are primarily predicted by the cognitive skill *PS* and the behavioral skill *PL*. Notably, *SB* and *LF* contribute little to the prediction of self-regulation, with some effects even negative.

The two external regulation constructs—*ERLP* and *ERLR*—show lower levels of explained variance, likely due to the absence of strong, consistent predictors. A minor exception is the significant role of *PL* in predicting *ERLP*. The model performs weakest in explaining *LACK*, where *SB* emerges as the most prominent predictor. Control variables continue to play a marginal role.

Table 2.6 Standardized beta coefficients and explained variance in structural equation models predicting learning regulation from adaptive skills

	SRLP	SRLC	ERLP	ERLR	LACK
SB	−0.004	−0.024*	−0.023*	0.086***	−0.165***
VS	0.086***	0.049***	0.074***	0.082***	−0.047***
LF	0.029*	0.022	0.052***	0.099***	0.122***
PL	0.199***	0.130***	0.131***	0.077***	−0.099***
SM	0.062***	0.031***	0.075**	0.052***	0.028*
PS	0.170***	0.214***	0.085***	0.062***	−0.096***
Female	0.009	0.001	0.050***	0.059***	0.070***
MathMajor	−0.021*	−0.040***	−0.025**	0.024**	−0.038***
MathEntry	0.062***	0.054***	0.036***	0.032***	−0.085***
R^2	0.187	0.126	0.104	0.126	0.081

Note ***$p < 0.001$; **$p < 0.01$; *$p < 0.05$

The predictive models remain robust across subgroups based on gender and prior education level. However, this robustness is substantially reduced when considering latent profile groupings. Structural equation power drops markedly in these subgroups. While Class 2 retains explained variance comparable to the full sample, for other profiles the explained variance for both self-regulation constructs fall below 3%, and most standardized beta coefficients lose statistical significance. These findings suggest the limits of the model's relative universalism, as the consistency in predicting self-regulation begins to weaken in certain learner profiles.

Learning Regulation as Predicted by Maladaptive Learning Regulation Skills

Table 2.7 presents the equations predicting various learning regulation constructs based on maladaptive regulation skills and control variables for the full sample. As expected, within this structural equation model, the maladaptive construct Lack of Regulation (Lack) shows the highest level of explained variance. Its main predictors are two cognitive-type motivational constructs: Anxiety (AN) and Uncertainty Control (UC).

A particularly noteworthy finding is the role of Anxiety, which contributes positively not only to the maladaptive strategy Lack of Regulation but also—albeit to a lesser degree—to the four adaptive regulation constructs, with the strongest effects observed for the external regulation facets (ERLP and ERLR).

The two maladaptive behavioral constructs, Self-Sabotage (SS) and Disengagement (DS), display a consistent pattern of associations: negative beta coefficients for the adaptive regulation strategies and positive coefficients for the maladaptive

Table 2.7 Standardized beta coefficients and explained variance in structural equation models predicting learning regulation from maladaptive skills

	SRLP	SRLC	ERLP	ERLR	Lack
AN	0.059***	0.066***	0.110***	0.077***	0.227***
FA	0.024*	0.036***	0.042***	0.036***	0.051***
UC	−0.077***	−0.073***	−0.014	−0.087***	0.258***
SS	−0.083***	−0.085***	−0.136***	−0.091***	0.067***
DS	−0.082***	−0.067***	−0.086***	−0.113***	0.057***
Female	0.067***	0.039***	0.065***	0.079***	−0.021*
MathMajor	−0.022*	−0.040***	−0.023*	0.029*	−0.032***
MathEntry	0.101***	0.090***	0.061***	0.052***	−0.063***
R^2	0.048	0.037	0.058	0.058	0.251

Note ***$p < 0.001$; **$p < 0.01$; *$p < 0.05$

strategy. When examining subgroup analyses, the patterns remain largely unchanged for groupings based on gender and prior education level. However, a notable decline in predictive power is observed when grouping by latent profiles. In these subgroups, the significance of predictors diminishes considerably, and many beta coefficients lose statistical significance. Still, given the relatively low explained variance already present in the full-sample models, caution is warranted in interpreting these subgroup-specific declines.

Learning Regulation as Predicted by Self-Determination Based Concepts

Table 2.8 displays the structural equations predicting various learning regulation constructs based on antecedents derived from Self-Determination Theory (SDT), along with control variables, for the full sample. A clear pattern emerges: Autonomous Motivation (AUTON) plays a dominant role, particularly in predicting the two self-regulation constructs, Self-Regulation of the Learning Process (SRLP) and Self-Regulation of Learning Content (SRLC).

Consistent with the tenets of SDT, Controlled Motivation (CONTROL) is positively associated with the two external regulation constructs (ERLP and ERLR) and negatively associated with both self-regulation constructs (SRLP and SRLC). The maladaptive motivational construct Amotivation (AMOTln, log-transformed) serves as a significant predictor of the maladaptive regulation strategy Lack of Regulation. Overall, the explained variance in these predictive models hovers around 10%.

Subgroup analyses confirm the patterns observed in previous sections. Groupings based on gender and prior education level yield minimal changes in model structure and explained variance. However, subgrouping by latent profiles reveals a

Table 2.8 Standardized beta coefficients and explained variance in structural equation models predicting learning regulation from self-determination concepts

	SRLP	SRLC	ERLP	ERLR	Lack
AUTON	0.352***	0.310***	0.144***	0.186***	−0.087***
CONTROL	−0.092***	−0.125***	0.105***	0.081***	0.113***
AMOTIn	0.007	0.011	−0.084***	−0.128***	0.217***
Female	0.039***	0.019*	0.068***	0.046***	0.104***
MathMajor	−0.019	−0.036***	−0.027**	0.032***	−0.046***
MathEntry	0.088***	0.080***	0.058***	0.049***	−0.103***
R^2	0.115	0.081	0.079	0.104	0.090

Note ***$p < 0.001$; **$p < 0.01$; *$p < 0.05$

different picture. In Classes 1, 3, and 4, the predictive power for both self-regulation constructs falls below 3%, and several previously significant predictors lose their statistical significance. These findings suggest that while SDT-based predictors function robustly across demographic subgroups, their explanatory power may not generalize across all learner profiles identified through LPA.

Learning Regulation as Predicted by Mindset Theory-Based Concepts

Table 2.9 presents the structural equations predicting various learning regulation constructs based on antecedents from Mindset Theory, along with control variables, for the full sample. Consistent with the authors' previous research, Effort Beliefs—both Positive Effort (PE) and Negative Effort (NE)—emerge as substantially stronger predictors than the Intelligence Beliefs, namely Incremental Theory (IT) and Entity Theory (ET). Unlike in prior sections, effort and intelligence beliefs contribute equally to the prediction of both adaptive and maladaptive learning regulation constructs, each explaining approximately 10% of the variance.

Subgroup analyses based on gender and prior education again replicate the stable patterns observed in earlier models, with prediction equations and levels of explained variance remaining largely unchanged. However, the findings diverge significantly when considering subgroups defined by latent profiles. To highlight the differences in structural models across these latent classes, Tables 2.10 and 2.11 present prediction equations for Self-Regulation of the Learning Process (SRLP) and Self-Regulation of Learning Content (SRLC), comparing the full sample with individual latent classes.

In the prediction of SRLP, only Positive Effort Belief (PE) retains a meaningful predictive role across most classes, while all other predictors lose significance in one or more latent profiles. Notably, the gender control variable even reverses sign in Class 1. The overall predictive power drops from 11.5% in the full sample to below 5% in the latent subgroups.

Table 2.9 Standardized beta coefficients and explained variance in structural equation models predicting learning regulation from mindset theory concepts

	SRLP	SRLC	ERLP	ERLR	Lack
IT	0.099***	0.029*	0.141***	0.136***	0.084***
ET	0.049***	−0.025	0.095***	0.114***	0.071***
EP	0.270***	0.204***	0.227***	0.249***	−0.051***
EN	−0.022*	−0.011	0.048***	−0.043***	0.284***
Female	0.069***	0.047***	0.099***	0.086***	0.073***
MathMajor	−0.028**	−0.041***	−0.028**	0.022*	−0.036***
MathEntry	0.096***	0.085***	0.051***	0.047***	−0.094***
R^2	0.115	0.065	0.083	0.106	0.121

Note ***$p < 0.001$; **$p < 0.01$; *$p < 0.05$

Table 2.10 Standardized beta coefficients and explained variance in structural equation models predicting SRLP from mindset theory concepts

SRLP	All	Class 1	Class 2	Class 3	Class 4	Class 5
IT	0.099***	0.090	0.131*	0.007	0.084*	0.054
ET	0.049***	0.048	0.040	0.003	0.058	0.024
EP	0.270***	0.002	0.127**	0.068**	0.129***	0.152***
EN	−0.022*	0.053	−0.021	−0.003	−0.021	0.031
Female	0.069***	−0.064*	0.010	0.036	−0.003	0.010
MathMajor	−0.028**	−0.021	0.013	−0.025	−0.029	0.015
MathEntry	0.096***	0.024	0.067	0.043	0.052*	0.049
R^2	0.115	0.011	0.043	0.009	0.028	0.030

Note ***$p < 0.001$; **$p < 0.01$; *$p < 0.05$

Table 2.11 Standardized beta coefficients and explained variance in structural equation models predicting SRLC from mindset theory concepts

SRLC	All	Class 1	Class 2	Class 3	Class 4	Class 5
IT	0.029*	−0.049	0.102	−0.020	−0.053	0.009
ET	−0.025	−0.075	0.018	−0.041	−0.125***	0.010
EP	0.204***	−0.011	0.058	0.036	0.042	0.086***
EN	−0.011	0.038	0.054*	−0.054*	0.074**	−0.004
Female	0.047***	−0.014	−0.048	−0.025	0.035	−0.041
MathMajor	−0.041***	−0.033	0.030	−0.063**	−0.027	−0.015
MathEntry	0.085***	−0.018*	0.084	0.049*	0.047*	0.034
R^2	0.065	0.005	0.026	0.012	0.013	0.011

Note ***$p < 0.001$; **$p < 0.01$; *$p < 0.05$

The lack of invariance is even more pronounced for SRLC. While in the full sample the adaptive beliefs Incremental Theory (IT) and Positive Effort (PE) are the main predictors, in the majority of latent classes (with the exception of Class 5), the maladaptive beliefs Entity Theory (ET) and Negative Effort (NE) emerge as the dominant predictors. Moreover, explained variance declines from 6.5% in the full sample to under 3% in the class-specific models. If anything, the relationships between mindset constructs and learning regulation show little evidence of relative universalism—unlike the more stable patterns observed in some of the models discussed in previous sections.

2.5 Discussion

This section synthesizes the findings derived from testing five alternative models linking self-perceived learning regulation to a diverse set of antecedents. Although the primary objective was to evaluate whether these antecedent–consequence relationships exhibit relative universalism across different subgroup decompositions, several broader insights emerged that carry implications for both theory and educational practice. In particular, the results highlight the need to move beyond a narrow focus on self-regulation of learning and toward a more comprehensive perspective on learning regulation, while also underscoring the limitations of conventional approaches to assessing generalizability. The subsections below elaborate these contributions.

Broadening the Focus: From SRL to Learning Regulation

In this study, we examined five alternative models that link self-perceived learning regulation to various types of antecedents. While our primary aim was to assess whether these antecedent–consequence relationships demonstrate relative universalism across different subgroup decompositions, some key findings extend beyond the question of generalizability.

One such finding is the importance of broadening the analytical focus from self-regulation of learning to the more comprehensive concept of learning regulation, which includes both self- and external regulation. Although this may seem self-evident, it is often overlooked in the current literature. To draw an analogy: assessing a soccer player's performance based solely on right-foot statistics would be incomplete without considering left-foot performance. Similarly, early research on SRL—particularly in the context of TEL and TELEs—frequently adopted a broader view that included both self- and external regulation (e.g., Azevedo et al., 2008; Witherspoon et al., 2008). However, in recent decades, the field has largely shifted toward studying self-regulation in isolation, with only a few exceptions (e.g., Bardach et al., 2023). This narrowing of focus is unfortunate and comparable to analyzing soccer performance based on one-sided data.

Although the empirical basis for comparing our work with studies on the integration of self- and external regulation is already limited, it becomes even more constrained when we turn to the central aim of this contribution: testing the relative universalism of SRL using profiling approaches. Similar to the present study, Shum et al. (2024) apply profiling to SRL disposition data; however, their analysis stops at reporting descriptive differences between profiles and does not extend to examining whether antecedent–consequence relationships within SRL vary across profiles. The only empirical study that employs a similar universalism-testing approach is a companion paper (Tempelaar & Niculescu, 2025), although that work focuses specifically on examining the universality of control–value theory.

The Limits of Dualistic Assumptions in Learning Research

The predominant assumption behind studying self-regulation in isolation is a dualistic one: that self-regulation and external regulation represent opposing and mutually exclusive learning approaches. According to this view, learners either self-regulate or rely on external regulation, but not both. This binary logic is not unique to learning regulation research. Similar dichotomies are seen in learning strategy studies (e.g., deep versus surface learning), self-determination theory (autonomous versus controlled motivation), and mindset theory (incremental versus entity beliefs, positive versus negative effort beliefs). Yet, our research—as well as prior studies—consistently challenges these assumptions.

In practice, students do not adhere strictly to one side of these theoretical dichotomies. When surveyed about their learning strategies, students typically report using both deep and surface approaches depending on the context. Similarly, learners often indicate that they employ self-regulation when feasible but rely on external regulation when needed. Indeed, our findings consistently show that the most adaptive students are those who make flexible and intensive use of all types of regulation and processing strategies, and who exhibit both high autonomous and controlled motivation.

Complementarity of Regulation Types and the Case for Integrated Models

The fact that different types of learning regulation tend to function as complementary rather than mutually exclusive processes strongly support the argument for studying them in an integrated manner. Focusing on one type in isolation not only oversimplifies learner behavior but also risks missing key dynamics that are crucial for understanding and supporting effective learning.

This finding aligns closely with outcomes of empirical applications of the Theory of Self- versus Externally-Regulated Learning (de la Fuente et al., 2021, 2022; see also de la Fuente & Kauffman, 2025), which emphasize that learning regulation can be fully understood only by considering the interplay between student regulation, the learning process, and external regulation, such as teacher guidance or other contextual supports.

Rethinking Relative Universalism: Why Natural Groupings are Not Enough

We now turn to the central contribution of this empirical study: the analysis of relative universalism in the antecedent relationships underlying learning regulation. We argue that the conventional approach to testing relative universalism—typically through comparisons across natural groupings such as gender or cultural background—is a necessary but insufficient condition for establishing true generalizability. A more rigorous assessment requires an additional step: evaluating whether these relationships hold across groups defined not by external characteristics, but by latent psychological or behavioral profiles.

To this end, we propose latent profile analysis as a stronger test of relative universalism. Unlike natural groupings, LPA is designed to minimize within-group variability and maximize between-group variability, offering a clearer lens through which to assess the consistency of structural relationships. Under a strict interpretation of relative universalism, the antecedent–consequence relationships identified in the full sample should also hold across all latent classes derived from the LPA.

However, our findings indicate that this condition is frequently violated. In several structural equation models, predictive power dropped sharply when moving from the full sample or natural groupings (e.g., gender, prior knowledge) to latent profile-based groupings. This pattern suggests that most of the explained variance in the models stems from interclass variation—differences in means between classes—rather than intraclass variation, which reflects differences among students within a single class.

Interclass Versus Intraclass Variation: Implications for Intervention Design

This distinction is practically important. Interclass variation may serve as a useful starting point for designing interventions targeted at relatively homogeneous student groups. However, for such interventions to be truly effective, they must be grounded in an understanding of intraclass variation—the differences that exist among individuals within each profile. For example, mindset-related constructs, together with control variables, account for 11.5% of the variance in SRLP—the crucial component of self-regulation of learning processes—across the full sample. Although this represents only a partial explanation, it highlights the potential for designing educational interventions. Table 2.4 shows that students in Class 1 exhibit the lowest levels of SRLP, suggesting that targeting this group would be a logical choice. However, Table 2.10 indicates that, within Class 1, mindset constructs explain only 1.1% of the variance in SRLP, less than one-tenth of the explanatory power observed in the full sample. Thus, even if an intervention successfully enhanced students' positive mindsets, its impact on self-regulation would likely be negligible.

As another example of an intervention that could yield unfavorable results, consider the final structural equation model based on mindset theory. If we relied solely on the full sample (or on gender and prior education subgroups), we might conclude that promoting incremental beliefs and positive effort beliefs is a promising intervention strategy. Yet the latent profiles tell a different story. In several classes, maladaptive beliefs (e.g., entity theory and negative effort beliefs) are more strongly associated with learning regulation outcomes than the adaptive constructs. This insight shifts the intervention focus from strengthening adaptive beliefs to addressing maladaptive ones—though whether the observed relationships are strong enough to inform effective interventions remains an open question.

2.6 Conclusions

The findings of this study carry important implications for both theoretical development and the design of educational interventions. Relying on full-sample averages to represent individual-level processes risks producing interventions that overlook the diverse needs of different learner profiles. Diversity research has partially addressed this challenge by examining differences across natural groups, such as gender, culture, ethnicity, socioeconomic status, or prior education. However, our findings suggest that such groupings are insufficient to capture the full complexity of learner variability.

A crucial next step is to divide heterogeneous samples into more homogeneous sections, offering a more precise test of theory and intervention relevance. Person-centered analyses, combined with a rigorous examination of the relative universality of educational theories, allow researchers to better capture individual variability and design targeted supports that more effectively promote student learning in authentic educational settings supported by technology. This approach helps prevent the application of uniform interventions aimed at strengthening adaptive learning dispositions, when in fact some students may benefit more from addressing elevated levels of maladaptive dispositions.

The significance of student heterogeneity in understanding and supporting SRL is well established. In their integrative review of the Learning patterns framework, Vermunt and Donche (2017) emphasize the value of person-centered approaches—such as cluster or latent profile analyses—to capture meaningful variation in students' learning patterns, rather than assuming uniform relationships across populations. While person-centered methods are increasingly applied in SRL research, most existing studies rely on behavioral indicators, such as trace data from TELEs. In contrast, relatively few studies have responded to Vermunt and Donche's (2017) call to identify profiles based on dispositional learning regulation and processing strategies. Building on previous work by Tempelaar et al. (2017), which demonstrated the role of learning dispositions in generating actionable learning analytics, the present study advances this line of research by identifying distinct dispositional profiles that imply differentiated pathways for targeted, actionable instructional interventions.

Another key takeaway of this study concerns the traditional focus on self-regulation in learning regulation research. While self-regulation is undoubtedly central, it cannot be fully understood without considering both the availability of external regulation and students' perceptions of its usefulness (de la Fuente et al., 2021, 2022; de la Fuente & Kauffman, 2025). This is especially important in technology-enhanced learning environments, where sophisticated regulatory processes are critical. More attention should therefore be directed toward the alignment of self- and external regulation in authentic contexts, including research on how these modes interact and how students evaluate the effectiveness of the full spectrum of regulatory strategies.

A limitation of the current study is its offline nature, as it was conducted only after the module had been completed. To enable instructional interventions during the module itself, the procedure would need to be implemented online, which would place considerable time pressure on data collection, data analysis, and the creation of optimally designed intervention groups.

The current study relies exclusively on self-reported dispositional data, which can be considered another limitation. In line with contemporary developments (Hadwin et al., 2025), an important next step for future research is to triangulate self-reports with multimodal behavioral data, including data collected from the TELE. A key challenge, however, lies in reconciling the requirements of a person-centered approach—which demands large samples—with the practical difficulties of collecting multimodal data on such a large scale. The main goal of this contribution is to demonstrate the important role the person-centered approach can play in establishing—or rejecting—the universal nature of antecedent relationships of self-regulated learning dispositions. To this end, our study concentrated on two key dispositional concepts—self-regulation of learning processes and of content—through which we could illustrate the differing outcomes between latent profiles decomposition and natural groupings, while leaving other dispositions beyond the scope of discussion.

References

Alexander, P. A. (1996). The past, present, and future of knowledge research: A reexamination of the role of knowledge in learning and instruction. *Educational Psychologist, 31*(2), 89–92. https://doi.org/10.1207/s15326985ep3102_2

Asparouhov, T., & Muthén, B. (2008). Multilevel mixture models. In G. R. Hancock & K. M. Samuelson (Eds.), *Advances in latent variable mixture models* (pp. 27–51). Information Age Publishing.

Asparouhov, T., & Muthén, B. (2014). Auxiliary variables in mixture modeling: Three-step approaches using Mplus. *Structural Equation Modeling: A Multidisciplinary Journal, 21*(3), 329–341. https://doi.org/10.1093/oso/9780197662359.001.0001

Azevedo, R., & Hadwin, A. F. (2005). Scaffolding self-regulated learning and metacognition: Implications for the design of computer-based scaffolds. *Instructional Science, 33*, 367–379. https://doi.org/10.1007/s11251-005-1272-9

Azevedo, R., Moos, D. C., Greene, J. A., Winters, F. I., & Cromley, J. G. (2008). Why is externally-facilitated regulated learning more effective than self-regulated learning with hypermedia? *Educational Technology Research and Development, 56*, 45–72. https://doi.org/10.1007/s11423-007-9067-0

Bardach, L., Yanagida, T., Goetz, T., Jach, H., & Pekrun, R. (2023). Self-regulated and externally regulated learning in adolescence: Developmental trajectories and relations with teacher behavior, parent behavior, and academic achievement. *Developmental Psychology, 59*(7), 1327–1345. https://doi.org/10.1037/dev0001537

Blackwell, L. S. (2002). Psychological mediators of student achievement during the transition to junior high school: The role of implicit theories. [Unpublished doctoral dissertation]. Columbia University.

Blackwell, L. S., Trzesniewski, K. H., & Dweck, C. S. (2007). Implicit theories of intelligence predict achievement across an adolescent transition: A longitudinal study and an intervention. *Child Development, 78*, 246–263. https://doi.org/10.1007/s10212-011-0062-9

Broadbent, J., & Poon, W. L. (2015). Self-regulated learning strategies and academic achievement in online higher education learning environments: A systematic review. *The Internet and Higher Education, 27*, 1–13. https://doi.org/10.1016/j.iheduc.2015.04.007

Buckingham Shum, S., & Deakin Crick, R. (2012). Learning dispositions and transferable competencies: Pedagogy, modelling and learning analytics. In S. Buckingham Shum, D. Gasevic, & R. Ferguson (Eds.), *Proceedings of the 2nd international conference on learning analytics and knowledge* (pp. 92–101). https://doi.org/10.1145/2330601.2330629

Butler, D. L., & Winne, P. H. (1995). Feedback and self-regulated learning: A theoretical synthesis. *Review of Educational Research, 65*, 245–281. https://doi.org/10.3102/00346543065003245

de la Fuente, J., & Kauffman, D. F. (2025). *The theory of self- versus externally-regulated behavior: Applicability to educational, clinical, health and organizational psychology contexts.* Nova Science Publishers. https://doi.org/10.52305/LUGJ1847

de la Fuente, J., Martínez-Vicente, J. M., Santos, F. H., Sander, P., Fadda, S., Karagiannopoulou, A., et al. (2022). Advances on self-regulation models: A new research agenda through the SR versus ER behavior theory in different psychology contexts. *Frontiers in Psychology, 13*, 861493. https://doi.org/10.3389/fpsyg.2022.861493

de la Fuente, J., Sander, P., Garzón-Umerenkova, A., Vera-Martínez, M. M., Fadda, S., & Gaetha, M. L. (2021). Self-regulation and regulatory teaching as determinants of academic behavioral confidence and procrastination in undergraduate students. *Frontiers in Psychology, 12*, 602904. https://doi.org/10.3389/fpsyg.2021.602904

Dweck, C. S. (1999). *Self-theories: Their role in motivation, personality, and development.* Psychology Press.

Dweck, C. S., & Master, A. (2008). Self-theories motivate self-regulated learning. In D. H. Schunk & B. J. Zimmerman (Eds.), *Motivation and self-regulated learning* (pp. 31–51). Routledge.

Fisher, A. J., Medaglia, J. D., & Jeronimus, B. F. (2018). Lack of group-to-individual generalizability is a threat to human subjects research. *Proceedings of the National Academy of Sciences, 115*(27), E6106–E6115. https://doi.org/10.1073/pnas.1711978115

Frenzel, A. C., Pekrun, R., & Goetz, T. (2007). Perceived learning environment and students' emotional experiences: A multilevel analysis of mathematics classrooms. *Learning and Instruction, 17*(5), 478–493. https://doi.org/10.1016/j.learninstruc.2007.09.001

Goetz, T., Stempfer, L., Pekrun, R., van Tilburg, W. A., & Lipnevich, A. A. (2024). Academic Boredom. In *The Routledge international handbook of boredom* (pp. 225–249). Routledge.

Hadwin, A. F., Rostampour, R., & Winne, P. H. (2025). Advancing self-reports of self-regulated learning: Validating new measures to assess students' beliefs, practices, and challenges. *Educational Psychology Review, 37*, 8. https://doi.org/10.1007/s10648-024-09977-9

Hamaker, E. L. (2012). Why researchers should think "within-person": A paradigmatic rationale. In M. R. Mehl & T. S. Conner (Eds.), *Handbook of research methods for studying daily life* (pp. 43–61). Guilford Press.

Hamaker, E. L., Kuiper, R. M., & Grasman, R. P. (2015). A critique of the cross-lagged panel model. *Psychological Methods, 20*(1), 102–116. https://doi.org/10.1037/a0038889

Hemmler, Y. M., & Ifenthaler, D. (2024). Self-regulated learning strategies in continuing education: A systematic review and meta-analysis. *Educational Research Review, 45*, 100629. https://doi.org/10.1016/j.edurev.2024.100629

Hertel, S., Reschke, K., & Karlen, Y. (2024). Are profiles of self-regulated learning and intelligence mindsets related to students' self-regulated learning and achievement? *Learning and Instruction, 90*, 101850. https://doi.org/10.1016/j.learninstruc.2023.101850

Howard, M. C., & Hoffman, M. E. (2018). Variable-centered, person-centered, and person-specific approaches: Where theory meets the method. *Organizational Research Methods, 21*(4), 846–876. https://doi.org/10.1177/1094428117744021

King, R. B., & McInerney, D. M. (2014). Culture's consequences on student motivation: Capturing cross-cultural universality and variability through personal investment theory. *Educational Psychologist, 49*(3), 175–198. https://doi.org/10.1080/00461520.2014.926813

Kline, R. B. (2023). *Principles and practice of structural equation modeling* (5th ed.). The Guilford Press.

Lodewyk, K., Winne, P. H., & Jamieson-Noel, D. (2009). Implications of task structure on self-regulated learning and achievement. *Educational Psychology, 29*, 1–25. https://doi.org/10.1080/01443410802447023

Lonka, K., Ketonen, E., & Vermunt, J. D. (2021). University students' epistemic profiles, conceptions of learning, and academic performance. *Higher Education, 81*(4), 775–793. https://doi.org/10.1007/s10734-020-00575-6

Marsh, H. W., Lüdtke, O., Trautwein, U., & Morin, A. J. S. (2009). Classical latent profile analysis of academic self-concept dimensions: Synergy of person- and variable-centered approaches to theoretical models of self-concept. *Structural Equation Modeling, 16*(2), 191–225. https://doi.org/10.1080/10705510902751010

Martin, A. J. (2007). Examining a multidimensional model of student motivation and engagement using a construct validation approach. *British Journal of Educational Psychology, 77*(2), 413–440. https://doi.org/10.1348/000709906X118036

Martin, A. J. (2011). *The motivation and engagement scale* (5th ed.). Lifelong Achievement Group.

Martin, A. J. (2023). Integrating motivation and instruction: Towards a unified approach in educational psychology. *Educational Psychology Review, 35*(2), 54. https://doi.org/10.1007/s10648-023-09774-w

Masyn, K. E. (2013). Latent class analysis and finite mixture modeling. In T. D. Little (Ed.), *The Oxford handbook of quantitative methods* (Vol. 2, pp. 375–393). Oxford University Press.

Moeller, J., Theobald, T., & Ziegler, M. (2021). Individual differences in intraindividual variability: A review and integration of the literature. *Perspectives on Psychological Science, 16*(6), 1248–1265. https://doi.org/10.1177/1745691620966789

Molenaar, I. (2022). The concept of hybrid human–AI regulation: Exemplifying how to support young learners' self-regulated learning. *Computers and Education: Artificial Intelligence, 3*, 100070. https://doi.org/10.1016/j.caeai.2022.100070

Molenaar, P. C. M. (2004). A manifesto on psychology as idiographic science: Bringing the person back into scientific psychology, this time forever. *Measurement Interdisciplinary Research and Perspectives, 2*(4), 201–218. https://doi.org/10.1207/s15366359mea0204_1

Molenaar, P. C. M., & Campbell, C. G. (2009). The new person-specific paradigm in psychology. *Current Directions in Psychological Science, 18*(2), 112–117. https://doi.org/10.1111/j.1467-8721.2009.01619.x

Moos, D. C., & Azevedo, R. (2008). Self-regulated learning with hypermedia: The role of prior domain knowledge. *Contemporary Educational Psychology, 33*(2), 270–298. https://doi.org/10.1016/j.cedpsych.2007.03.001

Morin, A. J. (2016). Person-centered research strategies in commitment research. In J. P. Meyer (Ed.), *The handbook of employee commitment* (pp. 490–508). Edward Elgar.

Morin, A. J. S., Bujacz, A., & Gagné, M. (2018). Person-centered methodologies in the organizational sciences. *Organizational Research Methods, 21*(4), 803–813. https://doi.org/10.1177/1094428118773856

Morin, A. J. S., Morizot, J., Boudrias, J. S., & Madore, I. (2011). A multifoci person-centered perspective on workplace affective commitment: A latent profile/factor mixture analysis. *Organizational Research Methods, 14*(1), 58–90. https://doi.org/10.1177/1094428109356476

Murayama, K., Pekrun, R., Lichtenfeld, S., & Vom Hofe, R. (2017). Predicting long-term growth in students' mathematics achievement: The unique contributions of motivation and cognitive strategies. *Child Development, 84*(4), 1475–1490. https://doi.org/10.1111/cdev.12036

Nota, L., Soresi, S., & Zimmerman, B. J. (2004). Self-regulation and academic achievement and resilience: A longitudinal study. *International Journal of Educational Research, 41*(3), 198–215. https://doi.org/10.1016/j.ijer.2005.07.001

OECD. (2015). *Skills for social progress: The power of social and emotional skills*. OECD Publishing. https://doi.org/10.1787/9789264226159-en

Pajares, F. (1996). Self-efficacy beliefs in academic settings. *Review of Educational Research, 66*(4), 543–578. https://doi.org/10.3102/00346543066004543

Pajares, F. (2002). Gender and perceived self-efficacy in self-regulated learning. *Theory Into Practice, 41*(2), 116–125. https://doi.org/10.1207/s15430421tip4102_8

Panadero, E. (2017). A review of self-regulated learning: Six models and four directions for research. *Frontiers in Psychology, 8*, 422. https://doi.org/10.3389/fpsyg.2017.00422

Pastor, D. A., Barron, K. E., Miller, B. J., & Davis, S. L. (2007). A latent profile analysis of college students' achievement goal orientation. *Contemporary Educational Psychology, 32*(1), 8–47. https://doi.org/10.1016/j.cedpsych.2006.10.003

Pekrun, R. (2009). Global and local perspectives on human affect: Implications of the control-value theory of achievement emotions. In M. Wosnitza, S. A. Karabenick, A. Efklides, & P. Nenniger (Eds.), *Contemporary motivation research: From global to local perspectives* (pp. 97–115). Hogrefe.

Pekrun, R. (2018). Control-value theory: A social-cognitive approach to achievement emotions. In R. Pekrun & L. Linnenbrink-Garcia (Eds.), *Handbook of emotions in education* (2nd ed., pp. 88–104). Routledge.

Pekrun, R. (2024). Overcoming fragmentation in motivation science: Why, when, and how should we integrate theories? *Educational Psychology Review, 36*(1), 5. https://doi.org/10.1007/s10648-024-09846-5

Pekrun, R., & Goetz, T. (2023). How universal are academic emotions? A control-value theory perspective. In G. Hagenauer, R. Lazarides, & H. Järvenoja (Eds.), *Motivation and emotion in learning and teaching across educational contexts: Theoretical and methodological perspectives and empirical insights* (pp. 85–99). Routledge.

Pintrich, P. R. (2004). A conceptual framework for assessing motivation and self-regulated learning in college students. *Educational Psychology Review, 16*(4), 385–407. https://doi.org/10.1007/s10648-004-0006-x

Prasse, D., Webb, M., Deschênes, M., Parent, S., Aeschlimann, F., Goda, Y., Yamada, M., & Raynault., A. (2024). Challenges in promoting self-regulated learning in technology supported learning environments: An umbrella review of systematic reviews and meta-analyses. *Technology, Knowledge, and Learning, 29*, 1809–1830. https://doi.org/10.1007/s10758-024-09772-z

Puustinen, M., & Pulkkinen, L. (2001). Models of self-regulated learning: A review. *Scandinavian Journal of Educational Research, 45*(3), 269–286. https://doi.org/10.1080/00313830120074206

Raković, M., Bernacki, M. L., Greene, J. A., Plumley, R. D., Hogan, K. A., Gates, K. M., & Panter, A. T. (2022). Examining the critical role of evaluation and adaptation in self-regulated learning. *Contemporary Educational Psychology, 68*, 102027. https://doi.org/10.1016/j.cedpsych.2021.102027

Rovers, S. F. E., Stalmeijer, R. E., van Merriënboer, J. J. G., Savelberg, H. H. C. M., & de Bruin, A. B. H. (2018). How and why do students use learning strategies? A mixed methods study on learning strategies and desirable difficulties with effective strategy users. *Frontiers in Psychology, 9*, 2501. https://doi.org/10.3389/fpsyg.2018.02501

Ryan, R. M., & Deci, E. L. (2017). *Self-determination theory: Basic psychological needs in motivation, development, and wellness*. Guilford Press.

Schunk, D. (2005). Self-regulated learning: The educational legacy of Paul R Pintrich. *Educational Psychologist, 40*, 85–94. https://doi.org/10.1207/s15326985ep4002_3

Schunk, D. H., & Ertmer, P. A. (2000). Self-regulation and academic learning: Self-efficacy enhancing interventions. In M. Boekaerts, P. R. Pintrich, & M. Zeidner (Eds.), *Handbook of self-regulation* (pp. 631–649). Academic.

Schunk, D. H., Pintrich, P. R., & Meece, J. L. (2008). *Motivation in education: Theory, research, and applications* (3rd ed.). Pearson.

Shum, A., Fryer, L. K., Vermunt, J. D., et al. (2024). Variable- and person-centred meta-re-analyses of university students' learning strategies from a cross-cultural perspective. *Higher Education, 87*, 1227–1250. https://doi.org/10.1007/s10734-023-01062-4

Tempelaar, D., Bátori, A., & Giesbers, B. (2024). Understanding self-regulation strategies in problem-based learning through dispositional learning analytics. *Frontiers in Education, 9*, 1382771. https://doi.org/10.3389/feduc.2024.1382771

Tempelaar, D., & Niculescu, A. (2023). Academic boredom(s): A person-centered investigation. *Frontiers in Sociology, 8*, 1190872. https://doi.org/10.3389/fsoc.2023.1190872

Tempelaar, D., & Niculescu, A. C. (2022). Types of boredom and other learning activity emotions: A person-centred investigation of inter-individual data. *Motivation and Emotion, 46*(1), 84–99. https://doi.org/10.1007/s11031-021-09909-y

Tempelaar, D., & Niculescu, A. C. (2025). *Testing the relative universalism of psychological theories: A person-centered analysis of control-value theory. Manuscript submitted*. Maastricht University.

Tempelaar, D., Rienties, B., Giesbers, B., & Nguyen, Q. (2023). Modelling temporality in person-and variable-centred approaches. *Journal of Learning Analytics, 10*, 2. https://doi.org/10.18608/jla.2023.7841

Tempelaar, D., Rienties, B., Mittelmeier, J., & Nguyen, Q. (2018). Student profiling in a dispositional learning analytics application using formative assessment. *Computers in Human Behavior, 78*, 408–420. https://doi.org/10.1016/j.chb.2017.08.010

Tempelaar, D., Rienties, B., & Nguyen, Q. (2020). Individual differences in the preference for worked examples: Lessons from an application of dispositional learning analytics. *Applied Cognitive Psychology, 34*(4), 890–905. https://doi.org/10.1002/acp.3652

Tempelaar, D. T., Rienties, B., & Giesbers, B. (2015). In search for the most informative data for feedback generation: Learning analytics in a data-rich context. *Computers in Human Behavior, 47*, 157–167. https://doi.org/10.1016/j.chb.2014.05.038

Tempelaar, D. T., Rienties, B., & Giesbers, B. (2017). Towards actionable learning analytics using dispositions. *IEEE Transactions on Learning Technologies, 10*(1), 6–16. https://doi.org/10.1109/TLT.2017.2662679

Usher, E. L., & Pajares, F. (2008). Self-efficacy for self-regulated learning: A validation study. *Educational and Psychological Measurement, 68*(3), 443–463. https://doi.org/10.1177/0013164407308475

Vallerand, R. J., Pelletier, L. G., Blais, M. R., Brière, N. M., Senécal, C., & Vallières, E. F. (1992). The academic motivation scale: A measure of intrinsic, extrinsic, and amotivation in education. *Educational and Psychological Measurement, 52*, 1003–1017. https://doi.org/10.1177/0013164492052004025

Vermunt, J. D. (1998). The regulation of constructive learning processes. *British Journal of Educational Psychology, 68*(2), 149–171. https://doi.org/10.1111/j.2044-8279.1998.tb01281.x
Vermunt, J. D., & Donche, V. (2017). A learning patterns perspective on student learning in higher education: State of the art and moving forward. *Educational Psychology Review, 29*(2), 269–299. https://doi.org/10.1007/s10648-017-9414-6
Voelkle, M. C., Brose, A., Schmiedek, F., & Lindenberger, U. (2014). Toward a unified framework for the study of between-person and within-person structures: Building a bridge between two research paradigms. *Multivariate Behavioral Research, 49*(3), 193–213. https://doi.org/10.1080/00273171.2014.889593
Williams, A., Sun, Z., Xie, K., Garcia, E., Ashby, I., Exter, M., Largent, D., Lu, P., Szafron, D., Ahmed, S., Onuczko, T., Smith, J., Tempelaar, D. T., Bitting, K. S., Olcott Marshall, A., Christensen, E., Tseng, H., & Walsh, J. (2016). Flipping STEM. In L. Santos Green, J. Banas, & R. Perkins (Eds.), *The flipped college classroom, conceptualized and re-conceptualized, part II* (pp. 149–186). Springer.
Winne, P. H., & Hadwin, A. F. (1998). Studying as self-regulated learning. In D. J. Hacker, J. Dunlosky, & A. C. Graesser (Eds.), *Metacognition in educational theory and practice* (pp. 277–304). Erlbaum.
Witherspoon, A. M., Azevedo, R., & D'Mello, S. (2008). The dynamics of self-regulatory processes within self-and externally regulated learning episodes during complex science learning with hypermedia. In B. P. Woolf, E. Aïmeur, R. Nkambou, & S. Lajoie (Eds.), *Intelligent tutoring systems* (Vol. 5091, pp. 677–686). Springer. https://doi.org/10.1007/978-3-540-69132-7_30
Wolters, C. A., Brady, A. C., & Lee, H. J. (2025). Time management and achievement motivation: A review of what we know and directions for where to go. *Educational Psychology Review, 37*, 58. https://doi.org/10.1007/s10648-025-10032-4
Zhao, R., & Ling, T. (2022). Latent profile analysis of university students' self-management and self-monitoring in the links among motivation, engagement, and wellbeing. *Frontiers in Psychology, 13*, 1023920. https://doi.org/10.3389/fpsyg.2022.102392
Zimmerman, B. J. (2000). Attaining self-regulation: A social cognitive perspective. In M. Boekaerts, P. Pintrich, & M. Zeidner (Eds.), *Handbook of self-regulation* (pp. 13–39). Academic.
Zimmerman, B. J. (2002). Becoming a self-regulated learner: An overview. *Theory Into Practice, 41*(2), 64–70. https://doi.org/10.1207/s15430421tip4102_2
Zimmerman, B. J., & Schunk, D. H. (2011). *Self-regulated learning and academic achievement: Theoretical perspectives* (2nd ed.). Routledge.
Zimmerman, B. J., & Schunk, D. H. (2012). Motivation: An essential dimension of self-regulated learning. In D. H. Schunk & B. J. Zimmerman (Eds.), *Motivation and self-regulated learning* (pp. 1–30). Routledge.

Chapter 3
A Learner Model of Self-Regulated Learning: A Three-Layer View

Alejandro Peña-Ayala, James L. McClelland, Antonio Romero-Hernández, and Karla Marlen Álvarez-Olvera

Abstract 21st-century education, both in-person and through eLearning, requires learners to possess the attitudes, cognitive skills, behaviors, social abilities, and digital literacy needed to master a wide range of scientific and domain knowledge content, diverse pedagogical practices, and the complex technological artifacts that support teaching and learning. In this context, *self-regulated learning* (SRL) represents a theoretical and practical construct that enables learners to be aware of their own learning endeavor occurring at both inner and external worlds during their performance in the academic scenario. Hence, many approaches, models, and processes that have been proposed to foster SRL only focus on particular subjects, leaving aside the characterization of learners' SRL practices. To address these practices themselves, this work designs a "*learner SRL model*" (LSRLM) to define basic *functionalities* that are in charge of *agents*, which represent components and roles depicted by means of *features* that group processes, strategies, and beliefs involved in the learning task. The LSRLM was applied to Higher Education learners to represent their SRL model, finding that the majority *often* apply SRL's leading during learning, and their customs privilege *soulful* and *scenery* functionalities. Further research should extend the LSRLM for improving academic performance.

A. Peña-Ayala (✉)
Artificial Intelligence & Data Science on Education Lab. WOLNM, 31 Julio 1859, No. 1099-B, Leyes Reforma, Iztapalapa, 09310, Ciudad de México, México
e-mail: apenaa@ipn.mx

A. Peña-Ayala · A. Romero-Hernández · K. M. Álvarez-Olvera
ESIME-Zacatenco, Instituto Politécnico Nacional, Unidad Profesional Adolfo López Mateos, Gustavo A. Madero, 07738, Ciudad de México, México
e-mail: anromeroh@ipn.mx

K. M. Álvarez-Olvera
e-mail: kalvarezo1300@alumno.ipn.mx

A. Peña-Ayala · J. L. McClelland
Department of Psychology and Center for the Neural Basis of Cognition, 450 Jane Stanford Way, Bldg. 420, Stanford University, 94305, Stanford, USA
e-mail: jlmcc@stanford.edu

A. Romero-Hernández
UPIICSA, Instituto Politécnico Nacional, Iztacalco, 08400, Ciudad de México, México

A. Peña-Ayala (ed.), *Self-Regulated Learning*, Cognitive Technologies,
https://doi.org/10.1007/978-981-92-0658-2_3

Keywords Learner · Learning · Self-regulation · Self-regulated learning · Cognition · Behavior · Domain knowledge

Abbreviations

HE	Higher education
RQ	Research question
SR	Self-regulation
SRL	Self-regulated Learning

3.1 Introduction

An overview at the purpose of education through last centuries is briefed by Smyle et al., (2008, p. 4), who assert: "since the mid-1600s up to the eighteenth century education was oriented to *religious* and *moral* growth; in the nineteenth century *vocational* education and *secular* teaching were the goal; and during the twentieth century, students were prepared for *jobs*, and for being *agents of socialization*".

Actually, "preparing youth for the professional, civic, and personal dares of adult life is the aim of twenty-first century education" (Baxter-Magolda, 2004, p. 1); whilst "twenty-first century learning fosters collaborative learning, and mastery of information as tools for domain knowledge acquisition and co-construction" (Chai & Kong, 2017, p. 1). In addition, "twenty-first century skills boost *soft skills* and dispositions including cross-cultural skills, critical thinking, and problem-solving to foment creativity and innovation, and prepare students for the digital age, where K-12 education plays a role for impressing such skills in learners" (Kennedy & Sundberg, 2020, p. 479).

In this context, *self-regulated learning* (SRL) emerges as a perspective withing the psychological and cognitive science of education that fosters learners to become aware of and responsible for their learning endeavors. "SRL refers to learning that results from student's self-regulated thoughts and behaviors systematically oriented toward the achievement of learning goals" (Zimmerman, 2000, p. 14), It is said, "SRL is behavior oriented toward the optimal execution of predefined task" (Thoutenhoofd & Pirrie, 2015, p. 72), highlighting "*self*" as an *agent* for the initiation, development, and continuation of SRL, where "students' will to engage in *self-regulation* (SR) is key, assuming they are aware of their faculties, creative agents, and responsible for and capable of reaching self-development and self-determination aims" (McCombs & Marzano, 1990, p. 51).

Hence, SR, as the core of SRL, is in charge of "leading efforts to start, direct, and strategically managing goal pursuit in situ via metacognitively planning, monitoring, evaluating, and adapting one's cognition, behavior, motivation, and affect to optimally proceed with goal attainment" (Greene et al., 2023, p. 314). In short, "SR refers to taking in information, weighing choices and consequences, and making adaptive choice to attain a particular goal" (McClelland et al., 2015, p. 7–8).

SRL emerges from *cognitive* and *behavioral* paradigms (Alam & Mohanty, 2024; Hidayati & Thompson, 2025; Ye et al., 2022), whose baseline lays on diverse theories, such as *phenomenological*, *operant*, and *social cognitive* that respectively concern to "explore subjective experiences and meaning construction" (Brziak & Urban, 2025, p. 1), "self-regulatory behaviors that are ultimately controlled by one's environment" (Carvalho-Filho, 2002, p. 438), and "behavior extensively motivated and regulated by the ongoing exercise of self-influence" (Bandura, 1991, p. 248).

Essentially, SRL is considered as an "*abstract phenomenon*" (Kaplan, 2008, p. 477), whose "practices are positively associated with academic performance" (Hadwin et al., 2025, p. 1), while "the development of SRL skills and strategies is a function of the bidirectional interaction of personal, behavioral, and setting factors" (Barnard-Brak et al., 2010, p. 62) that can be fostered by "e-learning tools that support SRL strategies" (García et al., 2018, p. 152), and its processes, particularly those oriented "to planning, monitoring, and strategy use, are related to prior domain knowledge" (Moos & Azevedo, 2008, p. 1).

In this concern, SRL "is object of stimulation in the workplace, as the clinical context" (Houten-Schat et al., 2018, p. 1008), "encapsulates autonomous navigation through learning content and enables for students to be successful in capitalizing on what online learning have to offer" (Ejubovic & Puška, 2019, p. 346), "has been developed as a pedagogy through the collective endeavors of teachers" (Kong & Lin, 2023, p. 1), and is necessary "to determine training needs of teachers in the area of strategies for SRL in order for them to successfully teach strategies for SRL to their learners" (Ortega-Ruipérez & Castellanos-Sánchez, 2023, p. 3).

With this in mind, diverse models have been outlined to reveal a basic idea of how SRL works, highlight its components, and draw relationships among them. In this sense, some reviews offer a landscape of the theoretical basics and research line of practitioners, such as: Puustinen and Pulkkinen (2001, p. 269), who present "diverse models of SRL, including those designed by Boekaerts, Borkowski, Pintrich, Winne and Zimmerman, which were compared on four criteria: background theories, definitions of SRL, components, and empirical work". Moreover, Panadero (2017, p. 1) analyzes "six models of SRL giving attention to history and development, description, empirical support, and instruments; comparing seven aspects: citations, phases and subprocesses, how they conceptualize (meta)cognition, motivation and emotion, top–down/bottom–up, automaticity, and context".

As for SRL and student or learner models, quite a few approaches are found to characterize SRL features that represent a given learner, where one is the "*Strategy model of student SRL*" tailored by Zimmerman and Martinez-Pons (1988, p. 284, 288), who recorded and analyzed "how students describe their use of 14 SRL strategies (e.g., self-evaluation, goal setting, seeking information, keeping records, rehearsing and memorizing, reviewing texts…) in six contexts (e.g., classroom, home, completing writing and mathematics assignments…)". The results show "the strategy of rehearsing and memorizing was the best predictor and one of the most highly correlated with teachers' ratings, despite its highly covert nature."

Lastly, the relationship between SRL and open learner models is instantiated by Long and Aleven (2017, p. 210), who wonder "how an open learner model enhances students' domain level learning outcomes through the scaffolding of SRL processes, self-assessment and study choice, in an Intelligent Tutoring System oriented to equation-solving". The open learner model depicts four traits: "students' equation-solving abilities, enjoyment of learning with the tutor, self-assessment accuracy, and problem selection decisions". The outcomes reveal that "students who had access to the open learner model learned better equation-solving skills than their counterparts when shared control over problem selection was offered in the system".

Although there are many models that depict SRL nature, components, and functioning, only a few describe how the learner approaches SRL during learning, reveal customs, and highlight preferences, including how aware he/she is of his/her learning process, strategies, and beliefs that are put into practice in classroom and online settings. Some of these concerns are addressed as the *research problem* that wonders: *How can the SRL practice that learner uses during learning endeavor be represented*? In addition, some *research questions* (RQ) are made to focus on specific aspects, such as: RQ-1: How can the diversity of aspects that must be taken into account for SRL practice be organized? RQ-2: What are the components, processes, attributes, strategies, and beliefs that depict SRL nature? RQ-3: Which are the privileged SRL practices that learners use for leading their learning affairs?

With this in mind, the present approach proposes the *learner SRL model*" (LSRLM) that features diverse attributes of learner's SRL practice under three *layers* of interrelation that represent *functionalities* exercised by the learner. The first is concerned with *soulful* traits, the second relates *leading* learning labor, and the third corresponds to the *scenery* where learning is performed. Such *functionalities* are carried out by several *agents* that represent *components* and *roles*, which are characterized through *features* that group *processes*, *strategies*, and *beliefs* that are respectively fulfilled, followed, and accepted by learners as SRL practices. Moreover, a survey is designed and conducted in a Higher Education (HE) setting, where undergraduates measure the frequency of practice for specific SRL features. As a result, interesting findings are uncovered to show SRL features that are preferable for learners, and those that should be instilled to enhance their use. All of this with the purpose of improving learners' performance.

The remainder of this chapter first defines in Sect. 3.2 the psychological baseline and the collection of related works used as referents. Section 3.3, outlines the design of the LSRLM and identifies the components that characterize diverse learner's features. Sect. 3.4 reports the learning modeling achieved through the application of the LSRLM to a sample of HE students. The discussion of the outcomes is expressed in Section 3.5, which is followed by the Conclusions to precise the achievements, constraints, and future work.

3.2 Theory and Models

The LSRLM is based on a theoretical frame composed of constructs stemming from diverse branches of the psychology, as well as from the SR and SRL domains, where some of them are briefed in the first subchapter. Moreover, the second describes a series of related works to highlight some of their features that are considered in the design of the proposed model.

Constructs

Basically, the baseline that grounds the LSRLM takes into account diverse branches of the psychology, and some theories that support SR, which is the main underlying element of SRL. Several of these fundamental elements compose the baseline of the model to set up its ideas, components, and architecture.

Psychological Baseline

Essentially, SRL rests on *psychology* as its baseline, whose meaning has evolved "with the passage of time as the *science of soul*, later to *science of mind*, after *science of consciousness*, and finally as *science of behavior*" (Aggarwal, 2010, p. 1), which "at the beginning of the twenty-first century has become a highly diverse field of scientific study and applied technology. Psychologists commonly regard their discipline as the *science of behavior*..." (Weiner et al., 2012, p. vii).

Particularly, two branches compose the essentials for SRL, where the first is the *cognitive psychology* that in the words of Braisby and Gellatly (2009, p. 2) is "the branch of psychology devoted to the scientific study of the mind", whilst Sternberg et al., (2009, p. 3) assert "*cognitive psychology* is the study of how people perceive, learn, remember, and think about information... why they remember some facts but forget others, or how they learn language".

The second branch is the *educational psychology*, which Samtrock (2011, p. 5) points out "has grown markedly in its 100 years and focuses on understanding learning and teaching in educational settings"; whereas, Tutoo (1998, p. 1) adds it "is a study of the human mind as it bears upon learning and teaching activities. It is an application of the principles of general psychology to the problems of education".

Self-regulation and Underlying Constructs

On top of the aforementioned baseline, SR appears as the core for SRL, whose building blocks are *cognitivism*, *behaviorism*, and *self*. The earliest "is roughly the position that intelligent behavior can (only) be explained by appeal to internal 'cognitive processes', that is, rational thought in a very broad sense" (Haugeland, 1978, p. 215). It is said, "cognitivism is an approach to the mind and behavior... to understanding psychological functioning, and... claim that mental activity should be modelled as the processing of information using an internal symbol system, with discrete abstract symbols" (Garnham, 2019, p. 99).

Behaviorism "was proposed by John B. Watson in 1913, as the classical stimulus–response, where behavior was a subject matter in its own right, to be studied by the observational methods common to all sciences" (Moore, 2011, p. 449). "Behaviorism is not the science of human behavior; it is the philosophy of that science. Some questions are: Can it account for every aspect of human behavior? What methods can it use?" (Skinner, 2011, p. 3). "The idea that behavior can be treated scientifically remains controversial because it challenges the notation that behavior arises from an individual's free choice" (Baum, 2017, p. 16).

The core of SR is the *executive function* of the "self" that according to Baumeister and Vohs (2003, p. 179) "is active, involved, and responsive, intentionally engaging in volitional processes to change, alter, or modify itself, as well as takes action, selects a response, filters information, and responsible for enactment". Such authors assert: "the aspect of the *self* that initiates behaviors and makes selections is called *executive function*". Such a function is "a form of behavior-to-the-*self* that evolved from overt to covert responses as a means of SR... they shift the control of behavior from the immediate context... and the temporal now to SR by internal representations regarding the hypothetical social future" (Barkley, 2001, p. 1).

As far as *regulation*, Vohs and Baumeister (2004, p. 1) state: it "carries the meaning of *control* with a hint of *regularity*, refers to the exercise of *control* over oneself, with regard to bringing the *self* into line with preferred standards". In addition, they precise "*SR* more broadly refers to goal-directed behavior or to feedback loops, whereas *self-control* may be associated with conscious impulse control". Gailliot et al., (2008, p. 472) insist: "*SR* (also commonly referred to as *self-control*) is the capacity to override one's thoughts, emotions, impulses, and automatic or habitual behaviors". Basically, "SR is fundamental to successful accomplishment of adaptive developmental tasks at all stages of life" (McClelland, 2017, p. 275).

Lastly, Schunk and Zimmerman (2012, p. 59) discuss "the role of SRL during learning... that results from students' SR thoughts", and they acknowledge five theoretical perspectives of SR, where the *Operant theory* and the *Social cognitive theory* have been already introduced in Sect. 3.1; and the remaining three are stated as follows: (1) "*Information processing theory* describes behavior as an interaction between an information-processing system, the problem solver, and a task environment" (Simon, 1978, p. 272); (2) "*Developmental theory* claims that the antecedents of SR are described in terms of discontinuous *developmental* phases, such as: neurophysiological modulation, sensorimotor modulation, control, self-control, and self SR" (Koop, 1982, p. 201); and (3) "*Social constructivist theory* recognizes the importance of learning in a *social* context and sees students as active *constructors* of their own learning environment" (Nithideechaiwarachok & Chano, 2024, p, 568).

Related Works

The proposed LSRLM characterizes learner's SRL attributes and practices that reveal main features of a collection of SRL models that are introduced in this subchapter, which are chronologically organized according to the work-line developed by researchers of SRL, who have participated in the development of the domain.

Zimmerman Approach

One of the contributors to extend the SRL arena is Barry J. Zimmerman and colleagues that since the last century have disseminated a diversity of models, workflows, and strategies that are worthy to be acknowledged, The first is the "Assessing student use of SRL strategies" (Zimmerman & Martínez-Ponz, 1986, p. 615), whose definition is: "SRL strategy means actions directed at acquiring information or skill that involve agency, purpose, and instrumentality self-perceptions by a learner". They define 15 categories of strategies: self-evaluation, organizing and transforming, goal-setting and planning, seeking information, keeping records and monitoring, environmental structuring, self-consequences, rehearsing and memorizing, seeking social assistance, reviewing records (e.g., tests, notes, textbooks), and other.

Simultaneously, Zimmerman (1986, p. 307) studies some "subprocesses in academic SR such as those involved in the self-system, metacognitive functioning, self-verbalization, instructional context management, and socialization of children". Later on, Zimmerman (1989, p. 329–330) offers a social cognitive view of SR academic learning that "assumes reciprocal causation among three influence processes *personal*, *behavioral*, and *environmental*, which are also known as *covert*, *behavioral*, and *environmental* self-regulation". Afterwards, Zimmerman and Martínez-Ponz (1990, p. 53), apply a "structured interview to assess the 15 categories of SRL strategies through eight learning contexts described to each student in classroom situations, when completing writing assignments to demonstrate the usefulness of two measures of students' academic efficacy in predicting their use".

Moreover, Zimmerman (1990, p. 5–6) identifies common features of definitions of students' SRL: "students are metacognitively, motivationally, and behaviorally participants in their own learning". Later, Zimmerman and Martínez-Ponz (1992, p. 663, 666, 668) depict a "*Causal model of students' self-efficacy beliefs and academic goals in self-motivated academic attainment*" that was applied to college students through "a survey composed by 11 and 9 inquiries respectively related to how well can they achieve self-efficacy for SRL and for academic achievement". Additionally, Zimmerman et al., (1996, p. 11) introduce a "*Cyclical model of SRL* to develop essential academic skills (e.g., planning, understanding, note taking, preparing for examinations, writing effectively) composed by four items: self-evaluation and monitoring, goal setting and strategic planning, strategy implementation and monitoring, strategic outcome monitoring".

During the present century, Zimmerman (2002, p. 67) wonders: "how does a student's use of specific learning processes, level of self-awareness, and motivational beliefs combine to produce SR-learners?" In order to answer the inquiry, he conceives the "*Structure of self-regulatory processes* in terms of three cyclical phases: (1) *forethought*, processes and beliefs that occur before efforts to learn; (2) *performance*, processes that occur during behavioral implementation; and (3) *self-reflection* processes that occur after each learning effort", which also include "sub-processes for each process" (Zimmerman & Campillo, 2003, p. 239; Zimmerman & Labuhn, 2012, p. 402; Cleary et al., 2012, p. 3; Panadero & Alonso-Tapia, 2014).

Boekaerts Trend

Monique Boekaerts is another researcher that also has contributed to enhance the SRL field with several models and frameworks proposed since the last century. Firstly, Boekaerts (1996, p. 100, 103) designs the "*Six-component model of SRL* that highlights the parallel and reciprocal relationships between components of the cognitive SR and motivational SR and centers on three levels of these repertoires: domain-specific knowledge, strategy use, and goals". Afterwards, Boakaerts (1997, p. 163–164) "suggests that each component (e.g., cognitive and motivational SR, cognitive and motivation strategies, content domain, and metacognitive knowledge and motivational beliefs) represents a specific type of *prior domain knowledge* that a student has potentially available at any given time".

Later, Boakaerts (1999, p. 445, 449) recognizes some schools of thought to ground SRL: "research on learning styles, research on metacognition and regulation styles, and theories of the self, including goal-directed behavior", which represent the baseline for a "*Three-layer model of SRL*" composed by "regulation of the self, regulation of the learning process, and regulation of processing modes that respectively choices goals and resources, uses metacognitive knowledge, and selects cognitive strategies". In this sense, Boakaerts (2017, p. 96) precises: "The core refers to the learning, how process information and select cognitive strategies; the middle refers to the regulation of the learning, the choice of metacognitive strategies; the outer refers to the way students protect the learning". After, Boekaerts and Niemivirta (2000, p. 417) claim "identification, interpretation, and appraisal processes are the gateways to SR". Hence, they extend the "*Model of adaptable learning* to add an identification process, two interpretation processes (task-focused interpretation and self-focused interpretation), and primary and secondary appraisal processes".

Moreover, Boekaerts and Corno (2005, pp. 203–204, 209–211) tailor the "*Model of classroom SR* composed by top-down SR and bottom-up SR parallel processes, and identify instruments that assess SR: self-report questionnaires, observations of behavior, interview evidence, think aloud, traces of mental events, situational manipulations, recording motivation strategies, keeping diaries". One year later, Boekaerts and Cascallar (2006, p. 200) wonder: "What key strategies do students need to guide and direct their own learning process?" As a response, they assert "SR involves multiple strategies (e.g., metacognitive, cognitive, motivation), successful students refer these strategies as *adaptive*, such self-strategies are orienting oneself before starting on an assignment, collecting resource material, integrating theoretical viewpoints, monitoring for comprehension, and assessing one's progress".

Diverse SRL Lines

In addition to the prior researchers, some others are worthy to be also recognized. First, Garcia and Pintrich (1991) tailor the "*Structural model of the relationships between intrinsic motivation, self-efficacy, and self-regulated learning*", where they put "the motivational constructs of intrinsic motivation (self-reports of value interest, and importance) and self-efficacy (evaluations of one's perceived competence and expectations for success) as temporally preceding SRL (a behavioral constellation of monitoring, elaboration, and effort management strategies)". Subsequently, Pintrich and Zusho (2007, p. 735) sketch the "*General model for student motivation and self-regulated learning in the college classroom*" composed by five elements: "student personal characteristics, classroom factors, motivational processes, self-regulatory processes, and outcome; where all the relations between components are reciprocal to reflect a social cognitive perspective" (Jayawardena et al., 2019). Another construct is the "*Metacognitive view of individual differences in SRL*", where Winne (1996, p. 330–331) presents a prospect that embraces two constructive and metacognitive phases: "(1) learners clarify a task, generate goals, and adopt a plan for reaching those goals or for juggling competing goals; and (2), learners achieve tactics to construct information that leads to self-generated and external feedback".

Furthermore, Kuiper (1999, pp. 4–5) outlines a "*SRL model in nursing*" based on the assumption that "behavior is a function of the discrepancy between a goal state and current state", which embraces three SR processes behavioral, metacognitive, and environmental that include subprocesses such as self-judgment, self-evaluation, and skills respectively". With this in mind she defines four propositions to describe the connections of the variables in her model: "*expectation*, the identification of a gain reduces a discrepancy; *choice*, the selection of behaviors produces gain; *response*, there are responses between producing gain and gathering information; *gain*, is produced by interactions between past gains, expectations, choices and responses". Afterwards, Kuiper and Pesut (2004, p. 382) update the "*SRL model in nursing*" as a theoretical structure that "explains how clinical reasoning skills are acquired through attention to reflective thinking and critical thinking acquisition, which suggests that cognitive processes (e.g., stimulus–response and memory storage) are enhanced, monitored, and controlled with the development of metacognitive knowledge and processes".

In line with Efklides (2011, p. 6), she believes metacognition, motivation, and affect are components of SRL that interact to make up the "*Metacognitive and affective model of SRL*" that distinguishes two levels of functioning: "the *Person level*, where interactions between trait-like characteristics guide top-down SR, attitudes…, in the form of expectancy-value beliefs and achievement goal orientations are hypothesized; and the *task* × *person* level leads bottom-up SR, at which SRL events take place". Whereas, Schunk and Greene (2011, pp. vii–x) published a representative "Handbook of SRL and performance" writing a chapter about "*Historical, contemporary, and future perspectives*" of both constructs, and organizing 30 works into five sections: "basic domains; in context; technology; methodology and assessment; and individual and group differences", which offer a broad and, up to that date, state of the art. While, Hamit (2014, pp. 74–75) asserts: "the degree and quality of SR processes that students exercise… depends on psychological dimensions of functioning that are depicted as a matrix composed by six questions and their dimensions, tasks conditions, SR attributes, and SR processes".

Lastly, several *holistic* and *cybernetic* contributions to the SRL field have been made by Alejandro Peña-Ayala and a colleague. The first is the "*Cybernetic method to regulate learning through learning strategies*" (Peña-Ayala & Cárdenas-Robles, 2019, pp. 198–199), where four sorts of cybernetic items are integrated: "*principles*: feedback controls behavior, realization of adaptive expediency function; *processes components*: observer, observed, system, input, disturbances, behavior, regulator, output…; *regulation mechanisms*: buffering, feedforward…; *processes*: lineal, iteration, SR, cybernetic…; in addition to three types of learning strategies: cognitive, metacognitive, resource management". At the same time, Cárdenas-Robles and Peña-Ayala (2019, p. 304) propose the "*Holistic self-regulated learning model*" organized into four layers: "*modes*: proactive, learning, reactive; *determinants*: learner, conduct, setting; *SR processes*; and *cognitive*, *self-regulated*, and *metacognitive methods* and *strategies*". As an enhanced version of the prior approaches, Peña-Ayala (2026) presents the "*Self–regulated learning* as a *holistic–cybernetic framework*" that is a *five–tier architecture* made up of: (1) *modes*: proactive, learning, reflective; (2) *determinants*: person, conduct, stage; (3) *cybernetic method*; (4) *SR processes*; and (5) *cognitive strategies*".

3.3 Design of the LSRLM

Once diverse constructs and related works that define, characterize, and study particular approaches of SRL have been introduced, in the present subchapter the design of the LSRLM is outlined. The sketch of the model considers four aspects, the first corresponds to the underlying concepts that establish the proposal, the second identifies the sorts of components that make up the approach, while the third shows the architecture that organizes the components through several layers, and the fourth reveals the complete set of features that characterizes the LSRLM.

Conceptual Baseline

A series of statements is enounced to ground the baseline of the LSRLM, where one corresponds to: "*learning is essentially both cognitive and behaviorist manifestations of a living being driven to goal attainment*". This means that *thought* and *conduct* are core functions of the living beings, who learn something through casualty, circumstance, or by their own will fostered by a specific interest.

Moreover, it is believed that: "*both cognition and behavior are immanent faculties of the living being that emerge as a result of its soul functioning embedded in its carnal body, particularly its nervous system for most species of the animal kingdom*". The statement reveals a special interest in the *soul* that is defined next.

The acknowledgment of the *living being's soul* existence is claimed by diverse domains of study, such as: the *biblical*, "...the man became a living being..." (Carroll & Prickett, 2008, Genesis 2.7); *theological*, "in traditional theology, the Creationist position has each new human soul as the direct creative act of God" (Greggo, 2005, p. 258); *philosophical*, "Plato's twofold to leverage soul view, as the subject of knowledge or of cognitive activity in general, and as the principle of movement or of life" (Roberts, 1905, p. 372); and *psychological*, "to write a history of psychology is to write a history of the soul, which is no less than the story of humankind from the beginning" (Rank, 1996, p. 193).

Constituent Elements

Plenty of *attributes* that characterize SRL *nature* and *functioning* are stemmed from the constructs and related works briefed, where several of them are taken into account to design the LSRLM. Specifically, those stated as *components*, *processes*, *functionalities*, *traits*, *strategies*, *beliefs*, and *interrelationships* are considered, and many are selected to be stratified into three sorts of *constituent elements*: *functionalities*, *agents*, and *features*, whose nature is explained as follows.

Chosen elements are classified into three *functionalities*: *soulful* personifies the abstract corpus, *leading* heads managing thinking, and *scenery* defines the nature of the performing environment. Such *functionalities* in turn embrace several *agents* that respectively: disclose intangible faculties (e.g., *consciousness*, *mind*, *feelings*, *will*), phases (e.g., *proactive*, *executive*, *reactive*), and observable performance (e.g., *inner*, *outer*, *setting*). These *agents* represent attributes and roles that are fulfilled by distinctive *features* of the SRL endeavor, such as *processes* (i.e., includes *functions*, *attributes*, *components*), *strategies*, and *beliefs*; whose presence or practice in / by the learner recreates a property of the LSRLM, where a sample of instances is shown in Section "Architecture" and the complete population is exhibited in Section "Whole Set of Features".

Architecture

Once the conceptual baseline and constituent elements of the LSRLM have been outlined, now the taxonomy that organizes them is sketched. Firstly, the *functionalities*, *agents*, and *features* are organized as a *descending hierarchy*, where *functionalities* contain *agents*, and *agents* embrace *features*, as Fig. 3.1 shows in the 2nd, 3rd, 4th columns. Secondly, the three *functionalities* interact *sequentially*, *cyclically*, and *recursively* to *start*, *develop*, and *control* SRL activity during the learning labor, as the 1st column of Fig. 3.1 illustrates. The hierarchical relationship is labeled by means of a numerical *Id* attached to each item.

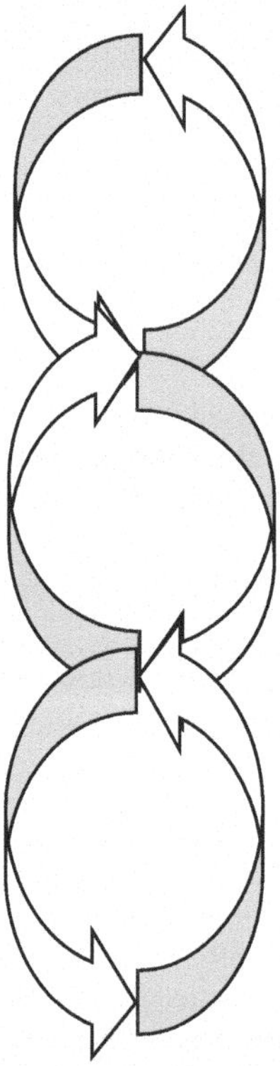

Functionalities — *Agents* — *Features*

- 1 soulful
  - 11 consciousness
    - 111 self-consciousness
    - 112 self-concept
    - 113 executive functions
  - 12 mind
    - 121 metacognition
    - 122 critical thinking
    - 123 reasoning
  - 13 feelings
    - 131 motivation
    - 132 emotions
    - 133 mood
  - 14 will
    - 141 attitude
    - 142 engagement
    - 143 resilience
- 2 leading
  - 21 proactive
    - 211 task analysis
    - 212 self-planning
    - 213 goals setting
  - 22 executive
    - 221 self-instruction
    - 222 self-monitoring
    - 223 self-directed
  - 23 reactive
    - 231 self-evaluation
    - 232 self-refection
    - 233 self-judgment
- 3 scenery
  - 31 inner
    - 311 domain knowledge
    - 312 skills development
    - 313 self-explanation
  - 32 outer
    - 321 meaningful learning
    - 322 competence
    - 323 performance
  - 33 setting
    - 331 socialization
    - 332 resource management
    - 333 collaboration

Fig. 3.1 LSRLM three-tier architecture

Whole Set of Features

Accordingly, with the *constructs* and related works that ground the LSRLM's baseline, as well as its *constituent* elements and *architecture*, in this subsection, the complete set of *features* is introduced. It is said, the whole LSRLM organizes the *features* into three kinds: *processes* (i.e., this kind also considers *functions, attributes*, skills, and *components*), *strategies*, and *beliefs*, associating them to the corresponding *agent* of each *functionality*, as it is edited in the Tables 3.1, 3.2, 3.3.

Such Tables respectively correspond to *soulful*, *leading*, and *scenery* functionalities, where the left column shows the kind of *feature*, the remaining columns identify the *agents* of a given *functionality*, and the cells enounce the *features* that pertain to a particular kind of *feature* (e.g., processes, strategies, beliefs) which owns its proper row, as it can be seen that the body table contains just three rows.

Table 3.1 Complete LSRLM: *Features* associated to the four *agents* (1.1, 1.2, 1.3, and 1.4) that compose the *1 soulful* functionality

Features	11 Consciousness	12 Mind	13 Feelings	14 Will
Processes Functions Attributes Components	Self-consciousness Self-concept Executive functions Self-responsibility Adaptation Comprehension Reflection Self-consequence Self-regulation Perception Recognition Reaction Personality Ego	Metacognition Critical thinking Reasoning Concentration Cognition Learning Aptitude Memory Short-term memory Long-term memory Metacognitive awareness, knowledge, skills, planning, regulation, and monitoring	Motivation Emotions Mood Character Affects Self-confidence Self-reward Temperament Sensitivity Frustration Selection Self-motivation	Attitude Commitment Resilience Initiative Discipline Procrastination Behavior Self-control Proactivity Habits Responsibility Persistence Abandonment Behavioral selection Volitional control
Strategies	Questioning	Mental strategies	Motivational and affective Fear management Self-confidence Self-praise Rejection management	Awaken interest Character strengthening Vigilance Volitional attention
Beliefs	Faith Values Ethics Honesty Good and evil	Strengths and weaknesses Learning styles Mental capacities	Rewards Prejudices Preferences	Behavioral patterns Personality

Table 3.2 Complete LSRLM: *Features* associated to the three *agents* (2.1, 2.2, and 2.3) that compose the *2 leading* functionality

Features	21 Proactive	22 Executive	23 Reactive
Processes Functions Attributes Components	Task analysis Self-planning Goal setting Task perception Framework construction Resource identification Organization and transformation Learning disposition Mastery-level specification Standard setting	Self-instruction Self-monitoring Self-directed Self-recording Self-control Self-response Metacognitive experience Self-experimentation Self-observation Strategic instruction Environmental structuring Personal consequences Plan maintenance Plan disengagement	Self-evaluation Self-reflection Self-judgment Goal-outcome discrepancies Feedback Progress-internal attributional Self-satisfaction Evaluation criteria Task performance Prospective, retrospective, and causal attributions
Strategies	Learning-strategy selection Domain knowledge modeling Performance-standard setting Learning interest Intention-behavior alignment Experience utilization Mental representation Developmental periods	Goal orientation Help seeking Attentional focus Resource utilization Time management Stress and emotion regulation Situational management Information seeking Comprehension monitoring	Contingency management Reward Exam review Tracking Correction Sanction
Beliefs	Self-efficacy Outcome expectations	Task interest Perceived task difficulty Incentive interest	Achievement grade Task utility Satisfaction Disappointment Indifference

3.4 Learning Modeling

After the description of the LSRLM, its application to a case study in a HE institution is briefed in this Section. Firstly, a *Three-stage frequency* to assess the practice of a feature is proposed to enhance the LSRLM; secondly the "Questionnaire to measure learner's SRL practices" is outlined; thirdly, the application of the questionnaire to undergraduates is reported; and lastly, descriptive statistics are informed according to the three constituent components that make up the architecture.

Table 3.3 Complete LSRLM: *Features* associated to the three *agents* (3.1, 3.2, and 3.3) that compose the *3 scenery* functionality

Features	31 Inner	32 Outer	33 Setting
Processes Functions Attributes Components	Domain knowledge: prior, in progress, acquired, conceptual, procedural, strategic, understood, and evaluated Skills development Self-explanation Cognitive processes Self-consequences Effort self-regulation Products Task change Renegotiation	Meaningful learning Competence Performance Self-verbalization Transformation Essay Task-change monitoring	Socialization: modeling, guidance, comparison, and knowledge activation Resource management Collaboration Cooperation Environmental interaction Context perception External feedback Co-regulation Social modeling Social comparison Social guidance Context monitoring Context evaluation Context change or abandonment
Strategies	Learning styles Selective attention Self-reinforcement Decoding Rehearsal Elaboration Structuring Questioning Rule activation Think-aloud Mental-process tracing Mental simulation	Private speech Record keeping Verbal description	Social-resource use Behavior observation
Beliefs	Intrinsic motivation Perceived autonomy Misconceptions Perceived competence	Behavioral pattern Performance climate	Learning climate Extrinsic motivation

Stages

Given the diversity of features that constitute the LSRLM, the *Three-stage* standard criterion is stated to assess their learner's use. Such a criterion identifies how frequently the learner is aware of and applies an SRL feature, *before*, *during*, and *after* its practice during learning. The stages represent a flow that drives the acquisition of domain knowledge, the development of a skill, or the exercise of a construct.

Hence, all features that compose the LSRLM, shown in Tables 3.1, 3.2, and 3.3, are assessed by means of the *Three-stage* criterion, making use of a suitable inquiry that asks how often the learner uses a specific feature at a particular stage (e.g., *before*, *during*, and *after*). Thus, three questions are made, one for each stage, to assess the frequency use of a feature, as the example stated in the following Section.

Instrument

As a tool to know the learner's custom to use the *features* that compose the LSRLM during the learning labor is designed the "Questionnaire to measure learner's SRL practices" that makes three inquiries to estimate the frequency of its application at three *stages* (e.g., *before*, *during*, and *after*), based on a Likert scale that identifies quantitative and qualitative values: 1 *never*, 2 *rarely*, 3 *sometimes*, 4 *often*, 5 *always*.

In this sense, Tables 3.4, 3.5, and 3.6 show respectively how to partially assess the *soulful*, *leading*, and *scenery* functionalities learner's practice by means of measuring two representative *features* of their *agents*. The appraisal is stated through a triplet of ad-hoc *questions*, where each of them represents one of the three *stages*, and its response corresponds to one of the five mentioned frequencies that is chosen by the learner according to how repeatedly he/she applies it during learning tasks.

Table 3.4 LSRLM: *Three-stage* frequency of two *features* associated to the four *agents* that compose the *1 soulful* functionality

11 Consciousness	12 Mind	13 Feelings	14 Will
111 *Self-consciousness* 1111 Are you aware of the purpose of the next learning activity?	121 *Metacognition* 1211 Do you define the mental processes to apply in the upcoming learning activity?	131 *Motivation* 1311 Do you consider your motivation for the next learning activity?	141 *Attitude* 1411 Do you value your readiness to initiate the following learning endeavor?
1112 Are you aware of the ongoing learning process?	1212 Do you monitor the mental processes in charge of the continuing learning activity?	1312 Do you think your motivation influences the learning in progress?	1412 Are you aware of changes in your attitude during the learning activity in progress?
1113 Were you aware of the achieved learning activity?	1213 Do you reflect on the mental processes used for the concluded learning activity?	1313 Do you consider that your motivation influenced the achieved learning?	1413 Do you question how your attitude influenced the attained learning?
112 *Self-concept* 1121 Do you relate your capabilities for the following learning activity?	122 *Critical thinking* 1221 Do you question the later learning topic?	132 *Emotions* 1321 Do you take into account your emotions prior to starting the learning labor?	142 *Commitment* 1421 Do you seriously commit to completing the following learning activity?
1122 Do your capabilities facilitate the current learning process?	1222 Do you examine the learning topic being acquired?	1322 Do you allow your emotions influence the ongoing learning process?	1422 Do you uphold your commitment during the current learning task?
1123 Did your capabilities contribute to the fulfilled learning activity?	1223 Do you evaluate the recently learning topic?	1323 Do you think your emotions influenced the completed learning?	1423 Do you reflect whether your commitment influenced the earned learning?

Table 3.5 LSRLM: *Three-stage* frequency of two *features* associated to the three *agents* that compose the *2 leading* functionality

21 Proactive	22 Executive	23 Reactive
211 *Task analysis* 2111 Do you define the tasks required for the nearest learning goal? 2112 Do you evaluate the tasks being developed during the learning process? 2113 Do you assess the usefulness of the task performed for the gained learning?	221 *Self-instruction* 2211 Prior to taking a lesson, do you usually consider self-instruction? 2212 Do you preserve your own instruction while the lesson is in progress? 2213 Do you evaluate whether the self-instruction fostered the achieved learning?	231 *Self-evaluation* 2311 Do you usually include the self-evaluation for the incoming learning task? 2312 Do you hang onto self-evaluation while doing the learning activities? 2313 Do you estimate the impact of self-evaluation on learning outcome?
212 *Self-planning* 2121 Do you plan the activities needed for the following learning task? 2122 Do you update the planning during the learning task execution? 2123 Do you evaluate how well the planning was followed during the learning?	222 *Self-monitoring* 2221 Do you plan to self-monitor the upcoming learning endeavor? 2222 Do you keep self-monitoring during the interim of the learning labor? 2223 Do you ponder how beneficial self-monitoring was for the learning gained?	232 *Self-reflection* 2321 Do you incorporate self-reflection for the ensuing learning topic? 2322 Do you adjust ongoing learning subject based on self-reflection? 2323 Do you examine the impact of self-reflection on the learning success?

Table 3.6 LSRLM: *three-stage* frequency of two *features* associated to the three *agents* that compose the *3 scenery* functionality

31 Inner	32 Outer	33 Setting
311 *Domain knowledge* 3111 Do you analyze the nature of the domain knowledge to be learned? 3112 Do you usually examine the domain knowledge that is being acquired? 3113 Do you weight the learned domain knowledge?	321 *Meaningful learning* 3211 Do you often identify the essential concepts to be learned? 3212 Do you contemplate how the basic concepts are being mastered? 3213 Do you define the core meaning of the learned key concepts?	331 *Socialization* 3311 Do you frequently involve peers for the forthcoming learning purpose? 3312 Do you encourage peers to retain their performance at the time of learning? 3313 Do you examine how the peers' participation contributes to the learning goal?
312 *Skills development* 3121 Do you identify your psychomotor skills to expand during the next learning? 3122 Do you perceive how your psychomotor skills evolve while learning? 3123 Do you appraise how your psychomotor skills raised during the achieved learning?	322 *Competence* 3221 Do you establish the level of competency to reach for the coming learning? 3222 Do you assess the gain of your competency while the learning is ongoing? 3223 Do you attain the gained competence as a result of the learning experience?	332 *Resource management* 3321 Do you identify the resources that facilitate and enrich the incoming learning? 3322 Do you incorporate new resources and ways of using them during learning? 3323 Do you examine how the used resources were useful to attain the gained learning?

Assessment

To reveal a natural LSRLM of undergraduates, who had never before received specialized training about the profile, logistic, and application of SRL to lead their learning endeavors, the "Questionnaire to measure learner's SRL practices" was administered to a random sample of $n = 110$ students taken from a population of $N = 200$. The learners pertained to several scholar grades of the B. Sc. in Informatics.

The survey took an hour to be completed by students who voluntarily agreed to answer the online form composed by 60 *questions* of five-option multiple-choice questions (i.e., five gray-level of *frequencies* that identify the aforementioned quantitative and qualitative values), according to the LSRLM architecture as follows: 1 triplet of *questions* (i.e., one per each *stage*) per 2 *features* of 10 *agents* (i.e., 4 of the *soulful*, 3 of the *leading*, and 3 of the *scenery* functionalities).

Outcomes

The survey of 60 *questions* administrated to $n = 110$ learners appears in Table 3.7, where the 1st column shows the inquires' *Id*, the columns 2nd to the 5th present the answers given by only 4 learners, due to space limitations, whose *Id* is in the header, and the remaining columns edit the descriptive statistics for each *question*. Similar statistics are shown in Table 3.8 for upper tiers: 3 *stages*, 20 *features*, 10 *agents*, 3 *functionalities*, and the *LSRLM.*; as Tables 3.9 exhibits the statistics for each learner. Lastly, Table 3.10 reports the *questions* with the weakest, strongest, and highest correlations, *r*; whilst Table 3.11 shows the *stages* and *features* that reached the weakest, strongest, and highest *r*; and Table 3.12 reveals the *r* for *agents* and *functionalities.*

3.5 Discussion

Once the application of the LSRLM to a sample of 110 undergraduates was briefed, this subchapter then examinates the outcomes. Firstly, the interpretation of the results is highlighted; secondly, a comparison of the proposed model is made against similar related works; thirdly, an analysis of benefits and requirements is pointed out; and lastly, the responses for the *research problem* and *questions* are given.

Table 3.7 LSRLM 3 *stages* rating for 2 *features* of *agents* for each *functionality*

(a)

Id	3	12	32	82	Σ	μ	σ	$\overline{x}$	*m*	*M*	*Mo*
1111	3	4	5	3	406	3.69	0.80	4	2	5	4
1112	3	3	4	3	396	3.60	0.87	4	1	5	4
1113	3	4	4	3	416	3.78	0.81	4	2	5	4
1121	4	4	4	2	405	3.68	0.85	4	2	5	4
1122	3	4	3	3	411	3.74	0.74	4	2	5	4
1123	4	4	4	3	429	3.90	0.75	4	2	5	4
1211	3	3	5	2	365	3.32	0.85	3	2	5	3
1212	3	3	4	2	385	3.50	0.90	4	1	5	4
1213	3	3	5	3	392	3.56	0.99	4	1	5	4
1221	4	2	5	1	365	3.32	1.08	3	1	5	3
1222	4	3	4	1	370	3.36	0.96	3	1	5	3
1223	4	3	5	3	389	3.54	1.09	4	1	5	4
1311	4	4	5	5	459	4.17	0.87	4	1	5	5
1312	3	4	4	2	387	3.52	0.85	4	1	5	3
1313	5	5	5	5	461	4.19	0.87	4	1	5	5
1321	4	2	4	2	360	3.27	1.22	3	1	5	3
1322	3	1	3	2	314	2.85	1.14	3	1	5	3
1323	3	2	4	3	375	3.41	1.14	3	1	5	4
1411	3	4	4	2	415	3.77	0.88	4	1	5	4
1412	4	2	5	2	393	3.57	0.93	4	1	5	4
1413	4	4	3	1	402	3.65	0.98	4	1	5	4
1421	3	3	4	2	425	3.86	0.87	4	1	5	4
1422	5	4	4	4	434	3.95	0.96	4	1	5	4
1423	4	4	5	4	472	4.29	0.78	4	2	5	5
2111	3	3	4	2	374	3.40	0.89	3	1	5	3
2112	3	5	3	1	350	3.18	1.04	3	1	5	3
2113	4	4	5	2	402	3.65	1.05	4	1	5	4
2121	3	4	4	1	383	3.48	1.02	4	1	5	4
2122	4	3	3	1	373	3.39	1.08	4	1	5	4
2123	3	3	4	1	372	3.38	1.04	3	1	5	4
2211	3	4	5	3	423	3.85	0.81	4	2	5	4
2212	3	4	3	2	408	3.71	0.76	4	2	5	4
2213	2	4	3	2	389	3.54	0.86	4	1	5	4
2221	4	3	2	3	345	3.14	0.99	3	1	5	3
2222	4	3	2	3	356	3.24	0.97	3	1	5	3
2223	4	2	4	3	366	3.33	1.09	3.5	1	5	4

(continued)

Table 3.7 (continued)

Id	3	12	32	82	Σ	μ	σ	x̄	*m*	*M*	*Mo*
2311	2	1	2	1	352	3.20	1.06	3	1	5	3
2312	2	2	1	1	315	2.86	1.17	3	1	5	3
2313	3	2	4	1	361	3.28	1.06	3	1	5	3
2321	3	2	4	1	344	3.13	1.19	3	1	5	2
2322	4	3	4	1	340	3.09	1.06	3	1	5	3
2323	3	3	5	1	363	3.30	1.17	3	1	5	3
3111	3	1	4	2	391	3.55	0.97	4	1	5	3
3112	4	4	3	2	419	3.81	0.91	4	1	5	4
3113	3	3	4	3	419	3.81	0.82	4	2	5	4
3121	4	3	4	2	390	3.55	1.02	3.5	1	5	3
3122	4	4	4	3	398	3.62	0.93	4	1	5	4
3123	3	3	4	3	415	3.77	0.91	4	1	5	4
3211	3	3	4	2	404	3.67	0.81	4	2	5	3
3212	3	4	3	2	395	3.59	0.85	4	2	5	4
3213	4	3	3	2	408	3.71	0.81	4	2	5	4
3221	3	2	4	2	402	3.65	1.01	4	1	5	4
3222	3	4	4	3	403	3.66	0.85	4	2	5	4
3223	2	3	4	2	389	3.54	0.92	4	1	5	4
3311	4	4	4	1	372	3.38	1.20	3.5	1	5	4
3312	3	3	5	1	382	3.47	1.24	4	1	5	4
3313	4	4	4	1	390	3.55	1.30	4	1	5	4
3321	3	4	4	2	422	3.84	0.87	4	2	5	4
3322	4	3	3	2	399	3.63	1.00	4	1	5	3
3323	3	4	4	3	440	4.00	0.86	4	1	5	4
Σ	203	193	233	131							
μ	3.38	3.22	3.88	2.18							
σ	0.67	0.92	0.87	0.98							
x̄	3	3	4	2							
m	2	1	1	1							
M	5	5	5	5							
Mo	3	4	4	2							

[a]n = 110, Σ sum, μ mean, σ standard deviation, x̄ median, *m* minimum, *M* maxi-mum, *Mo* mode

Table 3.8 LSRLM rate: 3 *stages*, 20 *features*, 10 *agents*, 3 *functionalities*, *model*

Id	*Stages/features/agents*	Σ	μ	σ	$\overline{x}$	*m*	*M*	*Mo*
...1	Before	7802	3.55	1.01	4	1	5	3
...2	During	7628	3.47	1.01	4	1	5	4
...3	After	8050	3.66	1.01	4	1	5	4
111	Self-consciousness	1218	3.69	0.83	4	1	5	4
112	Self-concept	1245	3.77	0.78	4	2	5	4
121	Metacognition	1142	3.46	0.92	3	1	5	4
122	Critical thinking	1124	3.41	1.05	3	1	5	3
131	Motivation	1307	3.96	0.92	4	1	5	4
132	Emotions	1049	3.18	1.19	3	1	5	3
141	Attitude	1210	3.67	0.93	4	1	5	4
142	Commitment	1331	4.03	0.89	4	1	5	4
211	Task analysis	1126	3.41	1.01	3	1	5	4
212	Self-planning	1128	3.42	1.04	4	1	5	4
221	Self-instruction	1220	3.70	0.82	4	1	5	4
222	Self-monitoring	1067	3.23	1.02	3	1	5	3
231	Self-evaluation	1028	3.12	1.11	3	1	5	3
232	Self-reflection	1047	3.17	1.14	3	1	5	3
311	Domain knowledge	1229	3.72	0.91	4	1	5	4
312	Skills development	1203	3.65	0.95	4	1	5	4
321	Meaningful learning	1207	3.66	0.82	4	2	5	4
322	Competence	1194	3.62	0.93	4	1	5	4
331	Socialization	1144	3.47	1.25	4	1	5	4
332	Resource management	1261	3.82	0.92	4	1	5	4
11	Consciousness	2463	3.73	0.81	4	1	5	4
12	Mind	2266	3.43	0.98	3	1	5	3
13	Feelings	2356	3.57	1.13	4	1	5	4
14	Will	2541	3.85	0.93	4	1	5	4
21	Proactive	2254	3.42	1.03	3	1	5	4
22	Executive	2287	3.47	0.95	4	1	5	4
23	Reactive	2075	3.14	1.13	3	1	5	3
31	Inner	2432	3.68	0.93	4	1	5	4
32	Outer	2401	3.64	0.87	4	1	5	4
33	Setting	2405	3.64	1.11	4	1	5	4
	Functionalities/ LSRLM							
1	Soulful	9626	3.65	0.98	4	1	5	4

(continued)

Table 3.8 (continued)

Id	*Stages/features/agents*	Σ	μ	σ	$\bar{x}$	*m*	*M*	*Mo*
2	Leading	6616	3.34	1.05	3	1	5	3
3	Scenery	7238	3.66	0.98	4	1	5	4
	LSRM	23,480	3.56	1.01	4	1	5	4

Interpretation of Results

According to the statistical results outlined in Sect. 3.4, in this subchapter a glance of the analysis is made, and the identification of relevant findings is achieved with the aim of recognizing the contribution of the approach about how learners consciously follow SRL guidance during their learning endeavors.

Analysis

Given the hierarchical perspective of the proposed LSRLM illustrated in Fig. 3.1 and edited in Tables 3.1, 3.2 and 3.3, the interpretation of the results is traced following a bottom-up order in Tables 3.4, 3.5 and 3.6: *questions* (i.e., 60 inquiries: "1111 Are you aware of the purpose of the current learning activity?", …), *stages* (i.e., x.y.z.1 *before*, x.y.z.2 *during*, and x.y.z.3 *after*, each characterized by 20 inquiries), *features* (i.e., 20 features, 2 per 10 agents, e.g., "111 *Self-consciousness*"…), *agent* (i.e., 10 agents, e.g., "11 Consciousness"…), *functionalities* (e.g., "1 soulful", "2 leading", "3 scenery"), *LSRLM*, and *learner*. The analysis of the statistics (e.g., n = 110, Σ, μ, σ, $\bar{x}$, *m*, *M*, Mo) edited in Tables 3.7 and 3.8 is made as follows.

Questions. Four clusters of *inquiries*, ordered as a Gaussian Bell, are found, where at the left side two questions with μ ≤ 3.00 *sometimes* appear (e.g., "1322 Do you allow your emotions influence the ongoing learning process?", "2312 Do you hang onto self-evaluation while doing the learning activities?"), and at the right side four inquiries with μ ≥ 4.00 *often* are used (e.g., "3323 Do you examine how the used resources were useful to attain the gained learning?", "1311 Do you consider your motivation for the next learning activity?", "1313 Do you consider that your motivation influenced the achieved learning?", "1423 Do you reflect whether your commitment influenced the earned learning?"); whilst 21 questions are inside of 3.00 < μ ≤ 3.50, and 33 inquiries meet 3.50 < μ < 4.00 that respectively reveal: many SRL practices are *sometimes* achieved, and *most* are *often* achieved during academic learning. This means, inquires related to the *after* stage tend to *sometimes* be considered; while some *soulful* questions are the ones most *often* followed by learners!

Stages. According to the following statistics respectively reached by the *before*, *during*, and *after* stages Σ 7,802, 7,628, 8,050; μ 3.55, 3.47, 3.66; and *Mo* 3, 4, 4; it is found that the least SRL practice is the one that occurs *during* the learning process; while the most is the one that happens *afterwards*.

Table 3.9 Statistics of the LSRLM for the 110 HE learners, which are estimated from their response frequencies across 60 *stages*

Id	1	2	3	4	5	6	7	8	9	10	11	12	13	14	15	16	17	18
Σ	187	170	203	167	212	186	196	123	219	169	178	193	269	211	235	196	264	254
μ	3.12	2.83	3.38	2.78	3.53	3.10	3.27	2.05	3.65	2.82	2.97	3.22	4.48	3.52	3.92	3.27	4.40	4.23
σ	0.87	1.11	0.67	1.01	0.68	0.82	1.19	1.03	0.82	0.72	0.49	0.92	0.75	1.05	0.50	1.13	0.87	0.89
$\bar{x}$	3	3	3	3	4	3	3	2	4	3	3	3	5	4	4	3	5	5
m	1	1	2	1	2	2	1	1	2	2	2	1	3	1	2	1	2	2
M	5	5	5	5	5	5	5	5	5	4	4	5	5	5	5	5	5	5
Mo	3	3	3	3	4	3	3	1	4	3	3	4	5	4	4	4	5	5
Id	19	20	21	22	23	24	25	26	27	28	29	30	31	32	33	34	35	36
Σ	229	209	163	174	199	232	222	247	232	219	206	187	187	233	166	218	248	210
μ	3.82	3.48	2.72	2.90	3.32	3.87	3.70	4.12	3.87	3.65	3.43	3.12	3.12	3.88	2.77	3.63	4.13	3.50
σ	1.00	0.50	0.85	1.24	0.54	0.72	0.77	0.76	1.03	0.90	0.62	1.09	0.87	0.87	0.74	0.76	0.89	0.75
$\bar{x}$	4	3	3	3	3	4	4	4	4	4	4	3	3	4	3	4	4	3
m	2	3	1	1	2	3	2	2	2	2	2	1	1	1	2	2	2	2
M	5	4	5	5	4	5	5	5	5	5	4	5	5	5	5	5	5	5
Mo	5	3	3	2	3	4	4	4	5	4	4	3	3	4	3	4	5	3

[a]n = 60, Σ sum, μ mean, σ standard deviation, $\bar{x}$ median, *m* minimum, *M* maximum, *Mo* mode

Table 3.9 (continued) Statistics of the LSRLM for the 110 HE learners, which are estimated from their response frequencies across 60 *stages*

Id	37	38	39	40	41	42	43	44	45	46	47	48	49	50	51	52	53	54
Σ	210	218	244	188	232	214	241	211	243	240	233	234	252	278	166	226	183	275
μ	3.50	3.63	4.07	3.13	3.87	3.57	4.02	3.52	4.05	4.00	3.88	3.90	4.20	4.63	2.77	3.77	3.05	4.58
σ	0.95	0.71	1.12	1.02	0.83	1.05	1.10	0.65	0.79	1.06	0.80	0.84	0.63	0.69	0.74	0.98	0.91	0.77
$\overline{x}$	4	4	5	3	4	4	4	4	4	4	4	4	4	5	3	4	3	5
m	1	1	1	1	2	1	1	2	1	1	2	2	2	2	1	1	1	2
M	5	5	5	5	5	5	5	5	5	5	5	5	5	5	4	5	5	5
Mo	4	4	5	4	4	4	5	4	4	4	4	4	4	5	3	4	3	5
Id	55	56	57	58	59	60	61	62	63	64	65	66	67	68	69	70	71	72
Σ	231	237	157	199	213	176	250	207	236	252	181	217	237	158	296	244	196	215
μ	3.85	3.95	2.62	3.32	3.55	2.93	4.17	3.45	3.93	4.20	3.02	3.62	3.95	2.63	4.93	4.07	3.27	3.58
σ	0.82	0.70	1.08	0.75	0.89	0.41	0.74	0.70	0.61	0.97	0.34	0.49	1.17	1.04	0.36	0.86	0.90	1.01
$\overline{x}$	4	4	3	3	4	3	4	3	4	4	3	4	4	3	5	4	3	4
m	2	2	1	2	2	2	2	2	3	1	2	3	1	1	3	2	1	1
M	5	5	5	5	5	4	5	5	5	5	4	4	5	4	5	5	5	5
Mo	4	4	3	3	4	3	4	3	4	4	3	4	5	3	5	4	3	4

[a] n = 110, Σ sum, μ mean, σ standard deviation, $\overline{x}$ median, *m* minimum, *M* maximum, *Mo* mode

Table 3.9 (continued) Statistics of the LSRLM for the 110 HE learners, which are estimated from their response frequencies across 60 *stages*

Id	73	74	75	76	77	78	79	80	81	82	83	84	85	86	87	88	89	90	91
Σ	252	224	263	197	176	270	271	174	223	131	207	259	211	203	209	208	209	200	186
μ	4.20	3.73	4.38	3.28	2.93	4.50	4.52	2.90	3.72	2.18	3.45	4.32	3.52	3.38	3.48	3.33	3.10	3.05	3.25
σ	0.94	0.90	0.78	1.15	0.94	0.54	0.62	1.27	0.76	0.98	0.65	0.93	0.70	0.88	0.65	0.81	0.75	0.93	1.22
$\overline{x}$	4	4	5	3	3	5	5	3	4	2	3	5	4	4	4	3	3	3	3
m	1	2	3	1	1	3	2	1	1	2	2	2	1	1	3	3	2	2	1
M	5	5	5	5	4	5	5	5	5	5	5	5	5	5	5	5	5	5	5
Mo	5	4	5	4	3	5	5	3	3	2	3	5	4	4	4	3	3	3	3
Id	92	93	94	95	96	97	98	99	100	101	102	103	104	105	106	107	108	109	110
Σ	183	195	243	150	231	239	176	243	225	216	205	192	226	207	242	179	226	206	220
μ	4.05	2.50	3.85	3.98	2.93	4.05	2.50	3.85	3.98	2.93	4.05	3.20	3.60	3.42	4.03	2.98	3.77	3.43	3.67
Σ	0.93	0.77	0.93	0.77	0.95	0.72	0.73	0.79	0.65	0.74	1.18	1.07	0.98	0.77	0.78	0.87	1.09	0.77	0.77
$\overline{x}$	3	3	4	2	4	4	3	4	4	4	4	3	4	3	4	3	4	4	4
m	2	2	1	1	1	3	1	3	2	2	1	1	2	2	2	1	2	1	2
M	5	5	5	5	5	5	4	5	5	5	5	5	5	5	5	5	5	5	5
Mo	3	3	4	2	4	4	3	4	4	4	4	3	4	3	4	3	5	4	4

[a] n = 110, Σ sum, μ mean, σ standard deviation, $\overline{x}$ median, *m* minimum, *M* maximum, Mo mode

Table 3.10 A sample of correlations estimated for the *questions* with the weakest, strongest, and highest correlations

Id	2221	Id	2222	Id	1311	Id	1322	Id	3113	Id	3211	Id	3312	Id	3313
1311	– 0.10	1311	– 0.02	2312	– 0.13	3222	– 0.22	1322	– 0.08	1323	0.11	1322	– 0.03	1322	– 0.10
1323	0.02	1313	0.01	2313	– 0.12	3122	– 0.16	1321	0.07	1322	0.12	1311	– 0.02	1311	– 0.01
1313	0.03	1322	0.01	2221	– 0.10	1111	– 0.13	1323	0.07	1311	0.12	1313	0.01	1323	0.05
1322	0.06	1323	0.09	1223	– 0.08	3313	– 0.10	1311	0.10	1313	0.14	1323	0.13	1313	0.11
3321	0.35	3321	0.35	1211	0.05	3323	– 0.02	2323	0.36	2121	0.37	2212	0.30	2222	0.31
3223	0.36	2313	0.36	3212	0.06	2122	– 0.01	1223	0.37	1312	0.38	1421	0.31	1421	0.32
2321	0.37	1422	0.37	3213	0.07	3221	0.00	1212	0.38	1223	0.39	3123	0.32	1222	0.33
2112	0.53	1213	0.53	1321	0.25	1311	0.21	3123	0.60	2111	0.61	3321	0.48	3222	0.49
2223	0.73	2223	0.75	1323	0.29	1323	0.68	3223	0.60	3111	0.61	3311	0.75	3311	0.79
2222	0.81	2221	0.81	1313	0.62	1321	0.70	3111	0.61	3212	0.69	3313	0.81	3312	0.81
Σ	21.11		21.80		4.75		2.36		22.28		22.69		18.81		19.46
μ	0.36		0.37		0.08		0.04		0.38		0.38		0.32		0.33
σ	0.15		0.14		0.12		0.15		0.14		0.12		0.14		0.15
$\overline{x}$	0.37		0.37		0.07		0.01		0.39		0.39		0.33		0.33
m	– 0.10		– 0.02		– 0.13		– 0.22		– 0.08		0.11		– 0.03		– 0.10
M	0.81		0.81		0.62		0.70		0.61		0.69		0.81		0.81

[a]n = 59, Σ sum, μ mean, σ standard deviation, $\overline{x}$ median, *m* minimum, *M* maximum

Table 3.11 A sample of correlations estimated for *stages* and *festures* with the weakest, strongest, and highest correlations

Id	Before	During	After	Id	131	Id	132	Id	211	Id	231	Id	232	Id	321
Before	1.00			212	0.06	322	0.01	132	0.24	131	0.16	132	0.15	132	0.07
During	0.60	1.00		222	0.07	111	0.02	111	0.25	111	0.20	131	0.15	131	0.21
After	0.58	0.63	1.00	311	0.10	312	0.04	131	0.28	142	0.23	111	0.23	111	0.23
				121	0.17	321	0.07	112	0.31	121	0.27	312	0.32	331	0.34
				132	0.19	142	0.08	221	0.34	221	0.28	311	0.34	142	0.35
				142	0.21	122	0.09	311	0.35	312	0.29	323	0.36	122	0.36
				141	0.27	131	0.19	321	0.47	222	0.45	322	0.43	211	0.47
				211	0.28	211	0.24	121	0.48	211	0.45	211	0.45	322	0.50
				332	0.29	231	0.25	222	0.48	232	0.56	231	0.56	311	0.52
n	2	2	2		19		19		19		19		19		19
Σ					3.52		2.06		7.00		6.14		6.50		6.71
μ					0.19		0.11		0.37		0.32		0.34		0.35
σ					0.07		0.07		0.08		0.10		0.10		0.11
$\overline{x}$					0.19		0.09		0.36		0.31		0.34		0.36
m					0.06		0.01		0.24		0.16		0.15		0.07
M					0.29		0.25		0.48		0.56		0.56		0.52

[a]n = count, Σ sum, μ mean, σ standard deviation, $\overline{x}$ median, *m* minimum, *M* maximum, *Mo* mode

Table 3.12 Correlations estimated for *agents* and *functionalities*

Id	11	12	13	14	21	22	23	31	32	33	Id	Soulful	Leading	Scenery
11	1										Soulful	1		
12	0.33	1									Leading	0.23	1	
13	0.11	0.12	1								Scenery	0.20	0.34	1
14	0.29	0.26	0.08	1										
21	0.21	0.40	0.16	0.31	1									
22	0.25	0.41	0.19	0.26	0.38	1								
23	0.27	0.29	0.13	0.28	0.43	0.33	1							
31	0.27	0.32	0.07	0.30	0.35	0.34	0.31	1						
32	0.27	0.34	0.09	0.29	0.37	0.43	0.39	0.45	1					
33	0.31	0.32	0.07	0.29	0.32	0.28	0.34	0.32	0.36	1				
n	9	9	9	9	9	9	9	9	9	9		2	2	2
Σ	2.30	2.79	1.05	2.35	2.93	2.75	2.78	2.74	2.89	2.61				
μ	0.26	0.31	0.12	0.26	0.33	0.31	0.31	0.30	0.32	0.29				
σ	0.06	0.08	0.04	0.07	0.09	0.07	0.08	0.10	0.10	0.09				
m	0.11	0.12	0.07	0.08	0.16	0.19	0.13	0.07	0.09	0.07				
M	0.33	0.41	0.19	0.31	0.43	0.41	0.43	0.45	0.45	0.36				

[a] n = count, Σ sum, μ mean, σ standard deviation, $\overline{x}$ median, *m* minimum, *M* maximum

Features. Three clusters of *features*, distributed in a Gaussian Bell, and one outlier are identified, within the least practiced getting a $\mu \leq 3.40$ (e.g., "231 self-evaluation", "232 self-reflection", "132 emotions", "222 self-monitoring"), the majority fall within $3.40 < \mu \leq 3.70$ (e.g., 122, 211, 212, 121, 331, 322, 312, 321, 141, 111, 221), and others, that tend to be often applied, appear within $3.71 < \mu \leq 4.00$ ("311 socialization", "112 metacognition", "332 resource management", "131 motivation"), while the outsider that often led learners is "142 commitment" with $\mu = 4.03$.

Agents. A Gaussian Bell distribution is appreciated, where the "23 reactive" and "14 will" are the *agents* least and most considered in learning due to respectively reaching the μ of 3.14 and 3.85, and the upper clusters (e.g., "21 proactive", "12 mind", "22 executive", "13 feelings") estimate $3.40 < \mu \leq 3.60$; and (e.g., "32 external", "33 setting", "31 internal", "11 consciousness") fall within $3.60 < \mu \leq 3.80$.

Functionalities. It can be seen that during learning labor, learners are least aware of the *leading* functionality, $Mo = 3$; but in contrast, they are more aware of *soulful* and *scenery* functionalities (i.e., both $Mo = 4$, $\mu = 3.65$ and 3.66 respectively).

Model. The LSRLM for the sample, $n = 110$, reveal a $\mu = 3.56$ that highlights an intermediate frequency between *sometimes* and *often*, with a $\sigma = 1.01$, privileges an $\overline{x}$ and Mo of 4, inducing to think that "learners often apply SRL to lead learning".

Learner. At both extremes, three outliers appear, e.g., $\mu = 2.05$, 2.18, and 4.93 to reveal: two people *rarely* and one *always* follow SRL, while the remaining 107 participants are organized into four sets to draw a Gaussian Bell, where the 1st cohort obtains $2.50 \leq \mu < 3.00$ for 17 learners that nearly *sometimes* consider SRL; the 2nd group reaches $3.00 \leq \mu < 3.50$ for 31 students who *sometimes* follow SRL; the 3rd cluster discloses $3.50 \leq \mu < 4.00$ for 37 individuals that are almost often led by SRL; and 4th team gets $4.00 \leq \mu < 4.65$ for 23 undergraduates who often account SRL.

Findings

Based on the previously explained hierarchical view of the LSRLM and the sample of the correlations, *r*, estimated in Tables 3.10, 3.11, and 3.12, in this subsection an example of findings is revealed for the seven layers in descending hierarchy, particularly taking into account the μ, *m* minimum, and *M* maximum statistics to highlight those with the *weakest*, *strongest*, and the *highest* correlations, where the most valuable finding is: "learners often practice SRL guide during learning labor".

Questions. There is a pair of questions with the *weakest correlation*: "1322 Do you allow your emotions influence the ongoing learning process?" and "1311 Do you consider your motivation for the next learning activity?" that respectively reached: $\Sigma = 2.36$ and 4.25; $\mu = 0.04$ and 0.08; $m = -0.22$ and $-$ 0.13; and a series of negative correlations = 27 and 15; in spite of $M = 0.70$ and 0.62. On another hand, the two questions " 3211 Do you often identify the essential concepts to be learned?" and " 3113 Do you weight the learned domain knowledge?" represent the *strongest* correlation due: $\Sigma = 22.69$ and 22.28; $\mu =$ both 0.38; $m = 0.11$ and -0.08; and a series of correlations = 59 and 60; even though $M = 0.69$ and 0.61; in contrast, the *highest* correlation is 0.81 for two pairs of questions: "2221 Do you plan to self-monitor the upcoming learning endeavor?"—"2222 Do you keep self-monitoring during the learning labor?", and "3312 Do you encourage peers to retain their performance at the time of learning?"—"3313 Do you examine how the peers' participation contributes to the learning goal?". This means, questions related to *feelings* reveal the *weakest* correlation effect with others, while questions concerned to *learning* and *domain knowledge* represent the *strongest* correlations with others; and particularly the *highest* correlations are about *self-monitoring* and *domain knowledge*!

Stages. The triplet of *stages* reaches a *moderate* correlation among them as it can be seen: the *lowest* correlation, $r = 0.58$, is the tide between *before* and *after*; in contrast, the relationship held by *during* and *after* discloses the *highest* $r = 0.63$. It uncovers the need to reinforce SRL practice *before* starting learning endeavors.

Features. Firstly, at this layer, there are no negative correlations. Secondly a couple of features reveals the *weakest correlation*, "132 Emotions" and "131 Motivation", with the following values: $\Sigma = 2.06$ and 3.52; $\mu = 0.11$ and 0.19; $m = 0.01$ and 0.06; and $M = 0.25$ and 0.29. In contrast, the *strongest correlation* pertains to "211 Task analysis" and "321 Meaningful learning" that respectively reached: $\Sigma = 7.00$ & 6.71; $\mu = 0.37$ and 0.35; $m = 0.24$ & 0.07; and $M = 0.48$ & 0.52; although the highest correlation was 0.56 for the tie "231 Self-evaluation" and "232 Self-reflection". Hence the prior findings are confirmed: "questions related to *feelings* reveal the *weakest* correlation effect with others", and "questions concerned to *learning* represent the *strongest* correlations with others"! Moreover, a new finding is exposed: "the strong correlation that exists between the pair of features, *self-evaluation* and *self-reflection*, that partially characterizes the *reactive* agent"!

Agents. Similarly to the prior layer, the *agents* with the *weakest* correlation are: "13 Feelings" and "11 Consciousness" that respectively scored: $\Sigma = 1.05$ and 2.30; $\mu = 0.12$ and 0.26; $m = 0.07$ and 0.11; and $M = 0.19$ and 0.33, confirming one of the aforementioned findings "questions related to *feelings* reveal the *weakest* correlation effect with others"! On the other hand, "21 Anticipator" and "32 External" *agents* get the strongest correlation with: $\Sigma = 2.93$ and 2.89; $\mu = 0.33$ and 0.32; $m = 0.16$ and 0.19; and $M = 0.43$ and 0.45. These results strengthen the previous finding "questions concerned to *learning* represent the *strongest* correlations with others"!

Functionalities. Special attention should be given to fact that the *soulful* functionality exhibits the *weakest correlation*, $r = 0.20$ and 0.23 for its ties with *scenery* and *leading* respectively; while both *scenery* and *managing* attain $r = 0.34$ to represent the highest one. This finding underscores the importance of offering cognitive psychology assistance to learners!

Model. In spite of both the $\overline{x}$ and Mo being 4 for the LSRLM, the $\mu = 3.56$ and $\sigma = 1.01$ represent a wide oscillation of frequency use of SRL guidance among the learners. In addition, the outcome reveals the high incidence of *sometimes* and *often* frequencies that were preferably chosen by learners. Such a tendency means a slightly superior mid-range learners' custom of following SRL practices during learning.

Learner. Based on the prior analysis made for *learner*, where the 3rd and 4th cohorts represent nearly 56% and the remaining almost reach 44% of the frequencies, it means that: learners are more *often* than *sometimes* prone to follow SRL counsel during academic learning labor.

Contrasting the Approach

With the aim of recognizing the contribution made by the proposed LSRLM to enhance the SRL field, in this subsection its constructs are assessed according to tenets introduced early, its baseline acknowledges diverse SRL essentials, and its properties are compared against the traits of some SRL models already stated.

Matching the SRL Concepts

Taking into account several concepts about the nature of SRL stated in the "3.1 Introduction" Section, in this subsection an account of how the LSRLM meets them is given. Firstly, this approach promotes the development of *soft skills* to "prepare students for the digital age" (Kennedy & Sundberg, 2020, p. 479) through the *setting* agent, where diverse *features* are considered, such as: *resource management*, *environmental interaction*, and *context perception*. The model fosters "learning that results from student's self-regulated thoughts and behaviors..." (Zimmerman, 2000, p. 14) by means of its *inner* and *outer* agents, leading learner's "behavior oriented towards the... execution of predefined tasks" (Thoutenhoofd & Pirrie, 2015, p. 72).

The approach rests on *cognitive* and *behavioral* paradigms (Alam & Mohanty, 2024; Hidayati & Thompson, 2025; Ye et al., 2022), considering principles of: the *phenomenological* theory to "explore subjective experiences and meaning construction" (Brziak & Urban, 2025, p. 1) as the essentials considered to design the model, the *operant theory* to head "self-regulatory behaviors that are ultimately controlled by one's environment" (Carvalho-Filho, 2002, p. 438) through the *scenery* functionality, and the *social cognitive theory*, where "behavior extensively motivated and regulated by the ongoing exercise of self-influence" (Bandura, 1991, p. 248) is described across the sequential, cyclical, and feedback flows shown in Fig. 3.1.

Basically, LSRLM depicts an "*abstract phenomenon*" (Kaplan, 2008, p. 477), whose "practices are either positively associated with academic performance" (Hadwin et al., 2025, p. 1), while its *scenery* functionality supports "the development of SRL skills and strategies" as "a function of the bidirectional interaction of personal, behavioral, and setting factors" (Barnard-Brak et al., 2010, p. 62).

Recognizing SRL Basis

Part of the soundness of the approach corresponds to the way it characterizes some principles stated in Section "Constructs". Firstly, as the *soulful* functionality, and the *consciousness* and *outer* agents demonstrate, this model is inspired by the progressive targets of the *psychology*, such as: the "science of *soul*, *consciousness*, *mind*, and *behavior*" (Aggarwal, 2010, p. 1; Weiner et al., 2012, p. vii). It also considers the aims of the *cognitive psychology* "...to study the mind" (Braisby & Gellatly, 2009, p. 2) and "the study of how people ...learn" (Sternberg et al., 2009, p. 3), and the *educational psychology* to "understanding learning... in educational settings" (Samtrock, 2011, p. 5) and the "study of the human mind as it bears upon learning" (Tutoo, 1998, p. 1), as the *mind* agent and the *purpose* of the model reveal.

In relation to *SR*, the approach defines *inner*, *mind*, and *outer* agents to recognize the *cognitivism* positions that "intelligent behavior can be explained by appeal to internal cognitive processes" (Haugeland, 1978, p. 215), and "cognitivism is an approach to the mind and behavior..." (Garnham, 2019, p. 99). The model also agrees with *behaviorism*, particularly the claims about: "the classical stimulus–response, where behavior was a subject matter in its own right" (Moore, 2011, p. 449), and "behavior arises from an individual's free choice" (Baum, 2017, p. 16), this why *outer* and *will* agents are taken into account. In addition, the *will* agent of the model represents the *executive function* of the "self" as "active, involved, and responsive, intentionally engaging in volitional processes...", where "the aspect of the *self* that initiates behaviors and makes selections is called *executive function*" (Baumeister & Vohs, 2003, p. 179), function that is a form "of behavior-to-the-*self* that evolved from *overt* to *covert* responses as a means of SR..." (Barkley, 2001, p. 1) that are represented by *inner* and *outer* agents. Lastly, concerning *regulation*, it "exercises the *control* over oneself, with regard to bringing the *self* into line with preferred standards" (Vohs & Baumeister, 2004, p. 1) as the *reactive* agent pursues.

As for SRL, the LSRLM meets three underlying items acknowledged by Schunk and Zimmerman (2012, p. 59) as follows: (1) *information processing theory* that "describes the *behavior* as an interaction between an *information-processing system*, the problem solver..., and a task *environment*" (Simon, 1978, p. 272), which are respectively characterized by *outer*, *inner*, and *setting* agents; (2) *developmental theory* affirms that "the antecedents of SR are described in terms of discontinuous *developmental* phases..." (Koop, 1982, p. 201), where those phases are represented by the three embodiments that follow sequential, cyclical, and feedback processes as they were illustrated in Fig. 3.1, and (3) *social constructivist theory* that affirms "the importance of learning in a *social* context and students as active constructors of their own learning *environment*" (Nithideechaiwarachok & Chano, 2024, p, 568), which are represented by *socialization* and *resource management* features.

Learner SRL Models

In regards to the SRL and learner models described earlier, some of them are chosen to highlight the attributes that distinguish the LSRLM. Firstly, in the "3.1 Introduction" Section a couple of proposals are considered. One corresponds to the "Strategy Model of Student SRL" designed by Zimmerman and Martinez-Pons (1988, p. 284, 288; 1986, p. 615; 1990, p. 53) that reveals "how students describe their use of 15 SRL strategies", which have been taken into account by the LSRLM as part of its dozens of *features* (i.e., they correspond to SRL processes, functions, attributes, components, strategies, and beliefs). The second approach is a kind of "Open Learner Model" that backs the study goal pursued by Long and Aleven (2017, p. 210), who wonder: "how an open learner model enhances students' domain level learning…". In this concern, the application of the designed instrument to the learners represented a kind of *open learner model* due to how its 60 questions triggered learners' reflection about how aware they are of SRL guidance during learning.

In regards to the SRL models reported in the Section "Related Works", some of them are referenced to highlight diverse attributes of the LSRLM, where the first is the proposal made by Zimmerman (1989, pp. 329–330), who "assumes reciprocal causation among three influence processes *personal*, *behavioral*, and *environmental*" that are considered by the proposal as the *inner*, *outer*, and *setting* agents respectively. Zimmerman (1990, pp. 5–6) also asserts "students are *metacognitively*, *motivationally*, and *behaviorally* participants in their own learning", such qualifications are respectively represented as *features* of the *mind*, *feelings*, and *will* agents. In the same way, the "*Cyclical model of SRL* to develop essential academic skills composed by four items: self-evaluation and monitoring, goal setting and strategic planning, strategy implementation and monitoring, strategic outcome monitoring" tailored by Zimmerman et al., (1996, p. 11), is also appreciated because its items are features of the *proactive*, *executive*, and *reactive* agents. In addition, such *agents* also respectively represent "the *forethought*, *performance*, and *self-reflection* cyclical phases of the *structure of self-regulatory processes*" conceived by Zimmerman (2002, p. 67) "to foster SR-learners" that also contains "sub-processes for each process" (Zimmerman & Campillo, 2003, p. 239; Zimmerman & Labuhn, 2012, p. 402; Cleary et al., 2012, p. 3; Panadero & Alonso-Tapia, 2014), which correspond to the diverse kinds of features: *processes*, *strategies*, and *beliefs*.

In another vein, the LSRLM is compared with the proposals made by Boekaerts, who tailored the "*Six-component model of SRL*" that establishes "three levels of repertoires: *domain-specific knowledge*, strategy use, and goals", which correspond to some features and strategies of the *inner* and *proactive* agents (Boekaerts, 1996, p. 100, 103). A similar case succeeds with "cognitive and motivational SR, cognitive and motivation strategies, content domain, and metacognitive knowledge and motivational beliefs" that "represent a specific type of *prior knowledge* that a student has available at any given time" Boakaerts (1997, p. 163–164). Similarly, Boakaerts (1999, p. 445, 449) organizes the "*Three-layer model of SRL*" in which "(1) the *inner* layer refers to the learning, processing information, and selecting cognitive strategies; (2) the *middle* refers to the regulation of the learning, using metacognitive knowledge; and (3) the *outer* refers to the regulation of the self, setting goals and resources". Those layers are respectively characterized by the following features: (1) goal setting; (2) metacognitive skills, planning, monitoring, regulation, and knowledge; and (3) learning-strategy selection. Moreover, Boekaerts and Cascallar (2006, p. 200) identify "*metacognitive, cognitive, motivation* key strategies students need to guide their own learning process", which are also considered as two kinds of features (e.g., processes and strategies) of the *mind* and feelings agents that are part of the *soulful* functionality.

On the other hand, the LSRLM is compared with the models designed by diverse authors, such as Garcia and Pintrich (1991), who tailor the "Structural model of the relationships between intrinsic *motivation, self-efficacy* and SRL", where the latter being understood as "a *behavioral* constellation of *monitoring*, elaboration, and effort *management strategies*", constructs that are part of the model as specific kinds of features (e.g., processes and beliefs) for *feelings, proactive, will, executive,* and *proactive* agents respectively. Concerning metacognition, the proposed model includes several features for the *mind* agent, such as: *metacognition, metacognitive skills, planning, monitoring, regulation, and knowledge* that meet some aims of the models "Metacognitive view of individual differences in SRL" that embraces "two constructive and metacognitive phases" (Winne, 1996, pp. 330–331), and the "Metacognitive and affective model of SRL" (Efklides, 2011, p. 6), which contains two levels of functioning: "the *person level* and the *task* × *person*" that in some sense correspond to the *soulful* and *scenery* functionalities.

Lastly, the diversity of *strategies* defined as *features* for the ten *agents* of the LSRLM include many of the instances organized into the *cognitive, metacognitive,* and *resource management* learning strategies identified in the "*Cybernetic method to regulate learning through learning strategies*" (Peña-Ayala & Cárdenas-Robles, 2019, p. 198–199). With regard to the proposed three-layer architecture, it adapts several tiers of the "Holistic self-regulated learning model" designed by Cárdenas-Robles and Peña-Ayala (2019, p. 304) and the "Self–regulated learning as a holistic–cybernetic framework" (Peña-Ayala, 2026) corresponding to *leading* for *modes*, and *scenery* for *determinants*, while the three kinds of *features* (e.g., *processes, strategies,* and *beliefs*) represent the ones defined as *self-regulatory processes* and *cognitive strategies.*

Examination of the Approach

As part of the *discussion* and considering the design and application of the proposed LSRLM, this subsection highlights the model's *benefits* and *requirements*. It acknowledges the contribution of the model and identifies its limitations to inspire future research aimed at overcoming the constraints and enhancing the scope.

Benefits

According to the statements, concepts, constructs, and description of SRL models, as well as the design and application of the proposed LSRLM, in this subsection an account of several *positive* attributes and advantages are identified in order to inspire future investigation and enhance the model to extend the SRL modeling of learners to foster their academic achievements.

Introduction. The approach fosters the development of twenty-first century skills, particularly those named *soft skills*, to be applied at any academic level and facilitate the acquisition of domain knowledge of any kind of subject. It rests on *cognitivism* and *behavioral* psychological lines, as the two main branches involved in leading learning labor. It takes into account diverse ideas and attributes of the introduced SR and SRL constructs, theories that support them, and SRL models.

Theory and models. It honors the four progressive objects of study in psychology: *soul*, *consciousness*, *mind*, and *behavior*, while also applying tenets from *cognitive psychology* and *educational psychology*. The model emphasizes the nature and role of the *executive function* of the *self*, as well as the aim of *regulation*. The approach principally considers two models mainly proposed by Zimmerman and three more designed by Peña-Ayala as part of its underlying elements, taking into account diverse constructs that characterize other SRL models.

Design. Its main basis acknowledges the prominent role of the *soul* and its interrelationship with the *living being's nervous system*. The diversity of stages, phases, processes, skills, strategies, beliefs, techniques... stated by SRL literature are classified and organized into three sorts of constituent elements: *functionalities*, *agents*, and *features*. Its three-tier architecture reserves the top layer for the *soulful* functionality that embraces four components (e.g., *consciousness*, *mind*, *feelings*, and *will*), named *agents*. Before the aforementioned variety of SRL terms, the model labels them as *features*, and defines three kinds: processes (i.e., it includes: *functions*, *attributes*, skills, and *components*), *strategies*, and *beliefs*.

Modeling. As an additional element of the LSRLM, a *three-stage* standard criterion is proposed to assess the frequency use of a given feature by the learner: *before*, *during*, and *after* its practice in the learning labor. Another contribution is the "Questionnaire to measure learner's SRL practices" for the features that characterize the agents of the three functionalities based on a Likert scale of five frequencies. An advantage of the assessment administrated to the sample of HE learners is the ease of answering the questionnaire. Although, undergraduates were unfamiliar with the SRL domain, they could understand the nature of the inquiries and responded readily, facilitating the gathering of raw data while characterizing how aware learners are of SRL practices.

Discussion. The analysis of the LSRLM is conducted from multiple views and levels of aggregation: from the fine-grained level, *questions* and *learners*, to the overall level, *model*, as well as the intermediate levels (e.g., *stages*, *features*, *agents*, *functionalities*). In this way, the approach allows a rich variety of views to be analyzed and valuable findings are uncovered, enabling suitable adjustments and enhancements. Furthermore, the LSRLM is sound and robust, whose baseline is composed of key concepts, main SRL theories, and valuable traits of some SRL models.

Demands

Similarly to the identification of the *benefits*, the *claims* are also recognized making use of the topics that make up this chapter; all of this in order to encourage potential subjects that demand additional attention, enhance their scope, delve deeper into the study, and develop new cases to add more empirical evidence.

Introduction. With the aim of fostering twenty-first-century education and instilling soft skills practices among learners, any initiative for describing SRL, designing models, and applying their guide to describe and lead learners' apprenticeship, as the one proposed in this work, requires the inclusion of a stage to train learners in its understanding and use before generating the learner model or guide their learning.

Theory and models. It is desirable to strengthen the baseline of the LSRLM, taking into consideration the support given by psychology, cognitivism, behaviorism, cognitive psychology, and educational psychology, as well other branches and disciplines such as: developmental and social psychology, and cognitive and learning sciences. Moreover, new functionalities, components, skills, strategies, and processes that are considered by a wide variety of SRL models are worthy to be examined, including those that enhance and enrich the essentials of the proposed model.

Design. Based on the prior needs, the constituent elements, features, questions, and the architecture of the LSRLM should be examined, discussed, reclassified, and redefined to enhance its nature, characteristics, and scope. What is more, new components, attributes, and inquiries could enrich the model, and even modify the architecture adding new perspectives and making the suitable amendments.

Modeling. There are pending tasks required to solve some weaknesses, such as: the estimation of the statistical reliability and validity of the "Questionnaire to measure learner's SRL practices" to appreciate its consistency, stability, and repeatability of measurements and findings. Additionally, several questions need to be rephrased to improve learner comprehension. Besides, inferential statistics and hypothesis tests are necessary to assess the confidence and reliability of the sample outcomes in order to draw meaningful inferences about the population.

Discussion. With the inclusion of the prior recommended statistics, wider, deeper, and better analysis of results and identification of new and valuable findings are expected to highlight the benefits and constraints of the LSRLM's current state with the aim of extending its scope and promoting the use of SRL as a natural practice.

Responses

Once the briefing of the design and application of the proposed model has been given, and the discussion of its outcomes is underway, it is now possible to provide a response for the research problem and the three specific questions to honor the commitment made in the "3.1 Introduction" Section as follows:

- Research problem "*How can the SRL practice that learner uses during learning endeavor be represented?*" The LSRLM gathers diverse constructs of several disciplines and SRL to propose a collection of constituent elements, organized into a three-layer hierarchy that characterizes essential *functionalities*, basic *agents*, and representative *features* of the SRL labor;
- RQ-1: "*How can the diversity of aspects that must be taken into account for SRL practice be organized?*" Basically, by means of *three-layer* architecture, where the constituent elements are hierarchically organized, and a *three-stage* series criterion is associated to the features for measuring the frequency use of SRL practice represented by specific features during learning endeavor;
- RQ-2: "*What are the components, processes, attributes, strategies, and beliefs that depict SRL nature?*" They are the constituent elements: *functionalities* (e.g., soulful, leading, and scenery), *agents* (e.g., consciousness, mind, feelings, will, proactive, executive, reactive, inner, outer, and setting), and *features* (e.g., self-consciousness…, critical metacognition…, motivation…, attitude…, task analysis…, self-instruction…, self-reflection…, domain knowledge, meaningful learning…, socialization…); and
- RQ-3: "*Which are the privileged SRL practices that learners use for leading their learning affairs?*" Specifically, questions concerning *motivation* (e.g., "1311 Do you consider your motivation for the next learning activity?" and "1313 Do you consider that your motivation influenced the achieved learning?"), *commitment* (e.g., "1423 Do you consider whether your commitment influenced the earned learning?"), and *resource management* ("3323 Do you examine how the used resources were useful to attain the gained learning?"). In addition, questions that learners recognize reveal the strongest ties with other SRL practices are: *meaningful learning* (e.g., " 3211 Do you often identify the essential concepts to be learned?") and *domain knowledge* (" 3113 Do you weight the learned domain knowledge?"). Lastly, the strongest ties between questions: *self-monitoring* (e.g., "2221 Do you plan to self-monitor the upcoming learning endeavor?"—"2222 Do you keep self-monitoring during the learning labor?"), and *domain knowledge* (e.g., "3312 Do you encourage peers to retain their performance at the time of learning?"—"3313 Do you examine how the peers' participation contributes to the learning goal?").

3.6 Conclusions

Even though the earliest works on SRL date back to the late 1980s, a growing number of publications have been produced since then, giving birth to diverse lines of research. However, modeling learners' SRL practices is one of the most promising areas requiring attention, and this chapter addresses this claim. Hence, the aim has been to *introduce a proposal*, whose key distinction is to consider the *learner's soul*.

With this in mind, the LSRLM is built on robust constructs from psychology, particularly SRL, taking into account solid concepts and theories, essential and novel models, and most common processes, skills, attributes, and components. Such items were stratified into three sorts of constituent elements: *functionalities*, *agents*, and *features*. Such items are organized into three hierarchical layers, where the bottom tier is measured through a *three-stage* standard criterion that reveals how frequently the learner is aware of and applies an SRL feature, *before*, *during*, and *after* its practice during learning endeavor. Empirical evidence is produced, gathered, and analyzed to highlight the benefits of characterizing learner's SRL customs.

Even though, some limitations of the introduced model demand its revision, amendment, and enhancement in order to: strength its baseline, include more constituent elements, refine the questions to facilitate their understanding by the learner, and estimate diverse inferential statistics to infer outcomes for the population.

As a future work, it is desirable to apply the proposed model to larger samples, undergraduates of other professional careers and HE institutions in order to confirm or refute current outcomes. An enhanced version of the model is convenient to extend its scope and identify new learners' SRL practices. Moreover, the use of artificial intelligence and data science is welcomed to automatize the generation of diverse learners' models for SRL and well adapt them to lead learners' labor.

Acknowledgements This research was partially funded by grants from SECIHTI-SNII-CVU-201000-36453, IPN-SIBE-2025-2026, IPN-SIP-EDI-2026-2028, IPN-SIP-2025-4112, IPN-SIP-2026-0613, and IPN Sabbatical Year DG-2023-342-1-8. Moreover, this work was conducted in part while the first author was a Visiting Scholar at the Department of Psychology of the Stanford University, hosted by the second author. A special mention and gratitude are given to native English speaker John Geoffrey Funk who achieved a thorough proof-reading to the manuscript.

Author Contributions Alejandro Peña-Ayala conceived, developed, and coordinated all aspects of the research effort and wrote the manuscript. James L. McClelland contributed to discussions during Alejandro Peña-Ayala's stay visit in his Center and participated in finalizing the manuscript for publication. Antonio Romero-Hernández collaborated in the design of the LSRLM and its application in the HE Schol where he works. Karla Marlen Álvarez-Olvera performed the analysis of empirical data.

Last but not least, the Alejandro Peña-Ayala expresses a testimony of the unction and strength given by his *Father*, *Brother Jesus*, and *Helper*, as part of the research projects performed by World Outreach Light to the Nations Ministries (WOLNM), and dedicates this work to the cherished memory of his mother, *María Teresa Ayala-Tinoco*.

References

Aggarwal, J. C. (2010). *Essentials of educational psychology*. Vikas Publishing House.
Alam, A., & Mohanty, A. (2024). Framework of self-regulated cognitive engagement (FSRCE) for sustainable pedagogy: A model that integrates SRL and cognitive engagement for holistic development of students. *Cogent Education, 11*(1), 2363157. https://doi.org/10.1080/2331186X.2024.2363157
Bandura, A. (1991). Social cognitive theory of self-regulation. *Organizational Behavior and Human Decision Processes, 50*(2), 248–287.
Barkley, R. A. (2001). The executive functions and self-regulation: An evolutionary neuropsychological perspective. *Neuropsychology Review, 11*, 1–29. https://doi.org/10.1023/A:1009085417776
Barnard-Brak, L., Paton, V. O., & Lan, W. Y. (2010). Profiles in self-regulated learning in the online learning environment. *International Review of Research in Open and Distributed Learning, 11*(1), 61–80. https://doi.org/10.19173/irrodl.v11i1.769.
Baum, W. M. (2017). *Understanding behaviorism: Behavior, culture, and evolution*. Wiley.
Baumeister, R. F., & Vohs, K. D. (2003). Self-regulation and the executive function of the self. In M. R., Leary and J. P. Tangney (Eds.), *Handbook of Self and Identity* (2 ed., p. 197–217). The Guilford Press.
Baxter-Magolda, M. B. (2004). Self-authorship as the common goal of 21st-century education. In M. B. Baxter-Magolda and P. M. King (Eds.), *Learning partnerships* (pp. 1–35). Routledge. https://doi.org/10.4324/9781003445685.
Boekaerts, M. (1996). Self-regulated learning at the junction of cognition and motivation. *European Psychologist, 1*(2), 100–112. https://doi.org/10.1027/1016-9040.1.2.100
Boekaerts, M. (1997). Self-regulated learning: A new concept embraced by researchers, policy makers, educators, teachers, and students. *Learning and Instruction, 7*(2), 161–186. https://doi.org/10.1016/S0959-4752(96)00015-1
Boekaerts, M. (1999). Self-regulated learning: Where we are today. *International Journal of Educational Research, 31*, 445–457. https://doi.org/10.1016/S0883-0355(99)00014-2
Boekaerts, M. (2017). Cognitive load and self-regulation: Attempts to build a bridge. *Learning and Instruction, 51*, 90–97. https://doi.org/10.1016/j.learninstruc.2017.07.001
Boekaerts, M., & Cascallar, E. (2006). How far have we moved toward the integration of theory and practice in self-regulation? *Education Psychology Review, 18*, 199–210. https://doi.org/10.1007/s10648-006-9013-4
Boekaerts, M., & Corno, L. (2005). Self-Regulation in the Classroom: A perspective on assessment and intervention. *Applied Psychology: An International Review, 54*(2), 199–231. https://doi.org/10.1111/j.1464-0597.2005.00205.x
Boekaerts, M., & Niemivirta, M. (2000). Self-regulated learning: Finding a balance between learning goals and ego-protective goals. In M. Boekaerts, P. R. Pintrich, & M. Zeidner (Eds.) *Handbook of self-regulation* (p. 417–451) Academic Press. https://doi.org/10.1016/b978-012109890-2/50042-1.
Braisby, N. & Gellatly, A. (2009). Foundations of cognitive psychology. In N., Braisby, & A. Gellatly (Eds.) *Cognitive psychology* (2nd ed., pp. 1–32) Oxford University Press.
Brziak, M., & Urban, K. (2025). Phenomenology meets self-regulated learning: Exploring the lived experience of learning. *Review of Education, 13*(1), e70063. https://doi.org/10.1002/rev3.70063
Cárdenas-Robles, L. A., & Peña-Ayala, A. (2019). A holistic self-regulated learning model: A proposal and application in ubiquitous-learning. *Expert Systems with Applications, 123*(1), 299–314. https://doi.org/10.1016/j.eswa.2019.01.007
Carroll, R., & Prickett, S. (Eds.). (2008). The Bible, Genesis, Chapter 2 verse 7: Authorized King James 1611 Version. Oxford Paperbacks.
Chai, C. S., & Kong, S. C. (2017). Professional learning for 21st century education. *Journal of Computers in Education, 4*(1), 1–4. https://doi.org/10.1007/s40692-016-0069-y

Cleary, T. J., Callan, G. L., & Zimmerman, B. J. (2012). Assessing self-regulation as a cyclical, context-specific phenomenon: Overview and analysis of SRL microanalytic protocols. *Education Research International, 2012*(1), 1–19. 428639 https://doi.org/10.1155/2012/428639

de Carvalho-Filho, M. K. (2002). A review on theories of self-regulation of learning. *Bulletin of the Graduate School of Education, Part III. No.* (50), 437–445.

Efklides, A. (2011). Interactions of metacognition with motivation and affect in self-regulated learning: The MASRL model. *Educational Psychologist, 46*(1), 6–25. https://doi.org/10.1080/00461520.2011.538645

Ejubovic, A., & Puška, A. (2019). Impact of self-regulated learning on academic performance and satisfaction of students in the online environment. *Knowledge Management & E-Learning, 11*(3), 345–363. https://doi.org/10.34105/j.kmel.2019.11.018

Gailliot, M. T., Mead, N. L., & Baumeister, R. F. (2008). Self-regulation. In O. P. John, R. W. Robins, & L. A. Pervin (Eds.), *Handbook of personality: Theory and research* (3rd ed., pp. 472–491). The Guilford Press.

Garcia, R., Falkner, K., & Vivian, R. (2018). Systematic literature review: Self-regulated Learning strategies using e-learning tools for computer science. *Computers and Education, 123*, 150–163. https://doi.org/10.1016/j.compedu.2018.05.006

García, T., & Pintrich, P. R. (1991). Student motivation and self-regulated learning: A LISREL model. In *Annual Meeting of the American Educational Research Association* (Chicago, Il, April 3–7).

Garnham, A. (2019). Cognitivism. In S. Robins, J. Symons, & P. Calvo (Eds.) *The Routledge companion to philosophy of psychology* (2nd ed., pp. 99–110). Routledge. https://doi.org/10.4324/9780429244629

Greene, J. A., Bernacki, M. L., & Hadwin, A. F. (2023). Self-regulation. In *Handbook of educational psychology* (pp. 314–334).https://doi.org/10.4324/9780429433726-17

Greggo, S. P. (2005). Soul origin: Revisiting creationist and traducianist theological perspectives in light of current trends in developmental psychology. *Journal of Psychology and Theology, 33*(4), 258–267.

Hadwin, A. F., Rostampour, R., & Winne, P. H. (2025). Advancing self-reports of self-regulated learning: Validating new measures to assess students' beliefs, practices, and challenges. *Educational Psychology Review, 37*, 8. https://doi.org/10.1007/s10648-024-09977-9

Hammit, L. (2014). Academic learning and personal skill achievement: The aspect of self-regulation. *Educational Psychologist, 34*(2/3), 73–86.

Haugeland, J. (1978). The nature and plausibility of cognitivism. *The Behavioral and Brain Science, 2*, 215–260.

Hidayati, N., & Thompson, W. (2025). The influence of self-regulated learning on academic achievement: A cognitive-behavioral perspective. *Innovative Journal of Educational Research and Insights, 2*(1), 21–30. https://doi.org/10.53623/ijeri.v2i1.69

Jayawardena, P. R., van Kraayenoord, C. E., & Carroll, A. (2019). Science teachers' practices: Teaching for self-regulated learning in relation to Pintrich and Zusho's (2007) model. *International Journal of Educational Research, 94*, 100–112. https://doi.org/10.1016/j.ijer.2018.09.022

Kaplan, A. (2008). Clarifying metacognition, self-regulation, and self-regulated learning: What's the purpose? *Educational Psychology Review, 20*(4), 477–484. https://doi.org/10.1007/s10648-008-9087-2

Kennedy, T. J., Sundberg, C. W. (2020). 21st century skills. In B. Akpan, & T.J. Kennedy (Eds.), *Science education in theory and practice: An introductory guide to learning theory* (pp. 479–496). Cham: Springer International Publishing. https://doi.org/10.1007/978-3-030-43620-9_32

Kong, S. C., & Lin, T. (2023). Developing self-regulated learning as a pedagogy in higher education: An institutional survey and case study in Hong Kong. *Heliyon, 9*(11). https://doi.org/10.1016/j.heliyon.2023.e22115

Koop, C. B. (1982). Antecedents of self-regulation: A developmental perspective. *Developmental Psychology, 8*(2), 199–214.
Kuiper, R. A. (1999). *The effect of prompted self-regulated learning strategies in a clinical nursing preceptorship* (PhD Thesis). University of South Carolina.
Kuiper, R. A., & Pesut, D. J. (2004). Promoting cognitive and metacognitive reflective reasoning skills in nursing practice: Self-regulated learning theory. *Journal of Advanced Nursing, 45*(4), 381–391. https://doi.org/10.1046/j.1365-2648.2003.02921.x
Long, Y., & Aleven, V. (2017). Enhancing learning outcomes through self-regulated learning support with an open learner model. *User Modeling and User-Adapted Interaction, 27*(1), 55–88. https://doi.org/10.1007/s11257-016-9186-6
McClelland, M. M., Geldhof, G. J., Cameron, C. E., & Wanless, S. B. (2015). Development and self-regulation. In R, M. Lerner (Ed.), *Handbook of child psychology and developmental science* (7th ed., pp. 1–43). Wiley. https://doi.org/10.1108/RR-10-2015-0245
McClelland, M. M., Geldhof, G. J., Morrison, F., Gestsdóttir, S., Cameron, C., Bowers, E., Duckworth, A., Little, T., and Grammer, J. (2017). Self-regulation. In N. Halfon, C. B. Forrest, R. M. Lerner, & E. M. Faustman (Eds.) *Handbook of life course health development* (pp. 275–298). Springer. https://doi.org/10.1007/978-3-319-47143-3_12
McCombs, B. L., & Marzano, R. J. (1990). Putting the self in self-regulated learning: The self as agent in integrating will and skill. *Educational Psychologist, 25*(1), 51–69. https://doi.org/10.1207/s15326985ep2501_5
Moore, J. (2011). Behaviorism. *The Psycholy Record, 61*, 449–463. https://doi.org/10.1007/BF03395771
Moos, D. C., & Azevedo, R. (2008). Self-regulated learning with hypermedia: The role of prior domain knowledge. *Contemporary Educational Psychology, 33*(2), 270–298. https://doi.org/10.1016/j.cedpsych.2007.03.001
Nithideechaiwarachok, B., & Chano, J. (2024). Socio-cultural and social constructivist theories and its application in EFL classroom for thai pre-service teachers: A review for further research. *International Journal of Language Education, 8*(3), 564–572. https://doi.org/10.26858/ijole.v8i3.66499
Ortega-Ruipérez, B., & Castellanos-Sánchez, A. (2023). Guidelines for instructional design of courses for the development of self-regulated learning for teachers. *South African Journal of Education, 43*(3), 1–13., https://doi.org/10.15700/saje.v43n3a2202
Panadero, E. (2017). A review of self-regulated learning: Six models and four directions for research. *Frontiers in Psychology, 8*, 422. https://doi.org/10.3389/fpsyg.2017.00422
Panadero, E., & Alonso-Tapia, J. (2014). How do students self-regulate? Review of Zimmerman's cyclical model of self-regulated learning. *Anales De Psicología, 30*(2), 450–462. https://doi.org/10.6018/analesps.30.2.167221
Peña-Ayala, A. (2026). Self–regulated learning: A holistic–cybernetic framework. *Education and Information Technologies 31, 3221-3253.* https://doi.org/10.1007/s10639-026-13919-z
Peña-Ayala, A., & Cárdenas-Robles, L. A. (2019). A cybernetic method to regulate learning through learning strategies: A proactive and reactive mechanism applied in U-Learning settings. *Computers in Human Behavior, 98*(1), 196–209. https://doi.org/10.1016/j.chb.2019.03.036
Pintrich, P. R., & Zusho, A. (2007) Student motivation and self-regulated learning in the college classroom. In R.P. Perry & J.C. Smart (Eds.), *The scholarship of teaching and learning in higher education: An evidence-based perspective* (pp. 731–810). Springer. https://doi.org/10.1007/1-4020-5742-3_16
Puustinen, M., & Pulkkinen, L. (2001). Models of self-regulated learning: A review. *Scandinavian Journal of Educational Research, 45*(3), 269–286. https://doi.org/10.1080/00313830120074206
Rank, O. (1996). Psychology and the Soul. *Journal of Religion and Health, 35*(3), 193–201.
Roberts, E. J. (1905). Plato's view of the soul. *Mind, 14*(55), 371–389.
Samtrock, J. W. (2011) *Educational psychology* (5th ed.). McGraw-Hill.
Schunk, D., H., & Greene, J. A. (Eds.) (2011). *Handbook of self-regulation of learning and performance* (2nd ed.). Routledge. https://doi.org/10.4324/9781315697048

Schunk, D., H., & Zimmerman, B. J. (2012). Self-regulation and learning. In W.M. Reynolds, G. E. Miller & I. B. Weiner (Eds.) *Handbook of psychology* (2nd ed., Vol. 7) Wiley.
Simon, H. A. (1978). Information-processing theory of human problem solving. In W. K. Estes (Ed.), *Handbook of learning and cognitive processes* (Vol. V, pp. 271–295). Lawarence Erlbaum Associates.
Skinner, B. F. (2011). *About behaviorism.* Vintage.
Smyle, M. A., Miller, C. L., & Westbrook, K. P. (2008) The work of teachers. In T. L. Good (Ed.) *21st Century education: A reference handbook* (Vol. 1, pp. 3–11). Sage Publications Inc. https://doi.org/10.4135/9781412964012.
Sternberg, R. J., Sternberg, K., & Mio, J. (2009). *Cognitive psychology* (6th ed.). Wadsworth Cengage Learning.
Thoutenhoofd, E. D., & Pirrie, A. (2015). From self-regulation to learning to learn: Observations on the construction of self and learning. *British Educational Research Journal, 41*(1), 72–84. https://doi.org/10.1002/berj.3128
Tutoo, D. N. (1998). *Educational psychology.* Sterling Publishers Pvt.
van Houten-Schat, M. A., Berkhout, J. J., Van Dijk, N., Endedijk, M. D., Jaarsma, A. D. C., & Diemers, A. D. (2018). Self-regulated learning in the clinical context: A systematic review. *Medical Education, 52*(10), 1008–1015. https://doi.org/10.1111/medu.13615
Vohs, K. D., & Baumeister, R. F. (2004). Understanding self-regulation. In R. Y., Baumeister and K. D., Vohs (Eds.) *Handbook of self-regulation* (Vol. 19, pp. 1–9). The Guilford Press.
Weiner, I. B., Reynolds, W. M., & Miller, G. E. (Eds.) (2012). *Handbook of psychology* (Vol. 7), Educational psychology (2nd ed.). Wiley.
Winne, P. H. (1996). A metacognitive view of individual differences in self-regulated learning. *Learning and Individual Differences, 8*(4), 327–353. https://doi.org/10.1016/S1041-6080(96)90022-9
Ye, Z., Jiang, L., Li, Y., Wang, Z., Zhang, G., & Chen, H. (2022). Analysis of differences in self-regulated learning behavior patterns of online learners. *Electronics, 11*(23), 4013. https://doi.org/10.3390/electronics11234013
Zimmerman, B. J. (1986). Becoming a self-regulated learner: Which are the key subprocesses? *Contemporary Educational Psychology, 11*(4), 307–313. https://doi.org/10.1016/0361-476X(86)90027-5
Zimmerman, B. J. (1989). A social cognitive view of self-regulated academic learning. *Journal of Educational Psychology, 81*(3), 329–339.
Zimmerman, B. J. (1990). Self-regulated learning and academic achievement: An overview. *Educational Psychologist, 25*(1), 3–17. https://doi.org/10.1207/s15326985ep2501_2
Zimmerman, B. J. (2000). Attaining self-regulation: A social cognitive perspective. In M. Boekaerts, P. R. Pintrich, & M. Zeidner (Eds.) *Handbook of Self-Regulation* (pp. 13–39). San Diego, C. A. Academic press. https://doi.org/10.1016/B978-012109890-2/50031-7
Zimmerman, B. J. (2002). Becoming a self-regulated learner: An overview, theory into practice. *Educational Psychologist, 41*(2), 64–70. https://doi.org/10.1207/s15430421tip4102_2
Zimmerman, B. J., Bonner, S., & Kovach, R. (1996). Developing self-regulated learners: Beyond achievement to self-efficacy. *American Psychological Association.*https://doi.org/10.1037/10213-000
Zimmerman, B. J., & Campillo, M. (2003). Motivating self-regulated problem solvers. In J. E. Davidson & R. J. Stember (Eds.) *The psychology of problem solving* (pp. 233–262). https://doi.org/10.1017/CBO9780511615771.009
Zimmerman, B. J., & Labuhn, A. S. (2012). Self-regulation of learning: Process approaches to personal development. In K. R. Harris, S. Graham, & T. Urdan (Eds.) *APA educational psychology handbook: Vol. 1. Theories, constructs, and critical issues* (pp. 399–425).
Zimmerman, B. J., & Martinez-Pons, M. (1986). Development of a structured interview for assessing student use of self-regulated learning strategies. *American Educational Research Journal, 23*(4), 614–628. https://doi.org/10.2307/1163093

Zimmerman, B. J., & Martinez-Pons, M. (1988). Construct validation of a strategy model of student self-regulated learning. *Journal of Educational Psychology, 80*(3), 284.
Zimmerman, B. J., & Martinez-Pons, M. (1990). Student differences in self-regulated learning: Relating grade, sex, and giftedness to self-efficacy and strategy use. *Journal of Educational Psychology, 82*(1), 51–59. https://doi.org/10.1037/0022-0663.82.1.51
Zimmerman, B. J., & Martinez-Pons, M. (1992). Self-motivation for academic attainment: The role of self-efficacy beliefs and personal goal setting. *American Educational Research Journal, 29*(3), 663–676. https://doi.org/10.1037/0022-0663.82.1.51

Part II
Approaches in Self-Regulated Learning

Chapter 4
The Role Model Effect in Self-Regulated Learning Development: A Review Study

Melek Karaca and Oktay Bektaş

Abstract The study examines the impact of role models (RM) on self-regulated learning (SRL) across various age groups from a comprehensive perspective. The problem is that the effects of RM, which provide direct and indirect learning experiences, on SRL development have not been sufficiently evaluated. The solution is to consider four studies examining the impact of RM on the SRL skills of middle school, high school, and university students by comparing them with the existing literature. The method is a qualitative systematic review. The results show that the impact of RM on SRL development changes at each stage of development. Gender also influences the effect of RM on SRL development. While parents' educational levels strongly influence SRL development, socioeconomic and sociocultural status, as well as parents' SRL skills and application levels, are also important. Students pay more attention to the behaviors of RM than their identities in SRL development. Educational policies can be developed that incorporate RM in academic settings to support students' SRL development. The impact of RM on SRL can be examined from a broad perspective, considering variables such as discipline, age, gender, socioeconomic and sociocultural status, and the qualities of the role model.

Keywords Learning · Perception · Role model (RM) · Self-regulation (SR) · Self-regulated learning (SRL)

Acronyms

RM	Role model
RM-SRL	Role model-self-regulated learning
RQ1	Research question 1

M. Karaca (✉)
Izmir, Türkiye
e-mail: melekkaraca38@gmail.com

O. Bektaş
Education Faculty, Mathematics and Science Education, Erciyes University, Kayseri, Türkiye
e-mail: obektas@erciyes.edu.tr

A. Peña-Ayala (ed.), *Self-Regulated Learning*, Cognitive Technologies,
https://doi.org/10.1007/978-981-92-0658-2_4

SR Self-regulation
SRL Self-regulated learning

4.1 Introduction

This section analyses the influence of RM on SRL skills from a multidimensional viewpoint, investigating how this influence is affected by developmental, demographic, and socio-cultural factors. The introduction outlines the theoretical underpinnings of the RM-SRL relationship and examines the influential roles of individual difference variables, including age, gender, and parental education levels, in this context. The methodologies section presents information on the four studies that underpinned the research, integrating them with data from the pertinent literature based on the inclusion criteria. The findings derived from the qualitative content analyses of these studies have yielded profound insights into how RM promotes SRL capabilities. Ultimately, recommendations and guidance for future research are provided based on the existing findings.

The organization of this section is as follows: initially, it presents the theoretical underpinnings of the research by emphasizing Bandura's social cognitive learning theory and Zimmerman's self-regulated learning model. Secondly, it elucidates the correlation between SRL and RM derived from the research. Thirdly, it encapsulates the methodological framework and details the authors' four cross-sectional studies. The findings of these four investigations are juxtaposed with existing literature results concerning demographic variables and subjected to qualitative analysis. Fifthly, the conclusions derived from these comparisons are encapsulated to address the study questions. The section finishes by summarizing the research contributions to the SRL field, its limitations, and recommendations for future studies.

RM-SRL Relationship Across Demographic Variables

SRL is a complex and dynamic process that includes planning, performance regulation, and self-reflection. According to Bandura's (1991) social cognitive theory and the SRL model proposed by Zimmerman (2002), SRL emphasizes how learners construct their unique educational experiences through the interplay of personal, behavioural, and contextual elements. The existence of RM is a crucial environmental component that contributes to the development and enhancement of lifelong self-regulated learning skills.

This section examines how learners with diverse demographic characteristics perceive RM and how these perceptions influence the development of SRL skills. This study comprises four thematically cohesive cross-sectional investigations, focusing on middle school, high school, and university students within the same geographical region, undertaken by the authors from 2021 to 2024. All investigations utilized the "Self-Regulation Scale for Science" and "Role Modeling Perception Scale," instruments created by the authors that have demonstrated validity and reliability. A uniform methodological framework has been constructed for the four basic subjects of the department.

This section examines the insufficient understanding of how the influence of RM on the development of SRL skills varies by age, gender, parental education level, and the attributes of the role model. Although data underscores the general efficacy of RM in cultivating SRL skills, existing studies' cross-sectional and inconsistent characteristics constrain developmental conclusions. A notable deficiency exists in the literature about a thorough synthesis that examines these impacts within a coherent theoretical and methodological framework. This section will cover the subsequent research questions:

- **RQ1**: How does the impact of RM on the development of SRL skills vary with age?
- **RQ2**: How does the impact of RM on the development of SRL skills vary by gender?
- **RQ3**: How does the impact of RM on the development of SRL skills vary according to parents' education level?
- **RQ4**: How does the impact of RM on the development of SRL skills vary according to the characteristics of the role model?

The literature consistently highlights the impact of RM on the development of SRL skills (Adıgüzel et al., 2023; Clark & Ste-Marie, 2007; Farley & Kim-Spoon, 2014; Nakanishi et al., 2019; Schunk & Zimmerman, 1997; White, 2017). Research indicates that observational learning through modelling is especially beneficial in cultivating self-regulated learning skills in early childhood. Conversely, most of these studies employ cross-sectional designs, which complicates the ability to derive developmental generalizations.

This section proposes a developmental theoretical framework by methodically analysing four experimental investigations that explore the relationship between perceived RM and SRL, while comparing their findings with existing literature. The authors aim to provide a comparative analysis that takes into account age, gender, parental educational attainment, and the characteristics of the RM. Consequently, advancing cross-sectional studies will establish a theoretical framework for curriculum design that incorporates RM into education and future implementations.

This study contributes to the field of SRL by establishing a theoretically grounded framework model that elucidates how the influence of RM on the development of SRL abilities differs depending on demographic characteristics. Another contribution is offering guidance to educators and program architects by providing a pragmatic theoretical framework that incorporates RM into education to cultivate enduring self-regulated learning skills. The proposed theoretical framework provides a foundation for further investigation of the RM notion in subsequent SRL research. This section primarily aims to illustrate the influence and characteristics of RM on the cultivation of SRL skills, highlighting variations based on demographic factors, to propose a cohesive theoretical framework that can inform educational methodologies and scholarly inquiry, and to underscore the significance of RM and students' developmental traits in the enhancement of SRL skills.

RM-SRL Implementations

RM's contribution to SRL development has been extensively examined through several research initiatives, including social cognitive learning theory. Zimmerman and Schunk (2001) emphasized the importance of modeling and observational learning in shaping individuals' learning styles. Subsequent studies indicate that various role models positively influence students' self-efficacy beliefs, goal-setting, and self-monitoring skills, which are associated with their SRL capabilities (Cleary & Zimmerman, 2004; Perry et al., 2002). These findings suggest that learners cultivate SRL techniques as both cognitive and social activities.

Recent investigations, however, have demonstrated that the RM-SRL interaction possesses a more intricate and dynamic structure. Panadero (2017) highlighted that the multifaceted nature of SRL continually interacts with the behavioral models that adolescents observe in their social context. Investigations into the influence of teacher or peer relational management on strategic planning, self-assessment, and motivational regulation abilities, particularly within digital and online learning contexts, are gaining interest (Dignath & Veenman, 2021; Rovers et al., 2022). Moreover, parental education level emerges as a socioeconomic element that indirectly affects students' adoption of SRL practices (Bai & Guo, 2022). This research seeks to provide a comprehensive perspective on how characteristics such as age, gender, and parental education level influence the impact of RM on SRL development, in contrast to prior findings, through qualitative content analysis.

A comprehensive assessment of the research indicates that the relationship between RM and SRL is not solely an observational learning process, but rather a complex framework influenced by the interplay of an individual's cognitive, affective, and motivational factors. The existing literature emphasizes the need for conceptual models that integrate social cognitive theory, motivational self-regulation theories, and sociocultural learning techniques to elucidate the influence of RM on the advancement of SRL. RM exhibited significant self-regulation skills pertinent to self-regulated learning development, including self-efficacy, goal setting, strategic planning, and self-monitoring; these skills manifested variably in relation to demographic factors such as age, gender, parental education level, and characteristics of role models. Consequently, contemporary research suggests that an interdisciplinary and multilevel theoretical framework should be employed to elucidate the interaction between RM and SRL. This work seeks to provide a comprehensive conceptual overview of the topic by addressing the identified theoretical gap.

4.2 Theory and Calculation

This section aims to provide an in-depth understanding of the topic by outlining the theoretical and conceptual foundations of the research, using explanations based on theory and calculation. Within the scope of this section, the nature and direction of the relationship between RM and SRL were first examined in detail. Subsequently, various factors influencing the nature of this relationship were systematically examined. Specifically, the effects of age, gender, parental education level, and RM characteristics on this relationship have been discussed, supported by literature findings. Thus, this section will provide a comprehensive structure that analyzes both the theoretical framework and the potential effects of demographic variables on the SRL-RM connection from a holistic perspective, in light of previous studies in the literature.

Theory

In this section, how individuals plan, direct, and evaluate their learning processes is examined within the framework of Social Cognitive Theory and SRL. Thus, the aim is to demonstrate how the concepts of observational learning and self-efficacy shape students' SRL skills through the behaviors and strategies they learn from the RM in their environment. Similarly, within the framework of SRL, the systematic organization of the three-stage cyclical process is explained. The theoretical framework presented in this section is designed to explain the role of RM in SRL development, to understand the impact of demographic variables on this relationship, and to provide a conceptual basis for subsequent analyses.

Social Cognitive Learning Theory

Bandura's (1991) social cognitive learning theory and Zimmerman's (2002) SRL model offer a comprehensive theoretical framework for elucidating the individual and social aspects of learning. RM, essential for developing learners' cognitive and motivational abilities, is integral to the self-regulated learning process.

In contrast to the orthodox behaviorist paradigm, which is centered on mechanical stimulus–response, Bandura (1986) asserts that learning occurs through modeling, incorporating the individual's cognitive processes and social context. This theory posits that SRL involves individuals observing their behavior, comparing it against established criteria, and adjusting their actions through evaluative processes (Bandura, 1986). Learners utilize and cultivate SRL skills through self-assessment, focusing on specific conditions, self-monitoring, decision-making, modeling, verbal persuasion, and environmental observation (Brainerd et al., 1989).

An individual who learns by contemplation, observation, recollection, and imitation of others' activities is crucial in the social cognitive learning framework (Joiner et al., 2002). The social cognitive learning theory emphasizes the interplay of cognitive, behavioral, and environmental elements in human behavior (Bandura, 1989). In social cognitive learning theory, this concept is known as the principle of triadic reciprocal determinism.

The social cognitive learning theory underscores the significance of four stages in observational learning. If a person fails to interact with or acknowledge the essential traits of a role model's conduct, they cannot derive significant learning from observation. Consequently, the initial component function of learning through modeling pertains to attentional processes. Certain members are likely to garner more attention in every social group than others. The functional significance of actions demonstrated by various models is highly efficient in ascertaining which models will be emulated and which will be disregarded. Certain modeling forms are intrinsically gratifying and can captivate individuals of all ages for extended periods. A prime example of this predicament is television. The models showcased on television are highly efficient in attracting attention, leading viewers to adopt the exhibited behavior, irrespective of additional incentives (Bandura et al., 1966).

The second crucial role in observational learning pertains to the long-term memory of modeled behaviors, known as retention mechanisms. The individual can remember and execute the pertinent behavior without the model by storing the observed behavior in their memory. This coding transpires either visually or audibly. The second representational system, which presumably elucidates the extraordinary rapidity of observational learning and the enduring retention of modeled information by individuals, pertains to the verbal encoding of seen occurrences. Most cognitive processes that govern behavior are verbal rather than visual. These codes enhance observational learning and memory retention, as they encapsulate substantial information in a readily storable fashion. Once the modeled behaviors are converted into visuals and accessible verbal symbols, these memory codes work as a reference for the subsequent reproduction of corresponding responses.

Research has shown that observational learning via symbolic coding improves in both children (Bandura et al., 1966; Coates & Hartup, 1969) and adults (Bandura et al., 1974; Gerst, 1971). Observers who encode modeled behaviors using words, succinct labels, or live visuals tend to acquire and remember the behavior better than those who watch others or are cognitively engaged while observing others' performance. The extent of observational learning that an individual may demonstrate behaviorally is contingent upon their mastery of fundamental skills. When the essential components are present, they can seamlessly integrate to generate novel behavioral patterns; nevertheless, the absence of response components will result in incorrect behavioral reproduction.

The proficient replication of modeled behaviors acquired through observation is the third phase of observational learning (motor reproduction processes). When positive incentives are offered, an individual can adeptly execute and preserve the demonstrated behavior in their memory. Consequently, a model that consistently exhibits the correct responses, trains individuals to replicate these responses, physically directs behavior when it fails to manifest, and then offers substantial rewards will guarantee that most individuals acquire the desirable behaviors.

The last phase referenced is reinforcement and motivational mechanisms (Bandura, 1991). Consequently, the four procedures must be effectively employed for successful modeling. The components include focusing on the model (attentional processes), memorizing the behavior to be emulated (retention processes), the ability to replicate observed behaviors (motoric reproduction processes), and possessing motivation to replicate (reinforcement and motivational processes) (Bandura, 1991; Malone, 2002). Individuals can capitalize on the potential to improve their skills in the SRL learning process by engaging in these four stages.

Zimmerman's SRL Model

Zimmerman's SRL model is based on a cyclical process that encompasses personal attributes, as well as contextual and behavioral factors, similar to social cognitive learning theory (Çokçalışkan, 2019). Consequently, Zimmerman has focused on Bandura's social cognitive learning theory to elucidate and define the SRL model. Zimmerman contends that the SRL process does not evolve autonomously from the social context but is bolstered by social modeling and feedback (Zimmerman, 2002). The learner observes SRL activities within their social context and subsequently internalizes and implements them. The internalization process transpires within a cyclical framework comprising three essential stages: forethought, performance/self-regulation, and self-reflection (Zimmerman, 2002; Fig. 4.1).

The pre-thinking phase preceding the learning action guarantees that the learner is psychologically and motivationally equipped for the task. In this preliminary phase, the learner identifies the learning aim, formulates strategic plans, and assesses the value, interest, intrinsic motivation, and self-efficacy of the task. At this juncture, RM assists the learner in establishing objectives and formulating strategies. Through observing RM, the learner acquires knowledge directly and indirectly regarding which goals are more attainable and the strategies to pursue them (Zimmerman & Schunk, 2001).

The second stage involves the learner executing their plans and implementing techniques while self-monitoring throughout the process. The student employs self-regulation and metacognitive strategies to maintain focus and motivation while

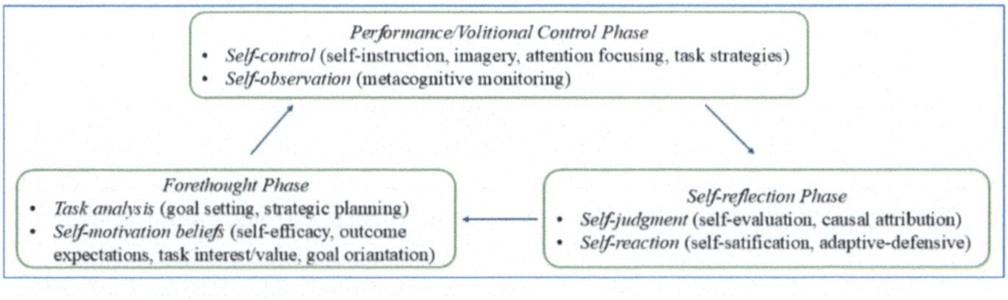

Fig. 4.1 Zimmerman's SRL model (Zimmerman, 2008)

managing their behavior. At this juncture, the learner may evaluate the RM regarding self-regulation and strategy execution. Consequently, individuals can acquire the ability to concentrate, sustain their attention, and identify the most effective technique (Schunk & Zimmerman, 2007).

Upon reaching the final stage, the learner cultivates cognitive and affective responses regarding the outcomes derived from assessing the learning process. Initially, they assess their advancement toward the established objective and scrutinize their achievements. In the event of failure, they attribute the cause to the employed strategies, revise their decisions, and recommend an alternative procedure. At this juncture, the learner cultivates their self-regulated learning capabilities by observing RM, analyzing the lessons they derive from personal experiences, the explanations they assign to success, and their methods for managing failure (Zimmerman, 2000). Consequently, learners can adopt a more intrinsic and development-oriented viewpoint while assessing their learning process and results.

Calculation

This section examines RM's role in SRL development from both theoretical and practical perspectives. RM plays a determining role in the development of SRL, which encompasses an individual's own learning processes. In the first six sections, the theoretical foundations of the relationship between RM and SRL are explained from a social cognitive theory perspective. In the second subsection, the relationship is examined in terms of how various demographic variables influence it.

The Relationship Between RM and SRL

Bandura (1986) demonstrated through his studies that humans can acquire knowledge without direct experience; they can learn by observing the experiences of others. Consequently, individuals can adopt numerous behaviors, particularly those imbued with cognitive, social, psychomotor, and moral values, by emulating suitable models. Recent studies indicate that RM promotes SRL by activating social support systems (Martínez-López et al., 2023). SRL entails learners actively overseeing their educational processes. At the same time, social factors such as encouragement, coaching, and feedback from RM can augment students' motivation, goal setting, and persistence in sustaining the learning journey. The form and source of support may differ. However, RM can bolster learners' self-confidence and sense of belonging, thereby enhancing self-regulated learning outcomes that are essential for academic achievement, such as personalized and independent learning (Martínez-López et al., 2023).

RM significantly promotes SRL by offering demonstrable instances of effective learning processes, goal formulation, and flexible behaviors. Recent empirical research suggests that when learners observe and reflect on the activities of RM, they invest more time in learning, exhibit improvements in self-regulated learning behaviors, and achieve superior academic outcomes compared to scenarios without such exposure (Lin et al., 2022). Training teachers to incorporate role modeling into the educational process resulted in notable enhancements in instructors' capacity to facilitate SRL and students' self-regulation skills within K-12 settings (Adıgüzel et al., 2023). Theoretical advancements, including the Metacognitive and Emotional Self-Regulated Learning Model (MASRL), highlight that observing RM can influence cognitive and metacognitive processes, as well as the regulation of motivation and emotions, which are crucial for effective SRL (Efklides & Schwartz, 2024). Consequently, pragmatic therapies utilizing RM can facilitate the acquisition and enhancement of abilities, including pre-thinking, imitation, self-reflection, recognition of adaptive learning strategies, and proactive engagement. Consequently, it illustrates that SRL can be more spontaneous, distinctive, accessible, and efficacious.

RM can substantially impact the advancement of self-regulation abilities, a significant factor in effective learning and individual development. Self-regulation, characterized as the capacity to control and coordinate one's thoughts, feelings, and actions in the interest of objectives, can be improved by observing how RM explores challenges and misfortunes. Whether youthful or more seasoned, students can learn to manage their time, set realistic goals, and adapt to setbacks by observing the RM approach to these life perspectives.

The impact of RM is not constrained by age, grade, or subject range. It has become apparent that RM can significantly impact students' career choices, scholarly accomplishments, and personality development. For illustration, inquiry has highlighted the significance of sex and age in part, demonstrating determination, with students regularly inclining toward RM with similar characteristics or backgrounds. In any case, the viability of a part show is closely tied to the alignment between the student's objectives and the characteristics of the role model (Fig. 4.2).

In conclusion, the concept of role models within Bandura's (1991) social cognitive theory highlights the importance of social influences on learning. Teachers, parents, peers, and other figures in a student's life can serve as capable RM, cultivating not, as it were, scholarly victory but, moreover, passionate and behavioral development. The capacity to self-regulate, an essential twenty first-century skill, is developed through watching and interacting with RM. Hence, the instructive environment should effectively integrate role modeling to support the advancement of students' cognitive, emotional, and social competencies, ensuring they are well-equipped to navigate their scholarly and personal lives successfully.

Factors Affecting the Relationship Between RM and SRL

Let us meticulously analyze the literature concerning the influence of RM on the cultivation of SRL skills, considering variables such as age, gender, parental educational attainment, and the attributes of the role model (Karaca & Bektas, 2023). First, let us examine how RM influences SRL skills across various age-related developmental stages. Following this, let us examine the potential differences RM brings about in

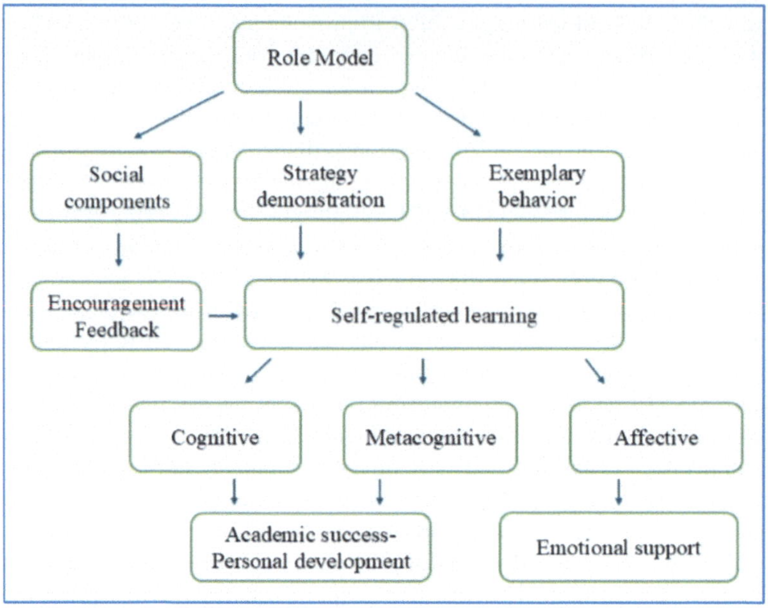

Fig. 4.2 The relationship between RM and SRL

SRL development from a gender perspective. Let us explain the role of parents' educational levels in supporting SRL skills through social transmission. Finally, let us address the characteristics of role models in terms of situations that support or hinder the internalization of SRL processes. Thus, we aim to identify the key factors that have a direct and/or indirect impact on RM's role in SRL development and to provide a theoretical framework.

The role of age in the RM-SRL relationship: The developmental aspect of SRL suggests that the significance of RM may vary with the learner's age. Literature indicates that the influence of RM on the development of SRL skills differs among age groups. During early infancy, particularly between the ages of 5 and 6 months, the efficacy of teachers and the learning environment, along with structured assistance and explicit feedback, significantly contributes to the development of SRL (Šūmane & Āboltiņa, 2021). As children mature, parental actions like autonomy support and conditional encouragement become crucial, establishing the groundwork for SRL before formal education (Dermitzaki & Kallia, 2021).

However, as people age, the nature of the influence of role models changes. In adolescence and high school, students' perceptions of RM markedly affect and elucidate their SRL skills (Bardach et al., 2023). Evidence indicates that the influence of RM on the development of SRL skills persists for pre-service teachers and young people (Karaca et al., 2024b). Thus, by prioritizing RM in the professional development of educators, the SRL skills of both instructors and students can be improved (Adıgüzel et al., 2023). In conclusion, while specific methods and pivotal figures evolve with age, the existence and caliber of RM from early childhood to adulthood consistently facilitate the development and enhancement of SRL abilities.

The role of gender in the RM-SRL relationship: The developmental aspect of SRL suggests that the significance of RM may be affected by the learner's gender. Literature indicates that learners' gender moderates the perception of RM and SRL (Study 2). Additionally, there is consistent evidence that female students demonstrate superior SRL skills in help-seeking, environmental structuring, and perseverance compared to male counterparts (Ablard & Lipschultz, 1998; Güneş, 2023; Liu et al., 2021; Refika, 2023; Virtanen & Nevgi, 2010). Conversely, research in online and game-based learning contexts suggests that while girls may initially possess lower perceived skills or experience, they can achieve performance comparable to that of boys when afforded equal opportunities. Furthermore, gender disparities in SRL may diminish when prior experiences are taken into account (Kuluşaklı, 2022; Nietfeld et al., 2014).

However, the effect of gender stems not only from individual differences but also from the structure of teaching environments. The nature of feedback and assistance offered by the teacher might variably influence the development of SRL skills according to gender. Certain feedback styles, such as scaffolding, can be more advantageous for girls (Guo, 2021). All individuals, regardless of gender, derive benefits from positive RM; however, females typically exhibit elevated SRL due to the influence of extensive sociocultural and familial factors (Ablard & Lipschultz, 1998; Refika, 2023). Research indicates that the influence of RM on the development of SRL skills is affected by gender, albeit the link is intricate.

The role of parental education level in the RM-SRL relationship: The influence of RM on cultivating SRL skills is markedly affected by parents' educational attainment. Parental educational support and involvement, mediated by resilience and performance objectives, are directly linked to the development of SRL skills. This association highlights the importance of the family environment in fostering SRL skills (Geduld, 2024; Thomas et al., 2019; Zhang & Ren, 2025).

Parents with advanced educational qualifications and who employ supportive, autonomy-enhancing parenting techniques are more proficient in fostering SRL competencies in their offspring; yet some aspects of SRL may still require supplementary assistance (Geduld, 2024; Žerak et al., 2024). Children with advanced educational attainment are more inclined to cultivate self-regulated learning skills by observing RM. The amount of parental education can moderate the influence of role modeling and the development of SRL skills. Higher parental education, particularly that of the father, enhances the positive correlation between students' perceptions of RM and their self-regulation skills, indicating that children of more educated parents may derive greater benefits from positive role modeling in the development of SRL skills (Geduld, 2024; Žerak et al., 2024; Zhang & Ren, 2025).

The role of role model characteristics in the RM-SRL relationship: The influence of RM on the cultivation of SRL skills is intricately linked to the attributes of the role model and the learner's perception of them. Research indicates that when learners view their RM as proficient, encouraging, and effectively exhibiting SRL strategies, their own SRL abilities markedly enhance (Adıgüzel et al., 2023; Dermitzaki & Kallia, 2021).

This situation becomes even more apparent, especially in digital learning environments. Educators trained in SRL methodologies, complemented by role modeling, are more proficient in cultivating these skills in students, underscoring the significance of the role model's education and expertise (Adıgüzel et al., 2023; Dermitzaki & Kallia, 2021). The notable success of RM in digital learning settings and platforms that render SRL behaviors observable to students further augments students' SRL skills. Consequently, the attributes and actions of RM that resonate with learners are crucial in cultivating SRL capacities (Lin et al., 2022). In essence, the more adept and purposeful a role model exhibits SRL skills, the more significant the favorable influence on the development of learners' SRL abilities.

4.3 Materials and Methods

In this section, the data used in the research, the sources referenced, and the methodological process followed are discussed in detail. Within the scope of this chapter, four fundamental studies that form the theoretical basis of the study and guide the research are introduced, and the content, objectives, and findings of these studies are explained. Additionally, the methodological framework of the current research was established in line with the methods and key findings obtained from these four studies. Thus, by explaining the theoretical background of the study, the method used, and the four studies that form the basis of the research, the structure of the research process is made clear and understandable.

Material

This study compares results from cross-sectional studies derived from data on learners of varying ages within the same socio-cultural context and comparable socio-economic status, with existing literature. This work is based on four investigations that collected quantitative data utilizing the "Self-Regulation Scale for Science" (Karaca & Bektaş, 2022) and the "Role Modeling Perception Scale" (Karaca & Bektaş, 2024).

Data from 500 students enrolled in three distinct middle schools in Kayseri, Turkey, during the spring semester of 2018 were reviewed for validity and reliability assessments for both scales. Confirmatory factor analysis was performed using data from a sample of 308 middle school children, which was separate from the group used for exploratory factor analysis.

The Self-Regulation Scale for Science, grounded in Bandura's (1991) social cognitive theory and Zimmerman's (2002) SRL model, comprises 26 items, accounting for 48% of the variance, and demonstrates Cronbach's alpha reliability of 0.94. The study comprises three components with Cronbach's alpha reliability of 0.94. The Role Modeling Perception Scale includes 30 questions derived from

Bandura's social cognitive theory, accounting for 41% of the variation and demonstrates Cronbach's alpha reliability of 0.96. The structure has three factors and exhibits Cronbach's alpha reliability of 0.91. The specifics of four research studies employing identical scales as data collection instruments are outlined below.

Study 1

The first study corresponds to the study titled "The relationship between perceived role models and self-regulation in Science," prepared by Karaca and Bektaş (2021). Study 1 investigated the correlation between middle school students' perceptions of RM and SRL skills.

The research sample, employing a mixed-methods explanatory-sequential design, consisted of 1100 students from each middle school grade level during the 2018–2019 academic year. The study group consisted of 12 kids from each grade level, along with an additional group of 17 who served as RM for these pupils. Quantitative data were obtained using scales employed in the other three studies, while qualitative data were acquired through semi-structured interviews and the "Role Model Self-Assessment Form."

The study concluded that the dimensions of reproduction and retention of role model perception predicted SRL; however, the motivation factor did not. These findings highlight the significance of incorporating RM in developing learners' SRL skills.

Study 2

The second study, titled "The relationship between role modeling perceptions and self-regulation with gender, grade, and parents' education levels as moderating variables," was developed by Karaca and Bektaş (2022). Study 2 examined the moderating effect of demographic variables (gender, grade, and parental education levels) on the relationship between middle school students' perceptions of RM and their SRL skills. Utilizing an explanatory correlational design within the relational quantitative research framework, the sample comprised 1100 middle school students in the 5th, 6th, 7th, and 8th grades during the 2018–2019 academic year.

The study concluded that gender and parental educational attainment moderate the association between role model perceptions and SRL capabilities; however, grade level does not moderate this relationship. The father's educational attainment exerts a more pronounced moderating influence. These findings enhance our understanding of the established influence of perceived RM on the development of SRL skills. Furthermore, it highlights the significance of using parental education level as an independent variable in the research.

Study 3

The third study was published by Karaca et al. (2024a) to analyze "The relationship between high school students' perceptions of role modeling and self-regulation for Science." In Study 3, a structural equation model was constructed to elucidate the correlation between high school students' perceptions of RM and their SRL skills. The sample, derived from a predictive correlation design, consisted of 362 students from a public high school who had given their consent to participate in the research.

The findings indicate that students' perceptions of RM in reproduction, retention, and motivation are significant determinants of SRL skills. These findings indicate that SRL capabilities commence in early childhood and persist throughout an individual's lifespan.

Study 4

"The relationship between preservice science teachers' perceived role modeling and self-regulation skills in science" is a study conducted by Karaca et al. (2024b). In Study 4, a structural equation model was constructed to elucidate the relationship between science teacher candidates' judgments of RM and their SRL skills. The research sample, employing a predictive correlation methodology, consisted of 242 volunteer science teacher candidates from two state institutions in Turkey.

The research findings indicate that teacher candidates' opinions of RM are major predictors of their SRL abilities. Notwithstanding their advanced age, the capacity of teacher candidates to cultivate their SRL skills through RM underscores the significance of emotional education and its enduring nature throughout life.

Method

The findings from the four studies that formed the basis of the research were descriptively compared with literature studies on the role of RM in SRL development. In this process, the results obtained from each study were analyzed descriptively, and their similarities and differences with the literature were highlighted. Thus, the role of RM in the development of SRL has been comprehensively evaluated.

The study results are detailed within the context of age, gender, parental education level, and the characteristics of the role model. Thus, the influence of RM on individuals' SRL development has been analyzed. The impact of RM on SRL development was evaluated from a developmental psychology perspective, considering age-related changes in strategies, gender-based motivational differences, and the opportunities provided by parents' educational levels.

The impact of RM characteristics on SRL development has also been thoroughly examined. A framework has been drawn outlining the conditions under which characteristics will positively impact SRL development. These comparisons allow us to see the potential contributions of RM to SRL development from a holistic perspective within a developmental theoretical framework.

4.4 Development

This section outlines the research design, inclusion criteria, and data analysis processes that form the foundation of the study. In this section, which outlines the methodological framework of the study, the research planning process is explained, including the criteria used to select studies from the literature and the methods employed to analyze the obtained data. Thus, the methodological approach employed in terms of validity, reliability, and scientific consistency of the research is presented.

Research Design

The findings of the four studies that formed the basis of the research were compared descriptively with the literature on the effect of RM on SRL development (Fig. 4.3). Thus, the aim was to develop a theoretical framework for the impact of RM on SRL development, considering variables such as age, gender, parents' educational level, and the characteristics of RM.

The study employed a qualitative systematic review approach. A systematic review is a methodical research design for gathering, assessing, and integrating published and unpublished pertinent material to address an articulated research topic

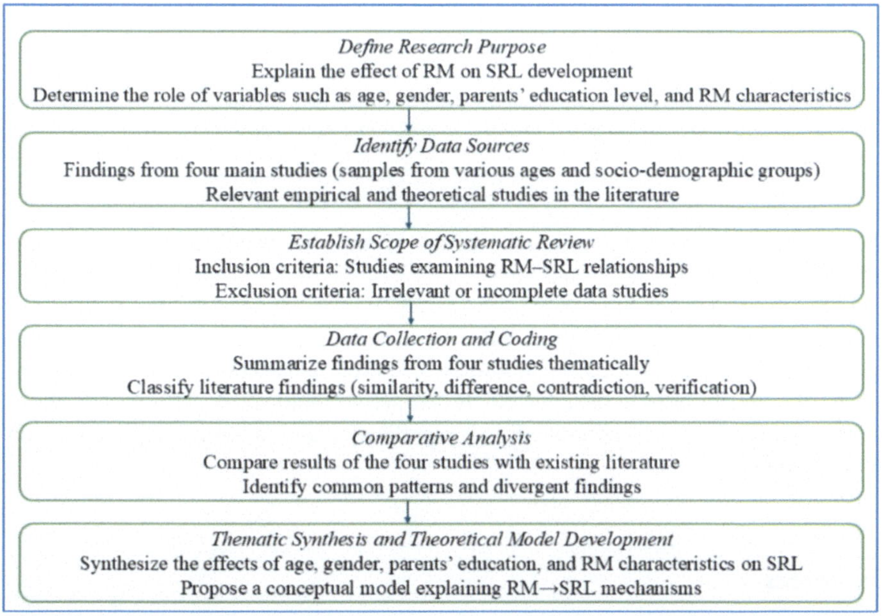

Fig. 4.3 Research design

(Taherdoost, 2022). This study contrasted the research findings on the role model influence in the authors' SRL skills development with existing literature, which justified the selection of this design. The outcomes derived from the four research studies referenced in the Materials section were examined descriptively by juxtaposing them with existing literature, highlighting similarities and discrepancies, as well as contradictory and corroborative scenarios.

Inclusion Criteria and Data Analysis

A systematic search was performed in prominent databases, including Springer, Elsevier, Wiley, Google Scholar, Web of Science, Scopus, and ERIC, to enhance methodological transparency. During this process, critical phrases including "role model," "self-regulated learning," "the impact of role models on the cultivation of SRL skills," "factors affecting the development of SRL," and "variables influencing the advancement of SRL" were employed. Studies employing experimental or quasi-experimental designs that explicitly investigate the relationship between RM and SRL, and that report measurable outcomes of SRL skills, were incorporated into the study based on the literature review. The study excluded theoretical analyses.

The obtained data were synthesized descriptively and comparatively to identify commonalities, contradictions, and complementary findings among them. Thus, the relationship between RM and SRL has been more clearly defined in light of the variables of age, gender, parents' education level, and characteristics of role models, and a solid and transparent theoretical framework has been established.

4.5 Results

This section presents the research results from a comprehensive perspective, providing a detailed analysis and interpretation of the findings and emerging trends. The data derived from four primary research studies, along with the overarching tendencies that emerged from this data, were assessed. Subsequently, the findings were juxtaposed with the theoretical framework and extant literature to underscore the research's contributions to the area and its distinctive conclusions. This part provided the research findings and examined their significance and potential implications for future studies.

Outcomes

The research generally examines various variables related to the impact of RM on SRL development. Previous studies have demonstrated the significant impact of

RM on individuals' learning motivation, self-efficacy beliefs, and strategic learning behaviors. In this context, the study's primary starting point was to examine how RM influences an individual's SRL capacity and the extent to which it serves as a guiding factor in learning processes.

This study specifically focuses on variables such as age, gender, parental education level, and the characteristics of role models. Thus, an opportunity was seized to examine the impact of RM on SRL from a multidimensional perspective. The combined evaluation of factors such as age, gender, parental education level, and the individual characteristics of RM reveals that learners' SRL processes are shaped not only individually but also within social and cultural contexts. This approach provides a deeper understanding of the developmental dynamics of SRL. It provides a theoretical framework for future research, enabling a comparative examination of the RM effect across various groups.

In this direction, the findings obtained will demonstrate the multidimensional and contextual structure of RM's impact on SRL development. In addition to demographic variables such as age, gender, and parental education level, the characteristics of RM shape learners' SRL skills in different ways. These results show that SRL is not only an individual and internal process but also develops in interaction with social and cultural contexts. Therefore, assessing the impact of RM on SRL development is crucial for designing effective learning processes and planning educational programs. These findings provide a conceptual basis for future research, enabling a comparative examination of the effects of RM on SRL across different demographic groups.

Analysis of Results

In this section, the impact of RM on SRL development has been systematically examined within the context of relevant variables. The study examined factors such as age, gender, parents' educational level, and the characteristics of role models, and the reflections of these variables in different studies were evaluated using a comparative approach. The analysis process was conducted considering both the theoretical framework and the previous literature, and the general trends and potential relationships of the findings were presented descriptively.

During the analysis of the findings, commonalities, differences, and complementary aspects between the studies were carefully examined. This approach not only summarized the results from individual studies but also provided a holistic framework for understanding how the impact of RM on SRL is shaped in a broader context.

This comprehensive assessment demonstrates that SRL development interacts with social, cultural, and demographic contexts, in addition to individual characteristics, and can be learned from RM. Each of the variables, such as age, gender, parents' education level, and the characteristics of the role model, shapes students' SRL skills in different ways. Therefore, the research shows that the impact of RM on SRL is multidimensional and that learning processes are enriched by interactions at both the interpersonal and societal levels. These results provide a comprehensive conceptual framework for future research, enabling a comparative examination of the effects of RM on SRL development across different demographic groups. Thus, the potential contributions of RM in designing educational programs and teaching strategies can be evaluated more systematically and holistically.

Interpretations

The findings of the four studies that underpin the research have been summarized concerning the targeted variables. A literature study in reputable databases, including Springer, Elsevier, Wiley, Google Scholar, Web of Science, Scopus, and ERIC, has discovered recent research examining the role of RM in developing SRL skills.

The investigations were rigorously analyzed, and their outcomes were systematically compared with those of the four trials. SRL is inherently connected to social and cultural circumstances. We emphasize the four studies because they are derived from data sets from the same social and cultural framework.

These assessments suggest that the impact of RM on SRL development is influenced by students' social and cultural contexts, in addition to their individual abilities. Research findings indicate that variables such as age, gender, parents' education level, and the individual characteristics of role models shape students' SRL processes in different ways. Additionally, four studies conducted on datasets from the same social and cultural framework emphasize that the impact of RM must be understood in conjunction with the social and cultural context. These results elucidate the multidimensional nature of the RM-SRL interaction in relation to demographic variables and offer a comprehensive conceptual framework for future research. This provides an opportunity to comparatively examine the effects of RM on SRL across different demographic and cultural groups for research purposes. Thus, the role of RM in designing education policies and teaching strategies can be evaluated more systematically and holistically.

Findings

This section presents the findings from the four studies that underpin the research, along with the results from the literature comparison regarding the influence of RM on the development of SRL skills. The results from Studies 1, 2, 3, and 4 concerning the age variable were compared, along with the data from studies examining the link between RM and SRL and the age variable. The results from Study 2 were compared with data from research investigating the association between RM and SRL, with an emphasis on the variables of gender, parental education level, and qualities of role models. The findings of studies on the utilization of artificial intelligence (AI) as a role model in the development of SRL, particularly in elucidating contemporary methodologies, have been emphasized.

The Role of Age in the RM and SRL Relationship

This section thoroughly examines the influence of RM on the development of SRL, specifically in relation to the age variable. A comparative analysis was conducted on the outcomes of 18 studies, encompassing various age groups, from the literature (Table 4.1). Consequently, an effort was made to obtain a systematic perspective from a developmental standpoint. Furthermore, investigations into the function of AI apps, for example, have also been analyzed. Consequently, an effort was made to establish a framework regarding the influence of both human and AI-assisted role models on the development of SRL, taking into account the age variable.

During early life and elementary education, instructors and classroom modeling are prevalent RM for students. Students at this age can acquire metacognitive methods with the instructor's assistance. The influence of teacher support in this age range is substantial. Consequently, childhood role modeling relies on external resources, with behavioral modeling taking precedence. Within this demographic, persons occupying the role model position must explicitly exhibit SRL processes using tactics such as task allocation, planning, and error monitoring to cultivate SRL competencies.

During the transition from infancy to adolescence, referred to as the adolescent era, behavioral imitation evolves into cognitive and motivational modeling. As the search for RM transitions from familial figures to both near and distant surroundings, it is advisable to help adolescents choose suitable peer exemplars. The inclination towards RM that promotes autonomy is on the rise. In adulthood, individuals tend to engage in more introspection and self-reflection. Consequently, the judicious selection of RM might enhance an individual's self-regulation and application of metacognitive methods. Adults typically select RM based on their expertise and competence. Furthermore, RM in technology-enhanced settings must be tailored to the respective age group. Research indicates that the influence of RM on the development of SRL skills is age-dependent; however, the findings are intricate. A study that included master's and doctoral students in Brazil initially hypothesized that participants' SRL levels would rise with age; however, the findings did not support this hypothesis (Lima Filho & Casa Nova, 2020).

The effectiveness of AI as a role model in SRL development varies by age. Younger students need more structure and human support, while older students benefit from AI that is personalized and supports autonomy. Teacher guidance and psychological needs remain important moderating variables, particularly for adolescents.

The Role of Gender in the RM and SRL Relationship

In this section, the impact of RM on SRL development is examined comprehensively in terms of the gender variable. The findings of nine studies focusing on the gender variable in the literature were analyzed comparatively (Table 4.2). Thus, an attempt was made to capture a systematic perspective on gender. Additionally, research findings on the role of AI applications as role models have also been examined. Therefore, an attempt was made to obtain a theoretical framework regarding the impact of both human and AI-supported role models on SRL development, specifically in terms of the gender variable.

Table 4.1 Example studies from literature on the role of age in the SRL-role model relationship

Study	Age group	RM and SRL by age
Dermitzaki and Kallia (2021)	Early childhood	Parent and teacher modelling is essential. Young children primarily internalize SRL strategies through imitation and scaffolding. SRL has developed less without external regulation
Zajda (2024)	Adolescents	This study, closely tied to Bandura's social learning theory, emphasizes the importance of imitating adult models in setting goals and motivating learning
Prasse et al. (2024)	All ages (review)	Meta-analysis suggested that RM in digital environments should be adapted according to age groups to remain effective in SRL interventions
Dörrenbächer-Ulrich and Bregulla (2024)	Adolescents	If modeling includes adaptive decision-making and reflection processes, especially during the transition from secondary to higher education, the execution and metacognition processes that form the basis of SRL develop
Hsu et al. (2023)	Elementary school	Young students benefit from clear and structured support, and because their SRL skills are still developing, they may need direct guidance and motivational support from AI
Study 1	Secondary school	The memory and reproduction skills of RM are practical in the development of SRL skills. However, the motivational aspect is not practical in the development of SRL
Study 2	Secondary school	The impact of RM varies by grade level. Older children benefit more from modelled SRL strategies
Study 3	High school	The dimensions of remembering, reproducing, and motivating RM are practical in developing SRL skills
Kubsch et al. (2025)	Secondary school	It shows that when digital frustration is not alleviated by teachers serving as RM in emotion regulation and perseverance, it affects SRL
Molenaar (2022)	Secondary school	For children aged 10–14, hybrid systems that gradually transfer regulatory control from AI to the student allow for a transition from AI-guided SRL to more independent SRL

(continued)

Table 4.1 (continued)

Study	Age group	RM and SRL by age
Chiu et al. (2023)	High school	Teacher guidance continues to be critically important for motivation and relationship building, which shows that AI should not replace human guidance at this stage, but rather complement it
Study 4	Preservice teacher	RM is effective in developing SRL skills. However, the sub-dimensions of the role model do not have a significant impact
Bittner et al. (2022)	Lifespan	From the observational-based youth period to the reflective and strategic-based adulthood period, role modeling remains valid at every age
Geier et al. (2025)	K-12 teachers	Teachers should adjust SRL strategies according to age to become more effective RM and emphasize technology-supported modeling for adolescent students
Vilkova (2022)	Young adults–older adults (MOOC participants)	The success of experiencing SRL varies significantly depending on prior education and the presence of peer RM. Older students benefit from clear, modeled task strategies
Lan and Zhou (2025), Jin et al. (2023)	Higher education	Students see AI as a partner or facilitator, enabling them to use it more effectively in self-directed SRL activities
Xu et al. (2010)	Higher education	In higher education, metacognitive support from AI enhances SRL, but the risk of over-reliance on technology is also considered, highlighting the need for balanced, human-centered AI integration

While both genders gain from exposure to RM in cultivating self-regulated learning skills, the extent and process of the impact vary. Women tend to exhibit a greater emotional attachment, while men are more responsive to indications of autonomy. The nature and closeness of the role model also result in varying SRL results between genders.

The gender variable influences AI's function as a role model in SRL development. Girls generally perceive AI support in terms of autonomy and competence, and benefit more from it in this regard. Men, on the other hand, need different strategies to use AI as a role model in SRL development. Designing AI applications to address gender differences can enhance AI's role as a model in SRL development.

Table 4.2 Example studies from the literature on the role of gender in the SRL-role model relationship

Study	Age group	RM and SRL by gender
Study 2	Secondary school	In the development of SRL skills, female students were more influenced by parental RM (especially mothers). Male students benefited more from structured teacher modelling
Wu (2025)	High school/ undergrad	Women showed stronger emotional engagement and goal setting through teacher RM, while men's SRL development was more strongly associated with autonomy and peer influence
Vilkova (2022)	Young adults–older adults (MOOC participants)	When exposed to peer RM, women exhibited better SRL skills, while men achieved higher SRL scores in environments that supported autonomy
Zajda (2024)	Adolescents	Girls benefited from social-emotional modeling (for example, motivational incentives), while boys responded to action-based, observable modeling such as task demonstrations and feedback on mistakes
Dörrenbächer-Ulrich and Bregulla (2024)	Adolescents	In developing SRL skills, women relied more on metacognitive modeling and planning, while men preferred self-regulation and strategic shortcuts
Geier et al. (2025)	K–12 teachers	In technology-supported SRL environments, gender influenced students' responses to RM. Relational RM, like empathetic teachers, influenced women, while men responded to task-oriented models
Mejeh and Held (2022)	Vocational schools	When female mentors guided women, they exhibited higher SRL behaviors such as strategic planning and effort
Xia et al. (2022)	High school	Girls tend to receive more AI support for AI-powered SRL compared to boys. Specifically, girls report greater satisfaction with their needs for autonomy, competence, and relatedness when interacting with AI tools
Liu et al. (2021)	High school	Girls generally exhibit stronger communication behavior strategies than boys in both traditional and AI-supported environments, such as goal setting, self-monitoring, and seeking help. However, men may exhibit more self-confidence (sometimes excessive self-confidence) in their self-evaluations, which can influence how they interact with AI feedback

The Role of Parental Education Level in the RM and SRL Relationship

This section thoroughly examines the influence of RM on the development of SRL in relation to parental education levels. The analysis compared findings from 10 studies that examined parental education level with socioeconomic position, parents' SRL competencies, and pertinent mediating processes (Table 4.3). Therefore, an effort was made to adopt a socio-culturally informed perspective. The research findings about the role of AI applications as exemplars have been analyzed. Thus, an endeavor was initiated to establish a theoretical framework regarding the impact of both human and AI-assisted resource management on SRL development, specifically with respect to the variable of parental education level.

The educational attainment of parents has a considerable influence on the effect of RM on children's SRL skills. Parents with elevated educational attainment tend to demonstrate more effective role modeling, especially in fostering metacognition, strategic goal planning, and independent learning. Conversely, children with parents who have a low educational level typically depend more on external resources, such as educators and peers, due to their limited access to academically enriching home environments. As the prevalence of external RM and SRL interventions increases, learners' advancement will occur naturally.

Current research has not yet addressed whether AI's role modeling status in SRL development varies according to parents' educational level. While parental support is important for SRL, there is no direct evidence in this context that AI reduces or increases its effectiveness as a role model.

In addition, parents' socioeconomic status, SRL proficiency, and involvement in the student's development directly and indirectly shape learners' SRL. Parental expectations, quality home interaction, and resilience have a mediating effect. Empowering practices in modeling and supporting SRL, especially for parents from low socioeconomic backgrounds, can help develop lifelong learning skills and minimize inequalities stemming from parents.

The Role of Role Model Characteristics in the RM and SRL Relationship

This section thoroughly examines the influence of RM on the development of SRL, with a focus on the attributes of the role model. A comparative analysis was conducted on the findings of 13 studies examining the qualities of role models in the development of SRL throughout the literature (Table 4.4). Consequently, an effort was undertaken to obtain a systematic understanding of the sense of possessing and embodying a role model. The findings also analyzed debates regarding the attributes that a good role model should embody in the context of AI applications fulfilling a role model function. An effort was made to establish a theoretical framework for understanding the impact of RM on SRL development, considering the attributes of role models as a variable applicable to both human and AI-assisted RM.

The influence of RM on learners' SRL skills varies significantly based on the qualities of RM, including authenticity, expertise, emotional support, instructional

Table 4.3 Example studies from literature on the role of parental education level in the SRL-role model relationship

Study	Age group	RM and SRL by parental education
Study 2	Secondary school	Students with parents possessing greater educational qualifications demonstrated superior SRL
Zajda (2024)	Adolescents	Children of highly educated parents typically cultivate SRL early due to modeling and guidance in autonomy. Children with parents with lower educational attainment necessitate systematic modeling for the development of SRL
Dörrenbächer-Ulrich and Bregulla (2024)	Adolescents	Students whose parents were more educated had stronger initial SRL core values
Wang et al. (2025)	Children learning online	Parents with advanced education offered supportive emotional and metacognitive advice, fostering the development of their children's SRL. Parents with lower educational attainment emphasized behavioural control, constraining their children's SRL development
Azevedo et al. (2022)	Elementary school	Parents with lower socioeconomic status are associated with fewer resources to support SRL. This can lead to inequalities in SRL development
Luo and Gao (2021)	Early childhood	Parental involvement is notably stronger in large families and among middle- to high-income socioeconomic groups
Xu et al. (2010)	Early childhood	Parental involvement in schoolwork, educational expectations, and autonomy support have a mediating effect between parents' SRL history and children's SRL development
Pino-Pasternak et al. (2010)	Elementary school	The emotional and instructional dimensions of parent–child interactions play a mediating role in the development of SRL
Žerak et al. (2024)	High school	Parents with strong SRL skills are more successful in modeling effective learning strategies, providing meta-cognitive talk, and laying the foundation for their children's development
Zhang and Ren (2025)	High school	Parenting education support promotes SRL by fostering resilience and performance goals in children, and it serves as a mediator in this relationship

Table 4.4 Example studies from the literature on the role of role model characteristics in the RM and SRL relationship

Study	Age group	RM and SRL by RM characteristics
Study 2	Secondary school	Students demonstrated optimal responses to RM that had organized self-regulated learning behaviours, including planning and self-regulation. Authoritative yet compassionate RM proved to be the most successful
Kubsch et al. (2025)	Secondary school	In the face of challenges within the digital environment, RM employed appropriate emotion regulation methods, such as resilience and transparency, to facilitate students' self-regulated learning progress
Ng et al. (2024)	High school	ChatGPT-powered digital tutors demonstrate that AI can potentially serve as an RM function, showing that they can improve students' SRL skills and performance in science education
Ngugi and Goosen (2021)	Higher education	Collaborative leadership is more effective than rigid authoritarianism in promoting students' SRL
Lan and Zhou (2025)	Higher education	AI can enhance motivation and self-efficacy by personalizing learning experiences and offering encouragement. However, it may be less effective than human RM in supporting the emotional and motivational aspects of SRL
Jin et al. (2023)	Higher education	AI can model effective SRL strategies such as goal setting, planning, monitoring, and reflection by guiding students and providing best practice examples
Jin et al. (2023), Lan and Zhou (2025)	Higher education	AI lacks the emotional mirroring and inspirational qualities of human RM, which can limit its impact on motivation and relationships in SRL development
Afzaal et al. (2023)	Higher education	AI excels at providing instant, data-driven feedback and recommendations, which are essential for the development of SRL. Explainable AI systems can provide explanations for the logic behind feedback, supporting students' understanding and self-correction, which are key elements of effective RM
Karlen and Hertel (2024)	All Ages (K-12)	Teachers' self-regulated learning competencies were revealed to be substantial predictors of students' self-regulated learning results. The teachers' involvement as strategic exemplars was essential for the sustained advancement of self-regulated learning (SRL)
Na et al. (2024)	Undergraduate students	Research indicates that Social Role Learning (SRL) is cultivated through collaborative modeling by dependable RM who emphasize involvement and community engagement
Mejeh and Held (2022)	Vocational schools	Students whose parents have a low level of education are compensated for the lack of RM at home by having career counselors act as SRL
Schunk and Mullen (2013)	General learners	RM with similar origins, elevated expectations, and exemplifying strategic learning practices have fostered enduring favorable impacts on SRL
Albelbisi et al. (2021)	Adult online learners	Personality factors, such as passion and clarity, enhanced the SRL modeling of digital instructors

clarity, and socio-demographic congruence (e.g., age, gender, socioeconomic status). Effective RM captures learners' attention through their titles (e.g., teacher, parent) and by demonstrating SRL behaviors, relatability, and consistent application of self-regulation.

AI can fulfill many, if not all, of the characteristics of an effective role model for SRL development. It can effectively identify and model appropriate strategies, provide feedback, and support personalized learning. On the other hand, its contribution to providing holistic and emotionally supportive guidance may be limited. SRL development can contribute more strongly when AI acts as a facilitator within a human-centered and interactive framework.

4.6 Discussion

In this section, the answers to the research questions are discussed comprehensively in light of the findings. First, the approach of the current study was evaluated under the heading "Response to Research Questions by Contrasting the Approach Against Related Works" by comparing it with the research findings in the literature. The relationship between RM&SRL has been examined in depth across the variables of age, gender, parental education level, and characteristics of role models. Finally, the strengths of the study's findings, potential opportunities for future research, the study's weaknesses, and risks have been systematically evaluated. Thus, this section provides a comprehensive assessment by addressing both the theoretical and practical aspects of the research from a holistic perspective, offering a thorough evaluation of the validity of the findings and their potential contributions to future research.

Response to Research Questions by Contrasting the Approach Against Related Works

In this section, four key study findings and relevant current literature are systematically examined to answer the research questions. The results, considering the findings, are discussed sequentially from the perspectives of age, gender, parents' education level, and the characteristics of the role model.

Response to RQ1

Research repeatedly demonstrates that the influence of RM on the development of SRL abilities varies with age, corresponding to advancements in cognition, metacognition, and autonomy, and this variation mirrors alterations in the primary sources of guidance and support (Fig. 4.4).

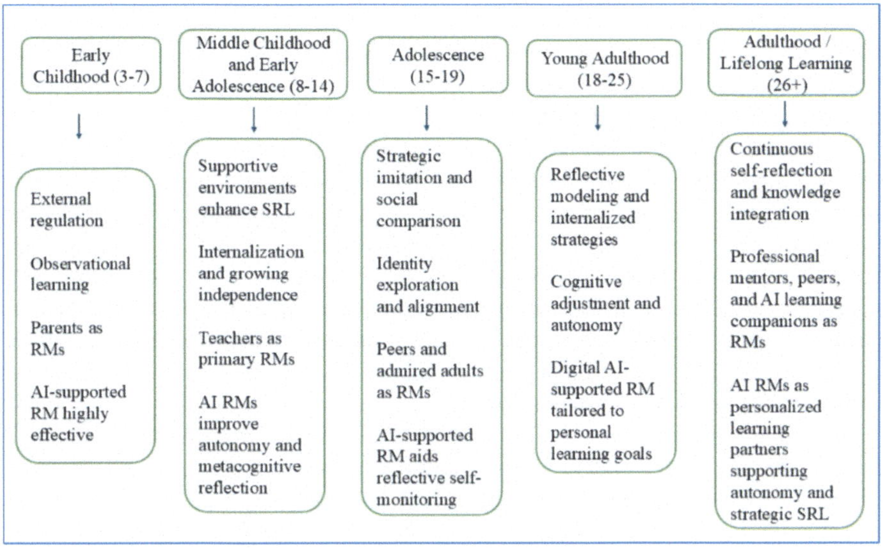

Fig. 4.4 Change in the effect of RM on SRL development according to age

Observational learning and external regulatory mechanisms are more efficacious during early childhood (ages 3–7) (Dermitzaki & Kallia, 2021). Consequently, parents significantly influence the development of SRL skills, and supportive approaches that promote the child's autonomy enhance this impact. Contrary to common perception, authoritarian parenting is more efficacious in fostering children's SRL skills, whereas less invasive techniques are comparatively ineffective (Lin et al., 2022).

During the transition from mid-childhood to early adolescence (approximately 8–14 years), mechanisms associated with the internalization of modeled behavior and enhanced independence become more prominent, contributing to the development of self-regulated learning skills (Study 2). At this developmental stage, children, influenced by their transition to formal education, increasingly regard their teachers as RM. The guidance they receive, the SRL strategies employed, and the learning environments established have a profound impact on the development of self-regulated learning (Karlen & Hertel, 2024; Matulaitienė et al., 2025). Nevertheless, most educators lack adequate training and self-evaluation in facilitating SRL, and their awareness of their responsibilities as RM. Consequently, they may exhibit inconsistent behavior or find it challenging to be RM for their pupils concerning SRL practices (Dermitzaki & Kallia, 2021; Karlen & Hertel, 2024).

During adolescence (ages 15–19), a transitional phase that concludes childhood, strategic imitation, social comparison, and identity development mechanisms become salient. At this age, learners typically seek RM they perceive as embodying their aspirations and identities. They might favor deriving advantages from peer and adult exemplars rather than parental and instructional models (Zajda, 2024). While the beneficial influence of parents and teachers on students is well-documented, several studies have failed to arrive at a uniform result about the evolution of these benefits during adolescence, a period when peers and individual methods gain significance (Li et al., 2023; Panadero, 2017).

During young adulthood (ages 18–25, University), mechanisms associated with reflective modeling, cognitive adjustment, and internalized strategies are prevalent (Na et al., 2024). In adulthood and subsequent stages, strategic integration and reflective learning mechanisms are more pronounced (Bittner et al., 2022). The processes and strength of the role model effect in the development of SRL are continually evolving, exhibiting inconsistencies particularly during transitional periods such as adolescence and adulthood. Specific research indicates robust adoption rates of the model (Na et al., 2024), but others propose that sensitivity diminishes owing to peers' aspirations for autonomy (Vilkova, 2022).

Given that most research has been undertaken in East or West Asia, comparative analyses are essential to understand how cultural norms regarding age and authority influence the efficacy of RM in cultivating SRL. Four studies and the existing literature, predominantly centered on relatively homogeneous groups, suggest that further investigation is required to understand how cultural and contextual factors influence the efficacy of various RM (Li et al., 2023). Moreover, there are contradictory results concerning the degree to which educators, as principal RM for students of all ages, can mitigate the effects of unsupportive home environments solely through modeling, and how teachers can be optimally trained to function as effective self-regulated learning RM (Dermitzaki & Kallia, 2021; Karlen & Hertel, 2024). The significance of RM in the cultivation of SRL is evident across all age groups; however, additional research is required to elucidate their functions across developmental stages and diverse contexts, as well as to ascertain effective strategies for fostering SRL, particularly during transitional phases such as adolescence (Dermitzaki & Kallia, 2021; Li et al., 2023; Panadero, 2017). The influence of avatars, AI educators, and recorded films on SRL across various age demographics remains inadequately studied.

On the other hand, it is known that younger students benefit more from AI-supported RM. In comparison, older students benefit more from AI role models that support autonomy, metacognitive reflection, and personalized feedback. As students get older, they prefer more detailed and personalized AI-supported digital role models for SRL development (Adıgüzel et al., 2023; Chang & Sun, 2024; Lan & Zhou, 2025; Lin et al., 2022). The absence of a standardized testing instrument that accurately assesses the role model effect on SRL development across different age groups is also significant. This also restricts the comparability among the investigations.

Response to RQ2

Research suggests that the influence of RM on the development of SRL skills may vary by gender, with additional variations occurring based on field, age group, socioeconomic status, and cultural context. Female students favor RM that offer emotional support, metacognitive transparency, and social connections. This also impacts the cultivation of planning, tenacity, and self-evaluation abilities in female students' SRL. Conversely, male students generally like authority personalities focused on tasks and achievements as RM. This also impacts the cultivation of male students' strategic time management and goal-oriented SRL competencies (Fig. 4.5).

In STEM, females are more impacted by RM than boys (Tal et al., 2024), although no gender disparities exist in engineering and online learning contexts (Apridayani et al., 2023; Khampirat, 2021). In language acquisition, it is noted that females are more predisposed to employ SRL processes than males and are affected by RM in diverse manners. Boys derive greater benefits from teacher ties, whereas peer relationships have a more significant impact on girls (Dan et al., 2024). In combining the research of Vilkova (2022) and Na et al. (2024), contradicting results emerge, indicating that university-aged male students are unaffected by modeling but significantly influenced by strategic modeling. Prasse et al. (2024) noted that most research in the literature has overlooked the consideration of gender variations in intervention programs.

The research results indicate that AI-powered digital RM varies by gender in SRL development. Female students, especially those without sufficient knowledge of AI, tend to benefit more from AI-powered digital RM in terms of autonomy and competence. In male students, this effect is weaker (Xia et al., 2022). The contradictory results underscore the domain's significance, the role model's nature, and the particular SRL processes assessed. Further study is essential to elucidate the conditions under which gender influences the development of SRL through RM, particularly across diverse cultural and educational contexts.

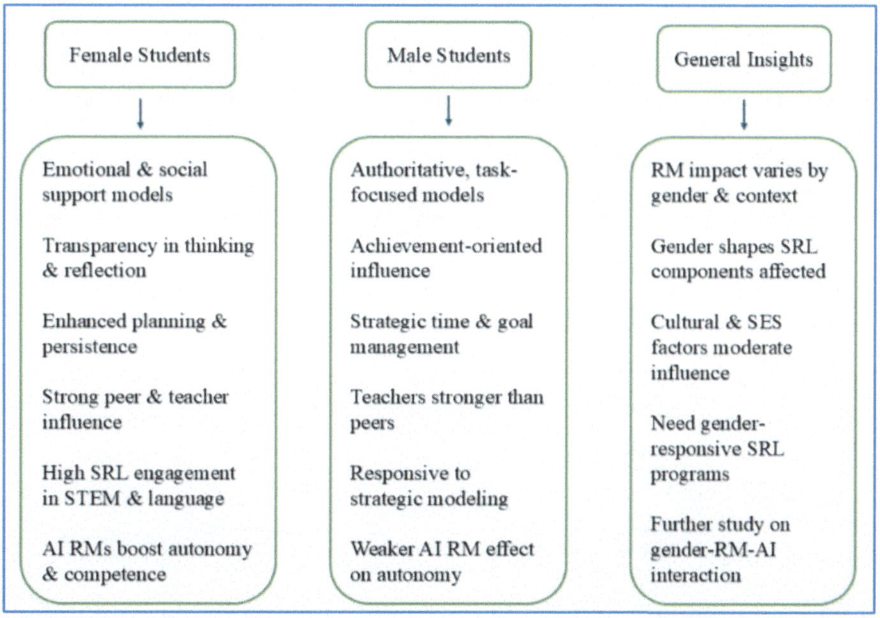

Fig. 4.5 Change in the effect of RM on SRL development according to gender

Response to RQ3

Research indicates that the influence of RM on the development of SRL skills is markedly affected by parents' educational attainment, with nuanced distinctions between mothers and fathers. Educated parents can foster self-awareness, task orientation, and time management SRL skills in their children by serving as RM through emotional support, strategic planning, goal setting, and task management. Parents with lower educational attainment often provide less guidance, resulting in their children favouring external models. Study 2 demonstrated that the SRL growth of middle school pupils is affected by their parents' educational attainment. Existing literature has not differentiated between mothers and fathers in evaluations; however, Study 2 robustly investigates both parental figures as distinct factors. This research indicated that fathers' educational levels exert a more significant influence on the role model SRL connection than those of mothers (Fig. 4.6).

Literature predicts that their educational expectations will increase when parental education levels rise, enabling them to offer more effective support for SRL (Xu et al., 2010). Specific findings suggest that further investigation is required to elucidate the distinct impact of parental education on SRL development (Study 2; Žerak et al., 2024). Consequently, further study is required to clarify the contradictory findings in the literature and establish a consistent correlation between parental education level and the role model's SRL relationship. In the literature, limited research, such as Study 2, has assessed mothers and fathers independently. Furthermore, a more precise methodology would be to assess mothers and fathers independently for daughters and sons.

Research investigating parental education fails to consider the influence of socioeconomic status on SRL. Research is needed to investigate the impact of RM on the development of SRL in highly educated yet low-income families. Parents with advanced educational qualifications may not consistently comprehend appropriate

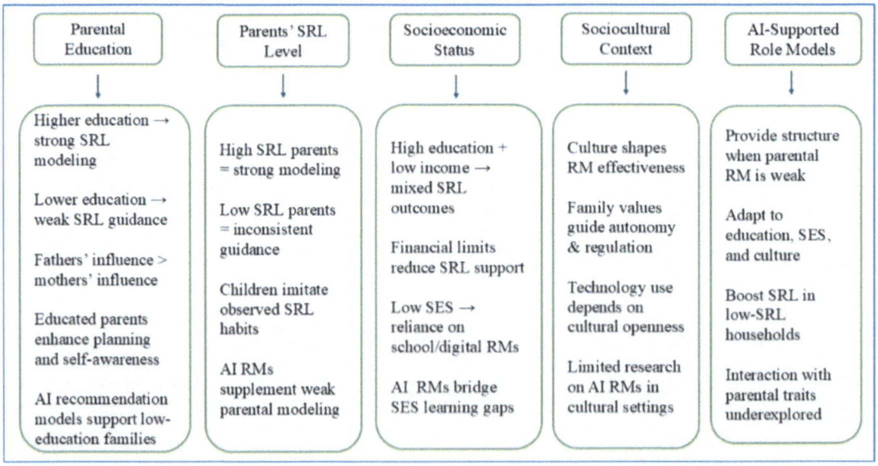

Fig. 4.6 Change in the effect of RM on SRL development according to parental factors

SRL procedures. Research that considers elements such as learning culture, values, and technology utilization represents a notable deficiency in the literature. Similarly, direct evidence regarding AI-powered digital RM is lacking, and more research is needed to clarify how parental education interacts with AI-powered SRL practices.

Response to RQ4

Research has unequivocally demonstrated that in the cultivation of self-regulated learning (SRL) skills, the influence of RM is contingent more upon their behaviours than their identities (Fig. 4.7). RM exhibiting strategic thinking, emotional support, authenticity, and the capacity to articulate metacognitive processes are more efficacious in fostering self-regulated learning (Karlen & Hertel, 2024; Matulaitienė et al., 2025). Conversely, the model's knowledge, shared attributes with the student (including experiences, age, and gender), communication style, and interaction methods in digital contexts influence self-regulated learning results (Li et al., 2023).

Research indicates that mere proficiency in the domain is inadequate for advancing SRL (Dermitzaki & Kallia, 2021). Conflicting findings exist regarding the significance of specific role model attributes and their influence on outcomes, particularly across diverse educational tiers and cultural settings (Karlen & Hertel, 2024; Žerak et al., 2024). Further research is necessary to examine the environmental and individual aspects influencing the effectiveness of role model features for various student groups in developing SRL (Dermitzaki & Kallia, 2021; Efklides, 2011). AI-powered digital RM that provides personalized, adaptive feedback, metacognitive systems, and goal-setting guidance may be more effective in improving SRL compared to general or unpersonalized models. The positive effects of RM support on SRL outcomes are further enhanced when it aligns with students' needs and learning levels (Chang et al., 2023; Jin et al., 2023; Lan & Zhou, 2025).

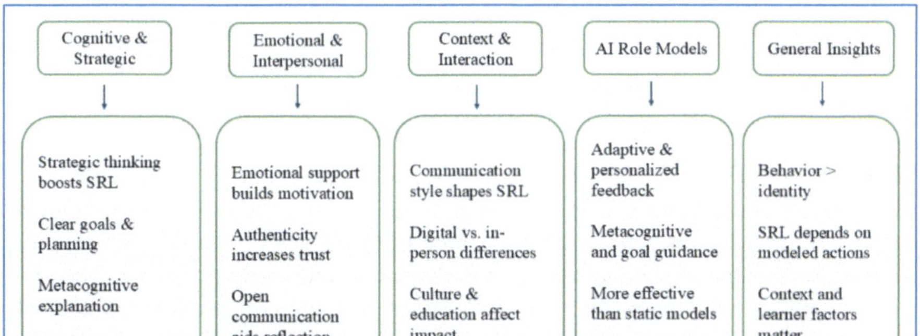

Fig. 4.7 Change in the effect of RM on SRL development according to role model characteristics

Strengths, Opportunities, Weaknesses, Risks

This section provides an assessment of the strengths, opportunities, flaws, and potential hazards associated with the research findings. This paper highlights its theoretical contributions while critically addressing its shortcomings and areas for enhancement. Consequently, an effort was made to conduct a comprehensive evaluation of the study's overall quality, its practical significance, and its impact on future research endeavors.

Strengths

This study, which focuses on the influence of RM in the development of SRL skills, has gained deep insight from a broad perspective by comparing the results of studies in the literature that address different age groups, genders, parental education levels, and qualities of role models. It has provided evidence clarifying the role of RM in SRL development from the perspectives of educational psychology, pedagogical approach, and developmental learning theories. By comparing four studies by the authors with the current literature, the authors have enabled conclusions based on a broad range of data. Considering the results obtained, recommendations for educational policies have been presented, demonstrating how theoretical findings can be applied in practice.

The study explored the potential of AI applications that do not rely solely on humans as role models. AI tools, such as adaptive feedback applications, intelligent tutors, and chatbots, can serve as digital role models by providing students with personalized experiences. In this regard, the study highlights the theoretical and practical roles of both human- and AI-supported RM in SRL development. Beyond summarizing a vast body of literature, recommendations for education policies and practices have been provided. Traditional and digital RM can complement each other, taking their contribution to SRL development to the next level.

Opportunities

The results obtained from this study may raise awareness among educational institutions and teacher training programs about the potential for integrating role-model-based SRL applications. This may contribute to the development of field-oriented programs such as mentoring, coaching, peer support, and teacher training. The variables examined in the study, such as age, gender, parental education level, and role model characteristics, may open the door to qualitative, quantitative, and mixed-method research exploring the role model effect on SRL development. It may also provide stronger reference information for the creation of new-generation digital RM, such as avatars, video teachers, and AI support, in digital education modeling applications, which are a necessity of the twenty-first century.

The study highlights AI-supported digital role models, in addition to traditional human role models who provide feedback and offer personalized support, as potential contributors to students' SRL development. Additionally, considering cross-cultural differences presents a significant opportunity to enhance the effectiveness of RM in SRL development. By conducting systematic cross-cultural comparisons, it can be determined which RM features are more effective for SRL development in different contexts, thus enabling the development of more effective and inclusive strategies for digital learning environments.

Weaknesses

The study's primary reliance on four studies by the authors may result in a limited data source, despite comparisons with the current literature. For example, these four studies focused on parental education level in the development of SRL. However, socioeconomic status, the parents' own SRL competencies, and potential mediating variables in this effect (such as the quality of parent–child interaction) were not included in these four studies. This deficiency has been addressed in relevant studies in the literature.

The descriptive nature of the qualitative systematic review, combined with the lack of a methodological coding framework in the content analysis, may reduce its systematicity. The non-standardization of the tools used to measure the effect of RM on SRL may limit the generalizability of the results. There is a lack of literature on how the role model effect differs among students from diverse cultural backgrounds. In addition, even if studies examine the same variables, the fact that they are conducted in different cultures is a disadvantage.

Risks

Comparing results in qualitative review studies can be subjective. To minimize this risk, two authors have attempted to reach a common conclusion through mutual and repeated discussions. The concentration of findings in certain cultures may limit the universal validity of these results. Although practical application recommendations based on theoretical findings are included, the lack of experimental testing of the effectiveness of educational policy recommendations poses a risk.

The effects of AI-supported RM, which is only recently being integrated into education, on SRL development have not been sufficiently examined in the literature. Therefore, application recommendations related to digital RM are subject to uncertainty and limitations. The influence of age, gender, and cultural factors on RM in the development of SRL limits the applicability of the recommended practices to the same extent in every context. These potential risks can be eliminated by conducting pilot applications.

4.7 Conclusions

The age of learners is a significant variable in the development of SRL skills in RM. Developmentally, the effect of RM on SRL development has also changed in each age period. As learners age, the influence of RM becomes more indirect. In addition to developmental characteristics, the cognitive and emotional development of learners should also be considered.

We concluded that the gender of learners is an important variable in the development of SRL skills through RM. Female students are influenced by RM who provide emotional support and close communication, while male students are influenced by authoritarian, task, goal, and success-oriented RM.

The educational level of parents is particularly influential in the development of SRL during childhood. Parents with higher education levels serve as role models (RM) for their children. Children of parents with low educational levels tend to turn to external models. There are very few studies that examine mothers and fathers as separate variables. Even if the level of education is high, this alone cannot prove that parents use SRL skills effectively. Therefore, variables such as socioeconomic status, parents' SRL levels, and the roles of different mediating variables must also be considered in studies focusing on educational levels.

When developing SRL skills, learners tend to focus more on the behaviors of their RM than on their own identities. In addition to the role model's advanced SRL skills, characteristics such as communication skills, commonalities with the learner, and digital literacy are also highly influential in the development of learners' SRL.

Although AI-assisted digital RM cannot supplant human role models, it will facilitate a tailored learning environment by enhancing guidance, feedback, and the design and monitoring of SRL processes. This effect may fluctuate according to age, gender, digital literacy, social status, and cultural influences.

Suggestion Based on Limitations of the Study

This section explores potential avenues for future research, drawing on the existing literature on the impact of RM on SRL development. Research indicates that RM in SRL development fluctuates based on developmental stages, individual traits, and learning environments. A thorough analysis of the roles of both traditional and digital RM in SRL development is necessary. This section's recommendations aim to elucidate the extent and sustainability of RM's influence on SRL development and to establish a perspective that will provide a foundation for both theoretical and applied studies.

- Most studies investigating the role model effect in SRL development in the literature have been conducted in East and West Asia, so cross-cultural validity is limited. To understand how role models affect and vary across cultures, studies should be conducted with multicultural samples.

- In the literature, the effect of parents on SRL has generally been evaluated as a single variable. There is a need for studies that analyze mothers and fathers as separate variables, considering their distinct roles and gender.
- There are very few studies on digital RM, which are still new to the education sector.
- There is a need for a standardized scale with validity and reliability controls that can measure the role model effect on SRL development by considering variables such as age, gender, parental education level, and role model qualities.
- The function of AI-supported RM in SRL development can be investigated.

Suggestions for Future Research

There are conflicting results regarding the impact of RM on SRL development in early and young adulthood, with some studies showing a decrease (Molenaar, 2022) and others indicating that it becomes more strategic with cognitive maturity (Žerak et al., 2024). Some studies have reported conflicting results, with some indicating that female students perceive more SRL support from RM (Xia et al., 2022), while others show no significant gender difference or a bias toward males (Liu et al., 2021). While some studies suggest that authoritarian and achievement-oriented models are more effective (Zhang & Ren, 2025), others report that relationship-based characteristics more strongly support learners' SRL motivation (Žerak et al., 2024). To address these contradictions and limitations in the literature.

- The reasons for the weakening/strengthening of the influence of RM during transitional periods such as adolescence and young adulthood should be investigated.
- The effects of RM, such as teachers, parents, peers, mentors, and digital RM, on SRL can be examined separately.
- Key concepts that RM should pay attention to be more effective in SRL development can be standardized for specific fields and age groups.
- The impact of digital RM on SRL can be examined by considering variables such as field, age, gender, socioeconomic status, and the qualities of the role model.
- Models can be developed that consider not only developmental characteristics but also learners' cognitive and emotional maturity and previous experiences.
- Longitudinal studies can be conducted to investigate the impact of RM on SRL development throughout the lifespan.

References

Ablard, K., & Lipschultz, R. (1998). Self-regulated learning in high-achieving students: Relations to advanced reasoning, achievement goals, and gender. *Journal of Educational Psychology, 90*(1), 94–101. https://doi.org/10.1037/0022-0663.90.1.94

Adıgüzel, T., Aşık, G., Bulut, M., Kaya, M., & Özel, S. (2023). Teaching self-regulation through role modeling in K-12. *Frontiers in Education, 8*, 1105466. https://doi.org/10.3389/feduc.2023.1105466

Afzaal, M., Zia, A., Nouri, J., & Fors, U. (2023). Informative feedback and explainable aı-based recommendations to support students' self-regulation. *Technology, Knowledge and Learning, 29*, 331–354. https://doi.org/10.1007/s10758-023-09650-0

Albelbisi, N. A., Al-Adwan, A. S., & Habibi, A. (2021). Self-regulated learning and satisfaction: A key determinants of MOOC success. *Education and Information Technologies, 26*(3), 3459–3481. https://doi.org/10.1007/s10639-020-10404-z

Apridayani, A., Han, W., & Waluyo, B. (2023). Understanding students' self-regulated learning and anxiety in online English courses in higher education. *Heliyon, 9*(6), Article e17469. https://doi.org/10.1016/j.heliyon.2023.e17469

Azevedo, R., Rosário, P., Magalhães, P., Núñez, J., Pereira, B., & Pereira, A. (2022). A tool-kit to help students from low socioeconomic status background: A school-based self-regulated learning intervention. *European Journal of Psychology of Education, 38*, 495–518. https://doi.org/10.1007/s10212-022-00607-y

Bai, B., & Guo, W. (2022). Parental involvement, self-regulated learning, and academic achievement: The mediating role of motivation in Chinese secondary students. *Frontiers in Psychology, 13*, Article 880937. https://doi.org/10.3389/fpsyg.2022.880937

Bandura, A., Jeffery, R. W., & Wright, C. L. (1974). Efficacy of participant modeling as a function of response induction aids. *Journal of Abnormal Psychology, 83*(1), 56–64. https://psycnet.apa.org/doi/10.1037/h0036258

Bandura, A. (1989). Human agency in social cognitive theory. *American Psychologist, 44*(9), 1175–1184. https://psycnet.apa.org/doi/10.1037/0003-066X.44.9.1175

Bandura, A. (1986). The explanatory and predictive scope of self-efficacy theory. *Journal of Social and Clinical Psychology, 4*(3), 359–373. https://doi.org/10.1521/jscp.1986.4.3.359

Bandura, A. (1991). Social cognitive theory of self-regulation. *Organizational Behavior and Human Decision Processes, 50*(2), 248–287. https://doi.org/10.1016/0749-5978(91)90022-L

Bandura, A., Grusec, J. E., & Menlove, F. L. (1966). Observational learning as a function of symbolization and incentive set. *Child Development, 37*(3), 499–506. https://doi.org/10.2307/1126674

Bardach, L., Yanagida, T., Goetz, T., Jach, H., & Pekrun, R. (2023). Self-regulated and externally regulated learning in adolescence: Developmental trajectories and relations with teacher behavior, parent behavior, and academic achievement. *Developmental Psychology, 59*(7), 1327–1345. https://doi.org/10.1037/dev0001537

Bittner, J. V., Stamov Roßnagel, C., & Staudinger, U. M. (2022). Educational self-regulation competence: Toward a lifespan-based concept and assessment strategy. *International Journal for Educational and Vocational Guidance, 22*(2), 307–325. https://doi.org/10.1007/s10775-021-09491-2

Brainerd, C. J., Zimmerman, B. J., & Schunk, D. H. (1989). *Self-regulated learning and academic achievement: Theory, research, and practice.* Springer. https://doi.org/10.1007/978-1-4612-3618-4

Chang, W.-L., & Sun, J. C.-Y. (2024). Evaluating AI's impact on self-regulated language learning: A systematic review. *System, 126,* Article 103484. https://doi.org/10.1016/j.system.2024.103484

Chang, D. H., Lin, M. P.-C., Hajian, S., & Wang, Q. Q. (2023). Educational design principles of using AI chatbot that supports self-regulated learning in education: Goal setting, feedback, and personalization. *Sustainability, 15*(17), Article 12921. https://doi.org/10.3390/su151712921

Chiu, T., Moorhouse, B., Chai, C., & Ismailov, M. (2023). Teacher support and student motivation to learn with Artificial Intelligence (AI) based chatbot. *Interactive Learning Environments, 32*, 3240–3256. https://doi.org/10.1080/10494820.2023.2172044

Clark, S., & Ste-Marie, D. (2007). The impact of self-as-a-model interventions on children's self-regulation of learning and swimming performance. *Journal of Sports Sciences, 25*, 577–586. https://doi.org/10.1080/02640410600947090

Cleary, T. J., & Zimmerman, B. J. (2004). Self-regulation empowerment program: A school-based program to enhance self-regulated and self-motivated cycles of student learning. *Psychology in the Schools, 41*(5), 537–550. https://doi.org/10.1002/pits.10177

Coates, B., & Hartup, W. W. (1969). Age and verbalization in observational learning. *Developmental Psychology, 1*(5), 556–562. https://psycnet.apa.org/doi/10.1037/h0027970

Çokçalışkan, H. (2019). *The effect of self-regulated science instruction on fourth-grade students' self-regulation skills, scientific process skills, and achievement* (Publication No. 539655) [Doctoral dissertation, Marmara University]. Council of Higher Education Thesis Center. https://tez.yok.gov.tr/UlusalTezMerkezi/

Dan, Q., Bai, B., & Huang, Q. (2024). Gender differences in the relations between EFL students' classroom relationships and English language proficiency: The mediating role of self-regulated learning strategy use. *System, 123*, Article 103311. https://doi.org/10.1016/j.system.2024.103311

Dermitzaki, I., & Kallia, E. (2021). The role of parents and teachers in fostering children's self-regulated learning skills. In D. Moraitou & P. Metallidou (Eds.), *Trends and prospects in metacognition research across the life span: a tribute to Anastasia Efklides* (pp. 185–207). Springer International Publishing. https://doi.org/10.1007/978-3-030-51673-4_9.

Dignath, C., & Veenman, M. V. J. (2021). The role of direct strategy instruction and indirect activation of self-regulated learning-Evidence from classroom observation studies. *Educational Psychology Review, 33*, 489–533. https://doi.org/10.1007/s10648-020-09546-2

Dörrenbächer-Ulrich, L., & Bregulla, M. (2024). The relationship between self-regulated learning and executive functions-a systematic review. *Educational Psychology Review, 36*(3), 95. https://doi.org/10.1007/s10648-024-09932-8

Efklides, A. (2011). Interactions of metacognition with motivation and affect in self-regulated learning: The MASRL model. *Educational Psychologist, 46*(1), 6–25. https://doi.org/10.1080/00461520.2011.538645

Efklides, A., & Schwartz, B. L. (2024). Revisiting the metacognitive and affective model of self-regulated learning: Origins, development, and future directions. *Educational Psychology Review, 36*(2), 61. https://doi.org/10.1007/s10648-024-09896-9

Farley, J. P., & Kim-Spoon, J. (2014). The development of adolescent self-regulation: Reviewing the role of parent, peer, friend, and romantic relationships. *Journal of Adolescence, 37*(4), 433–440. https://doi.org/10.1016/j.adolescence.2014.03.009

Geduld, B. (2024). Parental involvement in homework to foster self-regulated learning skills: a qualitative study with parents from selected higher quintile schools. *Cogent Education, 11*(1), 2343526. https://doi.org/10.1080/2331186X.2024.2343526

Geier, G., Ebner, M., & Burgsteiner, H. (2025, May). Empowering self-regulated learning through technology and the teacher's role–a systematic literature review. In *International conference on human-computer interaction* (pp. 61–76). Springer Nature Switzerland. https://doi.org/10.1007/978-3-031-93567-1_5

Gerst, M. S. (1971). Symbolic coding processes in observational learning. *Journal of Personality and Social Psychology, 19*(1), 7–17. https://psycnet.apa.org/doi/10.1037/h0031029

Güneş, H. (2023). Self-regulated learning skills of pre-service English language teachers. *European Journal of Education Studies, 10*(2), 113–122. https://doi.org/10.46827/ejes.v10i2.4661

Guo, W. (2021). Gender differences in teacher feedback and students' self-regulated learning. *Educational Studies, 50*, 341–361. https://doi.org/10.1080/03055698.2021.1943648

Hsu, T., Chang, C., & Jen, T. (2023). Artificial Intelligence image recognition using self-regulation learning strategies: Effects on vocabulary acquisition, learning anxiety, and learning behaviours of English language learners. *Interactive Learning Environments, 32*, 3060–3078. https://doi.org/10.1080/10494820.2023.2165508

Jin, S., Im, K., Yoo, M., Roll, I., & Seo, K. (2023). Supporting students' self-regulated learning in online learning using artificial intelligence applications. *International Journal of Educational Technology in Higher Education, 20*, 1–21. https://doi.org/10.1186/s41239-023-00406-5

Joiner, K. F., Malone, J. A., & Haimes, D. H. (2002). Assessment of classroom environments in reformed calculus education. *Learning Environments Research, 5*(1), 51–76. https://doi.org/10.1023/A:1015635122875

Karaca, M., & Bektas, O. (2022). Self-Regulation scale for science: a validity and reliability study. *International Journal on Social and Education Sciences, 4*(2), 236–256. https://doi.org/10.46328/ijonses.302

Karaca, M., & Bektas, O. (2024). Measuring role modeling perceptions of secondary school students: factor structure and reliability of scale. *Acta Didactica Napocensia, 17*(2), 153–168. https://doi.org/10.24193/adn.17.2.12

Karaca, M., & Bektas, O. (2021). The relationship between perceived role models and self-regulation in science. *International Journal of Educational Research, 110*, 101884. https://doi.org/10.1016/j.ijer.2021.101884

Karaca, M., & Bektas, O. (2023). The relationship between role modeling perceptions and self-regulation with gender, grade, and parents' education levels as moderating variables. *Current Psychology, 42*(36), 31736–31757. https://doi.org/10.1007/s12144-022-04172-x

Karaca, M., Bektas, O., & Eroglu, S. (2024a). The relationship between high school students' perceptions of role modeling and self-regulation for science. *Journal on Efficiency and Responsibility in Education and Science, 17*(1), 1–11. https://doi.org/10.7160/eriesj.2024.170101

Karaca, M., Bektaş, O., Öner Armağan, F., & Tor, D. (2024b). The relationship between preservice science teachers' perceived role modeling and self-regulation skills in science. *Psychology in the Schools, 61*(9), 3567–3588. https://doi.org/10.1002/pits.23243

Karlen, Y., & Hertel, S. (2024). Inspiring self-regulated learning in everyday classrooms: Teachers' professional competences and promotion of self-regulated learning. *Unterrichtswissenschaft, 52*(1), 1–13. https://doi.org/10.1007/s42010-024-00196-3

Khampirat, B. (2021). Relationships between ICT competencies related to work, self-esteem, and self-regulated learning with engineering competencies. *PLoS ONE, 16*(12), Article e0260659. https://doi.org/10.1371/journal.pone.0260659

Kubsch, M., Strauß, S., Grimm, A., Gombert, S., Drachsler, H., Neumann, K., & Rummel, N. (2025). Self-regulated learning in the digitally enhanced science classroom: Toward an early warning system. *Educational Psychology Review, 37*(2), 1–38. https://doi.org/10.1007/s10648-025-10011-9

Kulusaklı, E. (2022). Exploring self-regulated online learning skills of EFL learners in distance education. *Turkish Online Journal of Distance Education, 23*(1), 86–96. https://doi.org/10.17718/tojde.1050356

Lan, M., & Zhou, X. (2025). A qualitative systematic review on AI empowered self-regulated learning in higher education. *NPJ Science of Learning, 10*(21), 1–16. https://doi.org/10.1038/s41539-025-00319-0

Li, S., Miles, K., George, R. E., Ertubey, C., Pype, P., & Liu, J. (2023). A critical review of cultural competence frameworks and models in medical and health professional education: A meta-ethnographic synthesis: BEME Guide No. 79. *Medical Teacher, 45*(10), 1085–1107. https://doi.org/10.1080/0142159X.2023.2174419

Lima Filho, R. N., & Casa Nova, S. P. C. (2020). Differences in self-regulated learning in postgraduate students: An analysis relating age and gender to the use of strategies. *Revista Catarinense da Ciência Contábil, 19*, 1–19. https://doi.org/10.16930/2237-766220203075

Lin, J., Lin, H., & Chen, H. (2022). Developing an e-learning platform capable of being aware of self-regulated learning behaviors of role models. *IEEE Transactions on Learning Technologies, 15*, 697–708. https://doi.org/10.1109/TLT.2022.3200398

Liu, X., He, W., Zhao, L., & Hong, J. C. (2021). Gender differences in self-regulated online learning during the COVID-19 lockdown. *Frontiers in Psychology, 12*, Article 752131. https://doi.org/10.3389/fpsyg.2021.752131

Luo, L., & Gao, M. (2021). Family SES and self-regulated learning in Chinese preschoolers: a mediation analysis of parental educational expectation and home-based involvement. *Early Education and Development, 33*, 452–468. https://doi.org/10.1080/10409289.2021.1958580

Malone, D. (2002). Knowledge management: A model for organizational learning. *International Journal of Accounting Information Systems, 3*(2), 111–123. https://doi.org/10.1016/S1467-0895(02)00039-8

Martínez-López, Z., Nouws, S., Villar, E., Mayo, M. E., & Tinajero, C. (2023). Perceived social support and self-regulated learning: a systematic review and meta-analysis. *International Journal of Educational Research Open, 5*, Article 100291. https://doi.org/10.1016/j.ijedro.2023.100291

Matulaitienė, J., Kaminskienė, L., Monkevičienė, O., & Lehtinen, E. (2025, March). Teacher-and student-related factors supporting primary school students' self-regulated learning. *Frontiers in Education, 10*, 1503867. Frontiers Media SA. https://doi.org/10.3389/feduc.2025.1503867

Mejeh, M., & Held, T. (2022). Understanding the development of self-regulated learning: An intervention study to promote self-regulated learning in vocational schools. *Vocations and Learning, 15*(3), 531–568. https://doi.org/10.1007/s12186-022-09298-4

Molenaar, I. (2022). The concept of hybrid human-AI regulation: Exemplifying how to support young learners' self-regulated learning. *Computers and Education: Artificial Intelligence, 3*, Article 100070. https://doi.org/10.1016/j.caeai.2022.100070

Na, C., Lee, D., Moon, J., & Shin, Y. (2024). Modeling undergraduate students' learning dynamics between self-regulated learning patterns and community of inquiry. *Education and Information Technologies, 29*(15), 19621–19648. https://doi.org/10.1007/s10639-024-12527-z

Nakanishi, M., Yamasaki, S., Endo, K., Ando, S., Morimoto, Y., Fujikawa, S., Kanata, S., Takahashi, Y., Furukawa, T. A., Richards, M., & Hiraiwa-Hasegawa, M. (2019). The association between role model presence and self-regulation in early adolescence: a cross-sectional study. *PLoS ONE, 14*(9), e0222752. https://doi.org/10.1371/journal.pone.0222752

Ng, D. T. K., Tan, C. W., & Leung, J. K. L. (2024). Empowering student self-regulated learning and science education through ChatGPT: A pioneering pilot study. *British Journal of Educational Technology, 55*(4), 1328–1353. https://doi.org/10.1111/bjet.13437

Ngugi, J. K., & Goosen, L. (2021, April). Computer science and information technology students' self-regulated learning and knowledge sharing behavior as drivers of individual innovative behavior. In V. Skala (Ed.), Computer science online conference (pp. 593–608). Springer International Publishing. https://doi.org/10.1007/978-3-030-77442-4_50

Nietfeld, J., Shores, L., & Hoffmann, K. (2014). Self-regulation and gender within a game-based learning environment. *Journal of Educational Psychology, 106*, 961–973. https://doi.org/10.1037/A0037116

Panadero, E. (2017). A review of self-regulated learning: Six models and four directions for research. *Frontiers in Psychology, 8*, 422. https://doi.org/10.3389/fpsyg.2017.00422

Perry, N. E., VandeKamp, K. O., Mercer, L. K., & Nordby, C. J. (2002). Investigating teacher-student interactions that foster self-regulated learning. *Educational Psychologist, 37*(1), 5–15. https://doi.org/10.1207/S15326985EP3701_2

Pino-Pasternak, D., Whitebread, D., & Tolmie, A. (2010). A multidimensional analysis of parent-child interactions during academic tasks and their relationships with children's self-regulated learning. *Cognition and Instruction, 28*, 219–272. https://doi.org/10.1080/07370008.2010.490494

Prasse, D., Webb, M., Deschênes, M., Parent, S., Aeschlimann, F., Goda, Y., Yamada, M., & Raynault, A. (2024). Challenges in promoting self-regulated learning in technology supported learning environments: An umbrella review of systematic reviews and meta-analyses. *Technology, Knowledge and Learning, 29*(4), 1809–1830. https://doi.org/10.1007/s10758-024-09772-z

Refika, C. (2023). Differences in self-regulated learning among students in terms of gender. *Trend International Journal of Trends in Global Psychological Science and Education, 1*(1), 28–33. https://doi.org/10.62260/intrend.v1i1.88

Rovers, S. F. E., Stalmeijer, R. E., van Merriënboer, J. J. G., & de Bruin, A. B. H. (2022). How can self-regulated learning be supported in online learning environments? A systematic review. *Frontiers in Psychology, 13*, Article 845318. https://doi.org/10.3389/fpsyg.2022.845318

Schunk, D. H., & Mullen, C. A. (2013). Toward a conceptual model of mentoring research: Integration with self-regulated learning. *Educational Psychology Review, 25*(3), 361–389. https://doi.org/10.1007/s10648-013-9233-3

Schunk, D., & Zimmerman, B. (1997). Social origins of self-regulatory competence. *Educational Psychologist, 32*, 195–208. https://doi.org/10.1207/S15326985EP3204_1

Schunk, D. H., & Zimmerman, B. J. (2007). Influencing children's self-efficacy and self-regulation of reading and writing through modeling. *Reading & Writing Quarterly, 23*(1), 7–25.

Šūmane, I., & Āboltiņa, L. (2021). Promoting self-regulatory skills in self-regulated learning preschool education stage 3. In *Human, technologies and quality of education, 79th international scientific conference of the University of Latvia.* https://doi.org/10.22364/htqe.2021.45.

Taherdoost, H. (2022). What are different research approaches? Comprehensive review of qualitative, quantitative, and mixed-method research, their applications, types, and limitations. *Journal of Management Science & Engineering Research, 5*(1), 53–63. https://doi.org/10.30564/jmser.v5i1.4538

Tal, M., Lavi, R., Reiss, S., & Dori, Y. J. (2024). Gender perspectives on role models: Insights from STEM students and professionals. *Journal of Science Education and Technology, 33*(5), 699–717. https://doi.org/10.1007/s10956-024-10114-y

Thomas, V., De Backer, F., Peeters, J., & Lombaerts, K. (2019). Parental involvement and adolescent school achievement: The mediational role of self-regulated learning. *Learning Environments Research, 22*(3), 345–363. https://doi.org/10.1007/S10984-019-09278-X

Vilkova, K. (2022). The promises and pitfalls of self-regulated learning interventions in MOOCs. *Technology, Knowledge and Learning, 27*(3), 689–705. https://doi.org/10.1007/s10758-021-09580-9

Virtanen, P., & Nevgi, A. (2010). Disciplinary and gender differences among higher education students in self-regulated learning strategies. *Educational Psychology, 30*, 323–347. https://doi.org/10.1080/01443411003606391

Wang, J., Chen, S., & Bai, B. (2025). Cultivating children's online self-regulated learning: The role of parental mediation and support. *Education and Information Technologies, 30*, 1–32. https://doi.org/10.1007/s10639-025-13555-z

White, M. (2017). Cognitive modeling and self-regulation of learning in instructional settings. *Teachers College Record: THe Voice of Scholarship in Education, 119*, 1–26. https://doi.org/10.1177/016146811711901304

Wu, X. Y. (2025). Exploring the impact of blended collaborative learning on deep learning outcomes: A structural equation modeling approach. *Education and Information Technologies, 30*, 1–27. https://doi.org/10.1007/s10639-024-13202-z

Xia, Q., Chiu, T., & Chai, C. (2022). The moderating effects of gender and need satisfaction on self-regulated learning through Artificial Intelligence (AI). *Education and Information Technologies, 28*, 8691–8713. https://doi.org/10.1007/s10639-022-11547-x

Xu, M., Benson, S., Mudrey-Camino, R., & Steiner, R. (2010). The relationship between parental involvement, self-regulated learning, and reading achievement of fifth graders: A path analysis using the ECLS-K database. *Social Psychology of Education, 13*, 237–269. https://doi.org/10.1007/S11218-009-9104-4

Zajda, J. (2024). *Social learning, self-efficacy, and self-regulated learning in the classroom in engagement, motivation, and students' achievement* (pp. 117–128). Springer Nature Switzerland. https://doi.org/10.1007/978-3-031-61613-6_8

Žerak, U., Juriševič, M., & Pečjak, S. (2024). Parenting and teaching styles in relation to student characteristics and self-regulated learning. *European Journal of Psychology of Education, 39*(2), 1327–1351. https://doi.org/10.1007/s10212-023-00742-0

Zhang, Y., & Ren, X. (2025). Do resilience and performance goals mediate the relationship between parental educational support and Chinese high school students' self-regulated learning? Based on the social cognitive theory. *Psychology in the Schools, 62*(8), 2742–2754. https://doi.org/10.1002/pits.23496

Zimmerman, B. J. (2000). Attaining self-regulation: A social cognitive perspective. In M. Boekaerts, P. R. Pintrich, & M. Zeidner (Eds.), *Handbook of self-regulation* (pp. 13–39). Elsevier. https://doi.org/10.1016/B978-012109890-2/50031-7

Zimmerman BJ, Schunk DH (2001) Self-regulated learning and academic achievement-theoretical perspectives. Lawrence Erlbaum Associates, Publishers. https://doi.org/10.4324/9781410601032

Zimmerman, B. J. (2002). Becoming a self-regulated learner: An overview. *Theory into Practice, 41*(2), 64–70. https://doi.org/10.1207/s15430421tip4102_2

Zimmerman, B. J. (2008). Investigating self-regulation and motivation: Historical background, methodological developments, and future prospects. *American Educational Research Journal, 45*(1), 166–183. https://doi.org/10.3102/0002831207312909

Chapter 5
Promoting Self-Regulated Learning in Secondary Education Through Peer Observation and Feedback: Student Perspectives on a Classroom Practice

Daniela Pinto, Thiago Freires, Ana Eloisa Carvalho, and Ana Cristina Torres

Abstract Portuguese education policies and transnational frameworks promote student-centered pedagogies to prepare learners for complex and uncertain futures, yet secondary education practices continue to emphasize traditional approaches that limit opportunities for feedback and the development of learner agency. This chapter presents a project introducing a novel pedagogical practice to address this issue. This practice being tested in Portuguese secondary schools consists of peer observation and feedback among secondary education students (between 8 and 10th grade) as a promoter of self-regulated learning. A qualitative study was carried out. This included analyzing the 789 observation guides and conducting ten focus group discussions with students. The effects reported were explored, identifying strengths, improvements and how peer observation and feedback mediate the phases of forethought, performance and self-reflection in self-regulated learning. The results show that peer observation promotes self-regulated learning through reflection on learning practices and encouraging peer feedback. Students also report improvements in the development of transversal skills that reinforce the relationship between co-regulated learning and self-regulated learning. These results contribute to furthering self-regulated learning by demonstrating how peer observation and feedback can be integrated into different schools and educational levels and provide a basis for future research.

D. Pinto (✉) · T. Freires · A. E. Carvalho · A. C. Torres
Centre for Research and Intervention in Education (CIIE), University of Porto, Porto, Portugal
e-mail: danielapinto@fpce.up.pt

T. Freires
e-mail: tfreires@fpce.up.pt

A. E. Carvalho
e-mail: acarvalho@fpce.up.pt

A. C. Torres
e-mail: acctorres@fpce.up.pt

A. Peña-Ayala (ed.), *Self-Regulated Learning*, Cognitive Technologies,
https://doi.org/10.1007/978-981-92-0658-2_5

Keywords Self-regulated learning · Peer observation · Peer feedback · Collaboration · Secondary education

Abbreviations

CoRL	Co-regulated learning
DBR	Design-based research
FGD	Focus group discussion
ICAP	Interactive, constructive, active, and passive
WAY	"Who sAw You then and who sees you now"
SRL	Self-regulated learning
SSRL	Socially shared regulation of learning

5.1 Introduction

The chapter introduces a qualitative study developed within the project "Who sAw You then and who sees you now - promoting student self-regulated learning (SRL) in the classroom through peer observation" (WAY). The project aims to promote peer observation and feedback among secondary school students as a means to develop SRL skills. It is grounded in a design-based research (DBR) methodology (Nobre et al., 2017), characterized by iterative research cycles that allow for continuous refinement based on participants' feedback. Since its pilot phase, the model has been progressively adapted to meet the pedagogical and organizational needs of partner schools (Torres et al., 2024).

The study is the qualitative nature, focusing on students' perceptions and experiences with peer observation as a process that supports the development of SRL. This interpretative approach enables a deep understanding of how learners construct knowledge, regulate their learning, and engage collaboratively in classroom contexts. The analysis prioritizes meaning making and the situated nature of learning processes rather than quantitative measurement of outcomes.

There is broad agreement that to navigate complex, diverse, and constantly evolving environments, students benefit from strong critical thinking skills, particularly their metacognitive dimension related to SRL (Maksum et al., 2021) and observation (Silva et al., 2016). Social and emotional competencies, including empathy, collaboration, and active listening (OECD, 2018), are also central to this process. Within European educational frameworks, self-regulation, learner autonomy, and metacognition are fundamental to the learn-to-learn competence (Caena, 2019), which is closely related to collaboration, independence, tolerance, empathy, and perspective-taking. Research consistently links improvements in SRL to enhanced academic achievement and more positive classroom environments (Young, 2005).

Consequently, the promotion of SRL requires innovative and differentiated pedagogical approaches aligned with students' diverse learning needs (OECD, 2018). Despite the recognised importance of SRL in fostering academic success and learner autonomy, schools continue to face significant challenges in implementing pedagogical practices that effectively support its development in everyday classroom contexts.

The WAY project seeks to respond to this challenge by integrating peer observation and peer feedback into everyday classroom practices, positioning students as active participants in their own learning and in the transformation of teaching practices. Based on Zimmerman et al. (2015) cyclical model of SRL, the project explores how peer observation can function as a pedagogical strategy that fosters self- and co-regulation of learning. Regulation of learning is not an individual endeavour alone; it is influenced by teachers, peers, and the learning environment (Panadero & Järvelä, 2015), which gives rise to co-regulated learning (CoRL) and socially shared regulation of learning (SSRL) processes (Lobczowski et al., 2020). Through peer observation, the WAY project investigates how these dimensions of regulation can interact and reinforce each other.

From this perspective, the study aims to explore how peer observation contributes to the development of SRL competencies and to students' awareness of learning processes. The research questions guiding the study are formulated broadly to allow for interpretative depth:

(a) *How can peer observation and feedback among students support the development of SRL skills in classroom contexts?*
(b) *In what ways does students' reflection on peer observation experiences influence their ability to regulate their own learning and collaborate with others?*

To address these research questions, the chapter presents the WAY model, its pedagogical principles, and the tools used to implement peer observation. It also discusses the perceptions and reflections of participating students, highlighting how they interpret and experience the process. The results of the study may help deepen the understanding of how SRL develops through peer observation and feedback. The findings are analysed in relation to the theoretical frameworks of SRL, CoRL, and SSRL, and to the emerging connections between educational practice and Data Science—specifically, how qualitative data from student interactions and feedback can inform evidence-based educational innovation. The approach based on pedagogical practices and the attention to collaborative processes among students are the key aspects that differentiate the contributions of this study to the development of SRL processes.

The chapter is organized into a first section that presents the key theoretical concepts for this study, as well as their relevance in contemporary educational contexts. The second and third section presents the WAY project, its methodological design, and the instruments and methods used in data collection and analysis. The following section presents the results of the study, which are organized into two subsections: *Students' views on SRL practices* and *Perceived development of SRL and collaborative skills*. The fifth section discusses the results of the study, emphasizing students' perspectives on peer observation and its implications for the development of SRL. Finally, the concluding section reflects on the contributions of the WAY model to the broader field of SRL research.

5.2 Background and Related Works

The promotion of SRL has been recognised as a central element for academic success and for the development of lifelong learning skills, requiring students to mobilise cognitive, metacognitive, motivational, and social processes to manage their own learning. In this context, peer observation and feedback play a particularly relevant role, as they offer structured opportunities for interaction that can support the development of self-regulatory strategies, foster reflection, and enhance autonomy. This section first discusses the main contributions of Zimmerman's SRL model and related approaches, highlighting the cyclical and socially situated nature of self-regulation. It then explores how practices of peer observation and feedback among students can function as catalysts for these processes, promoting engagement, metacognitive awareness, and collaboration within educational contexts.

The SRL Model

SRL is increasingly recognised as a critical driver of academic success and lifelong learning. It encompasses cognitive, metacognitive, motivational, and behavioural dimensions that allow learners to plan, monitor, and adapt their learning strategies autonomously. Rooted in social-cognitive theory (Bandura, 1986; Zimmerman, 2000), SRL can be encouraged socially through collaboration, dialogue, or other relational processes, which is referred to as socially shared regulation (Panadero & Järvelä, 2015). With extensive research exploring SRL development and strategies, a wide number of models have been proposed and tested (Panadero, 2017), with one of the most popular being the cyclical phases model proposed by Barry J. Zimmerman (Zimmerman, 2000) and later updated (Zimmerman & Moylan, 2009; Zimmerman et al., 2015) which envisions self-regulation being incremented and refined through three sequentially repeated phases of strategies towards learning: forethought, performance, and self-reflection. Task analysis strategies and self-motivation beliefs like self-efficacy gain importance during the initial forethought phase. In the performance phase, self-control and self-observation strategies are emphasised. The self-reflection phase is developed through self-judgment and self-reaction strategies (Zimmerman & Moylan, 2009).

This cyclical phases' model explores mainly interactions between individual metacognitive and motivational processes. However, Zimmerman (2000) also took a more developmental approach proposing and refining a multilevel model of SRL that explains the individual development of self-regulatory skill as a set of four sequential stages: observation, emulation, self-control and self-regulation. Observation is highlighted as a first step for developing SRL under the assumption that students learn by watching skilled models that will be afterwards experimented by emulation or simple imitation. As such, models are crucial sources of the early stages of self-regulation's development. Modelling processes have been demonstrated to be related to skill acquisition and self-efficacy development, especially when the model is a peer with whom the observer can relate (Schunk & Zimmerman, 1997, 2007). In the classroom, observational learning often occurs implicitly during collaborative tasks, discussions, and peer assessments that require social interactions (Santos et al., 2025) as supported by a social-cognitive perspective (Bandura, 1986). When students engage in peer observation, they may be exposed to effective strategies, metacognitive routines, and alternative approaches to problem-solving that can inform their own learning practices (Santos et al., 2025).

Rather than being a passive process, observation appears to invite students to make evaluative judgments and reflect on the observed behaviours, which may contribute to greater metacognitive awareness related to goal setting and strategic planning. Motivation also seems to play an important role, as it can influence the extent to which students engage in modelling behaviours and sustain goal-directed activities during the performance and self-reflection phases of learning (Schunk & DiBenedetto, 2020). The development of autonomy may also play an important role within SRL. Thus, grounded in Zimmerman's cyclical model (Zimmerman et al., 2015), autonomy is understood as the deliberate capacity to plan, monitor, and evaluate one's own learning; and, drawing on Panadero and Järvelä (2015), it is conceived as a socially situated competence, which includes the ability to strategically mobilise resources (e.g. peers, feedback) to sustain this self-regulation of learning.

But not all types of modelling work equally well for all students. Research shows that students can benefit more from observing peer mastery and coping models than from adult models (Schunk & Zimmerman, 1997), but that some students benefit more from good models, while others benefit most from weak models (Braaksma et al., 2002). As such, observer students should be given the opportunity and intention, but also some degree of freedom in observing colleagues performing tasks in the classroom, so that they can focus their attention according to their learning needs and choose a model to which they relate. In the context of this chapter, peer observation refers to an intentional and structured process in which a student systematically attends to and documents another student's performance during a learning task, with the aim of making sense of strategies, decision-making and processes observable in action (Hendry & Oliver, 2012).

Peer Observation and Feedback Among Students

Peer observation and feedback thus constitute an opportunity for collaboration among students, which can represent an important contribution to interactive learning (Chi & Wylie, 2014; Vosniadou et al., 2023). Collaboration is defined here as coordinated joint work among peers oriented towards a common goal, in which meaning, strategies and knowledge are co-constructed through verbal and non-verbal social interaction (Chi & Wylie, 2014; Panadero & Järvelä, 2015).The authors of the ICAP (Interactive, Constructive, Active, and Passive) framework define the interactive mode as a deeper type of learning that depends on cognitive engagement in a group activity, with two key criteria: the nature of students' verbal contributions within the group should be primarily constructive, and the interaction should build upon and extend the previous contributions of each individual student (Chi & Wylie, 2014). Through peer observation and feedback, these two criteria can be met, as the observers' contributions are expected to enrich the learning processes of those being observed.

Peer observation, intentionally structured, can be an effective way of developing observation, reflection, feedback, and self-analysis skills, and encourage self-reflection and self-awareness about one's practices (Hendry & Oliver, 2012). Although most peer observation research is focused on activities with teachers, the project discussed here assumed that peer observation among students may have the same results, because of the reported effects of observation and modelling in the development of self-regulation skills. Peer feedback, on the other hand, is understood here as a dialogic process where learners provide comments to peers about the quality of performance in relation to shared criteria, with the purpose of supporting improvement and deepening understanding (Liu & Carless, 2006). When peer observation activities are accompanied by peer feedback, learners engage in participation and dialogue situations that trigger their reflection and communication skills.

In this chapter, reflection is taken as the deliberate metacognitive act of interrogating one's own or others' practice to interpret evidence, evaluate progress and make decisions on future action (Creswell & Creswell, 2018; Zimmerman & Moylan, 2009). According to Liu and Carless (2006), peer feedback is a dialogic process that encourages learners to reflect on performance and standards. As such, peer feedback extends SRL development by facilitating metacognitive engagement. Both giving and receiving feedback have been shown to promote metacognitive skills, as they require students to assess task quality, monitor understanding, and refine strategies. Often, students who provide detailed feedback demonstrate greater gains in SRL than those who only receive it (Zong et al., 2021). Furthermore, peer feedback also seems to be connected to motivational gains such as increased intrinsic motivation, self-confidence, and academic engagement, which are integral to the SRL cycle (Santos et al., 2025). When students act as observers in collaborative settings, they often report heightened motivation and ownership of the learning process. For example, Tamura and Uesugi (2019) found that when students led lesson reviews and observed peer engagement, they became more confident and proactive, thus reinforcing their self-regulatory capabilities.

On an integrative literature review about peer observation and peer feedback interventions to promote SRL (Santos et al., 2025), peer feedback was found to be explicitly present in most reviewed studies (n = 18), while peer observation was often embedded implicitly within collaborative tasks. However, key findings demonstrate that peer observation and feedback are positively associated with several SRL-related outcomes. Metacognitive gains include improvements in students' self-monitoring, goal setting, and self-evaluation (Newman, 2017; Zion et al., 2015). Other studies reported improved reasoning, academic self-regulation, and task comprehension (Kartono & Shora, 2020). Increased intrinsic motivation and emotional involvement were observed when peer interactions were structured (Mendieta et al., 2015; Michailidis et al., 2022). Furthermore, effective peer collaboration supported empathy, trust, and communication, essential skills for both SRL and CoRL (Lobczowski et al., 2020).

5.3 A Peer Observation and Feedback Model

Building on the theoretical underpinnings of SRL and the evidence supporting peer observation and feedback as catalysts for metacognitive and motivational growth, the WAY project sought to translate these concepts into a practical, student-centred framework. While SRL research has traditionally focused on individual processes, emerging perspectives highlight the value of socially shared and co-regulated learning experiences, where learners collaboratively engage in reflection, evaluation, and dialogue. Within this context, peer observation and feedback were envisioned as powerful mechanisms to promote awareness of learning strategies and self-evaluation. Drawing from previous initiatives that successfully implemented peer observation, the project extended this approach to students, aiming to foster SRL-related competencies through structured, dialogic, and reflective practices.

The WAY project bet on design-based research (McKenney et al., 2006; Nobre & Martin-Fernandes, 2021) to implement a scheme of peer observation and feedback for students enrolled in lower (8th and 9th grades) and upper secondary education (10th and 11th grades). This means it assembled diverse educational actors, particularly teachers, students, researchers and school leaders, to work collaboratively in designing learning environments which could support the fostering of SRL practices as well as knowledge in this field. Such an approach involves cyclical phases of analysis, design and evaluation that must consider the perspectives of all involved stakeholders.

Peer observation has been a focus of the research team in previous projects aimed at teachers' professional development. Over a period of six years, part of the research team implemented a multidisciplinary peer observation teaching programme for pedagogical supervision, which eventually attracted the interest of students (Mouraz et al., 2022; Torres et al., 2024). Building on the premise that the implementation of peer observation can promote incremental changes in classroom practices and foster more innovative, student-centred teaching approaches, the team was challenged by students of participating teachers to design an initiative in which they could take an active role (Torres et al., 2024). Triggered by the challenge, the team then designed a programme of peer observation and feedback, emphasising the acquisition of competences related to SRL (Torres et al., 2024).

The pilot programme was implemented in two school clusters (groups of schools working under the same educational project and management board) located in a predominantly urban area of northern Portugal in the school year of 2019/2020. At that time, 16 students were involved in the observation process concerning classes from eight teachers of diverse content areas (Portuguese, Natural Sciences, Physical Education, Mathematics, etc.). The design of this pilot was built under the consideration that peer observation among students, with feedback to peers and teachers, potentially enhances students' SRL skills by supporting self-reflection and amplifying their influence in the pedagogical improvement of teaching practices. Generally speaking, the idea was that students would observe their peers' engagement in teacher-assigned learning tasks, raising consciousness on the diverse learning strategies and approaches used to fulfil the activities, Fig. 5.1.

The pilot study results suggested that peer observation towards feedback have added potential in addressing the expectation that students develop SRL as part of their personal development and autonomy (Torres et al., 2024), in accordance with reference documents from the Portuguese Ministry of Education, such as the "Students' Profile by the End of Compulsory Schooling" (ME/DGE, 2017). Following this rationale, the WAY project resumes the scheme of peer observation and feedback among students in order to explore in-depth the programme's potential to equip students in the journey of becoming more active, participative and able to use metacognitive skills to self-regulate their learning (Panadero, 2017). For that purpose, two school clusters were added to the previous ones, which integrated the pilot study, as well as the research team was enlarged to effectively engage with all the involved partners.

Following the instances of the design-based research, the project focused the design process on the premise that peer observation between students, coupled with feedback to both peers and teachers, can enhance students' SRL skills. In terms

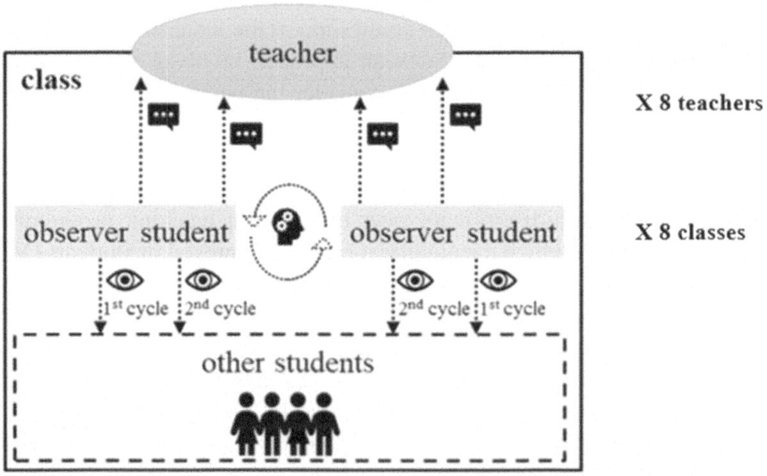

Fig. 5.1 Framework of students' peer observation and feedback in the pilot study

of operationalisation, the programme included a structured observation framework and detailed observation guides, as discussed with school teachers that serve the purpose of leading students in their focus of observation. Rather than approaching class content, the observation guides were aimed at building knowledge on how students responded to the learning tasks set by teachers, reflecting on the difficulties, the support materials and strategies that peers being observed relied on. Workgroup was therefore central in the application of the peer observation and feedback model.

It is important to highlight that the integration of the observation and feedback process within the class activities was entirely up to the teachers. They would decide when and for what tasks they wanted to apply the framework. On the basis of the design-based research, teachers participated in a training process focused on allowing room for discussion among teachers and researchers about the project development. The sessions were sometimes led by teachers and their concerns, challenges and initial outputs regarding the project activities. Earlier, teachers participated in sessions where the programme's objectives, operation, observation guidelines and key concepts were proposed and co-designed. Only then, the observation phase took place in both cycles, i.e., two school years (2023/2024 and 2024/2025).

As mentioned earlier, teachers participated in a training process, understood as joint collaborative sessions, which were also intended to co-create the programme framework. A total of six teaching training sessions were organised each year. The sessions are organised in accordance with the objectives of the observation and feedback model, aiming to meet the needs for support and joint reflection between teachers and researchers. These sessions take place throughout the school year, which corresponds to a cycle of observations, and aim to support teachers and listen to their recommendations for improving the model. The sessions are guided by researchers and organised by school/school group, although there is also a moment for joint sharing. Thus, the teacher training sessions are structured as follows:

Session 1 Presentation of the peer observation and feedback model, its aims, and its methodological foundations. In this session, teachers also discuss which types of learning tasks are more suitable for the implementation of peer observation and feedback (e.g., collaborative tasks).

Session 2 At this stage, peer observations among students have already taken place in the classroom. The purpose of this session is to discuss and jointly reflect on how the activities are unfolding (e.g., types of learning tasks proposed, students' reactions, initial effects perceived by teachers, challenges encountered, etc.).

Session 3 Conceptual and operational deepening of the model, focusing on how teachers' mediation strategies during lessons can foster students' self-regulation practices during observation and feedback.

Session 4 Presentation and discussion of the preliminary results emerging from the observation forms completed by students after observing lessons. The session focuses on a joint analysis of these data, to identify patterns, regularities and critical factors that can inform the continuous refinement of the model and the adjustment of the data collection instruments.

Session 5 Local public seminar hosted by one of the partner schools, involving the presentation and discussion of the overall results of the observation cycle. This seminar brings together teachers and students from all participating schools, promoting joint reflection on the implementation of the model.

Session 6 Focus group discussions with teachers from each school, aimed at critically analysing the peer observation and feedback processes between students, identifying positive and negative factors, and reflecting on opportunities to improve the model to enhance its effects.

The local seminar aims to bring together all teachers and students from the four educational institutions in a joint event to share experiences and reflect on the results of the project. Following the first session, the participating teachers began the intervention with their students. In class, the peer observation and feedback model was applied to group work activities. Students usually worked in groups of four: one student assumed the role of observer, while their peers worked collaboratively on completing the learning task (see Fig. 5.2). Forming groups of four allows one student to take on the role of observer while the other three jointly engage in the activity.

It was expected that throughout the year, each student would take on the observer role at least four times—although this did not always occur. In the first cycle of implementation, researchers recommended that the observer should not directly contribute to the completion of the learning task. Students questioned this positioning substantially; therefore, in the second cycle, teachers were encouraged to allow observers to decide whether they wished to actively engage in the task. After completing the learning task, the observer filled in an online observation form containing questions about the nature of the task, the group's action plan, emerging challenges, facilitators, barriers and strategies mobilised to overcome them. Teachers were also asked to upload a guide describing the learning task. This guide included questions about the context/location (e.g., regular classroom, Moodle, Teams, gym, library, lab…), the duration of the task, a description of the learning task performed, the reasons

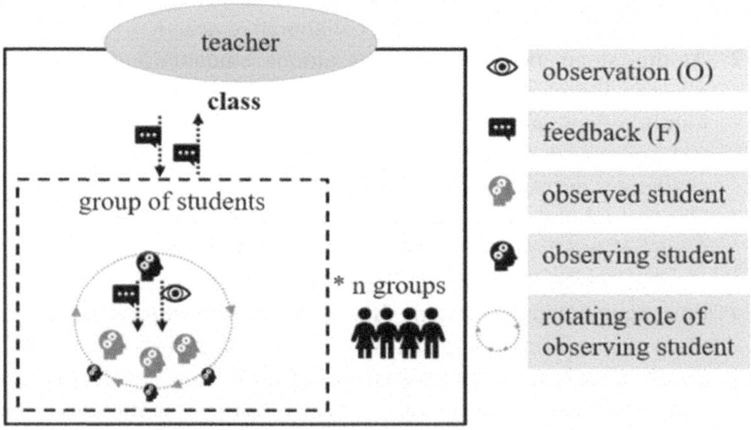

Fig. 5.2 Model of peer observation and feedback between students

why the learning task promotes SRL, what was observed while students worked on the task and observed each other, and a brief reflection on what could be changed for the next lesson based on the observation and feedback received from students.

As a methodological process grounded in DBR, the existence of a pilot study and the development of iterative cycles throughout the project were essential to introduce improvements and to adapt the model to the needs of students and teachers. The proximity generated by listening to students' and teachers' voices was crucial for the evolution and adjustment of the model.

Although the data presented in this chapter correspond to the first cycle of observations (school year 2023/2024), some adaptations were already introduced—based on students' and teachers' feedback—throughout the second cycle of observations, implemented in the following school year. For example, one important adaptation concerned students' participation in the learning tasks while acting as observers. In the first cycle of observations, to which the data presented in this chapter refer, students were instructed not to engage in the completion of the learning task when they were playing the role of observer. However, both students and teachers expressed discomfort with this "passive" role. Although scientific evidence emphasises the importance of maintaining attentional focus on observation in order to foster metacognitive awareness and self-regulatory growth (e.g., Panadero & Järvelä, 2015; Schunk & Zimmerman, 2007), an exception was introduced for situations in which students considered that their participation could, for example, support the peers being observed in completing the task more effectively. This change supported the improvement of collaborative work among students and, from the teachers' perspective, fostered students' autonomy when carrying out the learning tasks.

5.4 Study Design

The study design presented in this chapter reflects the iterative and collaborative nature of the WAY project, integrating methodological choices consistent with its aim of understanding how peer observation and feedback contribute to the development of SRL among secondary school students. Grounded in a DBR approach, the study deepens students' perspectives through multiple qualitative data sources to capture the complexity of learning processes as they unfold in classroom environments. The methodological framework seeks to document the co-regulatory dynamics and contextual conditions that shape students' engagement with SRL. In this section, we detail the participants, instruments, data collection procedures, and data analysis methods that structure the study, highlighting how these components contribute to a theoretically grounded interpretation of the emerging evidence.

Table 5.1 Characterization of the sample by distribution of the number of observation guides per school/school clusters

School	Number of completed observation guides
School cluster A (9 schools)	152
School cluster B (10 schools)	220
School cluster C (6 schools)	130
School D	287
Total	789

Participants

During the school year of 2023/2024, the first cycle of design and implementation of the project took place in the three school clusters and one secondary school. The school clusters are made up of several schools (see Table 5.1), but they only have one secondary school, so the project was developed in one school per school cluster. A total of 22 teachers from various scientific areas (e.g., Biology, Portuguese, Philosophy, Physics-Chemistry, Geography, Mathematics, History and Culture of the Arts, Marketing) and school paths (e.g., general education, vocational education) were involved. The classes of teachers who volunteered to participate in the project were involved.

Thus, their 8th and 10th grade students ($n = 422$) were informed about the project in a session with teachers and project researchers and invited to participate. The students involved had informed consent provided by their legal guardians, ensuring ethical principles of confidentiality and anonymity. The project results are shared with the participating schools to disseminate the findings in the school context and to promote pedagogical improvements that may be suggested based on the project outcomes.

Data Collection and Analysis

The data presented in this chapter are part of a more comprehensive study, which adopts a qualitative approach, grounded in a constructivist and interpretative research paradigm (Creswell & Creswell, 2018), with the aim of understanding how peer observation and collaborative feedback promote the development of SRL among secondary school students. To address the research questions, multiple data sources were mobilised. Besides the online observation guides, students submitted a pre- and post-test Motivated Strategies for Learning Questionnaire (MSLQ)[1] (Morais et al., 2025) and participated in focus groups in the middle and at the end of the school year.

[1] The MSLQ original version comprises 81 items divided into 15 dimensions. Six dimensions (31 items) are related to motivation (Intrinsic and Extrinsic goal orientation, Task value, Control of learning beliefs, Self-efficacy, and Test anxiety). The other nine dimensions (50 items) are related

Teachers also engaged in focus groups and provided reflective reports at the end of the collaborative sessions. These data were analysed to identify patterns in students' self-regulatory behaviours and in teachers' perceptions of the model. Importantly, the data emerging from the 1st cycle of implementation informed iterative adaptations of the peer observation and feedback model, which is coherent with the design-based nature of this research.

In the part of the study presented in this chapter, two data collection instruments were used: observation guides and focus group discussions (FGD). The observation guide consisted of structured online forms completed by students after observing their peers during classroom activities. These guides included categories related to task planning, execution strategies, time management, collaboration, self-reflection, and communication. To facilitate completion by students, these categories are closed-ended (yes/no, multiple choice, checkboxes). These categories are analysed quantitatively. For the purposes of this chapter, we focused the qualitative analysis on two open-ended questions from the guide: "*What did your peers do that made the learning task more difficult?*" and "*What did your peers do that helped them complete the learning task?*".

The data were analysed using content analysis (Bardin, 2011), combining both deductive and inductive procedures. First, a deductive coding grid was applied based on the components of the cyclical SRL model (Zimmerman et al., 2015). Subsequently, all remaining excerpts that did not fit these predefined categories were re-examined inductively. These excerpts were then coded open-endedly and discussed among the researchers until consensus was reached, resulting in a set of emergent categories grounded in the empirical material.

From the total number of coded references, 47.31% of the data were inductively coded into the emergent categories, while the remaining references were allocated to the deductive categories. This relatively high proportion of emergent codification is related to the fact that the cyclical SRL model conceptualises regulation as an individual process. In contrast, within this peer observation and feedback model, collaborative work is highly present in classroom learning tasks. Consequently, a substantial number of references were generated that capture the dynamics, interactions and co-regulatory processes emerging within the student work groups.

Data from the participating school/school clusters were analysed, as shown in Table 5.1. These data were organised into the categories presented in Table 5.2, which also shows illustrative examples of the type of references found in the observation guides that were coded into the categories of analysis.

Regarding the FGDs, these were conducted in ten sessions involving a total of 93 students after the implementation of the peer observation and feedback practices. The FGDs were guided by a semi-structured script, focusing on students' perceptions

---

to learning strategies that can be distinguished as cognitive and metacognitive strategies (Rehearsal, Elaboration, Organisation, Critical thinking, Metacognition) and resource management strategies (Time and study Environment, Effort regulation, Peer learning, Help-seeking) (Pintrich et al., 1991). All items used a 7-point Likert scale.

Table 5.2 Examples of student references in the observation guides for each phase of the SRL model

Phase/ dimension	Code	**Student reference example** What hindered the execution of the learning task?	**Student reference example** What facilitated the execution of the learning task?
Forethought phase	*Task analysis*		
	Goal-setting	*"[My colleagues had] difficulty maintaining a line of thought"*	*[a]
	Strategic planning	*"Poor division of the proposed tasks"*; *"They did not watch the video at home that served as support for the task"*	*"The colleague informed himself about the proposed task at home and was able to perform well in class"*
	Self-motivation beliefs/values		
	Self-efficacy	*"Final completion of the task; Waiting for responses"*; *"Being very nervous made it difficult to give a good presentation"*	*"The colleague is focused on completing the task, which has led him to achieve better results"*
	Outcome expectancies	*	*
	Task interest/ value/affect	*"They did not know all the contents"*	*"They were interested in what made for good work development"*
	Goal orientation	*"Production of the final objective"*	*"Everyone had the goal of finishing the task"*
Performance phase	*Self-control*		
	Task strategies	*"The disorganisation of your thoughts"*; *"Perhaps a little disorganisation"*; *"Confusion with work"*	*"They sought solutions to solve the problems"*
	Self-instruction	*	*"They developed a strategy for noting down keywords and then formed sentences"*
	Imaginary	*"Lack of creativity"*	*
	Time management	*"Taking too long to answer the questions"*; *"Research took too long, not enough time to put the work together"*; *"Had a little difficulty with time management"*	*"The group managed their time well and easily completed the tasks set for them"*; *"Good time management"*
	Environmental structuring	*"The confusion in the classroom"*; *"The noise from other classmates"*; *"Only one book for four people"*	*"Preliminary preparation for the presentation of the work"*; *"Use of a digital support"*

(continued)

Table 5.2 (continued)

Phase/ dimension	Code	**Student reference example** What hindered the execution of the learning task?	**Student reference example** What facilitated the execution of the learning task?
	Help-seeking	*"He consulted his notes too often"; "They weren't paying attention to the teacher's explanation"*	*"They made sure that the information used was correct"; "Book consultation"; "They asked the teacher for help"*
	Interest incentives	*	*
	Self-consequences	*	*
	Self-observation		
	Metacognitive monitoring	*"The disorganisation of your thoughts"; "Perhaps a little disorganisation"*	*"Be able to concentrate a little and get the work done"; "They were very organised and focused"*
	Self-recording	*"During multiple-choice questions, they did not point out important information"*	*"The notes they took and help finding more information"*
Self-reflection phase	*Self-judgment*		
	Self-evaluation	*	*
	Causal attribution	*	*
	Self-reaction		
	Self-satisfaction/ affect	*	*
	Adaptive/ defensive	*	*
Group dynamic	Collaboration	*"Too much individual work"; "Some didn't collaborate"; "They didn't work much as a group and only one member did the task"*	*"They discussed their doubts among the group, collaborated, and everyone participated"; "Everyone helped to obtain the items needed to complete the task, and everyone helped to carry out the task"*

(continued)

Table 5.2 (continued)

Phase/ dimension	Code	**Student reference example** What hindered the execution of the learning task?	**Student reference example** What facilitated the execution of the learning task?
	Communication	*"They didn't communicate well about the task"*; *"They had different opinions, which made it difficult to produce the final object"*; *"Lack of communication within the group"*	*"They were able to reconcile all opinions to achieve a better end result"*; *"Speak calmly and discuss the topic in an orderly manner"*; *"Exchange ideas about the proposed task until we reach a consensus"*
	Organization	*"They didn't organise their ideas"*; *"Lack of organisation within the group"*; *"The group lost its way a little while carrying out the work"*	*"They came together and organised themselves so that they could think together and arrive at the correct reasoning more easily"*; *"The division of labour was well done"*

[a] In the cells marked with *, there are no student responses in the observation guides for this combination of Phase/Dimension and Question

of the processes developed, the impact of the experience on their learning, self-regulation, and relationships with peers. The data were also analysed using content analysis; however, due to the more open-ended nature of the data collection elements, this was carried out through emergent categories. For this chapter, we focused on students' perceptions of the transversal skills developed during the implementation of the peer observation and feedback model. Transversal skills are understood as cross-cutting competencies that are not bound to one specific subject domain, but that are mobilised across learning situations and contexts. They include cognitive and metacognitive dimensions (e.g. critical thinking), as well as social and emotional dispositions such as collaboration, empathy, tolerance and perspective-taking, which enable learners to act autonomously and responsibly in complex and unpredictable environments (Caena, 2019; Maksum et al., 2021; OECD, 2018).

Issues and Constrains of the Work to Be Improved

The methodological design of this study presents two central constraints that should be acknowledged in order to contextualise the scope and interpretative reach of the findings. First, the research was implemented within a specific institutional and pedagogical ecosystem, characterised by particular organisational cultures and levels of collaborative maturity. This contextual specificity limits the transferability of the results to other educational settings that may differ substantially in their instructional practices, school climate, or readiness for peer-based learning interventions. As such, the findings should be understood as situated rather than universally generalisable.

Second, the qualitative nature of the design—although appropriate for capturing the richness and complexity of students' perceptions and interactions—does not permit causal inference. While the data reveal patterns that plausibly link peer observation, collaborative feedback, and the development of SRL competencies, the methodological approach supports interpretations grounded in association and theoretical coherence rather than causal determination. The emergent insights therefore highlight meaningful relationships without establishing directional or causal effects.

These constraints, however, serve as productive avenues for further methodological refinement. Future research may benefit from longitudinal designs with repeated measures, enabling a clearer understanding of the temporal evolution and durability of SRL-related changes. Moreover, implementing multimethod triangulation could strengthen the evidentiary base and deepen interpretative validity. Expanding the research to diverse socio-educational contexts would also help to examine the conditions under which peer observation and collaborative feedback strategies may be transferred, adapted, or scaled, ultimately contributing to stronger external validity and broader pedagogical applicability.

5.5 Results: Perceived Effects of Peer Observation and Feedback in SRL

This section presents the main findings of the study, focusing on how peer observation and feedback were perceived and experienced by students. Based on data from observation guides and FGDs, the analysis explores the ways in which these practices influenced students' SRL processes and the development of collaboration skills. The first subsection examines students' reports in the observation guides on the learning behaviours, strategies, and attitudes they observed in their peers, offering insights into how they interpret the development of SRL within the collaborative learning environment. The following subsection draws on data from the FGDs and presents students' descriptions of the changes they experienced when participating in these activities. Their descriptions include references to the cognitive, metacognitive, and social dimensions of learning, as well as the ways in which they generated their learning tasks and interacted with their peers.

What Do Students See in Their Peers' SRL Processes?

The analysis of data collected from the identification of components that hindered or facilitated the completion of a given task allows for an interpretation through the lens of cyclical model of SRL (Zimmerman et al., 2015), highlighting the learning components that stood out most to students during observation processes. Beyond the three cyclical phases of SRL (Zimmerman et al., 2015), an additional dimension emerged strongly in the data: group dynamics. Table 5.3 presents the distribution of student responses.

Regarding the forethought phase, the data suggest that 18.0% of student observers considered the absence of prior reflection to be a component that hindered task performance, while only 5.4% identified it as a facilitating element. A more detailed analysis of the forethought phase within the SRL model reveals important nuances about the processes that precede task execution. Table 5.4 shows the distribution of student responses across the subcategories of this phase.

When examining the subcomponents, issues related to self-motivation, beliefs, and values were reported most frequently, emerging as the most critical components influencing SRL in this phase. These dimensions were more often identified as

Table 5.3 Distribution of students' responses in the completed observation guides by phase of SRL model

SRL phase/dimension	What hindered the execution of the learning task?		What facilitated the execution of the learning task?	
Forethought phase	64	18.0%	35	5.4%
Performance phase	167	46.9%	264	40.6%
Self-reflection phase	0	0.0%	0	0.0%
Group dynamics	125	35.1%	351	54.0%
Total	356	100.0%	650	100.0%

Table 5.4 Distribution of students' responses categorized under the forethought phase

SRL phase	What facilitated the execution of the learning task?		What facilitated the execution of the learning task?	
Task analysis	**12**	**18.8%**	**21**	**60.0%**
Goal setting	2	3.1%	0	0.0%
Strategic planning	10	15.6%	21	60.0%
Self-motivation/beliefs/values	**52**	**81.25%**	**14**	**40.0%**
Self-efficacy	28	43.8%	11	31.4%
Outcome Expectancies	0	0.00%	0	0.0%
Task interest/value/affect	23	35.9%	2	5.7%
Goal orientation	1	1.6%	1	2.9%

hindering than facilitating, particularly due to a lack self-motivation, self-efficacy or task value among many students at the beginning of the activity. Conversely, 40.0% of observers perceived this component as a facilitator. Perceived self-efficacy was specifically cited as a hindering factor by 43.8% of observers. Task analysis and strategic planning, by contrast, were more frequently perceived as facilitators. Goal setting, an essential component of the forethought phase, was scarcely mentioned by students: only 2.9% identified it as a difficulty, and none as a facilitator. Also noteworthy is the low value attributed to task interest or value as a facilitator (only 5.7%), despite 35.9% identifying it as a hindering component. Another important finding is the very limited or absent reference to goal orientation and outcome expectancies, either as hindering or facilitating components.

The performance phase was perceived by students as one of the most evident stages for the exercise of SRL, concentrating both the main facilitators (40.6%) and hindering components (46.9%) identified in observation guides. This perception reflects variability in students' ability to mobilize self-regulatory resources during learning task execution. Those who managed to apply strategies such as self-control, self-observation, time management and metacognitive monitoring tended to experience this phase as supportive of learning. In contrast, students who reported difficulties related to disorganization, anxiety, or insecurity perceived this phase as particularly challenging. Table 5.5 presents the distribution of student responses within the performance phase.

Within this phase, self-control was the most frequently mentioned dimension—reported as a hindering component in 60.5% of cases and as a facilitator in 73.9%. Time management was also notable—identified as a difficulty in 31.7% of cases and as a facilitator in only 5.7%. Metacognitive monitoring also suggests relevant

Table 5.5 Distribution of students' responses categorized under the performance phase

SRL phase	What hindered the execution of the learning task?		What facilitated the execution of the learning task?	
Self-control	**– 101**	**60.5%**	**195**	**73.9%**
Task strategies	24	14.4%	1	0.4%
Self-instruction	0	0.0%	0	0.0%
Imagery	1	0.6%	0	0.0%
Time management	53	31.7%	15	5.7%
Environmental structuring	14	8.4%	31	11.7%
Help-seeking	9	5.4%	148	56.1%
Interest incentives	0	0.0%	0	0.0%
Self-consequences	0	0.0%	0	0.0%
Self-observation	**66**	**39.5%**	**69**	**26.1%**
Metacognitive monitoring	64	38.3%	67	25.4%
Self-recording	2	1.2%	2	0.8%

results. These functions are crucial for ongoing task adjustment and for detecting errors or gaps during execution. This component is mentioned in 38.3% of cases as an obstacle and in 25.4% as a facilitator of the learning task. Help-seeking was also mentioned, being identified as a hindrance in 5.4% of cases—when students reported not seeking or having difficulty seeking support—and as a facilitator in 56.1%, when students actively sought help from peers or teachers during learning task execution. SRL components such as task strategies, environmental structuring, self-recording, imagery, self-instruction, interest incentives, and self-consequences were rarely or never mentioned. The self-reflection phase was entirely absent from observers' observation guides—none mentioned it as having positively or negatively influenced learning task execution.

Data analysis point to that in collaborative contexts, interpersonal dynamics—particularly the way the group interactions—play a foundational and cross-cutting role in the self-regulatory process. Group dynamics were identified as both a hindering component (125 references) and a facilitating component (351 references), making it one of the most influential components of the learning experience (see Table 5.6). Positive dynamics, such as mutual support, open communication, and balanced participation, appeared to create an environment conducive to shared responsibility, co-regulation, and the collective achievement of goals. In contrast, negative dynamics, including conflict, lack of coordination, and unequal workload distribution, often disrupted workflow, reduced engagement, and hindered the development of both individual and collective autonomy.

The analysis of this category identified three key components: collaboration, communication, and organization (as shown in Table 5.6). Collaboration was perceived as a facilitator in 55.0% of cases and as a hindrance in 35.2%, reflecting its dual potential to either enhance or constrain the self-regulatory process. Communication is indicated by students in 30.5% of references as a facilitator and in 48.8% as an obstacle. Communication problems can compromise the clarity of instructions, lead to misunderstandings, create frustration, or block the natural flow of work. Group organization, though less frequently mentioned, also emerges as a relevant component influencing collaborative performance: it was cited as a difficulty in 16.0% of cases and as a facilitator in 14.5%. Factors such as clear role definition, equitable task distribution, and systematic progress tracking are not simply administrative concerns but structural conditions that directly affect the flow of tasks and the quality of group interactions.

Table 5.6 Distribution of students' responses categorized under group dynamics

Dimension	What hindered the execution of the learning task?		What facilitated the execution of the learning task?	
Collaboration	44	35.2%	193	55.0%
Communication	61	48.8%	107	30.5%
Organization	20	16.0%	51	14.5%

What Do Students Say About Their SRL and Collaboration Skills?

The analysis of the FGD's with students, conducted after the implementation of the observation and feedback phase, reveals a perceived and progressive development of skills related to autonomy and collaboration within the learning process, particularly as a result of engaging in peer observation during the execution of learning tasks. Students described this evolution not as an isolated or sudden change, but as a gradual transformation that became more evident over time as they repeatedly participated in the observation-feedback cycle.

These two factors—autonomy and collaboration—emerges several times across participant groups and were emphasised in students' reflections, indicating their centrality in how students perceived and described their learning experiences. Autonomy was expressed through an increased ability to self-assess, make independent decisions, and take responsibility for the quality of one's work. Collaboration, on the other hand, was reflected in the willingness to engage with peers constructively, share knowledge, and actively contribute to collective problem-solving. Taken together, these changes indicate alterations in students' individual school practices and a broader redefinition of how they position themselves in the learning context—moving from a more passive stance towards learning to a more active, responsible and socially engaged stance in the educational process. Regarding autonomy, many students report feeling more responsible for their own learning process, especially through observing their peers and reflecting on their own study and learning methods. One secondary school student stated: "*I think yes, we've become more autonomous, because by seeing others' mistakes, we can also improve our own*" (FGD1, Student A).

These practices appear to extend beyond the boundaries of the classroom, emerging in students' accounts as tangible signs of growing autonomy and self-regulation. The transfer of strategies from structured learning environments to personal study routines suggests that the skills developed through peer observation and feedback are not limited to specific tasks but are being internalised as part of students' broader approach to learning. As one student reports: "*Before, I didn't have the habit of studying every day and now I go home, I do some exercises on the subject, to stay on top of the material and be able to do the exercises more easily*" (FGD3, Student C). This testimony illustrates a shift from reactive learning to a more consistent and proactive engagement with learning process.

Students' autonomy appeared to be associated with the perception that the teacher's support is not the only available source of guidance. The students described seeking alternative resources or strategies when teacher guidance was limited. One student noted: "*When I have to do a task in class and I'm a bit lost, with no guidance, I tend to go to the teacher... and of course, we won't always have the teacher's support, later in life*" (FGD1, Student B). Statements such as this were interpreted as reflecting an emerging recognition of the need for independent problem-solving and preparation for contexts in which immediate guidance may be unavailable. By seeking solutions through personal initiative or peer collaboration, students demonstrated behaviours aligned with self-directed learning, resilience, and adaptive learning strategies, which are considered important for lifelong learning and professional autonomy. Another student reinforces this idea by emphasizing the value of observation as a reflective practice: *"I think it's possible to improve our autonomous work with this project because when we're observers, we can understand what we're doing while we're working, and so we can identify the strategies we're using at the moment and the ones we might use in the future to work better"* (FGD4, Student C). Here, the role of the observer is not limited to evaluating others but extends to the development of metacognitive skills.

Within this framework, peer feedback and support emerged as a central element. The data suggest that students began to view their classmates not merely as co-participants but as valuable learning resources, capable of offering guidance, clarification, and constructive feedback. One student illustrated this shift: "*Before the implementation of this project, it was always the teacher who cleared up our doubts or gave us feedback... and now we have our classmates helping each other*" (FGD2, Student A). This change signals a reconfiguration of the learning environment, in which feedback ceases to be a strictly vertical, teacher-to-student process, and becomes a horizontal, peer-to-peer exchange.

In the same vein, a student acknowledged that "*it's a way... it's beneficial for both sides, in terms of autonomy*" (FGD1, Student B), referring to the idea that by collaborating with one another, students not only strengthen their own capacity for autonomous work but also engage in a process where the teacher's role shifts from providing constant guidance to facilitating and supporting student-led problem-solving. This reciprocal benefit underlines a shift in classroom dynamics, where responsibility for learning is more evenly distributed and where peer interaction becomes a recognised and valued source of guidance. Another student highlights the role of peers as active sources of support: "*We end up not depending so much on the teacher because we have more people to help us than if we were working alone*" (FGD4, Student C). This statement captures the essence of a collaborative learning culture in which students begin to view their classmates as legitimate partners in the problem-solving process.

Finally, the diversity of approaches observed among peers emerged as a particularly enriching element for the development of autonomous learning. Exposure to different problem-solving methods, organisational strategies, and cognitive approaches was associated with students broadening their repertoire of learning techniques and adapting them to suit their own preferences and needs. One student illustrated this point clearly: "*By seeing what other students were doing, I was also able to see different ways of doing things. When the teacher would do an exercise in only one way, if I was observing two different students, they might each be doing it in a different way*" (FGD3, Student D). This statement reflects the variety of strategies in practice and the active process of comparison, selection, and adaptation that is central to SRL. The opportunity to witness alternative methods appeared to support cognitive flexibility, encourages openness to experimentation, and foster a reflective stance toward one's own learning processes. Students' accounts also highlighted the role of peer learning in exposing them to diverse strategies and perspectives, which differs from teacher-provided guidance by allowing students to actively share, compare, and evaluate approaches among themselves. Across FGD, students consistently expressed the view that the structured implementation of observation and feedback methodologies contributes to the development of autonomy and collaborative skill.

5.6 Discussion of Results

The results presented suggest that peer observation and feedback were associated with positive outcomes in the development of SRL and transversal skills, particularly regarding autonomy and collaboration. Students involved in these practices reported a greater ability to take responsibility for their own learning, greater awareness of effective learning strategies, and greater adaptability of their approaches to different tasks. These developments are aligned with Zimmerman's cyclical model of SRL (Zimmerman et al., 2015), which identifies three interdependent phases—anticipation, execution, and self-reflection—that together form a continuous cycle of planning, action, and evaluation (see Fig. 5.3). By actively participating in observation and feedback, students were able to engage more meaningfully in each of these phases, using the knowledge gained through interaction with peers to inform both their immediate performance and their longer-term learning strategies.

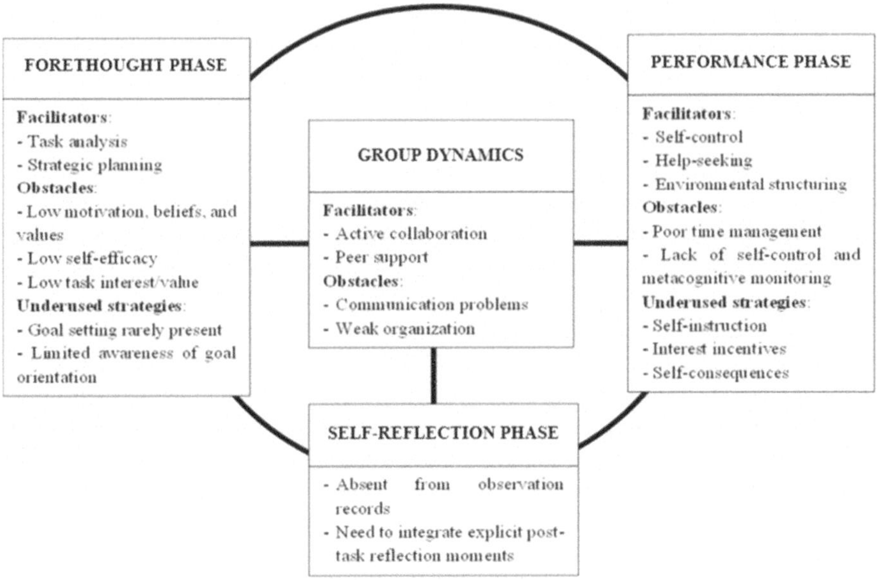

Fig. 5.3 Summary of students' perceptions regarding peer observation and feedback in cyclical model of SRL (Zimmerman et al., 2015)

Peer Observation and Feedback in the Development of Self-regulation

These findings are consistent with the four-level model of SRL development—observation, emulation, self-monitoring, and self-regulation—which emphasizes the central role of social modelling in the learning process (Bandura, 1986; Braaksma et al., 2002; Schunk & Zimmerman, 1997). Peer observation and feedback gave students the opportunity to see a variety of learning approaches in action, identify models of effective practice, and recognize less productive strategies to avoid. This exposure strengthened their cognitive and metacognitive processes, while also promoting motivational gains, namely greater self-efficacy and persistence. The integration of collaborative feedback further reinforced these effects by creating spaces for dialogue, negotiation of meaning, and co-construction of knowledge. In summary, these results reinforce a central point of this study: SRL is both an individual and socially situated process (Lobczowski et al., 2020; Panadero & Järvelä, 2015), and peer-based practices—such as observation and feedback—can function as a mediating mechanism that allows students to progress from modelling and guided reflection to greater autonomy and self-regulation of their own learning.

Peer observation and feedback can be understood as a tool to support the development of SRL, as proposed by Zimmerman et al. (2015). In the early stages of SRL development, students acquire new skills and strategies by closely observing other peers in action. In the context of this study, the observation process offered students opportunities to learn both from the demonstration of effective models and from the challenges, hesitations, and mistakes observed in their peers' performances—a dynamic also emphasized by Braaksma et al. (2002) as an important, yet often overlooked, source of learning. Observing strengths and difficulties allowed students to develop a deeper understanding of the learning task, recognizing that success does not result from perfect execution, but rather from a continuous process of refinement and adjustment. The students' reports highlight the formative value of peer observation for SRL, especially in promoting greater awareness of learning strategies through observation of others. Thus, students recognize the importance of identifying effective strategies that are worth replicating, as well as less productive strategies that should be avoided in their own learning processes.

Furthermore, the diversity of approaches captured in the observation guides seems to have further reinforced the development of SRL. Seeing diverse strategies in action increased students' ability to identify with the models presented, as they observed factors like their own learning style reflected in their peers' work. This identification facilitated the internalization of adaptive strategies. Over time, this repeated exposure to varied models can expand students' metacognitive repertoire (Newman, 2017; Zion et al., 2015), encouraging them to select, adapt, and combine strategies according to task demands—thus creating a solid foundation for progression to subsequent stages of SRL.

Students' Perceptions of SRL Practices in Peer Observation and Feedback

The results suggest that the forethought phase is less frequently mentioned by students in the observation guides. This disparity suggests that, for a considerable percentage of students, there is a tendency to neglect or undervalue the forethought phase of the learning process. Instead, the focus often shifts prematurely to execution and rapid delivery of results, without devoting sufficient time to the analysis and planning processes necessary to achieve those results effectively.

Analysis of the subcomponents included in this phase points to the importance of adaptive beliefs—such as self-efficacy and outcome expectations—during the forethought phase. However, the data also indicate that these components were more often referred to as barriers that arise during task execution than as facilitators of engagement. This pattern suggests that insufficient belief in one's own abilities may limit students' willingness to engage deeply and strategically in the learning task. At this stage, the components of task analysis and strategic planning were considered more as facilitators, suggesting that when students clearly understand the requirements of the task and develop action strategies in advance, they feel more prepared to engage in the task.

The setting of goals was rarely mentioned by students in the observation guides. In the context of the learning tasks implemented, the main learning goals were set by teachers, which may explain the limited references to goal setting in the students' observation guides. It is possible that students did not perceive the formulation of intermediate or personal goals as part of their self-regulatory process, or that they considered goal setting to be an element external to the task structure. The interest or value attributed to the task was also mentioned as a factor that hindered the execution of the tasks. This may indicate a mismatch between the task proposal and the individual interests of the students or the perceived relevance of the activity. These difficulties in attributing value to the learning task may be related to negative indicators of self-motivation.

The scarcity of references to components related to goal orientation and outcome expectations suggests that, for many students, these dimensions may not yet be consciously integrated into their learning processes. This may reflect a lack of awareness of how outcome expectations influence readiness to act, or a difficulty in anticipating task outcomes based on planned strategies. Without a clear understanding of what they want to achieve and how their effort can translate into results, students are more likely to approach tasks reactively rather than proactively, which may limit their ability to self-regulate effectively.

These results highlight the need to provide explicit support to students in formulating and monitoring clear, specific, and personally meaningful goals, as well as in developing the ability to anticipate potential outcomes. Encouraging students to articulate expected outcomes before beginning a learning task can strengthen their sense of direction, increase motivation, and facilitate ongoing self-monitoring during the execution phase.

During the performance phase, observation guides revealed that students emphasized key dimensions such as time management, self-control, and decision-making while actively engaged in the task. Observers recorded these behaviours, demonstrating an increased awareness of the essential components of self-regulation as they unfolded in real time—particularly self-monitoring, in which students track their progress, and self-instruction, which involves the internal dialogue that guides ongoing actions. This careful attention to detail suggests that students were not mere passive spectators but were actively engaged in the cognitive processes that underpin effective task management and adaptive learning.

The high number of student references associated with this phase also suggests that students perceived the task execution as the moment in the self-regulation cycle when the use of SRL strategies is most visible and significant for the learning process. Self-control emerges as a particularly salient component. This is in line with the idea that the ability to regulate cognitive, emotional, and behavioural processes is central to task success (Zimmerman et al., 2015).

Time management is also a key dimension, mostly referred to as an obstacle to learning processes. This suggests that many students encountered challenges in organizing and distributing their time effectively while performing the task. However, this imbalance may also reflect observers' limited awareness of the specific time management strategies used by their peers, as these behaviours are not always visible during classroom observation. Time management plays a central role in task completion, allowing effort to be distributed efficiently, deadlines to be met, and last-minute pressure to be reduced.

The presence of the metacognitive monitoring component in the students' observation guides points to some level of awareness of their own cognitive processes. The students' references suggest that the presence or absence of help-seeking behaviours was perceived as influencing task performance. Other components of SRL—such as task strategies, environment structuring, self-recording, imagery, and self-instruction—were rarely mentioned, which may indicate limited awareness or use of these strategies. The total absence of references to incentives of interest and self-consequences also suggests that students are not consciously incorporating self-motivation mechanisms during task performance. This absence of references to the self-reflection phase is notable, pointing to the neglect of an essential step in the consolidation of learning.

These observations are supported by data from the FGDs, where students reported that their roles as observers increased their sensitivity to the different strategies used by their peers during learning tasks. This increased attention allowed them to recognize patterns of successful behaviour, as well as areas that required adjustment, ultimately enabling them to transfer the learning resulting from observation to their own learning practices. This reflective process promotes deeper metacognitive awareness, encouraging students to become more deliberate and strategic in regulating their own actions.

The development of this metacognitive awareness through active peer observation is aligned with existing literature that highlights the intentional use of observation as a powerful tool for promoting cognitive regulation and self-awareness

(Hendry & Oliver, 2012; Santos et al., 2025). By observing others while performing tasks, students engage in a form of learning that informs their understanding of the task requirements while supporting the internalization of self-regulation skills critical for autonomous learning and problem solving.

The coexistence of difficulties—particularly in time management and metacognitive monitoring—which reveals the need for more structured training in self-regulation strategies. At the same time, the emphasis that students placed on self-control and seeking help as facilitating components shows that effective performance does not depend exclusively on individual cognition, but also on interaction with others and the environment.

Another important finding concerns the absence of references to post-task reflection in the observation guides, which seems to highlight its lesser relevance, from the students' point of view, during classroom observations and feedback. This result may suggest the need to incorporate explicit moments of post-task reflection into teaching practices to make these processes more regular and routine for students. In contrast, the dynamics established in the working group play a key role in students' observations of their peers' learning processes. Regarding group dynamics, the observation guides documented behaviours indicative of shared responsibility, active collaboration, and effective communication. Students' attention to collaborative processes demonstrates the relevance of CoRL and SSRL processes, where social and contextual interactions are a fundamental component of SRL development (Lobczowski et al., 2020; Panadero & Järvelä, 2015).

These results, although deepened by the content analysis that the qualitative approach allowed, may be limited by the specific contexts in which the study was conducted. The schools that implemented the peer observation model among students are specific contexts, located geographically, socially, and culturally, which limits the generalisation of the results of this research. However, we consider that the results achieved are effective clues for more innovative and active pedagogical practices that promote the development of SRL.

Perceived Development of SRL and Collaboration Skills Through Reflection

The collaborative dimension was also evident in the FGDs, where students reported that mutual support among classmates had become more common and that peers were now seen as legitimate and valuable resources for learning. These reports suggest a shift in focus from exclusive dependence on the teacher to more distributed forms of involvement in the learning process. These patterns of interaction generated by observation and feedback point to the presence of co-regulation and socially shared regulation (Panadero & Järvelä, 2015), both of which are critical for understanding the development of self-regulation of learning in collaborative contexts. Peer observation seems to have functioned as an effective catalyst for dialogic and metacognitive processes, in which students negotiated meanings, exchanged constructive feedback, and collaboratively constructed shared understandings. This dynamic process creates opportunities for learners to externalize their thinking, critically reflect on different perspectives, and refine cognitive strategies. In this sense, Liu and Carless (2006) show that peer feedback facilitates metacognitive engagement and improves learning outcomes for both the observer and the observed, reinforcing the reciprocal nature of peer learning.

Furthermore, the collaboration observed and reported by students appears to have had a significant motivational impact. Students expressed greater engagement, increased confidence, and a greater sense of initiative—motivational components that Schunk and DiBenedetto (2020) recognize as essential for sustaining self-regulation over time. The diversity of strategies observed among peers, evident in both observation guides and focus groups, also allowed students to expand their cognitive flexibility. This exposure to multiple approaches enabled them to adopt more personalized and adaptive problem-solving methods, supporting creativity and resilience in their learning processes (Tamura & Uesugi, 2019). These enriched social and motivational experiences underscore the transformative potential of peer observation and collaborative feedback as integral components of effective educational practices.

The structured practice of peer observation, combined with collaborative feedback, supported the development of self-regulation strategies for learning, while also promoting greater awareness among students of their active role in learning processes. These results support the idea that self-regulation, although manifested at the individual level, is social and collaborative in nature, confirming the relevance of pedagogical contexts that intentionally integrate peer observation and feedback as formative strategies to promote self-regulation. The results of this study demonstrate the considerable potential of peer observation and collaborative feedback practices in supporting the development of SRL. Analysis of the observation guides and focus groups revealed that active observation was associated with metacognitive awareness, recognition of effective learning strategies, and adjustment of behaviours in the three phases of the cyclical model of self-regulation: forethought, performance, and self-reflection.

These practices go beyond merely improving the immediate execution of tasks; they promote a lasting ability for students to plan, monitor, and evaluate their own learning processes in a more strategic and reflective manner. In doing so, they create opportunities for learners to internalize key self-regulation habits that can be transferred to other academic and non-academic contexts. The combination of structured observation and peer feedback also appears to reinforce students' sense of agency, supporting confidence in their ability to make informed decisions about learning. This suggests that peer observation, in line with Santos et al. (2025), when integrated into supportive and collaborative environments, improves the quality of current learning experiences while equipping students with essential skills for lifelong learning, preparing them to adapt effectively to future personal, academic, and professional challenges.

Students consistently reported gains in autonomy, self-assessment, and strategic planning, reinforcing the idea that self-regulation is not an innate characteristic but a set of skills that can be intentionally developed through social modelling and deliberate reflective analysis of different learning approaches. Once developed, these skills can be flexibly applied to a variety of academic and everyday situations, allowing learners to adapt more effectively to new challenges.

In line with the results presented by Tamura and Uesugi (2019), our results suggest that the opportunity to observe peers in action created authentic and contextualized learning moments, in which students could compare strategies, recognize successful and less effective approaches, and integrate this knowledge into their own practice. This exposure broadened their repertoire of strategies while encouraging critical thinking about why certain methods work better in specific contexts. This process of comparative observation and selective adoption reflects the adaptive cycles central to SRL theory, in which learners refine their approaches through continuous interaction between planning, performance, and reflection. Over time, these experiences appeared to strengthen students' confidence in autonomous decision-making and support an orientation toward continuous improvement and lifelong learning.

The observation and feedback processes seem to promote a culture of shared responsibility, in which the success of the learning process is seen as a collective goal, and each member's contribution has tangible value. In this way, collaborative skills are simultaneously practiced and internalized, reinforcing students' ability to work productively in diverse team-based contexts. The results also seem to reflect the understanding that autonomy does not mean working in isolation; on the contrary, it implies knowing how to mobilize and integrate various forms of support—whether from peers or other resources—to work more effectively and confidently. These results are in line with the ICAP framework (Chi & Wylie, 2014), which conceptualizes interactive learning as a form of cognitive engagement that arises from constructive and reciprocal exchanges between colleagues. The students' discourses illustrate this interaction, as they begin to see their colleagues as legitimate partners in problem solving and knowledge building. This recognition is consistent with the interactive mode proposed by ICAP, in which learning is enhanced through the co-construction of understanding and the extension of peer contributions. In this sense, peer observation and feedback can provide a structured opportunity for collaboration and promote interpersonal and metacognitive dimensions that support interactive learning. The development of mutual trust, collective responsibility, and the ability to integrate various forms of support reflects the movement from individual autonomy to a socially situated form of self-regulation—consistent with the theoretical principles of interactive engagement.

Through these processes, learners become better able to set goals independently, monitor progress, and adjust strategies, while developing the interpersonal skills necessary for effective group work. This dual development enhances academic content acquisition and retention, while equipping students with essential transferable skills for navigating complex personal and professional contexts. Student discourses suggest that engagement with these approaches provided opportunities to exercise initiative, collaboration, critical thinking, and adaptability. Participants described these experiences as supporting their ability to respond to challenges beyond the classroom and develop behaviours aligned with self-directed and collaborative learning in dynamic contexts. The qualitative nature of the study, which allowed for a deeper understanding of the students' perceptions of how they experienced and developed skills throughout the observation processes, limited the extent of the research to more contexts and students. However, the correlation with other scientific literature in the field seems to consolidate the results of the study.

In addition, despite the specificity of the contexts in which the study was conducted, the study highlights the accessibility and adaptability of peer observation and collaborative feedback. These strategies do not require complex resources, can be implemented in different subjects and levels of education, and benefit from the practicality of the tools used in this project. The structured yet flexible nature of the model ensures its adaptability to different classroom contexts while maintaining its fundamental principles. Its success lies in facilitating authentic peer interactions, allowing students to take an active role in their own learning and in the learning of others, transforming the classroom into a space for shared reflection and co-construction of knowledge.

5.7 Conclusions

The results support the notion that SRL is both an individual and social process, and that its development can be enhanced through structured collaborative practices. Peer observation and feedback function as mechanisms for the development of students' metacognitive, motivational, and social skills. Thus, these practices should be understood not as isolated pedagogical techniques, but as essential components of a teaching culture that values autonomy, shared reflection, and peer learning.

This study aims, through the analysis of students' perceptions in observation guides and FGDs regarding their experiences of observation and feedback, to answer two research questions:

(a) *How can peer observation and feedback among students support the development of SRL skills in classroom contexts?*

The results suggest that peer observation and feedback have significant potential to support the development of SRL. Students' engagement in these practices enhanced their ability to observe peers across the different phases of self-regulation processes. This awareness of peers' practices can foster self-reflection and the development of their own capacities to plan, monitor, and evaluate their learning (Zimmerman et al., 2015).

Through observation, students were able to identify effective strategies, recognize less successful approaches, and help peers adjust their learning practices accordingly. Collaborative feedback reinforced these processes by enabling dialogue, negotiation of meaning, and co-construction of knowledge. These practices contributed to autonomy, self-efficacy, and persistence, demonstrating that SRL is not only an individual skill set but also a socially mediated process (Bandura, 1986; Schunk & Zimmerman, 1997).

The structured interaction enabled by peer observation and feedback reduced exclusive dependence on the teacher, promoted mutual support, and fostered students' responsibility for their own learning. These results align with the ICAP framework, which highlights that interactive learning arises from constructive and reciprocal peer exchanges (Chi & Wylie, 2014). Thus, peer observation and feedback appear to represent an important mechanism for developing metacognitive, motivational, and social skills that are transferable to other academic and real-life contexts.

(b) *In what ways does students' reflection on peer observation experiences influence their ability to regulate their own learning and collaborate with others?*

Reflection on learning practices and students' awareness of peers' strategies appears to have impacted the development of SRL skills. Observing peers provided a mirror for self-assessment and served as a catalyst for strategy adaptation, an effect also noted in previous studies on observational learning and modelling (Braaksma et al., 2002; Hendry & Oliver, 2012). Observing peers' planning, monitoring, and evaluation of task performance seemed to lead students to think about and redirect their own learning strategies as well. According to students' accounts, this reflective practice increased metacognitive awareness, promoted deliberate planning, and supported strategic decision-making (Santos et al., 2025). Moreover, students' reflections on observed strategies extended beyond learning tasks, influencing personal study habits and demonstrating the transfer of learning strategies to independent contexts—a process that reflects the cyclical and transferable nature of SRL (Panadero, 2017). The diversity of approaches observed fostered cognitive flexibility and encouraged selective adoption of strategies, strengthening students' capacity to engage proactively with different learning challenges. This reinforces the idea that awareness and reflection on peers' practices are essential for the internalization of self-regulatory skills and the development of adaptive learning behaviours (Schunk & DiBenedetto, 2020).

Overall, SRL emerges as both an individual and socially mediated process (Panadero & Järvelä, 2015). Embedding structured peer observation and feedback in classroom practice promote interactive engagement, student responsibility for learning processes, and transferable learning skills. Integrating them systematically into educational practice has the potential to strengthen students' capacity to regulate their learning in ways that are transferable, sustainable, and responsive to the complex challenges of contemporary education.

Although the study provides insights into how peer observation and feedback support the development of SRL, several limitations must be acknowledged. First, the research was conducted in a small number of schools with specific geographical, social, and cultural characteristics, which limits the generalisability of the findings. The qualitative nature of the study, while allowing for an in-depth understanding of students' perceptions, also restricts the extent to which conclusions can be extended to broader populations. In addition, students' observation guides revealed limited awareness of certain SRL components, such as goal setting, metacognitive monitoring, or post-task reflection, suggesting that some processes may not have been fully captured or may have been underreported due to students' emerging self-regulatory skills. The absence of references to the self-reflection phase, for example, may reflect not only students' neglect of this component but also the constraints of observing such processes in real time. Likewise, differences in task structure, teacher involvement, and group dynamics across classrooms may have influenced the consistency of implementation and students' engagement with the peer observation model.

Future research should expand the scope of research to include a wider range of educational levels, subject areas, and school contexts to deepen understanding of how peer observation and feedback work in diverse learning environments. Longitudinal studies would be especially valuable for examining the long-term effects of these practices on students' SRL development, motivational beliefs, and the transfer of strategies to independent learning contexts. Furthermore, future work could explore interventions that explicitly strengthen the underdeveloped SRL components identified in this study, such as goal setting, strategic planning, or post-task reflection, testing whether support structures improve students' ability to engage in these phases. Investigating the role of digital tools, may also provide new opportunities for scalable and flexible implementation. Finally, research could examine how teachers' professional development influences the successful integration of peer observation and feedback, helping to establish sustainable pedagogical models that promote SRL in contemporary educational contexts.

Acknowledgements This work was funded by national funds through the Foundation for Science and Technology (FCT), I.P., under the WAY project (2022.01025.PTDC). The research was also funded by FCT under the multi-annual funding awarded to CIIE [grants UID/00167/2023, UIDP/00167/2020 and UIDB/00167/2020]. Ana Cristina Torres acknowledges FCT funding for her contract established under the transitional rule of Decree-Law 57/2016, amended by Law 57/2017 (SFRH/BPD/108950/2015). Thiago Freires acknowledges FCT funding for his contract established under the Stimulus of Scientific Employment Individual Support.

References

Bandura, A. (1986). Social foundations of thought and action: A social cognitive theory. Prentice Hall.

Bardin, L. (2011). *Análise de conteúdo*. Edições 70.

Braaksma, M. A., Rijlaarsdam, G., & Van den Bergh, H. (2002). Observational learning and the effects of model–observer similarity. *Journal of Educational Psychology, 94*(2), 405–415. https://doi.org/10.1037/0022-0663.94.2.405

Caena, F. (2019). Developing a European framework for the personal, social and learning to learn key competence (LifEComp). In Y. Punie (Ed.), *EUR 29855 EN*. Publications Office of the European Union.

Chi, M. T. H., & Wylie, R. (2014). The ICAP framework: Linking cognitive engagement to active learning outcomes. *Educational Psychologist, 49*(4), 219–243. https://doi.org/10.1080/00461520.2014.965823

Creswell, J. W., & Creswell, J. D. (2018). *Research design: Qualitative, quantitative, and mixed methods approaches*. SAGE Publications.

Hendry, G., & Oliver, G. (2012). Seeing is believing: The benefits of peer observation. *Journal of University Teaching & Learning Practice, 9*(1), 1–9. http://ro.uow.edu.au/jutlp/vol9/iss1/7

Kartono, & Shora, R. Y. (2020). Effectiveness of process oriented guided inquiry learning with peer feedback on achieving students' mathematical reasoning capabilities. *International Journal of Instruction, 13*(3), 555–570. https://doi.org/10.29333/iji.2020.13338a

Liu, N.-F., & Carless, D. (2006). Peer feedback: The learning element of peer assessment. *Teaching in Higher Education, 11*(3), 279–290. https://doi.org/10.1080/13562510600680582

Lobczowski, N. G., Allen, E. M., Firetto, C. M., Greene, J. A., & Murphy, P. K. (2020). An exploration of social regulation of learning during scientific argumentation discourse. *Contemporary Educational Psychology, 63*, Article 101925. https://doi.org/10.1016/j.cedpsych.2020.101925

Maksum, A., Widiana, I. W., & Marini, A. (2021). Path analysis of self-regulation, social skills, critical thinking and problem-solving ability on social studies learning outcomes. *International Journal of Instruction, 14*(3), 613–628. https://doi.org/10.29333/iji.2021.14336a

McKenney, S., Nieveen, N. M., & van den Akker, J. (2006). Design research from a curriculum perspective. In J. van den Akker, K. Gravemeijer, S. McKenney, & N. Nieveen (Eds.), *Educational design research* (pp. 67–90). Routledge.

ME/DGE—Ministério da Educação/Direção-Geral da Educação. (2017). *Perfil dos alunos à saída da escolaridade obrigatória*. Ministério da Educação.

Mendieta, J., Múnera, L., Olmos, T., Onatra, C., Pérez, P., & Rojas, E. (2015). Fostering reading comprehension and self-directed learning in a collaborative strategic reading (CSR) setting. *Íkala, Revista de Lenguaje y Cultura, 20*(1), 15–42. https://doi.org/10.17533/udea.ikala.v20n1a02

Michailidis, N., Kapravelos, E., & Tsiatsos, T. (2022). Examining the effect of interaction analysis on supporting students' motivation and learning strategies in online blog-based secondary education programming courses. *Interactive Learning Environments, 30*(4), 665–676. https://doi.org/10.1080/10494820.2019.1678487

Morais, E., Santos, A. C., & Mouraz, A. (2025). Validation and proposal of a short version of the Motivated Strategies for Learning Questionnaire (MSLQ) for Portuguese adolescent students. *Frontiers in Education, 10*, 1445548. https://doi.org/10.3389/feduc.2025.1445548

Mouraz, A., Pinto, D., & Torres, A. C. (2022). Effects of a model for multidisciplinary peer observation of teaching in teacher professional development and in nurturing a reflective school. *Reflective Practice, 24*(1), 45–58. https://doi.org/10.1080/14623943.2022.2130225

Newman, R. (2017). Let's talk talk: Utilising metatalk for the development of productive collaborative dialogues. *Thinking Skills and Creativity, 26*, 1–12. https://doi.org/10.1016/j.tsc.2017.04.006

Nobre, A., Mallmann, E., Mazzardo, M., & Martin-Fernandes, I. (2017). Princípios teórico-metodológicos de design based research (DBR) na pesquisa educacional tematizada por Recursos Educacionais Abertos (REA). *Revista San Gregorio, 1*(16), 128–141. https://doi.org/10.36097/rsan.v1i16.425

Nobre, A., & Martin-Fernandes, I. (2021). Abrir caminhos para a investigação em educação: Design-based research. *Práxis Educacional, 17*(48), 234–254. https://doi.org/10.22481/praxisedu.v17i48.8821

OECD. (2018). *The future of education and skills: Education 2030. The future we want* [Position paper]. OECD. https://www.oecd.org/content/dam/oecd/en/about/projects/edu/education-2040/position-paper/PositionPaper.pdf

Panadero, E. (2017). A review of self-regulated learning: Six models and four directions for research. *Frontiers in Psychology, 8*, 422. https://doi.org/10.3389/fpsyg.2017.00422

Panadero, E., & Järvelä, S. (2015). Socially shared regulation of learning: A review. *European Psychologist, 20*(3), 190–203. https://doi.org/10.1027/1016-9040/a000226

Pintrich, P. R., Smith, D., Duncan, T. & Mckeachie, W. (1991). *A Manual for the use of the Motivated Strategies for Learning Questionnaire (MSLQ)*. National Center for Research to Improve Teaching and Learning, School of Education: The University of Michigan.

Santos, A., Torres, A. C., Mouraz, A., & Nobre, A. (2025). Peer observation and peer feedback to promote self-regulated learning: An integrative review. *International Journal of School & Educational Psychology, 13*(4), 1–20. https://doi.org/10.1080/21683603.2025.2567885

Schunk, D. H., & DiBenedetto, M. K. (2020). Motivation and social cognitive theory. *Contemporary Educational Psychology, 60*, Article 101832. https://doi.org/10.1016/j.cedpsych.2019.101832

Schunk, D. H., & Zimmerman, B. J. (1997). Social origins of self-regulatory competence. *Educational Psychologist, 32*(4), 195–208. https://doi.org/10.1207/s15326985ep3204_1

Schunk, D. H., & Zimmerman, B. J. (2007). Influencing children's self-efficacy and self-regulation of reading and writing through modeling. *Reading & Writing Quarterly, 23*(1), 7–25. https://doi.org/10.1080/10573560600837578

Silva, H., Lopes, J., Dominguez, C., Payan-Carreira, R., Morais, E., Nascimento, M., & Morais, F. (2016). Fostering critical thinking through peer review between cooperative learning groups. *Revista Lusófona de Educação, 32*, 31–45. https://revistas.ulusofona.pt/index.php/rleducacao/article/view/5511

Tamura, T., & Uesugi, Y. (2019). Involving students in lesson study: A new perspective. *International Journal for Lesson and Learning Studies, 9*(2), 139–151. https://doi.org/10.1108/IJLLS-04-2018-0026

Torres, A. C., Duarte, M., Pinto, D., & Mouraz, A. (2024). Self-regulated learning in secondary school: Students' self-feedback in a peer observation programme. *Studies in Educational Evaluation, 83*, Article 101407. https://doi.org/10.1016/j.stueduc.2024.101407

Vosniadou, S., Lawson, M. J., Bodner, E., Stephenson, H., Jeffries, D., & Darmawan, I. G. N. (2023). Using an extended ICAP-based coding guide as a framework for the analysis of classroom observations. *Teaching and Teacher Education, 128*, Article 104133. https://doi.org/10.1016/j.tate.2023.104133

Young, M. (2005). The motivational effects of the classroom environment in facilitating. *Journal of Marketing Education, 27*(1), 25–40. https://doi.org/10.1177/0273475304273346

Zimmerman, B. J. (2000). Attaining self-regulation: A social cognitive perspective. In M. Boekaerts, P. R. Pintrich, & M. Zeidner (Eds.), *Handbook of self-regulation* (pp. 13–39). Academic Press. https://doi.org/10.1016/B978-012109890-2/50031-7

Zimmerman, B. J., & Moylan, A. R. (2009). Self-regulation: Where metacognition and motivation intersect. In D. J. Hacker, J. Dunlosky, & A. C. Graesser (Eds.), *Handbook of metacognition in education*. Routledge.

Zimmerman, B. J., Schunk, D. H., & DiBenedetto, M. K. (2015). A personal agency view of self-regulated learning: The role of goal setting. In F. Guay, H. Marsh, D. M. McInerney, & R. G. Craven (Eds.), *Self-concept, motivation and identity: Underpinning success with research and practice* (pp. 83–114). Information Age Publishing.

Zion, M., Adler, I., & Mevarech, Z. (2015). The effect of individual and social metacognitive support on students' metacognitive performances in an online discussion. *Journal of Educational Computing Research, 52*(1), 50–87. https://doi.org/10.1177/0735633114568855

Zong, Z., Schunn, C. D., & Wang, Y. (2021). What aspects of online peer feedback robustly predict growth in students' task performance? *Computers in Human Behavior, 124*, Article 106924. https://doi.org/10.1016/j.chb.2021.106924

Chapter 6
Self-Regulated Learning in University Students with Specific Learning Disabilities

Li-Chih Wang and Kevin Kien Hoa Chung

Abstract This chapter addresses a two-fold gap: most self-regulated learning (SRL) research centers on K-12, but growing numbers of undergraduates report specific learning disabilities (SLD). We conduct an integrative narrative review (2010–2025) of SRL among university students with SLD, organized around five Self-Regulated Online Learning Questionnaire (SOL-Q) dimensions salient in contemporary, especially online study: metacognitive skills, time management, environmental structuring, persistence/effort, and help-seeking. We first advance a cognitive–motivational framework that foregrounds working memory and processing speed as proximal constraints on SRL, then synthesize empirical findings comparing students with and without SLD and examining cognitive predictors. Across studies, students with SLD typically report lower metacognitive regulation, time management, environmental structuring, and persistence, with help-seeking often comparable to peers. Evidence indicates working memory positively predicts SRL for all students, whereas processing speed predicts SRL specifically within SLD samples. We translate these insights into practice via targeted strategy instruction, assistive technologies, accommodations and Universal Design for Learning, and data-informed supports (e.g., early-warning systems). Contributions are fourfold: (i) aligning SLD-relevant cognitive bottlenecks with five SRL dimensions; (ii) clarifying differential roles of working memory versus processing speed; (iii) articulating design principles for course-level

L.-C. Wang (✉)
Department of Special Education and Counselling at The Education University of Hong Kong, Tai Po, N.T, Hong Kong
e-mail: wanglca@eduhk.hk

Integrated Centre for Wellbeing at The Education University of Hong Kong, Tai Po, N.T, Hong Kong

K. K. H. Chung
Department of Early Childhood Education, The Education University of Hong Kong, Tai Po, N.T, Hong Kong
e-mail: kevin@eduhk.hk

Centre for Child and Family Science, The Education University of Hong Kong, Tai Po, N.T, Hong Kong

A. Peña-Ayala (ed.), *Self-Regulated Learning*, Cognitive Technologies,
https://doi.org/10.1007/978-981-92-0658-2_6

scaffolds that embed SRL; and (iv) setting an agenda for multimethod, profile-based, and longitudinal research to sharpen tailoring by SLD subtype and academic year.

Abbreviations

ADHD	Attention-deficit/hyperactivity disorder
EWS	Early Warning System (learning-analytics-based risk/alert system)
SLD	Specific learning disabilities
SRL	Self-regulated learning
TD	Typically developing
UDL	Universal Design for Learning

6.1 Introduction

This chapter reviews self-regulated learning (SRL) in university students with specific learning disabilities (SLD), advances an integrative cognitive–motivational framework, and synthesizes empirical evidence, especially in online/blended study, on how working memory and processing speed shape five SRL dimensions (metacognition, time management, environmental structuring, persistence, help-seeking). We translate implications into design and support principles.

Conceptualizing SRL in Higher Education

SRL refers to the active process by which learners plan, monitor, and adapt their behaviors and strategies to achieve academic goals. In the social-cognitive view, SRL involves "self-generated thoughts, feelings, and behaviors that are oriented to attaining goals" (Zimmerman, 2002, p. 65). Successful university students tend to be self-regulated learners who can manage their time, set appropriate goals, employ effective learning strategies, and persist in the face of challenges.

In higher education, SRL is enacted under conditions of greater autonomy, heavier reading and writing loads, and increasingly digital course delivery. Adopting a cyclical view, we treat planning and time management (forethought), metacognitive monitoring and environmental structuring during study (performance), and self-evaluation with adaptive strategy change (self-reflection) as mutually reinforcing processes that students must orchestrate on a week-to-week basis. To keep the theory close to practice, this chapter operationalizes SRL with five facets from the Self-Regulated Online Learning Questionnaire (SOL-Q), metacognitive skills, time management, environmental structuring, persistence/effort regulation, and help-seeking, which capture the study behaviors most diagnostic of contemporary university success. These facets provide a common vocabulary for subsequent comparisons between students with and without SLD, as well as for translating evidence into course-level supports.

SLD in Adulthood: Definition and Core Cognitive Features

However, students with SLD often face unique barriers that can impede their SRL processes. SLD is a neurodevelopmental disorder that affects skills such as reading (dyslexia), writing (dysgraphia), or mathematics (dyscalculia), and is not due to intellectual disability or lack of opportunity (American Psychiatric Association, 2013). Many individuals with SLD, compared to typically developing (TD) peers, experience difficulties with cognitive functions like working memory and processing speed (Kibby et al., 2004; Swanson, 2000), which can pose additional challenges in the largely self-directed learning context of higher education.

Two cognitive characteristics, working memory and processing speed, are especially consequential for SRL in adult learners with SLD. Working memory supports the maintenance and manipulation of task goals and intermediate products during planning and monitoring. When constrained, students may lose track of subgoals, experience greater interference, or struggle to compare their progress against standards. Processing speed influences the time cost of core academic operations (reading, note-making, composing), thereby shaping how realistic study schedules are and how much strategy enactment can occur within a given week. Consequently, a reduction in these two cognitive abilities can emerge across the SRL cycle, resulting from over-reliance on habitual strategies, reduced metacognitive checking, slower adaptation after feedback, and increased vulnerability to time pressure. At the same time, there is substantial heterogeneity: many students with SLD develop compensatory routines and benefit from assistive technologies and accommodations that help decouple cognitive constraints from SRL behavior.

Why Online/Blended Contexts Amplify SRL Demands

The transition to university demands greater autonomy and self-management from students. This is especially true in online learning environments, which became increasingly prevalent in the wake of the COVID-19 pandemic and the expansion of distance education. Online courses often lack the structure and immediate feedback present in face-to-face classrooms, placing a heavier emphasis on students' capacity for self-regulation (Selmeczy et al., 2021). For students with SLD, the combination of core cognitive challenges and reduced external scaffolding can lead to struggles with tasks such as keeping up with coursework, organizing study materials, monitoring comprehension, and completing assignments on time. Indeed, research indicates that postsecondary students with SLD frequently report challenges in areas that align with SRL, including time management, concentration, and adjusting study strategies (Goegan et al., 2022; Mortimore & Crozier, 2006). At the same time, many students with SLD have developed compensatory strategies and benefit from support services (e.g., tutoring, assistive technology, accommodations) to help them succeed academically. Understanding how these students self-regulate—and where they may diverge from their typically developing peers—is critical for designing effective supports in higher education.

We conducted an integrative narrative review focused on tertiary-level SLD and SRL. Searches (January 2010–September 2025) in PsycINFO, ERIC, Scopus, and Web of Science combined terms for SLD (and learning disabilities) with SRL and the five SRL dimensions (e.g., metacognitive skills, time management, environmental structuring, persistence/effort, help-seeking), plus working memory and processing speed. Inclusion criteria: (a) participants enrolled in higher education; (b) group status includes SLD (or diagnosed subtypes); (c) SRL assessed via validated self-report and/or behavioral/trace data; and/or (d) studies relating cognitive predictors to SRL in university students. Exclusions: K-12 samples, non-tertiary adult populations, purely clinical case reports without SRL measures. We prioritized peer-reviewed articles in English and Chinese and included foundational syntheses to contextualize findings (e.g., meta-analyses of SRL-achievement links and online SRL). This chapter positions itself by explicitly aligning SLD-relevant cognitive constraints (working memory, processing speed) with SRL dimensions most consequential in online/blended university contexts, thereby extending prior reviews that have treated SRL predominantly in general student populations.

Empirical Anchor and Chapter Contributions

A recent study by Wang and Chung (2024) provides empirical insight into SRL among university students with SLD in an online learning context. They examined how two key cognitive abilities—working memory and processing speed—influence self-regulated learning in a sample of Chinese undergraduates with and without SLD. Their findings shed light on specific SRL components that students with SLD struggle with (such as metacognitive regulation, time management, environmental structuring, and persistence) and highlight differences between learners with and without disabilities. Notably, working memory and processing speed were found to play distinct roles in SRL outcomes for these groups. These results, alongside other emerging literature, underscore the interplay between cognitive factors and self-regulatory skills in the postsecondary learning of students with SLD.

This chapter explores self-regulated learning in university students with specific SLD through several lenses. First, we present a theoretical framework outlining the constructs of SRL and SLD, and how cognitive abilities like working memory and processing speed are hypothesized to impact SRL. Next, we review empirical evidence, including the core findings of Wang and Chung (2024) and related studies, to identify key SRL patterns, strengths, and weaknesses observed in students with SLD. In subsequent sections, we discuss practical implications for supporting and improving SRL in this population—for example, through targeted strategy instruction, technology supports, and accommodations in online and face-to-face settings. Finally, we consider future directions for research and practice, highlighting gaps in the current knowledge and promising avenues to enhance the educational experiences of university learners with SLD. By integrating the findings of recent research with established theory, the goal is to provide a comprehensive understanding of how university students with SLD self-regulate their learning and how educators can foster their success in higher education environments.

Scope and Review Methodology

We adopted an integrative narrative review approach appropriate for synthesizing conceptually related yet methodologically heterogeneous literatures (diagnostic SLD subtypes; SRL self-reports; cognitive tests; trace data). Searches (January 2010–September 2025) in PsycINFO, ERIC, Scopus, and Web of Science combined controlled vocabulary and free-text terms for SLD (specific learning disabilities, learning disabilities, dyslexia, dysgraphia, and dyscalculia), self-regulated learning and SOL-Q dimensions (metacognition, time management, environmental structuring, persistence/effort, help-seeking), and working memory/processing speed.

We included peer-reviewed studies or graduate theses in English or Chinese with participants enrolled in higher education that (a) compared undergraduates with and without SLD on SRL constructs, and/or (b) related working memory or processing speed to SRL outcomes. We excluded K–12 samples, non-tertiary adult populations, and clinical case reports without SRL measures. Title/abstract screening was followed by full-text review; forward–backward citation chasing augmented database results. For each study, we extracted sample characteristics (SLD definitions/subtypes, year of study), SRL instruments or behavioral indicators, cognitive measures, and key effect directions/magnitudes. Given heterogeneity in instruments and reporting, we qualitatively synthesized convergent patterns and highlighted points of inconsistency, reserving formal meta-analysis for future work.

In the following sections, Section 6.2 outlines the SRL framework we adopt and its alignment with five operational facets used throughout the chapter. Section 6.3 organizes the empirical review by facet (metacognition, time management, environmental structuring, persistence, help-seeking), highlighting where effects are strongest. Section 6.4 translates the synthesis into actionable recommendations for course design, assessment, accommodations, and learning analytics. Section 6.5 outlines unresolved questions and methodological priorities for future directions, and 6.6 presents the conclusion of this chapter.

6.2 Theoretical Framework

This section (1) introduces the SRL model we adopt (Zimmerman's cyclical phases and the Self-Regulated Online Learning Questionnaire [SOL-Q] mapping), (2) specifies why working memory and processing speed warrant focus for SLD in university settings, and (3) proposes an integrative framework linking cognitive constraints to five SRL dimensions in online/blended study.

Model of Self-regulated Learning Adopted in this Chapter

In this chapter, we adopt Zimmerman's social-cognitive, cyclical model of self-regulated learning as our theoretical backbone, because it explicitly links forethought (goal setting, strategic planning, self-efficacy), performance (strategy enactment, self-monitoring), and self-reflection (self-evaluation, causal attributions, adaptive strategy change) in an iterative loop of improvement (Zimmerman, 2002, 2008). In parallel, we recognize the close correspondence with Pintrich's four-phase articulation (planning, monitoring, control, reaction/reflect; Pintrich, 2004) and Winne and Hadwin's event-level account (task definition, goal setting & planning, enacting, and adaptation), which emphasize monitoring/control as mechanisms operating within each phase.

Because our focus is university study, often online, we operationalize SRL with the SOL-Q dimensions most diagnostic in that context (Jansen et al., 2017): metacognitive skills, time management, environmental structuring, persistence/effort regulation, and help-seeking. Table 6.1 shows how these indicators map onto the cyclical model and typical online behaviors.

Table 6.1 Self-regulated learning components: comparison of typically developing students versus students with specific learning disabilities

SOL-Q component	Group difference (TD vs. SLD)
Metacognitive skills	TD > SLD (TD students showed significantly stronger metacognitive regulation than SLD students)
Time management	TD > SLD (TD students managed time and study schedules significantly better than SLD students)
Environmental structuring	TD > SLD (TD students were more effective in structuring their learning environment than SLD students)
Persistence	TD > SLD (TD students demonstrated higher persistence/effort in learning tasks than SLD students)
Help-seeking	TD $\approx$ SLD (no significant difference; both groups reported similar levels of help-seeking)

Note TD Typically developing, *SLD* Specific learning disabilities

In our framework (Fig. 6.1), working memory and processing speed function as proximal cognitive constraints on strategy planning, monitoring, and adaptation; motivational beliefs (e.g., self-efficacy, task value) moderate whether constraints translate into behavior; and proximal outcomes (consistent logins, on-time submissions, course success) close the loop. We analyze SRL at the individual level; co–/socially shared regulation is acknowledged as a contextual influence rather than a focal construct in this chapter.

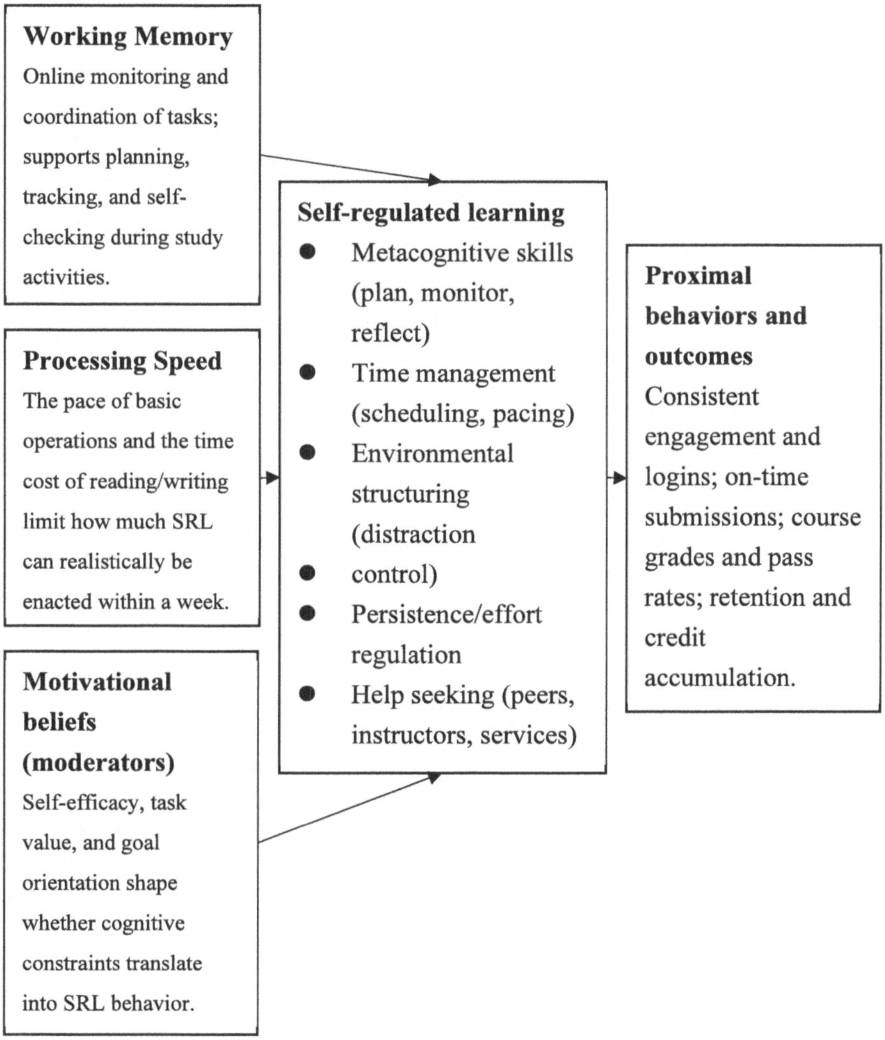

Fig. 6.1 Conceptual framework of SRL and the relevant factors. Solid rectangles denote focal constructs (cognitive constraints, SRL, outcomes)

This explicit model underlies our synthesis, presented following, in which we (1) compare SLD vs. non-SLD SRL by dimension, (2) test the expected links from working memory to broad SRL and from processing speed to time-intensive facets (time management, persistence), and (3) translate each mapped facet into course-level supports and accommodations.

Self-regulated Learning: Concepts and Models

This section consolidates the conceptual foundations that undergird the model adopted above. We first define SRL and summarize the shared cyclical architecture emphasized across leading accounts, then review evidence linking strategy enactment to academic outcomes in higher education. We next differentiate metacognitive knowledge from metacognitive regulation and consider motivational drivers—self-efficacy, goal orientation, and task value, that sustain persistence. Finally, we discuss task and context dependence in online/blended study and explain our use of the SOL-Q as a pragmatic operationalization of five SRL facets that organize the remainder of the chapter. Sections 6.2.2.1–6.2.2.5 address these elements in turn.

Definitions and Cyclical Phases

SRL is a multifaceted construct encompassing cognitive, metacognitive, motivational, and behavioral processes. Broadly, SRL can be understood as the degree to which learners are active participants in their own learning, monitoring their progress, and adjusting their approaches as needed to reach academic goals (Pintrich, 2004).

Classical models of SRL, such as Zimmerman's (2002) social cognitive model, describe SRL as a cyclical process with phases including forethought (e.g., planning, goal-setting, self-motivation), performance (e.g., use of strategies, self-monitoring), and self-reflection (e.g., self-evaluation, adjusting strategies).

As used in this chapter, SRL refers to learners' proactive planning, monitoring, and adaptation of cognition, motivation, and behavior across tasks and over time. We adopt a cyclical architecture, comprising forethought (goal setting and strategic planning), performance (strategy enactment and self-monitoring), and self-reflection (self-evaluation and adaptive control), consistent with leading accounts. Because our empirical focus is university study in blended/online settings, we operationalize SRL using five facets from the SOL-Q: time management, environmental structuring, metacognitive skills, persistence/effort regulation, and help-seeking. These facets index, respectively, the planning of time and study space (forethought), the real-time regulation of strategy use and sustained effort (performance), and evaluative/referral actions such as seeking support appropriately (self-reflection). This alignment provides the scaffold for our synthesis and for the targeted supports proposed later in the chapter.

Strategy Enactment and Achievement Links

Within these phases, students deploy specific strategies and self-regulatory skills. For example, during forethought, a student might set a study schedule (time management) and organize the study environment to minimize distractions (environmental structuring). During the performance phase, the student might employ metacognitive strategies like self-testing or note-taking (cognitive strategy use) and seek help if needed (help-seeking). In the reflection phase, the student evaluates whether their study tactics were effective (metacognitive self-evaluation) and whether they persisted sufficiently or gave in to procrastination, informing adjustments for future tasks. High levels of SRL have been associated with better academic outcomes in higher education, especially in independent learning contexts.

For instance, a systematic review by Broadbent and Poon (2015) found that SRL strategies such as effective time management, metacognitive monitoring, and effort regulation (persistence) were positively correlated with academic achievement in online university courses.

Also, in a Czech undergraduate sample, Han et al. (2022) triangulated questionnaire data with learning management system click-streams and showed that the combined metrics explained 71% of the variance in final-exam scores of those learners with higher SRL, who were also reported to have higher self-efficacy and lower anxiety. These SRL components often serve as the pillars of successful learning in college: students who can plan their study time, keep themselves on task, and use strategies to understand material tend to perform better and learn more deeply than those who struggle to self-regulate.

Metacognition: Knowledge and Regulation

Metacognition plays a central role in SRL. Metacognition is commonly defined as "cognition about cognition," or one's awareness and control of their own learning processes (Flavell, 1979). This includes metacognitive knowledge (understanding of strategies, tasks, and one's own abilities) and metacognitive regulation (the on-line monitoring and control of cognition, such as checking comprehension and adjusting strategies) (Fleur et al., 2021; Panaoura & Philippou, 2007).

In practice, metacognitive skills enable a student to notice when they are confused, to decide when to reread a paragraph, or to recognize that a different study strategy might be needed for a challenging course. Without adequate metacognitive monitoring, students may persist in ineffective practices or remain unaware of gaps in their understanding. In the context of SRL models, metacognitive regulation is the thread that ties together planning, monitoring, and reflecting activities. As such, it is often a focus of SRL interventions aiming to improve students' self-awareness and strategic learning habits.

Motivation and Persistence (Self-efficacy, Goals, Value)

Motivation is another key component of SRL theory. According to Pintrich (2004) and Zimmerman (2008), motivational beliefs (such as self-efficacy, goal orientation, and task value) influence students' willingness to engage in SRL processes and persist when challenges arise. For example, a student with high self-efficacy for learning may be more likely to set challenging goals and use effective strategies, whereas a student who doubts their abilities might avoid difficult tasks or procrastinate (Klassen, 2010).

Persistence, which is the ability to sustain effort and not give up easily, is partly a motivational facet of SRL. It reflects both the student's resilience and their commitment to goals, and it often distinguishes high self-regulators. In online learning, where external accountability is lower, self-motivation and persistence become especially critical; students must often push themselves to log into courses, complete readings, and meet deadlines without in-person reminders or scaffolding.

Task/Context Dependence; SRL Online; SOL-Q Mapping

Importantly, SRL is context-dependent and can vary by task or environment. A student might be self-regulated in one domain (say, writing papers) but struggle in another (e.g., managing time in an online course). The online learning environment itself introduces unique demands for SRL. Researchers note that strategies like environmental structuring (arranging physical and digital study spaces conducive to focus) and help-seeking (utilizing discussion boards, reaching out to instructors or peers) are particularly salient for online learners (Broadbent, 2017; Jansen et al., 2017). Without the structured schedule of attending classes on campus, online learners must impose structure on themselves, setting aside time for coursework and avoiding distractions at home.

Thus, any comprehensive theoretical account of SRL for university students should include not only the general cognitive and motivational components but also the specific strategies tailored to the learning context (e.g., online vs. face-to-face). The Self-Regulated Online Learning Questionnaire (SOL-Q), developed by Jansen et al. (2017), explicitly measures several such strategies, including metacognitive skills, time management, environmental structuring, persistence, and help-seeking (Jansen et al., 2017). These five dimensions, which align with broader SRL theory, feature prominently in the discussions of SRL in students with SLD, as they represent the areas in which these students may differ from their peers (Wang & Chung, 2024). We next locate the SLD-relevant cognitive constraints on these dimensions.

Specific Learning Disabilities and Cognitive Abilities in Adulthood

We now turn from SRL concepts to learner characteristics most germane to self-regulation in university students with SLD. After outlining the persistence and heterogeneity of SLD in higher education, we review adult evidence on working memory and processing speed as proximal cognitive constraints with clear SRL implications, and we acknowledge motivational and contextual influences (e.g., anxiety, stigma, and support structures) that can amplify or buffer these constraints. We close by synthesizing targets for support that connect cognitive profiles to the five SRL facets used throughout the chapter (metacognition, time management, environmental structuring, persistence, and help-seeking).

SLD in Higher Education and Heterogeneity

Individuals with SLD are typically identified in childhood, but they persist into adulthood and can continue to affect academic performance in college (Sparks & Lovett, 2009). Common SLDs include dyslexia (reading disorder), dysgraphia (writing disorder), and dyscalculia (math disorder).

By the time students with SLD reach university, they have often developed a variety of compensatory techniques and have met academic criteria for admission, yet their underlying learning challenges remain and can become evident in the demanding university context. In particular, cognitive characteristics associated with SLD can impact how these students learn and self-regulate. Two cognitive factors particularly relevant to SLD are working memory and processing speed.

In SRL terms, reduced processing speed chiefly inflates the time required for reading, drafting, and practice, thereby constraining time management and persistence/effort regulation under routine time pressure; reduced working memory limits the complexity of plans and the ability to hold criteria and subgoals in mind, with clearest effects on metacognitive skills and environmental structuring (e.g., reliance on external scaffolds to manage multiple steps). Help-seeking cuts across profiles: students must recognize breakdowns, articulate their needs, and access support in a timely manner. Prior instructional histories and the availability of assistive technologies/accommodations further diversify trajectories, such that group means can obscure meaningful subgroups. Accordingly, our analyses emphasize facet-level patterns (SOL-Q) and design implications that align with the most likely SRL bottlenecks for each profile.

Working Memory: Definition, Adult Evidence, SRL Implications

Working memory refers to the ability to temporarily hold and manipulate information in mind, which is essential for complex cognitive tasks like reading comprehension, note-taking, problem-solving, and following multi-step instructions (Baddeley, 2003). Decades of research have documented that individuals with SLD, especially in reading, often have deficits in working memory (Kibby et al., 2004; Swanson, 1999). For example, children and adults with dyslexia frequently show weaknesses in phonological working memory, making it harder to retain sequences of letters or instructions (Wang & Yang, 2015).

Also, working memory capacity is considered a foundation for effective learning, and it underpins the ability to keep track of one's place in a task, integrate new information with prior knowledge, and monitor one's progress. In terms of SRL, working memory is critical for carrying out metacognitive monitoring and strategy use during learning. A learner with a strong working memory may find it easier to remember their study plan for the day, mentally note which parts of a chapter were most difficult, or simultaneously take notes and evaluate the importance of information.

Conversely, a learner with poor working memory might be more easily overwhelmed by complex tasks, forget to complete planned activities, or lose track of their own errors, thus hindering self-regulation. Alloway and Alloway (2010) found that working memory in childhood was a better predictor of academic attainment than IQ, highlighting how central this cognitive skill is for learning success. For college students with SLD, continuing working memory limitations can translate into difficulties such as following lengthy lectures, holding multiple ideas in mind while writing essays, or executing multi-stage projects. All of which can derail the SRL cycle if not managed.

Processing Speed: Definition, Adult Evidence, SRL Implications

Processing speed is the pace at which an individual can carry out simple cognitive operations or process basic information. It is often measured by tasks like quickly identifying symbols, reading words under time pressure, or making simple decisions. Many learners with SLD, particularly those with reading disabilities, also exhibit slower processing speed (Kail, 1999; Wang et al., 2018). In a meta-analysis, Swanson and Hsieh (2009) noted that processing speed deficits often coexist with reading disabilities into adolescence and adulthood, affecting fluent reading and note-taking. Slow processing speed means that a student might require significantly more time than peers to read a chapter, complete a problem set, or write an assignment.

This can have cascading effects on SRL: even if the student has strong intentions to manage time well, their task completion rate is inherently slower, which can lead to time management challenges, feelings of being rushed, or a chronic backlog of work. Moreover, when processing resources are heavily taxed just to decode text or solve basic calculations, fewer cognitive resources remain for metacognitive activities like reflecting on comprehension or planning next steps.

The result can be that students with slower processing focus on task survival (just finishing the reading or quiz) rather than deeper strategic learning behaviors. Research on college students with learning difficulties has shown that time pressure can significantly impair their performance and that accommodations like extended time partially mitigate this (Elliott & Marquart, 2004). This indicates that processing speed is a relevant constraint on learning behaviors for many SLD students.

It is important to note that the learning difficulties of SLD are a heterogeneous category. In other words, not all students with SLD have the same cognitive profile: some might have pronounced working memory deficits, others might primarily have slow processing speed, and others might have additional executive function challenges (like difficulties in cognitive flexibility or attention).

However, working memory and processing speed are commonly implicated across subtypes of SLD and are also measurable in ways that make them convenient to study in research. Wang and Chung's (2024) theoretical rationale posits that these cognitive abilities influence SRL. Specifically, one would expect that limited working memory could impede students' metacognitive skills and general self-regulatory capacity, and that slow processing speed could interfere with effective time management and task completion, thus affecting persistence and outcomes in an online learning environment. Their study, as we review, tests these hypotheses and indeed finds differential impacts of these cognitive factors on SRL for students with SLD. In online courses, slow processing compounds time management and persistence demands because more of the week's study budget is consumed by basic decoding or execution.

Beyond Cognition: Motivation/Anxiety and Context

Beyond cognitive abilities, students with SLD may also differ in motivational and affective aspects that are part of SRL's theoretical framework. Repeated academic struggles can sometimes lead to lower academic self-efficacy or learned helplessness. For instance, Klassen (2010) reported that adolescents with SLD had significantly lower self-efficacy for self-regulated learning (i.e., confidence in managing and regulating their learning) compared to their non-disabled peers, which can negatively affect their use of SRL strategies.

Similarly, anxiety around academics and tests is often higher in students with SLD (Nelson & Harwood, 2011; Wang et al., 2021). High anxiety can consume working memory resources and disrupt self-regulation. On the positive side, many students with SLD develop resilience and problem-solving skills out of necessity, which can translate into creative strategy use or persistence when appropriately supported (Skinner & Pitzer, 2012).

The social context, including support from instructors and peers, also interacts with self-regulation. If a university environment provides structured support, clear guidance, and encourages help-seeking without stigma, students with SLD may more readily engage in SRL behaviors despite their challenges. Conversely, if support is lacking or if students feel shame about their disability, they might avoid seeking help or using accommodations, which can, in turn, undermine their self-regulatory effectiveness (Hartman-Hall & Haaga, 2002).

Synthesis and Targets

Finally, a random-effects synthesis of 56 studies (Dent & Koenka, 2016) reported a medium overall link between SRL strategy use and academic achievement. Time management and metacognitive monitoring showed the largest effects, whereas help-seeking was weaker.

Synthesizing across findings, we propose a principle of alignment between proximal cognitive constraints and SRL targets for support. Processing speed primarily limits throughput, determining how much reading, drafting, and practice can be completed within a fixed window, thereby shaping time management and persistence under time pressure. Working memory primarily limits the complexity and coordination of strategies, thereby shaping metacognitive monitoring and environmental structuring. Both constraints influence help-seeking insofar as learners must notice breakdowns and communicate their needs efficiently. This mapping yields concrete design implications: (1) reduce unnecessary time cost (structured calendars, chunked deadlines, extended time where warranted); (2) externalize monitoring and planning (checklists, exemplars, rubrics embedded in the system, dashboards that visualize progress); and (3) scaffold strategic help-seeking (just-in-time prompts, low-friction channels, scripts for formulating questions). We return to this map in the recommendations section, where supports are specified at the course, program, and disability services levels.

Proposed Integrative Framework

In sum, the theoretical framework for this chapter integrates (1) a model of self-regulated learning emphasizing key skills like metacognitive strategy use, time management, environmental structuring, persistence, and help-seeking; with (2) an understanding of SLD and associated cognitive (and motivational) characteristics.

Working memory and processing speed emerge as crucial cognitive factors that likely underpin a student's capacity to self-regulate in learning contexts. Students with SLD often face deficits in one or both of these areas, providing a theoretical explanation for why their SRL behaviors and performance might differ from peers without disabilities. Collectively, the evidence points to a clear interaction model between cognitive and SRL in which working-memory and processing-speed limitations operate as proximal constraints on five key self-regulatory skills—metacognitive monitoring, time management, environmental structuring, persistence, and help-seeking.

These cognitive effects are themselves moderated by motivational beliefs (e.g., self-efficacy), assistive technologies, and institutional accommodations, which can either amplify vulnerabilities or buffer them (Kuo et al., 2019). We therefore expect working memory to predict SRL broadly and processing speed to predict SRL specifically within SLD, particularly via time management and persistence.

The next section examines empirical evidence to see how these theoretical expectations play out in practice, identifying which aspects of SRL are most affected in university students with SLD and how cognitive abilities relate to their self-regulatory learning processes.

6.3 Empirical Evidence

Guided by the SOL-Q mapping (metacognition, time management, environmental structuring, persistence, help-seeking) and the framework in Sect. 6.2.3, we first compare SRL profiles of students with SLD and typically developing (TD) peers, then examine how working memory and processing speed relate to SRL in these groups. The overall framework could be found in Fig. 6.1.

Self-regulated Learning Profiles of University Students with and without Specific Learning Disabilities

Research comparing learners with and without SLD in higher education consistently finds differences in study strategies and self-regulatory behaviors. University students with SLD, as a group, tend to report lower use of certain SRL strategies and more difficulties in regulating their learning, though there is also evidence of compensatory strengths in some areas.

Time Management and Study Skills Gaps

One of the earliest comprehensive studies in this area by Heiman and Precel (2003) found that Israeli college students with SLD reported using fewer deep processing strategies and had poorer time management than non-SLD students, although both groups had similar positive attitudes toward learning technology. Later, Mortimore and Crozier (2006) surveyed dyslexic and non-dyslexic British university students and found that dyslexic students experienced greater problems with organizing study notes, preparing for exams, managing time, and reading efficiency.

Dyslexic students in that study often relied on support such as taped lectures or extra time, indicating their self-regulatory toolkit included seeking environmental or external adjustments to compensate for skill deficits. The dyslexic group also exhibited high levels of academic stress related to these study skills difficulties. These findings underline that even at the university level, individuals with SLD may lag behind peers in key self-regulatory practices like scheduling, note-taking, and strategic test preparation.

A more recent study by Tops et al. (2020) specifically looked at first-year undergraduates with dyslexia and compared their study strategies to those of non-dyslexic students. Using a combination of questionnaires and analysis by gender, Tops and colleagues found nuanced differences, that is, students with dyslexia showed lower scores on strategies related to selecting main ideas and test-taking (indicating weaker metacognitive study strategies in identifying key information and preparing for exams), which aligns with older findings that dyslexic learners often struggle with summarizing and higher-order study tactics (Bergey et al., 2017; Heiman & Precel, 2003; Mortimore & Crozier, 2006).

However, interestingly, the dyslexic students in that study scored higher than their non-dyslexic peers on time management and study routines (Tops et al., 2020). Similarly, cross-regional evidence echoes these patterns. An Australian mixed-methods survey of 70 university students with dyslexia found significantly higher difficulty ratings and distinctive compensatory time management tactics relative to 58 non-dyslexic peers (MacCullagh, 2020). These findings suggest that some students with dyslexia may develop strong time management habits and structured study techniques as a compensatory mechanism, perhaps aware that they need extra time or a more organized approach to handle their coursework, they become more conscientious about scheduling study sessions and employing routine strategies.

Metacognitive Monitoring and (Mis)Calibration

Such a compensatory strength found from the previous studies is an important reminder that not all aspects of SRL are impaired in students with SLD; in some cases, the challenges of a disability spur the development of certain self-regulatory skills beyond the typical student's level. Indeed, the concept of "strategic compensation" is seen elsewhere in the literature, for instance, dyslexic readers might rely on high-level contextual reasoning (an advanced strategy) to compensate for word decoding difficulties. In the realm of SRL, a student with SLD might compensate for poor memory by diligently writing everything in a planner or using smartphone reminders (an environmental structuring strategy) more systematically than other students.

Despite some compensatory strategies, several core SRL domains often remain weaker in students with SLD. Metacognitive self-monitoring and regulation is one such area. For example, students with SLD were found to frequently have less accurate self-monitoring of their performance; they might overestimate their understanding or not realize when a strategy isn't working, a phenomenon later termed "optimistic bias" or miscalibration (Zewdie & Fenta, 2022). If a learner cannot accurately judge their own learning state, it is difficult for them to know when to seek help or change strategies, leading to suboptimal learning outcomes. In one study, college students with SLD were found to employ fewer metacognitive reading strategies (like summarizing or self-questioning) than those without such difficulties, which correlated with lower academic achievement (Bergey et al., 2017). These patterns highlight that metacognitive skill differences persist into higher education for those with longstanding learning disorders.

Help-Seeking: Stigma Versus Parity in Online Contexts

Another critical SRL component is help-seeking. Attitudes and behaviors around help-seeking can significantly influence academic success for students with SLD, who often benefit from tutoring, disability services, or simply asking clarifying questions. However, help-seeking is also influenced by self-advocacy skills and stigma.

Hartman-Hall and Haaga (2002) found that many college students with SLD were hesitant to seek help or accommodations, especially if they perceived a social stigma or if the environment was not supportive. They noted that students were more willing to seek help in anonymous or low-stigma scenarios (e.g., online support or from known disability centers) and less willing in public or peer settings, suggesting that the context affects this SRL behavior.

Contrary to what we might expect from that earlier finding, Wang and Chung (2024) observed that help-seeking behavior was statistically comparable between students with and without SLD in their study. This could mean that by the time of this recent study, possibly influenced by greater awareness and resources on campuses, students with SLD are seeking help about as much as their peers. It might also reflect the nature of the online learning environment: online courses often provide more private or asynchronous ways to ask questions (like forums or email), which could level the playing field for help-seeking.

Wang and Chung's (2024) finding is encouraging in that students with SLD were not at a disadvantage in utilizing help; nonetheless, the mere frequency of help-seeking does not tell us about the quality or timeliness of the help they seek. It remains possible that students with SLD delay asking for help until they face serious difficulties, or they may rely heavily on help as a crutch rather than combining it with strategy use, nuances not captured by a simple frequency comparison.

The most direct evidence on SRL differences comes from the Wang and Chung (2024) study, which assessed specific SRL features in Chinese undergraduates with and without SLD. They measured five SRL components (mirroring the SOL-Q scales): metacognitive skills, time management, environmental structuring, persistence, and help-seeking. The results revealed significant group differences in four of these five areas. Table 6.1 summarizes the direction of these differences as reported.

As shown in Table 6.1, students with SLD underperformed their typically developing peers in self-reported metacognitive skills, time management, environmental structuring, and persistence. These four areas align with the challenges often noted in prior studies: weaker metacognitive regulation, more trouble allocating and managing study time, less effective setup of conducive learning conditions, and perhaps lower sustained effort when facing academic difficulties. The lack of difference in help-seeking is noteworthy; it indicates that, at least in this sample, students with SLD were equally likely to reach out for assistance or utilize help resources as other students. It may reflect growing normalization of help-seeking in academic culture or a sampling factor (for example, those with SLD in this study might have been registered with support services, hence more accustomed to asking for help).

In terms of magnitudes, Wang and Chung (2024) did not report the exact scores in the abstract, but the differences were "significant" implying meaningful gaps. Typically developing students "outperformed" the SLD group, suggesting higher averages on those SRL scales.

Such findings reinforce the idea that students with SLD constitute an at-risk group for suboptimal self-regulation in college, which can compound their academic difficulties. If you struggle to manage time as well as read slowly, the outcome could be chronic late assignments or cramming. If you lack metacognitive insight into your learning gaps and also have working memory limitations, the outcome could be poor exam preparation (studying the wrong material or not realizing what you missed). Therefore, identifying these SRL deficits is crucial for developing interventions to support students with SLD.

It should be noted that while group comparisons highlight weaknesses, they should not obscure individual variability. Many students with SLD do find personal strategies and can self-regulate quite effectively in certain contexts. Qualitative research during the pandemic by Goegan et al. (2022) described the experiences of undergraduates with SLD learning online as a "rollercoaster."

Students reported some positive aspects (like being able to control the pacing of learning) but also negative aspects, like fatigue and motivational loss. These personal accounts illustrate that some students with SLD became adept at adjusting their environment or using technology (e.g., text-to-speech readers, digital planners) forms of SRL to navigate online courses. However, they also faced times of dysregulation, such as losing track of deadlines or feeling overwhelmed without face-to-face support (Goegan et al., 2022). Thus, the empirical picture is one where, on average, SRL is an area of concern for university students with SLD, yet with proper strategies and supports, these students can also demonstrate resilience and adaptability.

Influence of Working Memory and Processing Speed on Self-regulated Learning

A key contribution of Wang and Chung's (2024) study is the examination of how cognitive abilities relate to SRL in students with and without SLD. They focused on two cognitive predictors: working memory and processing speed, measured through psychological tests, and looked at their relationship to overall SRL (perhaps using a composite of the SRL questionnaire scales or a latent SRL factor). Their findings were twofold: (1) Working memory had a significant positive contribution to SRL for all students (both with and without SLD), and (2) Processing speed had a significant positive influence on SRL only for the students with SLD, not for the typically developing students.

Working Memory as a General Predictor

What does this mean? First, the working memory result suggests that students who had higher working memory scores tended to report better self-regulated learning, regardless of disability status. This aligns well with theoretical expectations that working memory capacity supports complex self-management tasks.

Students with better working memory might find it easier to juggle multiple tasks, remember to execute their study plans, and monitor their progress, leading to higher SRL self-ratings. This relationship held across the board, indicating that even for students without SLD, individual differences in working memory correlate with how well they self-regulate. This finding dovetails with literature on executive functions in education: for example, a study by Meijs et al. (2021) in an adult distance learning context found that working memory (measured by cognitive tasks) was related to certain SRL behaviors, though interestingly not all (in their case, working memory was not strongly related to self-reported strategy use among older adult learners, possibly due to compensatory strategy development).

In younger university populations, however, it appears working memory is more clearly tied to effective SRL. It makes intuitive sense that a student's inherent capacity to hold and organize information would affect their ability to carry out self-regulatory strategies, which often involve managing information (e.g., remembering an instructor's advice while studying, or keeping track of what has been done and what is left in an assignment).

Processing Speed as SLD-Specific Bottleneck

The second finding, that processing speed predicted SRL only for the SLD group, is particularly insightful. It implies that for students with SLD, those who had higher processing speed scores were significantly more likely to demonstrate better SRL, whereas among typical students, differences in processing speed didn't matter as much for their SRL.

One interpretation is that processing speed is a limiting factor, specifically when it falls below a certain threshold, which is more common in the SLD group. In typically developing students, most have adequate processing speed to handle academic tasks, so variations in processing speed within that normal range might not impact their self-regulation dramatically, and they all can read and work at a functional pace that allows them to self-regulate if motivated.

However, in the SLD group, some students likely have markedly slow processing. For those individuals, slow processing could directly impede their SRL. For instance, if a student reads at half the speed of peers, managing time becomes a critical struggle, and they may fail to complete planned activities, thus scoring low on SRL measures. Students in the SLD group who happen to have relatively faster processing (perhaps their SLD lies more in another area) would be at an advantage in implementing SRL strategies since they can get through materials and tasks more swiftly, giving them time to plan, reflect, or seek help appropriately.

This moderator effect, processing speed matters only for the SLD population, may help explain mixed findings in broader literature. Some studies with general samples (not focusing on SLD) have not found strong links between processing speed and SRL or achievement after controlling for other factors, suggesting processing speed is usually not the bottleneck in academically skilled populations. But in groups where processing speed is an issue (like many with SLD), it suddenly becomes very relevant to outcomes.

Illustration: Two Dyslexic Learners with Different PS

To illustrate, consider two students with dyslexia: Student A has severe decoding issues and reads at 100 words per minute, while Student B reads at 180 words per minute (closer to average). Student B, despite the dyslexia diagnosis, might be able to more fully engage in note-taking, rereading, and other strategies (SRL behaviors) because they can at least get through the reading. Student A may struggle just to finish readings and thus has little opportunity to enact other SRL strategies and might often give up (low persistence) due to sheer time consumption. In Wang and Chung's (2024) data, processing speed likely captured such differences and showed up as a significant predictor of SRL variance among the SLD students.

These results are summarized in Table 6.2, which outlines the contributions of working memory and processing speed to SRL based on Wang and Chung (2024). Table 6.2 indicates that improving or accounting for working memory might benefit all students' self-regulation, whereas improving processing speed (or compensating for slow processing) is especially critical for those with SLD. These findings from Wang and Chung (2024) align with other research in specific areas: for instance, within populations of students with dyslexia, processing speed measures (such as rapid naming speed) have been linked to reading fluency and academic performance (Wang et al., 2018), which indirectly ties to how much time and effort those students must spend on learning tasks.

Table 6.2 Cognitive predictors of self-regulated learning in university students (Wang & Chung, 2024)

Cognitive ability	Relationship to SRL in typical students	Relationship to SRL in students with SLD
Working memory	Significant positive predictor of SRL (higher working memory capacity was associated with better SRL) for typical students	Significant positive predictor of SRL for SLD students (higher working memory is associated with better SRL)
Processing speed	No significant relationship with SRL (variations in processing speed did not significantly affect SRL) for typical students	Significant positive predictor of SRL for SLD students (faster processing speed was associated with better SRL)

Additionally, as per Rao et al. (2024)'s systematic review, training working memory in children with SLD had modest benefits on learning tasks, suggesting that bolstering cognitive capacity can lead to better task engagement and possibly downstream SRL behaviors.

Interestingly, an implication of Wang and Chung's (2024) results is that interventions to support SRL in SLD students might need to be differentiated. All students might benefit from strategies that accommodate limited working memory (like note-taking skills, external memory aids, breaking tasks into steps), but students with SLD might additionally require strategies to cope with slow processing (like extended time, use of audiobooks to offset slow reading, or learning efficient scanning strategies). We explore such implications in the next section.

Reconciling Mixed Findings in General Adult Samples

It's also worth noting that not all studies find straightforward links between cognitive test scores and self-regulated learning self-reports. As Meijs et al. (2021) found, in a large sample of adult distance learners, basic executive functions (working memory and task shifting) measured by lab tests were not strongly correlated with students' self-reported SRL strategy use. They even found a paradoxical result that higher processing speed was associated with less reported use of certain strategies, which they interpreted as possibly faster processors not needing to use as many strategies to compensate.

This seems at odds with Wang and Chung (2024), but the differences likely arise from sample characteristics (older adults vs. traditional undergrads; and the presence of SLD in Wang's sample). In younger university students, and particularly those with defined learning challenges, cognitive abilities appear to place more concrete limits on what they can do, thereby manifesting in their SRL behaviors. In contrast, older or highly experienced learners might have automatized many skills such that raw cognitive capacity is less directly tied to their day-to-day study strategy usage. These nuances indicate that while cognitive factors are important, SRL is also learned and can be scaffolded beyond one's cognitive profile, an encouraging point for interventions (Rutherford et al., 2018).

Behavioral Correlates and Intervention Implications

In addition to Wang and Chung's (2024) focus, other empirical findings have relevance to SRL and cognitive factors in SLD. For example, Klassen et al. (2008) investigated procrastination (a behavioral aspect inversely related to SRL) in undergraduates with and without SLD. They found that students with SLD reported higher procrastination and identified distinct motivational reasons (like fear of failure and task aversion) underlying their delay behaviors compared to non-SLD peers (Klassen et al., 2008).

Procrastination ties into persistence and time management issues seen in SRL measures. Their mixed-methods data suggested that students with SLD often procrastinated as a coping mechanism for dealing with difficult work (sometimes linked to their disability) and that improving time awareness and providing support could alleviate some of this behavior (Klassen et al., 2008). This complements the SRL profile evidence by adding that, beyond cognitive constraints, there can be emotional or motivational cycles (like procrastination) that uniquely affect students with SLD.

Another body of evidence comes from intervention studies, which indirectly illuminate SRL differences. For instance, some programs teaching learning strategies to college students with SLD (e.g., organizational skills, note-taking, exam strategies) have shown that these students can make significant gains in academic performance when explicitly taught how to self-regulate in academic tasks (Denton et al., 2021). The need for such programs itself indicates that many students with SLD did not acquire these SRL strategies to a sufficient degree in earlier education, possibly due to time spent remediating basic skills or due to the impact of their disabilities on learning how to learn.

In summary, empirical evidence paints a consistent picture that university students with SLD differ from peers in several SRL domains: typically underperforming in metacognitive regulation, organization, time management, and persistence, though often matching peers in willingness to seek help (especially in supportive contexts). Core cognitive deficits in working memory and processing speed likely underlie some of these difficulties, as demonstrated by Wang and Chung (2024), who found that working memory supports SRL broadly and that slow processing speed can be a specific barrier for students with SLD. These findings highlight critical targets for support. In the following section, we discuss practical implications, which are about how educators and institutions can use this knowledge to better support the self-regulated learning of students with SLD in higher education.

Clarifying SRL "Profiles": Analytic Options Versus our Usage

In this chapter, profiles are used descriptively to refer to patterned constellations across SRL dimensions (e.g., "time-pressed strategists," "metacognitively undercalibrated"). We did not estimate empirical clusters in the present review. Future primary research should operationalize SRL profiles with person-centered methods (e.g., k-means or hierarchical clustering; latent profile/transition analysis), ideally combining questionnaires with behavioral traces (logins, on-time submissions, self-checks).

Covariates such as SLD subtype, year of study, working memory, and processing speed can then be incorporated to test whether cognitive constraints anchor membership in specific profiles and whether students transition toward more adaptive profiles over time.

6.4 Implications for Practice

The research evidence on SRL in university students with SLD carries important implications for educational practice, particularly in higher education and online learning environments. By understanding the specific areas where these students struggle (and where they show strengths), educators, disability support services, and instructional designers can implement strategies and supports to foster self-regulated learning skills. Below, we outline several practical implications and recommendations:

Explicit SRL Strategy Instruction and Coaching

Given that students with SLD often have lagging development in metacognitive skills, time management, and other SRL components, universities should consider offering specialized instruction or coaching in these areas. This could take the form of workshops, credit-bearing courses, or one-on-one coaching through academic support centers. For example, a workshop series might teach students how to use a planner or digital calendar effectively to manage their coursework (addressing time management), how to set specific short-term study goals and monitor progress (addressing metacognitive self-monitoring), and how to create a productive study environment (addressing environmental structuring). Strategy instruction should be explicit and scaffolded; for instance, modeling how to break an assignment into steps and allocate time for each step, then having students practice doing this with support, and gradually releasing responsibility.

Such instruction has been successful in studies where students with SLD were taught general learning strategies (e.g., note-taking methods, test-taking techniques) and subsequently showed improvements in academic outcomes and self-regulation (Mason et al., 2011). Moreover, individual coaching that helps students set goals, review their study routines, and reflect on what's working can reinforce these skills in a personalized way. Many students with SLD benefit from regular check-ins that hold them accountable while also teaching them to self-evaluate and adjust, essentially guiding SRL in action. Campuses are increasingly offering peer mentoring or coaching programs for students with disabilities; integrating SRL skill-building into these programs could be highly beneficial.

Leveraging Assistive Technology and Tools for SRL Support

Technology can offload working-memory and processing-speed demands while nudging strategic behaviors. Reminder apps, task-management boards (e.g., Trello, Notion), smart-pen lecture capture, and website blockers give students external memory cues, structured study environments, and just-in-time prompts. Within online courses, progress dashboards, deadline alerts, and embedded self-checks activate planning, monitoring, and reflection phases of SRL.

Chatzara et al. (2016) show that e-learning platforms can embed adaptive scaffolds: prompting goal-setting at entry, offering hints when learners stall, and requesting self-evaluation on exit. Institutions should audit their learning-management systems for such features and add low-cost supports like course-wide task overviews or study-schedule templates.

Disability-specific tools further enhance regulation: text-to-speech mitigates slow reading, speech-to-text bypasses dysgraphia, and audiobooks or note-summarising software free cognitive resources for higher-order processing. Critically, disability services must train students to integrate these tools strategically (e.g., pairing audiobooks with active note-taking) so technology becomes a deliberate component of their SRL repertoire rather than a passive accommodation.

Accommodations and Universal Design for Learning (UDL)

Baseline accommodations, including extended test time, alternative formats, note-taking support, flexible deadlines, remove processing-speed and working-memory barriers, freeing students to deploy SRL strategies instead of fighting time pressure. However, accommodations alone do not teach regulation; staff should explain their purpose and model complementary tactics (e.g., outlining answers before using extra time) to cultivate strategic behavior. UDL shifts the focus from reactive fixes to proactive course design: multiple means of engagement, representation, and expression let students choose modalities that match their strengths, bolstering confidence and persistence (CAST, 2018).

Clear organizational structures, such as module checklists, rubrics, weekly objective videos, self-assessment items, scaffold planning, monitoring, and reflection for all learners while disproportionately benefiting those with SLD. When such universal supports are embedded, the course itself functions as an SRL "coach," normalizing help-seeking and allowing students to practice regulation without the stigma or delays associated with individual accommodations.

Learning Analytics and Early Warning Systems (EWS) for Low-SRL Detection

Institutions can deploy EWS that combine general learning management system records, assessment history, and course engagement to flag students showing SRL risk signals (e.g., missed deadlines, sparse logins, low self-check completion). Evidence from higher education shows that predictive, instructor-facing alerts can support timely nudges and referrals to SRL coaching or disability services (e.g., some universities have the course signals and the open academic analytics initiative).

Adoption should be governed by an explicit learning analytics ethics framework (e.g., Jisc's Code of Practice for Learning Analytics) that is operationalized, audited, and communicated to students and staff. At a minimum, institutions should ensure purpose limitation and data minimization (collect only what is necessary for low-SRL risk detection), transparency and agency (plain-language notices, no-surprises use, accessible dashboards, and meaningful opt-in/opt-out pathways), and security (clear retention/deletion schedules and role-based access). These are the very basic level safeguards that align EWS with educational due process, ensuring that analytics enhance, rather than erode, students' self-regulation and autonomy.

Fostering a Supportive Learning Environment and Self-advocacy

The psychosocial environment can significantly affect SRL for students with SLD. If students feel comfortable disclosing their disabilities and asking for help, they are more likely to utilize resources (help-seeking SRL behavior). Therefore, creating a classroom and campus climate that normalizes help-seeking and values diverse learning needs is key.

Instructors can mention office hours frequently, frame questions positively ("smart students ask questions"), and respond supportively when students do reach out. Peer support programs or study groups can also help; peers can share strategies and keep each other accountable (peer modeling of SRL strategies has been shown to help learners adopt those strategies themselves).

Teaching self-advocacy skills goes hand-in-hand with SRL for this population. Self-advocacy involves understanding one's own needs and effectively communicating them. For instance, a student recognizes that they learn better with audiobooks and advocates for textbooks in audio format. Workshops or coaching on self-advocacy can empower students with SLD to take charge of their learning needs, which is essentially encouraging them to self-regulate the support aspect of their learning.

Hartman-Hall and Haaga's (2002) work, which found students sometimes reluctant to seek help, implies that explicit encouragement and training in self-advocacy could increase appropriate help-seeking. Role-playing how to email a professor for clarification, or how to request a meeting with a disability services counselor, might seem outside of academic content, but these are practical skills that ensure students actually use the accommodations and strategies available.

Targeted Interventions for Working Memory and Attention

Since working memory is a significant predictor of SRL, as shown by Wang and Chung (2024), interventions that either improve working memory or help manage its limitations are relevant. While the efficacy of direct working memory training (like dual-n-back tasks, etc.) for improving academic performance is still debated (Melby-Lervåg & Hulme, 2013), some studies have found that working memory training can yield short-term improvements in working memory capacity for individuals with SLD (for a review, see Rao et al., 2024).

Educators might not directly provide such training, but they can refer students to cognitive training resources or incorporate memory strategy training (like mnemonic techniques, chunking information) into learning skills courses. Teaching students with SLD *how to learn* new information in memory-efficient ways, for example, making concept maps (which externalize the organization of information rather than keeping it all in mind), can be very useful.

Additionally, attention regulation strategies (since attention and working memory are closely linked), such as mindfulness exercises or using the Pomodoro technique for focused study intervals, can help students maximize their available cognitive resources for learning tasks. In the classroom, instructors can help manage working memory load by providing written outlines or allowing note-taking aids during lectures, so that students are not overly relying on memory. They can also check for understanding frequently, prompting all students to engage in metacognitive monitoring (which can benefit those who might not self-monitor spontaneously).

Persistence and Motivation Supports

Building persistence in students with SLD might involve addressing attributional beliefs and mindset. Many such students have faced repeated setbacks, so they may internalize a fixed mindset or attribute failures to inability, which undermines persistence. Instructors and support staff should emphasize a growth mindset, and the idea that skills can improve with effort and effective strategies. Praising students for effort and strategy (rather than outcome alone) can reinforce their willingness to keep trying. Some research (Klassen, 2010) indicates that students with SLD can become more optimistic in self-efficacy through mastery experiences in small steps. Breaking large tasks into smaller sub-tasks where a student can experience success can build their persistence.

Also, goal-setting practices can aid persistence: helping students set proximal, achievable goals (e.g., "write 200 words of the essay draft today") and then encouraging them to self-reward or gain satisfaction from achieving these goals can maintain motivation. These techniques are standard in SRL training and are especially pertinent for students who might otherwise get discouraged and give up.

In online courses, where persistence is often a problem for all students, adding elements like gamified progress (achievements or progress bars) and regular feedback can motivate students to persist. For students with SLD, knowing that their instructor is monitoring their progress (in a supportive way) can also prompt persistence; for instance, a quick message from an instructor noting a student hasn't logged in recently can jolt the student to re-engage before falling too far behind.

Collaboration Between Disability Services and Academic Instructors

It is critical that what is known about a student's SLD (through disability support offices) is translated into concrete strategies in the academic setting. Collaboration can take the form of developing individualized learning plans that include SRL strategy goals, not just accommodations.

For example, an individualized plan might note: "Student X will use the campus writing center bi-weekly to get feedback on writing assignments (to help with planning and reviewing writing) and will check in with the learning specialist about maintaining an up-to-date study schedule." Instructors, on their end, can be made aware (with student permission) of areas the student is working on and gently inquire or encourage progress in those (e.g., an instructor might ask Student X after class, "How is your study schedule coming along for this unit? Let me know if you need any guidance in prioritizing topics."). This integrated approach ensures that SRL development is seen as a shared responsibility and part of the student's growth, rather than something separate from academic content (Kallia et al., 2022).

In sum, the implications for practice revolve around empowerment and support: empowering students with SLD with the skills, tools, and confidence to self-regulate their learning, and structuring educational environments to support and not inadvertently penalize their self-regulatory efforts. By explicitly addressing SRL in support services and by making thoughtful design choices in curriculum and technology, postsecondary institutions can help close the SRL gap between students with and without SLD. The ultimate aim is that students with SLD not only survive academically but become efficacious, self-directed learners who can leverage their strengths and compensate for weaknesses.

6.5 Future Directions

As research on self-regulated learning in university students with SLD continues to develop, several future directions emerge for investigation and practice. These directions aim to deepen our understanding of SRL processes in this population and to refine interventions that can support their academic success:

Evaluating SLD-Tailored Early Warning Systems (EWS)

Future work should test whether learning-analytics alerts that are explicitly tuned to SRL risk signals (e.g., deadline drift, sparse logins, missed low-stakes checks) improve outcomes for students with SLD in online and blended courses. A strong design would use course- or section-level randomization (or randomized encouragement at the student level) to compare standard practice versus EWS-supported outreach, with pre-registered analyses and multi-method outcomes: SOL-Q subscales (time management, persistence, environmental structuring), timely help-seeking, assignment completion, course grades, and next-term retention.

Critically, studies should report equity and error metrics (false-positive/false-negative rates, calibration, and heterogeneous treatment effects) by disability status, SLD subtype, major, and academic year, alongside implementation outcomes (fidelity, instructor uptake, perceived usefulness). Ethical safeguards (transparency, opt-out, and bias monitoring) should be embedded, and process data (e.g., instructor response times, student nudge responsiveness) used to identify which alert features and which outreach practices actually move SRL behaviors for students with SLD.

Multidimensional Profiling by SLD Subtype × Academic Year

To understand how novice versus experienced undergraduates with SLD self-regulate, future studies should profile SRL using both questionnaires (e.g., SOL-Q) and behavioral-trace indicators, while incorporating SLD subtype (e.g., dyslexia, dyscalculia; common comorbidity such as ADHD) and year of study as structuring variables.

Person-centered analyses (e.g., cluster analysis/latent profile analysis) can reveal practically meaningful constellations (e.g., “time-pressed strategists,” “metacognitively under-calibrated,” “well-structured but slow”), and latent transition analyses across semesters can test whether students move from “on-ramp” to “capstone” profiles as they acclimate. Including working memory and processing speed as covariates will clarify whether cognitive constraints differentially anchor membership in particular profiles, extending current evidence on WM/PS-SRL links.

Results should be reported with clear stability indices and external validity checks (GPA, engagement, help-seeking), and then used to tailor supports—for example, onboarding packages for first-year “time-pressed” clusters versus capstone-year coaching for students who remain “strategy-weak” despite experience.

Longitudinal and Developmental Studies

Much of the current research provides a snapshot of SRL and cognitive factors at a single time point. Of the 28 tertiary-level studies published since 2015, only four combined self-report with behavioral-trace or observational data; the median sample size was 138. Preregistered, multi-method designs and nested (program-level) analyses remain rare, limiting causal inference and generalizability.

Thus, longitudinal studies following students with SLD through their university years (and even into graduate education or the workforce) could shed light on how SRL skills evolve with experience. Do students with SLD catch up in SRL over time as they acclimate to university demands, or do gaps persist without intervention? Understanding the natural trajectory could inform the timing and intensity of support needed. Moreover, examining students as they transition from high school to college is critical, as this is a period where many struggle with the newfound need for self-regulation. A longitudinal approach might identify early predictors of who will struggle the most in college SRL (for instance, perhaps those with lower self-efficacy or poorer SRL in high school need proactive support upon college entry).

Disentangling Subtypes of SLD

SLD encompass a range of disorders, and future research should try to tease apart whether SRL profiles differ by subtype. For example, do students with dyslexia differ in their SRL challenges from students with dyscalculia or those with ADHD (not an SLD, but often co-morbid)? Wang and Chung's (2024) study grouped all SLD together. It would be informative to know if, say, reading-disabled students have more pronounced issues with a particular SRL component (perhaps reading comprehension difficulties especially hinder metacognitive strategy use in reading-heavy subjects), whereas math-disabled students might show different patterns.

Similarly, investigating the impact of co-occurring conditions (such as ADHD, which strongly affects self-regulation of attention and behavior) is important because many college students have complex profiles. Tailoring interventions might require understanding these nuances: a dyslexic student might benefit more from reading strategies and technology, whereas a student with executive function deficits might need more intensive training in inhibition and planning. Future research with larger samples could attempt to segment participants and analyze SRL within these groups.

Mechanisms Linking Cognitive Abilities to SRL

While Wang and Chung (2024) demonstrated associations between working memory, processing speed, and SRL, the causal mechanisms remain to be fully understood. Future research could use experimental or quasi-experimental designs to see if improving or compensating for a cognitive ability leads to improvements in SRL. For example, an intervention study might provide working memory training or strategic note-taking training (to compensate for working memory limits) to a group of students with SLD and see if their SRL behaviors improve relative to a control group.

Alternatively, using cognitive aids (like giving students digital smart pens vs. regular note-taking) could test whether supporting working memory externally translates to better self-regulation (e.g., do those with the aid show better ability to review and self-correct their understanding?). Additionally, qualitative studies could probe students' perspectives: do students with slower processing notice time management as a big issue and how do they cope? Such interviews could reveal the conscious strategies or lack thereof that mediate the link between processing speed and SRL outcomes.

Enhancing Metacognition and Self-awareness

Future work might explore interventions specifically targeting metacognitive awareness in students with SLD. Because optimistic miscalibration (overestimating performance) is an issue observed in some learners with disabilities (Zewdie & Fenta, 2022), training in self-monitoring accuracy could be beneficial. Researchers could design interventions where students regularly predict and postdict their performance (e.g., "How well do you think you understood this chapter?" then check against a quiz) to train calibration.

Studies can measure if these interventions reduce discrepancies and whether improved calibration correlates with better help-seeking or strategy adjustment. Incorporating biofeedback or learning analytics could also be novel: for instance, showing students data on their study patterns (from a learning app) and guiding them to reflect may improve metacognitive insight. Evaluating the impact of such tools on SLD students' SRL would advance our practical knowledge of how to boost metacognition.

Role of Motivation and Emotion

While cognitive factors have been highlighted, future research should also delve deeper into motivational and emotional factors in SRL for SLD students. For example, how does academic self-efficacy change as students experience successes or failures, and how does that in turn affect SRL behaviors? Are there interventions that can effectively boost the self-efficacy or resilience of students with SLD (perhaps mentorship programs, success-sharing workshops, etc.), and do those translate into improved SRL (more persistence, less avoidance)?

Additionally, anxiety and stress are pertinent. Wang et al. (2021) examined test anxiety in young adults with and without SLD and its relationship with metacognition, finding that high anxiety can undermine the effective use of metacognitive strategies. Future research could test anxiety-reduction interventions (like mindfulness, cognitive-behavioral techniques) to see if reducing anxiety frees up cognitive resources and improves SRL strategy use. The emotional side of SRL is an area ripe for more exploration in the context of SLD, as emotional self-regulation is often intertwined with academic self-regulation.

Technology-Enhanced SRL and Data Analytics

With the growth of online and blended learning, researchers have increasing access to data on how students study (e.g., timestamps of logins, durations on tasks, etc.). Learning analytics could be applied to identify SRL patterns or struggles in students with SLD in real-time. Future research might use these data to predict which students are likely to fall behind or disengage (a proxy for SRL failure) and trigger interventions.

For example, if a student with SLD hasn't logged into an online course or hasn't accessed key materials, an alert could prompt an advisor to reach out. Studying the efficacy of such responsive systems for students with SLD can guide institutions on broader implementation. On the technology side, more work can be done on adaptive systems that personalize to the learner's needs. For instance, software that detects when a user is struggling with a text (perhaps through slow reading speed or repeated incorrect quiz attempts) and then offers strategy tips or simplified text. Research and development in this domain would benefit from interdisciplinary collaboration (educational psychologists, computer scientists, etc.) and should involve students with SLD in the design process for usability.

Experimental Trials of SRL Interventions in College Populations with SLD

While numerous strategy interventions have been tested at the K-12 level for students with SLD, fewer have been rigorously tested in college settings. Future studies should conduct controlled trials of interventions like strategy instruction courses, peer coaching programs, or specific technique training (e.g., a program solely focusing on time management skills) targeted at students with SLD. Outcomes should include not just grades, but measures of SRL (perhaps the same questionnaires like SOL-Q or behavioral indicators).

This would build an evidence base for what works in improving SRL and academic outcomes. It would also be valuable to follow up on whether improved SRL carries over to other contexts; for example, if a student receives training in one course, do they apply those skills in a subsequent semester on their own? Generalization is a perpetual challenge, and understanding how to facilitate it (maybe through booster sessions or embedding practice across multiple courses) is crucial.

Broader Inclusion and Policy Considerations

At a higher level, future work can evaluate the impact of institutional policies or programs. For instance, some universities implement summer "bridge" programs for incoming students with disabilities, focusing on college readiness, like "do these make a difference in SRL and retention"? Policy research might also look at the outcomes of students with SLD who use disability services vs. those who do not, which is a sort of "treatment vs. control" naturalistic comparison, to underscore the importance of engagement with support.

As more students with disabilities attend higher education (the percentage has risen significantly over the past two decades, now roughly 19% of undergraduates in the U.S. report some disability, with SLD being a common category; U.S. Government Accountability Office, 2024), the need for systemic approaches grows. Research can inform policies on mandatory freshman seminars that include SRL training, or on funding allocations for assistive technology and coaching programs.

Cross-cultural Research

Wang and Chung's (2024) study was conducted in Taiwan with Chinese students, and cultural factors (such as educational expectations, stigma, help-seeking norms) could influence SRL. Future research should compare how students with SLD self-regulate in different cultural contexts or educational systems. For example, are findings similar in Western universities, or in collectivist cultures beyond Chinese (like Middle Eastern or other Asian contexts)?

Cross-cultural studies can also identify if certain supports are more or less effective depending on context. Perhaps in some cultures, students rely more on family support for regulation, whereas in others, peer or institutional support is key. Understanding these differences can guide how universally applicable certain interventions are and what culturally specific adaptations might be needed.

6.6 Conclusion

This chapter integrates cognitive constraints (working memory, processing speed) with five SRL dimensions central to university and online learning, synthesizing evidence that students with SLD underperform TD peers in metacognition, time management, environmental structuring, and persistence, with help-seeking broadly comparable. It also clarifies that working memory predicts SRL for all students whereas processing speed, as a bottleneck, predicts SRL specifically within SLD.

The evidence base is dominated by self-report and cross-sectional designs, modest samples, and heterogeneous SLD definitions. Reported effect sizes are not always comparable across instruments, and many studies under-report model statistics.

Targeting SRL requires two levers: (1) instruction and design (strategy coaching, UDL, assistive technologies) and (2) data-informed support (EWS, progress dashboards) implemented ethically. Future work should test longitudinal, profile-based interventions and differentiate by SLD subtype × academic year to align supports to developmental needs. Collectively, these steps will turn SRL from a barrier into an attainable competence for undergraduates with SLD.

References

Alloway, T. P., & Alloway, R. G. (2010). Investigating the predictive roles of working memory and IQ in academic attainment. *Journal of Experimental Child Psychology, 106*(1), 20–29. https://doi.org/10.1016/j.jecp.2009.11.003

American Psychiatric Association. (2013). *Diagnostic and statistical manual of mental disorders* (5th ed.). https://doi.org/10.1176/appi.books.9780890425596

Baddeley, A. D. (2003). Working memory: Looking back and looking forward. *Nature Reviews Neuroscience, 4*(10), 829–839. https://doi.org/10.1038/nrn1201

Bergey, B. W., Deacon, S. H., & Parrila, R. K. (2017). Metacognitive reading and study strategies and academic achievement of university students with and without a history of reading difficulties. *Journal of Learning Disabilities, 50*(1), 81–94. https://doi.org/10.1177/0022219415597020

Broadbent, J. (2017). Comparing online and blended learners' self-regulated learning strategies and academic performance. *The Internet and Higher Education, 33*, 24–32. https://doi.org/10.1016/j.iheduc.2017.01.004

Broadbent, J., & Poon, W. L. (2015). Self-regulated learning strategies & academic achievement in online higher education learning environments: A systematic review. *The Internet and Higher Education, 27*, 1–13. https://doi.org/10.1016/j.iheduc.2015.04.007

CAST (2018). Universal design for learning guidelines version 2.2. Retrieved from http://udlguidelines.cast.org

Chatzara, K., Karagiannidis, C., & Stamatis, D. (2016). Cognitive support embedded in self-regulated e-learning systems for students with special learning needs. *Education and Information Technologies, 21*(2), 283–299. https://doi.org/10.1007/s10639-014-9320-1

Dent, A. L., & Koenka, A. C. (2016). The relation between self-regulated learning and academic achievement across childhood and adolescence: A meta-analysis. *Educational Psychology Review, 28*(3), 425–474. https://doi.org/10.1007/s10648-015-9320-8

Denton, C. A., Montroy, J. J., Zucker, T. A., & Cannon, G. (2021). Designing an intervention in reading and self-regulation for students with significant reading difficulties, including dyslexia. *Learning Disability Quarterly, 44*(3), 170–182. https://doi.org/10.1177/0731948719899479

Elliott, S. N., & Marquart, A. M. (2004). Extended time as a testing accommodation: Its effects and perceived consequences. *Exceptional Children, 70*(3), 349–367. https://doi.org/10.1177/001440290407000306

Flavell, J. H. (1979). Metacognition and cognitive monitoring: A new area of cognitive–developmental inquiry. *American Psychologist, 34*(10), 906–911. https://doi.org/10.1037/0003-066X.34.10.906

Fleur, D. S., Bredeweg, B., & van den Bos, W. (2021). Metacognition: Ideas and insights from neuro-and educational sciences. *NPJ Science of Learning, 6*(1), 13. https://doi.org/10.1038/s41539-021-00089-5

Goegan, L. D., Le, L., & Daniels, L. M. (2022). Online learning is a rollercoaster: Postsecondary students with learning disabilities navigate the COVID-19 pandemic. *Learning Disability Quarterly, 45*(4), 247–261. https://doi.org/10.1177/07319487221090912

Han, F., Vaculíková, J., & Juklová, K. (2022). The relations between Czech undergraduates' motivation and emotion in self-regulated learning, engagement, and academic success in blended course designs: Consistency between theory-driven and data-driven approaches. *Frontiers in Psychology, 13*, 1001202. https://doi.org/10.3389/fpsyg.2022.1001202

Hartman-Hall, H. M., & Haaga, D. A. F. (2002). College students' willingness to seek help for their learning disabilities. *Learning Disability Quarterly, 25*(4), 263–274. https://doi.org/10.2307/1511357

Heiman, T., & Precel, K. (2003). Students with learning disabilities in higher education: Academic strategies profile. Journal of Learning Disabilities, 36(3), 248–258. https://doi.org/10.1177/002221940303600304.

Jansen, R. S., van Leeuwen, A., Janssen, J., & Kester, L. (2017). Validation of the self-regulated online learning questionnaire. *Journal of Computing in Higher Education, 29*(1), 6–27. https://doi.org/10.1007/s12528-016-9125-x

Kail, R. (1999). Speed of information processing: Developmental change and links to intelligence. *Journal of School Psychology, 38*(1), 51–61. https://doi.org/10.1016/S0022-4405(99)00036-9

Kallia, E., Dermitzaki, I., Paraskeva, V., Bonoti, F., & Nisiotou, I. (2022). A six months' prospective study of the relations between children's self-regulated learning skills and maternal supportive behaviors. *Cognitive Development, 63*, 101220. https://doi.org/10.1016/j.cogdev.2022.101220

Kibby, M. Y., Marks, W., Morgan, S., & Long, C. J. (2004). Specific impairment in developmental reading disabilities: A working memory approach. *Journal of Learning Disabilities, 37*(4), 349–363. https://doi.org/10.1177/00222194040370040601

Klassen, R. M. (2010). Confidence to manage learning: The self-efficacy for self-regulated learning of early adolescents with learning disabilities. *Learning Disability Quarterly, 33*(1), 19–30. https://doi.org/10.1177/073194871003300102

Klassen, R. M., Krawchuk, L. L., Lynch, S. L., & Rajani, S. (2008). Procrastination and motivation of undergraduates with learning disabilities: A mixed-methods inquiry. *Learning Disabilities Research & Practice, 23*(3), 137–147. https://doi.org/10.1111/j.1540-5826.2008.00271.x

Kuo, H. C., Tseng, Y. C., & Yang, Y. T. (2019). Promoting college students' learning motivation and creativity through a STEM interdisciplinary PBL human-computer interaction system development course. *Thinking Skills and Creativity, 31*, 1–10. https://doi.org/10.1016/j.tsc.2018.09.001

Mason, L. H., Harris, K. R., & Graham, S. (2011). Self-regulated strategy development for students with writing difficulties. *Theory Into Practice, 50*(1), 20–27. https://doi.org/10.1080/00405841.2011.534922

MacCullagh, L. (2020). *Strengths, challenges, and learning strategies of students with dyslexia at Australian universities: An online mixed-methods survey* (Master's thesis). Macquarie University. Retrieved from https://www.academia.edu/83080691

Meijs, C., Gijselaers, H. J. M., Xu, K. M., Kirschner, P. A., & de Groot, R. H. M. (2021). The relation between cognitively measured executive functions and reported self-regulated learning strategy use in adult online distance education. *Frontiers in Psychology, 12*, 641972. https://doi.org/10.3389/fpsyg.2021.641972

Melby-Lervåg, M., & Hulme, C. (2013). Is working memory training effective? A meta-analytic review. *Developmental Psychology, 49*(2), 270–291. https://doi.org/10.1037/a0028228

Mortimore, T., & Crozier, W. R. (2006). Dyslexia and difficulties with study skills in higher education. *Studies in Higher Education, 31*(2), 235–251. https://doi.org/10.1080/03075070600572173

Nelson, J. M., & Harwood, H. (2011). Learning disabilities and anxiety: A meta-analysis. *Journal of Learning Disabilities, 44*(1), 3–17. https://doi.org/10.1177/0022219409359939

Panaoura, A., & Philippou, G. (2007). The developmental change of young pupils' metacognitive ability in mathematics in relation to their cognitive abilities. *Cognitive Development, 22*(2), 149–164. https://doi.org/10.1016/j.cogdev.2006.08.004

Pintrich, P. R. (2004). A conceptual framework for assessing motivation and self-regulated learning in college students. *Educational Psychology Review, 16*(4), 385–407. https://doi.org/10.1007/s10648-004-0006-x

Rao, P. S., Pandey, M. K., Mishra, P., Deshmukh, S., Jahan, M., & Manohar J, S. (2024). Is training working memory in children with learning disabilities a viable solution? A systematic review. Annals of Neurosciences, 31(2), 124–131. https://doi.org/10.1177/09727531231198639.

Rutherford, T., Buschkuehl, M., Jaeggi, S. M., & Farkas, G. (2018). Links between achievement, executive functions, and self-regulated learning. *Applied Cognitive Psychology, 32*(6), 763–774. https://doi.org/10.1002/acp.3462

Selmeczy, D., Ghetti, S., Zheng, L. R., Porter, T., & Trzesniewski, K. (2021). Help me understand: Adaptive information-seeking predicts academic achievement in school-aged children. *Cognitive Development, 59*, 101062. https://doi.org/10.1016/j.cogdev.2021.101062

Skinner, E. A., & Pitzer, J. R. (2012). Developmental dynamics of student engagement, coping, and everyday resilience. In S. L. Christenson et al. (Eds.), *Handbook of research on student engagement* (pp. 21–44). Springer. https://doi.org/10.1007/978-1-4614-2018-7_2

Sparks, R. L., & Lovett, B. J. (2009). College students with learning disability diagnoses: Who are they and how do they perform? *Journal of Learning Disabilities, 42*(6), 494–510. https://doi.org/10.1177/0022219409338746

Swanson, H. L. (1999). What develops in working memory? A life span perspective. *Developmental Psychology, 35*(4), 986–1000. https://doi.org/10.1037/0012-1649.35.4.986

Swanson, H. L. (2000). Are working memory deficits in readers with learning disabilities hard to change? *Journal of Learning Disabilities, 33*(6), 551–566. https://doi.org/10.1177/002221940003300604

Swanson, H. L., & Hsieh, C.-J. (2009). Reading disabilities in adults: A selective meta-analysis of the literature. *Review of Educational Research, 79*(4), 1362–1390. https://doi.org/10.3102/0034654309350931

Tops, W., Callens, M., Van Cauwenberghe, E., Adriaens, S., & Brysbaert, M. (2020). Study strategies of first-year undergraduates with and without dyslexia and the effect of gender. *European Journal of Special Needs Education, 35*(3), 398–413. https://doi.org/10.1080/08856257.2019.1703580

U. S. Government Accountability Office (2024). *GAO analysis of National Postsecondary Student aid Study (NPSAS) data.* (GAO-24-105614).

Wang, L.-C., & Chung, K. K. H. (2024). The influences of cognitive abilities on self-regulated learning in online learning environment among Chinese university students with learning disabilities. *The Internet and Higher Education, 62*, 100947. https://doi.org/10.1016/j.iheduc.2024.100947

Wang, L.-C., Li, X. N., & Chung, K. K. H. (2021). Relationships between test anxiety and metacognition in Chinese young adults with and without specific learning disabilities. *Annals of Dyslexia, 71*(1), 103–126. https://doi.org/10.1007/s11881-021-00218-0

Wang, L.-C., Liu, D., Chen, J.-K., & Wu, Y.-C. (2018). Processing speed of dyslexia: The relationship between temporal processing and rapid naming. *Reading and Writing, 31*(7), 1645–1668. https://doi.org/10.1007/s11145-018-9857-2

Wang, L.-C., & Yang, H.-M. (2015). Diverse inhibition and working memory of word recognition for dyslexic and typically developing children. *Dyslexia, 21*(2), 162–176. https://doi.org/10.1002/dys.1490

Zewdie, K., & Fenta, A. (2022). Self-esteem, self-efficacy and academic achievement of students' with disabilities in selected universities of Ethiopia. *SN Social Sciences, 2*(9), 189. https://doi.org/10.1007/s43545-022-00500-x

Zimmerman, B. J. (2002). Becoming a self-regulated learner: An overview. *Theory Into Practice, 41*(2), 64–70. https://doi.org/10.1207/s15430421tip4102_2

Zimmerman, B. J. (2008). Investigating self-regulation and motivation: Historical background, methodological developments, and future prospects. *American Educational Research Journal, 45*(1), 166–183. https://doi.org/10.3102/0002831207312909

Chapter 7
Promoting Self-Regulation Learning in Informal Digital English Learning: Insights on Dual-Focus Engagements from Perceptions and Emotions

Lihang Guan and Mingyue Michelle Gu

Abstract Informal digital learning of English (IDLE) is the self-regulated, self-directed digital learning of English independent of formal contexts, in which the dual-focus engagement (DFE) of the semantic content and linguistic input significantly predicts learning outcomes. We lack an understanding, however, of the factors that elicit this dual focus. From the perspective of self-regulation learning in technological learning environments, we identified the potential effects of technological perceptions and learning affections and employed the Technology Acceptance Model and the Attitude and Motivation Test Battery to assess the influence of personal perceptions and affections on DFE among 155 Chinese university students. We conducted path analysis, finding that: (1) both personal perceptions and affections were significantly correlated with DFE, but (2) only variables of attitude toward usages and active learning strategies in these factors contributed significantly to this relationship. This study develops theoretical understandings of quality self-regulated learning engagement and guides the practical application of IDLE for English acquisition. We also reasoned across frameworks of self-regulated learning behaviors and engagements to suggest the complexity of self-regulated learner engagements with digital technologies and the indirect effects of personal variables in the negotiation among the learner, others, and environments that drive DFE in self-regulated IDLE.

Keywords Self-regulated learning · Informal digital learning of English · Idle quality · Technology acceptance model · Attitude and motivation test battery · Dual-focus engagement

---

L. Guan
School of Foreign Languages, Ludong University, Yantai, Shandong, China
e-mail: s1136696@s.eduhk.hk

M. M. Gu (✉)
Department of English Language Education, The Education University of Hong Kong, Tai Po, Hong Kong
e-mail: mygu@eduhk.hk

A. Peña-Ayala (ed.), *Self-Regulated Learning*, Cognitive Technologies,
https://doi.org/10.1007/978-981-92-0658-2_7

Abbreviations

AEL	Attitudes toward English learning
ALS	Active learning strategies
AU	Attitude toward using
CET-4	College English Test-4
CET-6	College English Test-6
DFE	Dual-focus engagement
EFL	English as a foreign language
GDL	Goals and desire to learn
IDLE	Informal digital learning of English
IEL	Interest in the English language
MI	Motivation intensity
PEU	Perceived ease of use
PU	Perceived usefulness
SRL	Self-regulated learning
TAM	Technology acceptance model

7.1 Introduction

Self-regulated learning (SRL) clearly constitutes a major part of students' educational journeys and affects their academic achievements. SRL may be especially important for foreign- or second-language education, with digital technologies, such as the Internet, social media, video streaming, and, most recently, artificial intelligence (AI), being used outside of classrooms. With digital technologies' increasing accessibility to learners of foreign languages, these learners gain individualized input exposure to their target language in rich environments (Zadorozhnyy & Lee, 2025b) and additional multimodality practice opportunities through language socialization (Soyoof et al., 2023), both of which allow for more observation and imitation, both factors that are critical in foreign-language acquisition in contemporary education (Guan et al., 2025).

Specific to English as a foreign language (EFL) contexts, self-regulation in digital learning environments has been argued to be a key moderator in academic achievements (Qi & Derakhshan, 2024). Compared to in-class instructor-led EFL learning experiences, studies have found that self-regulation is closely related to students' participation, engagement, and reflection in autonomous out-of-class digital English learning (Yang et al., 2023), benefitting students' EFL proficiency across learning and pragmatic contexts (Guan et al., 2024).

We must also acknowledge, however, that the instrumentalist view of EFL education that prevails across many countries and cultures (Sun et al., 2025) challenges students' self-regulation in such learning environments. With both teachers and students seeing EFL education as a means to an end (Sun et al., 2025), they are little motivated to engage in the learning process but nonetheless desire the results. In this light, students' "mental effort can be effective or ineffective, depending on whether it was invested in germane or extraneous cognitive processing" (Wang & Lajoie, 2023, p. 69), an argument supported by out-of-class digital EFL learning studies.

Termed as the *informal digital learning of English* (IDLE), *out-of-class digital EFL learning* is defined as students' self-regulated autonomous uses of digital devices and information in EFL contexts (Lee, 2019). Seminal studies, such as those by Lee (2019) and Lai et al. (2025), have long suggested that student engagements in both contextual meaning and linguistic form the dual-focus engagements (DFE) in IDLE activities that are significant predictors of learning outcomes. As argued by many scholars (e.g., Lai et al., 2025; Niu et al., 2022), DFE is a strategic cognitive engagement that promotes language-learning outcomes (e.g., vocabulary, willingness to communicate) among EFL students, as DFE is a significant antecedent of students' deep cognitive processing in self-regulated digital language learning and directs students' attention to both linguistic accuracy and language use in authentic contexts (Zhang & Liu, 2024). More importantly, it is not easy for students to self-achieve DFE. As suggested by the IDLE profile (Lee & Xie, 2023), 89% of EFL students would self-regulate their IDLE activities solely for gaming and entertainment purposes, thus focusing on meaning and language use only. Therefore, given the significance of DFE in self-regulated IDLE activities for EFL students, in this study we examined the significance of potential drivers of DFE.

Most publications investigating IDLE engagement have focused on the psychological factors that motivate students' self-regulated IDLE (e.g., Zadorozhnyy & Lee, 2024; Zhang & Liu, 2024). For example, Zadorozhnyy and Lee (2024) identified language needs, and Liu et al. (2024a) identified the influence of IDLE enjoyment in motivating students to engage in IDLE activities. As the IDLE profile found, however, IDLE engagement is not synonymous with high-quality self-regulated informal digital learning; rather, DFE must be encouraged.

In the IDLE research context, however, studies have mainly focused on the adaptation of technologies in self-regulated learning. For example, Zhang and Liu (2024) found that how users envision what they can do with digital technologies affects their adaptation of such technologies. Moreover, such adaptation is significantly affected by individual differences, such as learner background, language proficiency, and learning needs (Zadorozhnyy & Lee, 2025a; Zhang & Liu, 2025). These studies investigated students' adaptation of self-regulated IDLE practices in general or by type (e.g., receptive or productive). Despite, however, the found significance of DFE (Lai et al., 2025; Lee, 2019; Niu et al., 2022) and the significant lack of DFE in IDLE (Lai et al., 2025; Lee & Xie, 2023), strategies for encouraging DFE have been under-investigated.

Therefore, we summarize that recent studies have increasingly integrated self-regulation theory, technology acceptance, and affective motivation to explain students' digital English learning behaviors. However, little empirical research directly connects these frameworks to the quality dimension of IDLE—particularly dual-focus engagement (DFE). While TAM-based studies (e.g., Dizon, 2024;

Liu & Ma, 2024) successfully predict usage behaviors, and AMTB-based studies (e.g., Han, 2023; He et al., 2024) emphasize affective factors, few have explored how these perceptions and emotions jointly influence strategic engagement such as DFE. The current state of research, therefore, calls for an integrated approach bridging perception, affection, and engagement quality in self-regulated digital English learning.

To address this research gap, we grounded this study in two well established behavioral-prediction frameworks—the technology acceptance model (TAM; Davis, 1989) and the Attitude/Motivation Test Battery (AMTB; Gardner, 2004) —to examine what drives students to engage in DFE in self-directed learning from both the perception and affection perspectives. Theoretically, this study bridges the DFE research gap of self-regulated informal digital language learning, contributing to the scholarly understanding of the effects of student perceptions and affections. Practically, this study guides practitioners in designing self-regulated informal digital language learning to encourage DFE for desired learning outcomes. Furthermore, the chapter contributes by identifying attitudes toward using technology and active learning strategies as critical predictors of high-quality SRL engagement in IDLE, thus enriching theory and practice.

In addition to introducing the study's origin, research gap and research significance in the introduction section, this chapter moves onto literature review, which presents the theoretical foundations of the TAM and the AMTB, together with their relevance to IDLE and DFE in SRL. Following up, the method section describes the research design, participants, data collection procedures, and analytical approaches adopted in this study for other studies' reproduction. After that, the results and discussion section is presented to interpret the key findings, placing and comparing the key findings with current literature, and highlighting the significance of key findings in eliciting DFE. Moreover, the conclusion section summarizes the key findings and the study's contributions, which later extends to recommendations for further studies focusing on longitudinal, cross-context, and intervention-based explorations. At the end, the references section provides details of the cited work.

7.2 Literature Review

As previous studies on SRL have suggested, learner autonomy is at the center of such learning activities, as it is the most important determinant of student engagement behaviors and learning outcomes in SRL (Chang & Sun, 2024). Learner autonomy is also at the core of IDLE (Lee, 2019), the differences being that IDLE conceptualizes the learning contexts beyond SRL into digital technologies and EFL. Therefore, the present study views IDLE as a learning context for SRL that helps focus the investigation into digital and EFL learning environments for DFE.

As EFL digital learning studies have suggested, learner autonomy is closely associated with student perceptions of the digital technologies and student affections toward the target language (Guan et al., 2025). For example, at the heart of all behavioral frameworks of educational technology (e.g., TAM, the unified theory of acceptance and use of technology), student perceptions of ease of use, usefulness, and attitudes are the predictive factors of actual technological uses (Zadorozhnyy et al., 2025). Moreover, from the perspective of social cognitive theory (Bandura, 2012) to the ideal L2 self (Dörnyei, 2010) and AMTB (Gardner, 2004), the motivational theories behind second- and foreign-language acquisition have repeatedly argued for the role of students' language affections in learner autonomy. In this study, we adopted the TAM and AMTB to bridge the effects of perceptions and affections with actual weekly self-regulated IDLE time.

Technology Acceptance Model

Many quantitative questionnaires, such as the TAM (Davis, 1989), the Learning Management System Acceptance Scale (Sezer & Yilmaz, 2019), and the unified theory of acceptance and use of technology model (Venkatesh et al., 2003) have been proposed to correlate with self-regulated behaviors in technology adaptation. Among these scales, the TAM is one of the most accepted measures not only for its reliability in measuring both internal and external influences that negotiate technology uses (Sprenger & Schwaninger, 2021) but also for its quantifications of personal perceptions of technology for learning, which underlines a fundamental path from perception to behavior (Tverskoi et al., 2023).

In the existing literature, TAM's three categories of measuring items, "Perceived Usefulness" (PU), "Perceived Ease of Use" (PEU), and "Attitude Toward Using" (AU), have been repeatedly used to quantify technology-adaptation intentions (e.g., Liu et al., 2024a) as well as predict usage behaviors in quantified time and length (e.g., Lai et al., 2025). For example, Dizon's study (2024) suggests that the PU, PEU, and AU variables all significantly affect the frequency and length of self-regulated uses of chatbots for English learning. Additionally, Chen and Zhao (2022) have suggested that the PU and PEU variables of TAM positively affect the frequency and duration of uses of gamified content for English learning.

The TAM also has a wide adaptation in IDLE research, with many studies suggested its sufficiency in predicting IDLE practices with various digital technologies (e.g., Hoi & Mu, 2021; Liu & Ma, 2024). For example, in artificial intelligence (AI)-mediated IDLE practices, Liu and Ma (2024) found that Chinese EFL students' perceptions of technology and intention toward using the technologies predicted their actual uses in self-regulated autonomous IDLE practices. Moreover, in a large-scale experimental study, Liu et al. (2024a) found that perceptions and intentions were shaped by technological affordances in actual uses and engagement behaviors, negotiating learning through balancing perceptions and technological advantages (and disadvantages) to strategically develop their intention and actual behaviors.

Therefore, we found a possible correlation between personal perceptions (as measured by the TAM factors) and hours spent on IDLE activities in the previous literature. It remains unclear, however, whether TAM variables are correlated with dual-focus learning in self-regulated IDLE—in other words, whether the more a student considers digital technology to be "useful," "easy to use," or "positively desiring for learning," the more the student would spend their digital-learning hours focusing on both meaning and form. Since the IDLE profile suggests that most EFL students would self-initiate IDLE activities for entertainment and gaming purposes (Lee & Xie, 2023), we hypothesized that the perception variables of PU, PEU, and AU would at least partly affect students' participation in IDLE activities, marking at least an initial step of DFE engagements. Moreover, we hypothesized that a student might self-regulate their attention more on linguistic forms rather than contextual meaning when motivated with affections toward the language. In other words, we imagined that the TAM could be a starting point for DFE because it promotes the uses of technology for all types of focuses in self-regulated IDLE practices.

Attitude and Motivation Test Battery

As identified in the previous literature, affective factors play a crucial role in shaping how students engage with IDLE activities (Lee & Drajati, 2019), often focusing more sustained attention on form-focused input and deeper processing of linguistic material (Lai et al., 2025). Evidence of the affective domain's effects on language-learning engagement has been repeatedly documented across diverse contexts. With respect to SRL supported by digital technologies, He et al. (2024) demonstrated that language anxiety and motivation jointly determine the extent of EFL students' engagement in online self-regulated reading practices. Likewise, Han (2023) observed that a reduction in anxiety, accompanied by stimulated motivation, fosters learner autonomy, thereby enabling deeper engagement in online collaborative writing. These findings align with Gardner's AMTB framework, which underscores the centrality of motivation and affect in sustaining language-learning behaviors.

Academic discussions, however, have thus far primarily concentrated on how digital technologies optimize students' affective experiences to increase the quantity of their learning (e.g., Han, 2023; Lai et al., 2025), often neglecting the quality and depth of engagement in digital foreign-language environments. This is a critical gap because affective factors in traditional classroom contexts (e.g., motivation, interest, anxiety) have been shown to influence both engagement styles and the processing of input and output (Yang et al., 2022). Moreover, in SRL contexts, learner engagement is inherently self-directed and requires the regulation of affective states to sustain autonomous interaction with learning resources (Li et al., 2021). Recognizing these theoretical premises, the present study investigates how key EFL-related affective constructs—specifically motivation, interest, and anxiety—shape learners' autonomous engagement with digitalized learning materials. By situating the analysis within the AMTB framework, we aim to uncover the affective mechanisms that underlie self-regulated participation in technology-mediated language learning.

To determine the correlation between affective factors and hours spent on dual-focus learning, motivation and anxiety must be quantified. This study adopts the

AMTB (Gardner, 2004) for its comprehensive coverage of both positive emotions (e.g., motivation) and negative emotions (e.g., anxiety; Dewaele et al., 2023), as well as for its validated reliability in Chinese culture (Su, 2018). Compared to the other quantification scales commonly used in EFL learning (e.g., the ideal L2 self), the AMTB is more robust in capturing the dynamics of foreign-language teaching and learning with more critically examined empirical evidence (McClelland & Larson-Hall, 2025).

Of course, specific to SRL and IDLE, not all factorial variables in the AMTB are suitable. The questionnaire comprises 104 items interpreting 10 latent variables: "interest in the English language," "motivation intensity," "English class anxiety," "English teacher evaluation," "attitudes toward learning English," "active learning strategies," "learning environment," "goals and desire to learn," "English course evaluation," and "ease in using English" (Wongsa & Son, 2022). To suit the research context of self-regulated digital English learning, the AMTB questionnaire was trimmed to just those variables and items that apply to out-of-class autonomous English learning. For this purpose, the modification leaves out 63 question items about English classes, choosing courses, attitudes toward English teachers, peer pressure in classrooms, and output generation, leaving 41 questions measuring five variables: "interest in the English language" (IEL), "motivation intensity" (MI), "attitudes toward English learning" (AEL), "active learning strategies" (ALS), and "goals and desire to learn" (GDL).

Therefore, based on the review of the previous literature, this study proposes the following research hypotheses, which Fig. 7.1 also illustrates.

H1: Factors of personal perception toward technology for learning are significantly correlated with weekly average hours spend on self-regulated dual-focus digital learning.

H2: The affective factors for English learning are significantly correlated with weekly average hours spent on self-regulated dual-focus digital learning.

H3: Each variable among the personal-perception factors is significantly correlated with weekly average hours spent on self-regulated dual-focus digital learning.

H4: Each variable among the affective factors is significantly correlated with weekly average hours spent on self-regulated dual-focus digital learning.

7.3 Method

As detailed in the literature review, this study was bounded in the theoretical frameworks of TAM (Davis, 1989) and AMTB (Gardner, 2004). Therefore, the methodological design allows this study to examine both perceptual and affective influences on DFE, represented by TAM and AMTB respectively. Specifically, the TAM questionnaire included 12 items covering PU, PEU, and AU, representing students' cognitive–perceptual orientations toward technology adaptation. Moreover, the AMTB

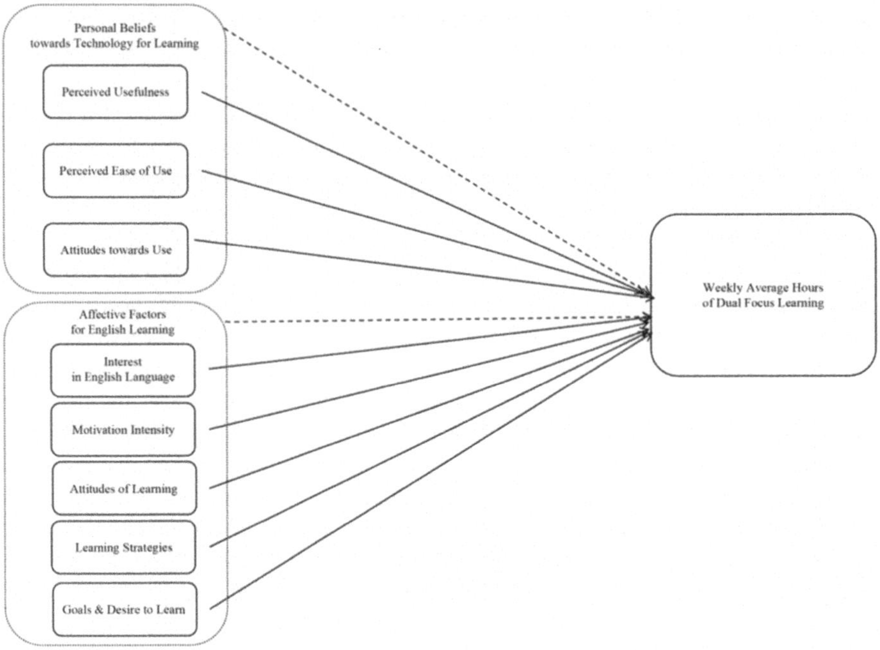

Fig. 7.1 Research hypotheses to be examined

scale, after trimming, contained 41 items from five subscales—IEL, MI, AEL, ALS, and GDL—which together captured learners' affective–motivational influences toward DFE.

Moreover, data collection adopted the digital diary technique with a sequential six-week design. The data collection was grounded with a quantitative logistic integration linked to the theoretical and empirical components of TAM and AMTB through the dependent variable average weekly DFE hours. Participant mean scores in perceptual factors (PU, PEU, AU) and affective factors (IEL, MI, AEL, ALS, GDL) were matched to their diary-based DFE data accordingly. Using R Studio's lavaan package, a pathway structural equation model tested perception–affection relationships predicting DFE. This logistic structure ensures that the operational flow of the study directly reflects both TAM's perception–use pathway and AMTB's attitude–motivation framework within self-regulated informal digital English learning.

Sampling

With the help of university English teachers, 231 students showed initial interest in this incentive-provided research project, among whom 171 participants signed the consent form. Sixteen, however, dropped out during the study, leaving a participation size of 155 (97 females and 58 males). All research participants were bachelor's-degree students from five first-tier universities (一本) with a mean age of 20.69 years (*SD* = 0.88). The sample's composition is considered representative of the Chinese university EFL student population in that participating students came from various cultural regions and were studying various majors (e.g., architecture, biology, English, commerce, and tourism).

Data Collection

To quantify perceptions toward technology and affection for the English language, the TAM and AMTB was adopted to examine the correlations on a four-point Likert scale, with 1 being "least true for me" and 4 being "most true for me." The questionnaires were distributed to participants via Wenjuanxing (问卷星), a popular online distribution system in Chinese academia that the students already knew how to use. Because of the monetary incentives given to students and the requirements for participation quality (i.e., they were to submit true and detailed data or would not get paid), all 155 final participants spent an appropriate amount of time assigning Likert ratings and passed the questionnaires' quality-control tests. Seven of the 171 did not pass the quality-control stage and were asked to leave the study. The questionnaires were given in week 0, before their diary-keeping of their daily IDLE practices, as all of them, as digital natives (Ng, 2012) had participated in IDLE practices before (Lee & Xie, 2023).

To quantify dual-focus learning time, the digital-diary technique was adapted form Lai et al. (2022). This technique involves a journal in which students write in detail for their daily English engagement with digital tools so that the researchers could learn what the students had focused on during their digital learning activities. For example, if a student recorded that s/he paid attention to the meaning of a television show and noticed some vocabulary or grammatical input during the process, then this student was conducting DFE in learning (for an example, see Fig. 7.2). The differences among meaning focus, form focus, and DFE were taught before students began recording their activities as well so that they could record their activities correctly. To enhance research validity, we followed the precise steps in Lai et al.'s (2022) study. We not only checked the entries each night and sent reminders the next morning but also asked those who missed at least one page of their entries (nine of the 171) to leave the study after one opportunity to backfill this missing information. The digital journal lasted six weeks before their College English Tests-4/6 (CET-4/6, two semi-mandatory tests for college students' graduation and application to master's-degree programs in China). Students were asked to count in the minutes they spent on each activity, which were later converted into the average weekly hours of DFE for each participant to avoid data-range mismatch.

The data collection methods not only followed the convention of other DFE studies (e.g., Lai et al., 2022; Reinhardt, 2019) by adapting the digital diary technique for

Vidhub视频库	下午在宿舍	观看《汉尼拔》第一集	45分钟	我在观看的时候，主要还是集中注意力于字幕上。对于我来说，这是一部新的剧，我最开始还是看字幕去了解主要的人物以及他们的人物性格，所以在看的时候主要看着视频和字幕。同时对于一些不认识的单词我也会记录到我的平板上面。同时这也是一部悬疑犯罪类型的美剧，我在观看的时候有些地方可以不看字幕就能了解故事的主要剧情。

VidHub Video Bank	In the afternoon at my dorm	Watching *Hannibal*, season 1, episode 1	45 minutes	Because this is a new show for me, I focused on the subtitles when watching to familiarise myself with the main characters. Meanwhile, I transcribed new vocabulary onto my tablet.

Fig. 7.2 Sample recording of dual-focus engagement with translation

cross-sectional data to state the significance of form focus in IDLE, but also developed on such studies (e.g., Lai et al., 2025; Zadorozhnyy & Lee, 2025a, 2025b) to find the eliciting factors of DFE, providing scholarly understanding and practical insights into promoting students' DFE in self-regulated digital learning of English. Specifically, this study bridges technological acceptance, language learning affect, and DFE behavior, thereby shedding light on the antecedents of quality IDLE. It further consolidates the argument for the significance and feasibility of quality IDLE and DFE in self-regulated autonomous foreign language learning.

Data Analysis

To address the hypotheses in the proposed theoretical model, a pathway structural equation modeling was deemed fit because all the variables were observed (Hair et al., 2018). Some have argued that the preferred sample size for structural equation modeling is at least 200 participants (Sideridis et al., 2014). Since, however, all the variables in this theoretical construct were observed rather than latent, with a participant-to-parameter ratio approaching 14:1, this study provides reliable parameter estimates for hypothesis testing with pathway analysis (Hair et al., 2018). Data were input into Lavaan's structural equation modeling functions in R Studio for pathway analysis.

7.4 Results and Discussion

With quantitative data from questionnaires and digital diaries, we were able to test our hypotheses. Further discussions of the found significance and non-significance were also conducted.

Table 7.1 Path-analysis results of perceptions and affective factors predicting DFE hours

Factor	B	SE(B)	β
Personal perceptions	0.204***	0.050	0.210
Affective factors	0.676***	0.047	0.732
R^2			0.522

* $p < 0.05$; ** $p < 0.01$; *** $p < 0.001$

Personal Perceptions and Affective Factors in Relation to DFE Hours

Using Lavaan's structural equation modeling function in R studio, we first conducted a path analysis, with DFE hours being the dependent variable and the two factors (perceptions and affections) being the independent variables. The results (Table 7.1) indicate that both factors can significantly predict one's weekly average hours of DFE ($F(2, 152) = 185.661, p < 0.001$). The two predictors together can explain 73.2% of the total variance in DFE hours. Moreover, both factors are significant in predicting DFE, with personal perceptions at $b = 0.204$, $t = 4.101$, $p < 0.001$, $\beta = 0.210$, and affective factors at $b = 0.676$, $t = 14.295$, $p < 0.001$, $\beta = 0.732$. Thus, hypotheses 1 and 2 are supported.

Significant and Non-significant Variables in TAM and AMTB Scales

All variables on the two scales, however, contributed to the discovered statistical significance. The Wald test reveals that only one variable in each factor can significantly predict DFE hours in a statistical sense: "attitudes toward using" (AU; $b = 0.260$, $t = 4.510$, $p < 0.001$, $\beta = 0.322$) for perception factors and "active learning strategies" (ALS; $b = 0.548$, $t = 8.914$, $p < 0.001$, $\beta = 0.637$) for affective factors (Table 7.2). After trimming the insignificant variables, AU and ALS can still significantly explain 88.3% of weekly average DFE hours ($\Delta R^2 = -0.004$, F_{change} (2, 152) $= 513.993$, $p < 0.001$). Figure 7.3 shows the hypothesis-testing results.

Attitudes, Learning Strategies, and Their Relationship to DFE

Although there is limited existing research on what drives DFE in IDLE, our findings align with previous studies that have explored the factors influencing the quality of autonomous SRL (e.g., Niu et al., 2022; Wang & Zhang, 2022). In essence, the results of this study support the notion put forth by many scholars (e.g., Liu et al.,

Table 7.2 Wald test results identifying significant predictors of DFE hours from perceptions and affective factors

	Model 1			Model 2		
Variable	B	SE(B)	β	B	SE(B)	β
Perceived usefulness	− 0.027	0.028	− 0.031			
Perceived ease of use	0.006	0.020	0.009			
Attitude toward using	0.265***	0.061	0.328	0.260***	0.058	0.322
Interest in English language	0.057	0.044	0.078			
Motivation intensity	− 0.065	0.045	− 0.084			
Attitudes toward English learning	0.021	0.117	0.025			
Active learning strategies	0.552***	0.133	0.641	0.548***	0.062	0.637
Goals and desire to learn	− 0.031	0.021	− 0.049			
R^2		0.887***			0.883***	
ΔR^2		0.887***			− 0.004***	

* $p < 0.05$; ** $p < 0.01$; *** $p < 0.001$

2021; Wang & Zhang, 2022) that the self-regulated nature of IDLE necessitates an acceptance perception of educational technology and a level of language affection sufficient to negotiate usage behaviors in SRL, which were the two factors measured in this study.

Specifically, this study finds a positive and significant predictive relationship between the independent variable "attitude toward using" and the dependent variable "weekly average DFE hours." Just as the TAM (Davis, 1989) delineated, the PU and PEU variables are predictive of AU, which determines the behavioral intention of usage. Although some studies using the TAM for the predictors of behavioral intention (e.g., Balouchi & Samad, 2021) have found that PU, PEU, and AU can all be correlated with behavioral intention, a significant number have reported that AU directly influences students' intention and behavior in IDLE (as evidenced by larger *b*-value in Mailizar et al., 2021). One Asian study even suggested that attitudinal factors were most crucial in predicting behavioral intention of technology in learning (Hsu & Lin, 2022), which further emphasizes the significance of AU toward educational technology in autonomous digital-assisted language learning.

This study also discovered a significant positive relationship between ALS and DFE. When students are conducting DFE in IDLE, they are active in devoting more engagement and involvement to their cognitive processing, as they need to focus

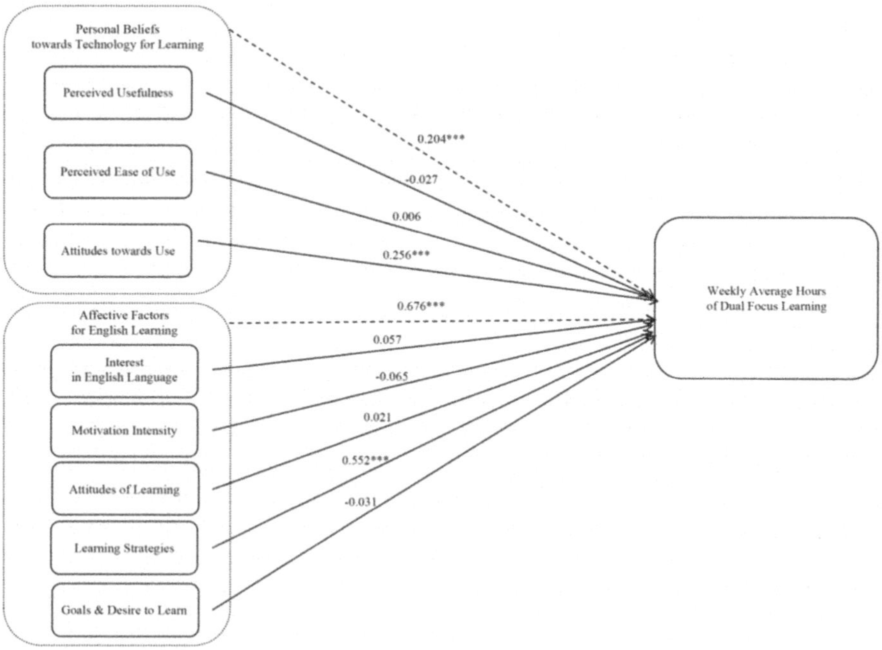

Fig. 7.3 Hypothesis-testing results

on two types of input (Lai et al., 2022; Lee, 2019); this could explain the correlation between ALS and DFE hours. Therefore, we argue that, to prepare Chinese college EFL students for important English tests, self-regulation and autonomy can be extended to IDLE by fostering positive technological attitudes and active learning strategies.

Such fostering may be especially important under the instrumentalist view of EFL education (Sun et al., 2025). Both teachers and students engage in EFL teaching and learning for performance goals (e.g., grades) rather than mastery goals (e.g., actual English proficiency in authentic communications), leading them to "emphasize the instrumental utility or achievement value of academic activities or outcomes" (Xu et al., 2023; p. 4). This instrumentalist view explains why students do not regulate themselves to engage in DFE; as many scholars have pointed out (e.g., Guan et al., 2025; Lee & Xie, 2023), EFL students want to experience fun and enjoyment in SRL without extrinsic regulators (e.g., major upcoming tests). Therefore, fostering language and learning affections in educational-technology uses can be significant in promoting students' language and learning enjoyment (Wang et al., 2024), thus supporting more focus on linguistic forms in everyday IDLE practices.

As digital natives, students may already possess positive technological attitudes, although they still need to be taught with educational perspectives about these uses (Ng, 2012). Moreover, the digital nativity of these young adults also means that they possess various digital technologies that can be used as resources for their self-regulated EFL learning (Wang, 2025). Therefore, from the perception and affection perspectives, fostering EFL students' DFE appears to have an educational solution for which teachers and researchers can and should foster students' strategic uses of digital technologies through the autonomy that this study provides as one possible educational solution. As evidenced by the 155 daily learning diaries collected for this study, students' DFEs were attained through a cognitive reflection of their daily IDLE after being taught about the differences in learning focuses. In other words, Chinese EFL students actively and strategically applied DFE in self-regulated IDLE by understanding the concept of meaning and linguistic focus, leading to DFE, especially when they had major tests upcoming.

The significant correlations found in this study have both theoretical and practical implications. Theoretically, not only have we shown the effectiveness of the TAM (Davis, 1989) and AMTB (Gardner, 2004) in promoting DFE in self-regulated IDLE contexts, thereby contributing to the long ongoing discussion of IDLE quality (Lai et al., 2022, 2025; Lee, 2019) on the eliciting factors of DFE, but we also bridge the gap between knowing the significance of DFE and stimulating DFE practices in Chinese college EFL IDLE contexts with the instrumentalist view of EFL education, thereby advancing scholarly discussion on SRL and engagement quality. This study can thus also guide practitioners practically to promote quality engagements in digital SRL by teaching students the educational use of technological advantages and the affective affordances they create (Jeon, 2024) in self-regulated digital EFL learning, which in turn promote learners' learning engagements and academic achievements (Zou et al., 2025) through promoted learner autonomy in cognitive processing (Namaziandost et al., 2024). To offer a humble suggestion upon which for others to build, practitioners may adopt peer reflection as a metacognitive learning strategy to influence learning attitudes through positive and critical evaluations (Alharbi, 2025) in the EFL learning ecosystem.

Non-significant Variables in Relation to DFE

Other variables (PU, PEU, IEL, MI, AEL, and GDL) were found not to significantly correlate with DFE. These findings seemed contradictory to some IDLE studies' findings (e.g., Balouchi & Samad, 2021; Liu et al., 2024b). For example, Liu et al. (2024b) found that, when EFL students have affections toward the language or its users, they practice IDLE more intensively. By finding insignificant relationships, however, between these variables and IDLE quality (i.e., DFE), we argue that, although they may be directly predictive of self-regulated IDLE quantity (e.g., frequency and duration), affections may not be indirective (versus ineffective) in promoting DFE in SRL. Much like how PU and PEU are considered prerequisites for actual system use in the TAM's perception–attitude–behavior logic (Davis, 1989; Mailizar et al., 2021), IEL, MI, AEL, and GDL could also be viewed as independent variables for ALS.

The argument among affection variables, such as IEL, MI, AEL, and GDL, is also supported by the existing literature. As other publications have suggested, an individual's adoption of ALS is correlated with their learning interests (Guan et al., 2024), motivation (Chang et al., 2022), and learning goals and desires (Rezai et al., 2025). Moreover, in Jiang et al.'s (2024) model, actual deep learning engagements with favoritist cognitive processing in online SRL were found to be the mediated results of one's intrinsic motivation (e.g., affections) and learning environment (e.g., upcoming major tests) with "the processes and strategies that facilitate or hinder deep learning" (p. 3104) detailing the directive effects of learning strategies in predicting actual engagements initiated with the negotiation of personal and environmental factors.

Furthermore, we consider that the insignificant correlational findings can yield more implications for theories and practice than the significant ones. Much like the logic used after the call for the immediate cessation of the use of the L2 ideal self for affection-based motivation in education (McClelland & Larson-Hall, 2025), personal perceptions and affections are purely personal factors that neglect the social, interactional dynamics among stakeholders in education and between learning contexts. Correlating this logic to other motivation–behavior frameworks like Jiang et al.'s environment–person–mediation–behavior model (2024), we call for more holistic theoretical proposals of students' SRL behaviors not only within personal factors (e.g., perception and affection) but also across learning contexts (e.g., formal and informal) and strategic learning abilities (e.g., meta-cognitive reflections). Only in this way can we bridge learning contexts through strategic teaching and learning, thus bridging instructor-led and student self-regulated EFL learning together and holistically. For practitioners, this study suggests that the holistic EFL learning in all contexts could be achieved through a reflection diary between instructors (in this case, the researcher) and learners so that the practitioners can better consider learners' informal SRL in English acquisition and design suitable formal EFL teachings accordingly. Just as suggested by Peña-Ayala (2021), twenty-first-century education should be holistically supported by human, physical, and digital resources across all teaching and learning contexts to boost the twenty-first-century skills that students need to succeed in education, career, and life (e.g., learning, motivation, media, and technology; Trilling & Fadel, 2009).

Therefore, we consider the promotion of DFE to be a complex construction that requires not only considerations of perception and affection variables but also how these variables interact with each other and with environmental factors to shape the final engagements. As suggested by Guan et al. (2025), students who find technology useful and easy to use drop their use of it very quickly after changes in learning spaces and environments. Therefore, we suggest that the drivers shaping IDLE DFE could be considered together as a social practice negotiated among oneself, others, and one's environment, with self-regulation and autonomy at the core of engagement decisions changing through time and space. With such negotiations, the entertainment-oriented IDLE practices in SRL could be promoted to be more learning-oriented, with more DFE that helps EFL students obtain the English performance they desire (Galvin & Greenhow, 2019; Teng et al., 2022).

Contrasting Findings Between Studies

Although not much studies have focused on what elicits DFE, we do acknowledge that one study by Lai et al. (2025) dabbled on how student intentions impacts their uses of digital technologies. Similar to this study, Lai et al., (2025) found very little eliciting factors in student intentions that predict DFE, with only the socialization purpose being significant. However, different from Lai et al.'s study (2025), which found instructional intentions not significant to provoke DFE, this chapter reveals that students' active learning strategies in self-regulation learning is a significant predictor. Considering that samples from both studies are all Chinese Mainland university students, we deliberate that the differences lies within the environment-led extrinsic motivation. In this study, students face imminent CET-4/6 tests, which are mandatory for graduation and further education purposes. However, in Lai et al.'s study (2025), 95% of the sampled students had passed CET-4 and 33% had passed CET-6, marking a major difference in students' test demands. Considering the IDLE profile by Lee and Xie (2023) which found the majority of students do not engage in IDLE for learning purposes, we deliberate that college students' authentic DFE engagement in self-regulation learning is contingent to environmental factors such as coming tests, for most EFL learners hold instrumentalism views (Sun et al., 2025). This contrast of sample and findings is detailed in Table 7.3.

Table 7.3 Comparison of samples and findings of IDLE engagements

	Sample	Environmental factor	Significant predictors	Non-significant predictors
This study	Chinese Mainland university students	With CET-4/6 tests coming	Attitude toward use Learning strategies	Perceived ease of use Perceived usefulness Interest in the English language Motivation intensity Attitudes toward English learning Active learning strategies; Goals and desire to learn
Lai et al., 2025	Chinese Mainland university students	With no major test coming	Socialization purpose	Instructional purpose Informational purpose Entertainment purpose

7.5 Conclusion and Recommendations for Further Studies

This study set out to investigate the predictors of DFE in self-regulated learning (SRL) within an informal digital learning of English (IDLE) context. Drawing on questionnaires adapted from the TAM (Davis, 1989) and the Attitude/Motivation Test Battery (AMTB; Gardner, 2004), together with a digital-diary technique (Lai et al., 2022), quantitative data were collected from Chinese EFL college students about their personal perceptions, affective orientations, and weekly IDLE engagement hours. Pathway analysis revealed that both perception and affective factors significantly predicted self-regulated DFE, although not all variables within these constructs contributed meaningfully. The findings highlight the mediating significance of attitudes and learning strategies, suggesting that the indirect effects of perceptions and affective factors may be more influential than direct paths alone.

Despite its contributions to the field, the study is not without limitations. First, to secure detailed diary data across 48 consecutive days, the research was scheduled in the six weeks preceding major examinations. This context likely gave students extrinsic motivation to engage more meaningfully with self-regulated IDLE. The existing research shows that such exam-related engagement often diminishes once exams conclude (Guan et al., 2025), yet little is known about how extrinsic motivation is negotiated into or out of everyday DFE behaviors throughout an entire semester. Future studies should, therefore, adopt longitudinal designs to map the rise and fall of DFE behaviors across academic cycles, clarifying how extrinsic and intrinsic motivational factors interact over time.

Second, the social negotiation of DFE within IDLE remains insufficiently studied. While the literature suggests that motivation, interest, and anxiety influence students' individual behaviors, little empirical, practice-based evidence explores how peer collaboration, online communities, or teacher interventions shape DFE in digital contexts (Guan et al., 2024). Examining these social dimensions could offer valuable insights for enhancing learner autonomy and promoting reflective, strategy-based engagement in IDLE.

Third, although participants were drawn from multiple universities and majors across China, they were limited to first-tier undergraduate students. This restricts the generalizability of the results to other age groups and educational levels. Replicating the study in different EFL populations—including K–12 learners, vocational students, and postgraduates—and in diverse cultural contexts would enable stronger validation of the mediating roles of attitudes and learning strategies (AU and ALS).

Finally, methodological extensions are also warranted. Mixing quantitative analyses with qualitative approaches, such as interviews, think-aloud protocols, or digital ethnography, could illuminate the nuanced ways that perceptions and affective factors shape DFE. Moreover, technology-specific investigations (e.g., mobile applications versus adaptive platforms) and intervention-based studies (e.g., reflective journals, scaffolding for motivation regulation, or peer-support systems) could clarify not only how DFE is predicted but also how it may be systematically cultivated.

In sum, this research demonstrates that both perceptual and affective factors play important, if different, roles in shaping digital engagement for EFL learning. Subsequent studies are encouraged to adopt longitudinal, cross-cultural, methodological, and intervention-focused perspectives to advance a more comprehensive understanding of DFE within students' self-regulated digital learning.

Acknowledgements The authors received no funding and declare no competing interests.

References

Alharbi, A. S. (2025). Hidden dialogues: The power of informal peer feedback in EFL online reflective blogging. *Education and Information Technologies, 30*, 20821–20850. https://doi.org/10.1007/s10639-025-13593-7

Balouchi, S., & Samad, A. A. (2021). No more excuses, learn English for free: Factors affecting L2 learners intention to use online technology for informal English learning. *Education and Information Technologies, 26*(1), 1111–1132. https://doi.org/10.1007/s10639-020-10307-z

Bandura, A. (2012). Going global with social cognitive theory: From prospect to paydirt. In S. I. Donaldson, D. E. Berger, & K. Pezdek (Eds.) *Applied psychology* (pp. 53–79). Psychology Press.

Chang, J. C., Wu, Y. T., & Ye, J. N. (2022). A study of graduate students' achievement motivation, active learning, and active confidence based on relevant research. *Frontiers in Psychology, 13*, 915770. https://doi.org/10.3389/fpsyg.2022.915770/full

Chang, W. L., & Sun, J. C. Y. (2024). Evaluating AI's impact on self-regulated language learning: A systematic review. *System, 126*, 103484. https://doi.org/10.1016/j.system.2024.103484

Chen, Y., & Zhao, S. (2022). Understanding Chinese EFL learners' acceptance of gamified vocabulary learning apps: An integration of self-determination theory and technology acceptance model. *Sustainability, 14*(18), 11288. https://www.mdpi.com/2071-1050/14/18/11288

Davis, F. D. (1989). Perceived usefulness, perceived ease of use, and user acceptance of information technology. *MIS Quarterly, 13*(3), 319–340. https://doi.org/10.2307/249008

Dewaele, J. M., Saito, K., & Halimi, F. (2023). How foreign language enjoyment acts as a buoy for sagging motivation: A longitudinal investigation. *Applied Linguistics, 44*(1), 22–45. https://doi.org/10.1093/applin/amac033

Dizon, G. (2024). ChatGPT as a tool for self-directed foreign language learning. *Innovation in Language Learning and Teaching*, 1–17.https://doi.org/10.1080/17501229.2024.2413406

Dörnyei, Z. (2010). Researching motivation: From integrativeness to the ideal L2 self. In S. Hunston & D. Oakey (Eds.), *Introducing applied linguistics: Concepts and skills* (pp. 74–83). Routledge.

Galvin, S., & Greenhow, C. (2019). Educational networking: A novel discipline for improved K-12 learning based on social networks. In A. Peña-Ayala (Ed.), *Educational networking: A novel discipline for improved learning based on social networks* (pp. 3–41). Springer International Publishing.

Gardner, R. C. (2004). *Attitude/motivation test battery: International AMTB research project* (pp. 1–12). The University of Western Ontario.

Guan, L., Li, S., & Gu, M. M. (2024). AI in informal digital English learning: A meta-analysis of its effectiveness on proficiency, motivation, and self-regulation. *Computers and Education: Artificial Intelligence, 7*, 100323. https://doi.org/10.1016/j.caeai.2024.100323

Guan, L., Zhang, E. Y., & Gu, M. M. (2025). Examining generative AI–mediated informal digital learning of English practices with social cognitive theory: A mixed-methods study. *ReCALL, 37*(3), 315–331. https://doi.org/10.1017/S0958344024000259

Hair, J. F., Black, W. C., Babin, B. J., & Anderson, R. E. (2018). *Multivariate data analysis* (8th ed.). Cengage Learning.

Han, S. (2023). The contribution of blog-based writing instruction to enhancing writing performance and writing motivation of Chinese EFL learners. *Frontiers in Psychology, 13*, 1069585. https://doi.org/10.3389/fpsyg.2022.1069585

He, J., Wang, H., Xia, J., & He, X. (2024). An ecological perspective on learner agency: The case of Chinese tertiary-level EFL students in peer reviews. *System, 121*, 103222. https://doi.org/10.1016/j.system.2024.103222

Hoi, V. N., & Mu, G. M. (2021). Perceived teacher support and students' acceptance of mobile-assisted language learning: Evidence from Vietnamese higher education context. *British Journal of Educational Technology, 52*(2), 879–898. https://doi.org/10.1111/bjet.13044

Hsu, H. T., & Lin, C. C. (2022). Extending the technology acceptance model of college learners' mobile-assisted language learning by incorporating psychological constructs. *British Journal of Educational Technology, 53*(2), 286–306. https://doi.org/10.1111/bjet.13165

Jeon, J. (2024). Exploring AI chatbot affordances in the EFL classroom: Young learners' experiences and perspectives. *Computer Assisted Language Learning, 37*(1–2), 1–26. https://doi.org/10.1080/09588221.2021.2021241

Jiang, L., Lv, M., Cheng, M., Chen, X., & Peng, C. (2024). Factors affecting deep learning of EFL students in higher vocational colleges under small private online courses-based settings: A grounded theory approach. *Journal of Computer Assisted Learning, 40*(6), 3098–3110. https://doi.org/10.1111/jcal.13060

Lai, C., Liu, Y., Hu, J., Benson, P., & Lyu, B. (2022). Association between the characteristics of out-of-class technology-mediated language experience and L2 vocabulary knowledge. *Language Learning & Technology, 26*(1). 1–24. https://hdl.handle.net/10125/73485

Lai, C., Liu, Y., & Lin, Y. (2025). Purpose and strategic engagement in informal English digital activities and aspects of vocabulary knowledge. *Applied Linguistics, 46*(1), 128–145. https://doi.org/10.1093/applin/amad075

Lee, J. S. (2019). Informal digital learning of English and second language vocabulary outcomes: Can quantity conquer quality? *British Journal of Educational Technology, 50*(2), 767–778. https://doi.org/10.1111/bjet.12599

Lee, J. S., & Drajati, N. A. (2019). Affective variables and informal digital learning of English: Keys to willingness to communicate in a second language. *Australasian Journal of Educational Technology, 35*(5), 168–182. https://doi.org/10.14742/ajet.5177

Lee, J. S., & Xie, Q. (2023). Profiling the affective characteristics of EFL learners' digital informal learning: A person-centered approach. *Innovation in Language Learning and Teaching, 17*(3), 552–566. https://doi.org/10.1080/17501229.2022.2085713

Li, H., Majumdar, R., Chen, M. R. A., & Ogata, H. (2021). Goal-oriented active learning (GOAL) system to promote reading engagement, self-directed learning behavior, and motivation in extensive reading. *Computers & Education, 171*, 104239. https://doi.org/10.1016/j.compedu.2021.104239

Liu, G., & Ma, C. (2024). Measuring EFL learners' use of ChatGPT in informal digital learning of English based on the technology acceptance model. *Innovation in Language Learning and Teaching, 18*(2), 125–138. https://doi.org/10.1080/17501229.2023.2240316

Liu, G., Zhang, Y., & Zhang, R. (2024a). Bridging imagination and informal digital learning of English: A mixed-method investigation. *Journal of Multilingual and Multicultural Development, 45*(10), 4533–4553. https://doi.org/10.1080/01434632.2023.2173214

Liu, G. L., Darvin, R., & Ma, C. (2024b). Unpacking the role of motivation and enjoyment in AI-mediated informal digital learning of English (AI-IDLE): A mixed-method investigation in the Chinese context. *Computers in Human Behavior, 160*, 108362. https://doi.org/10.1016/j.chb.2024.108362

Liu, Y. C., Wang, W. T., & Lee, T. L. (2021). An integrated view of information feedback, game quality, and autonomous motivation for evaluating game-based learning effectiveness. *Journal of Educational Computing Research, 59*(1), 3–40. https://doi.org/10.1177/0735633120952044

Mailizar, M., Burg, D., & Maulina, S. (2021). Examining university students' behavioural intention to use e-learning during the COVID-19 pandemic: An extended TAM model. *Education and Information Technologies, 26*(6), 7057–7077. https://doi.org/10.1007/s10639-021-10557-5

McClelland, N., & Larson-Hall, J. (2025). Why you should stop using the ideal L2 self and the L2 motivational self-system to measure motivation (Reaction to Al-Hoorie, Hiver & In'nami, 2024). *Studies in Second Language Acquisition*, 1–12.https://doi.org/10.1017/S0272263124000779

Namaziandost, E., Çakmak, F., Heydarnejad, T., & Rezai, A. (2024). The predictive effects of learner autonomy and academic engagement on willingness to communicate, foreign language learning self-esteem, and L2 grit in an EFL context. *Acta Psychologica, 250*, 104528. https://doi.org/10.1016/j.actpsy.2024.104528

Ng, W. (2012). Can we teach digital natives digital literacy? *Computers & Education, 59*(3), 1065–1078. https://doi.org/10.1016/j.compedu.2012.04.016

Niu, L., Wang, X., Wallace, M. P., Pang, H., & Xu, Y. (2022). Digital learning of English as a foreign language among university students: How are approaches to learning linked to digital competence and technostress? *Journal of Computer Assisted Learning, 38*(5), 1332–1346. https://doi.org/10.1111/jcal.12679

Peña-Ayala, A. (2021). A learning design cooperative framework to instill 21st century education. *Telematics and Informatics, 62*, 101632. https://doi.org/10.1016/j.tele.2021.101632

Qi, S., & Derakhshan, A. (2024). Technology-based collaborative learning: EFL learners' social regulation and modifications in their academic emotions and academic performance. *Education and Information Technologies, 30*, 1–26. https://doi.org/10.1007/s10639-024-13167-z

Reinhardt, J. (2019). Social media in second and foreign language teaching and learning: Blogs, wikis, and social networking. *Language Teaching, 52*(1), 1–39. https://doi.org/10.1017/S0261444818000356

Rezai, A., Ahmadi, R., Ashkani, P., & Hosseini, G. H. (2025). Implementing active learning approach to promote motivation, reduce anxiety, and shape positive attitudes: A case study of EFL learners. *Acta Psychologica, 253*, 104704. https://doi.org/10.1016/j.actpsy.2025.104704

Sezer, B., & Yilmaz, R. (2019). Learning management system acceptance scale (LMSAS): A validity and reliability study. *Australasian Journal of Educational Technology, 35*(3). https://doi.org/10.14742/ajet.3959

Sideridis, G., Simos, P., Papanicolaou, A., & Fletcher, J. (2014). Using structural equation modeling to assess functional connectivity in the brain: Power and sample size considerations. *Educational and Psychological Measurement, 74*(5), 733–758. https://doi.org/10.1177/001316441452539

Soyoof, A., Reynolds, B. L., Vazquez-Calvo, B., & McLay, K. (2023). Informal digital learning of English (IDLE): A scoping review of what has been done and a look towards what is to come. *Computer Assisted Language Learning, 36*(4), 608–640. https://doi.org/10.1080/09588221.2021.1936562

Sprenger, D. A., & Schwaninger, A. (2021). Technology acceptance of four digital learning technologies (classroom response system, classroom chat, e-lectures, and mobile virtual reality) after three months' usage. *International Journal of Educational Technology in Higher Education, 18*(1), 8. https://doi.org/10.1186/s41239-021-00243-4

Su, Y. C. (2018). Assessing Taiwanese college students' intercultural sensitivity, EFL interests, attitudes toward native English speakers, ethnocentrism, and their interrelation. *The Asia-Pacific Education Researcher, 27*(3), 217–226. https://doi.org/10.1007/s40299-018-0380-7

Sun, Y., Chen, Z., & Li, L. (2025). Teaching creative thinking in the ELT context: Beliefs and practices. *SAGE Open, 15*(1), 21582440251315236. https://doi.org/10.1177/21582440251315235

Teng, M. F., Wang, C., & Zhang, L. J. (2022). Assessing self-regulatory writing strategies and their predictive effects on young EFL learners' writing performance. *Assessing Writing, 51*, 100573. https://doi.org/10.1016/j.asw.2021.100573

Trilling, B., & Fadel, C. (2009). *21st century skills: Learning for life in our times*. John Wiley & Sons.

Tverskoi, D., Guido, A., Andrighetto, G., Sánchez, Á., & Gavrilets, S. (2023). Disentangling material, social, and cognitive determinants of human behavior and beliefs. *Humanities and Social Sciences Communications, 10*(1), 236. https://doi.org/10.1057/s41599-023-01745-4

Venkatesh, V., Morris, M. G., Davis, G. B., & Davis, F. D. (2003). User acceptance of information technology: Toward a unified view. *MIS Quarterly, 27*(3), 425–478. https://doi.org/10.2307/30036540

Wang, T., & Lajoie, S. P. (2023). How does cognitive load interact with self-regulated learning? A dynamic and integrative model. *Educational Psychology Review, 35*(3), 69. https://doi.org/10.1007/s10648-023-09794-6

Wang, Y. (2025). Exploring self-regulated learning within online informal language learning: a case study. *Computer Assisted Language Learning*, 1–37.https://doi.org/10.1080/09588221.2025.2497506

Wang, X., Pang, H., Wallace, M. P., Wang, Q., & Chen, W. (2024). Learners' perceived AI presences in AI-supported language learning: A study of AI as a humanized agent from community of inquiry. *Computer Assisted Language Learning, 37*(4), 814–840. https://doi.org/10.1080/09588221.2022.2056203

Wang, X., & Zhang, W. (2022). Improvement of students' autonomous learning behavior by optimizing foreign language blended learning mode. *SAGE Open, 12*(1), 21582440211071108. https://doi.org/10.1177/21582440211071108

Wongsa, M., & Son, J. B. (2022). Enhancing Thai secondary school students' English speaking skills, attitudes and motivation with drama-based activities and Facebook. *Innovation in Language Learning and Teaching, 16*(1), 41–52. https://doi.org/10.1080/17501229.2020.1853134

Xu, J., Yang, J., & He, D. (2023). Control-value appraisals, academic emotions, and student engagement: A case of Chinese EFL undergraduates. *Language Teaching Research*, 13621688231215276. https://doi.org/10.1177/13621688231215276

Yang, S., Xu, W., Liu, R., & Yu, Z. (2023). Influencing and moderating variables in informal digital learning of English through a structural equation model. *Computer Assisted Language Learning*, 1–36.https://doi.org/10.1080/09588221.2023.2280645

Yang, Y. F., Hsieh, W. M., Wong, W. K., Hong, Y. C., & Lai, S. C. (2022). Reducing students' foreign language anxiety to improve English vocabulary learning in an online simulation game. *Computer Assisted Language Learning, 37*(3), 410–432. https://doi.org/10.1080/09588221.2022.2039203

Zadorozhnyy, A., & Lee, J. S. (2024). Linking EFL students' psychological needs to engagement in informal digital learning of English: A structural equation modeling analysis. *Computer Assisted Language Learning*, 1–25.https://doi.org/10.1080/09588221.2024.2387269

Zadorozhnyy, A., & Lee, J. S. (2025a). Comparing classroom and digital settings: The role of basic psychological needs on EFL students' IDLE engagement. *ReCALL, 37*(3), 403–420. https://doi.org/10.1017/S0958344025000059

Zadorozhnyy, A., & Lee, J. S. (2025b). Informal digital learning of English and willingness to communicate in a second language: Self-efficacy beliefs as a mediator. *Computer Assisted Language Learning, 38*(4), 669–689. https://doi.org/10.1080/09588221.2023.2215279

Zadorozhnyy, A., Winsy, L. W. Y., & Lee, J. S. (2025). EFL teachers' ecological barriers to integrating informal digital learning of English. *TESOL Quarterly*.https://doi.org/10.1002/tesq.3400

Zhang, Y., & Liu, G. (2024). Revisiting informal digital learning of English (IDLE): A structural equation modeling approach in a university EFL context. *Computer Assisted Language Learning, 37*(7), 1904–1936. https://doi.org/10.1080/09588221.2022.2134424

Zhang, Y., & Liu, G. L. (2025). Examining the impacts of learner backgrounds, proficiency level, and the use of digital devices on informal digital learning of English: An explanatory mixed-method study. *Computer Assisted Language Learning, 38*(5–6), 1113–1140. https://doi.org/10.1080/09588221.2023.2267627

Zou, M., Azari Noughabi, M., Sabouri, M., & Zhou, L. (2025). The contribution of informal digital learning of English (IDLE) to achievement emotions and willingness to communicate: a cross-cultural investigation. *Journal of Multilingual and Multicultural Development*, 1–19.https://doi.org/10.1080/01434632.2025.2490076

Chapter 8
Self-Regulated Learning Strategies in EFL Students' Collaborative Academic Writing

Candradewi Wahyu Anggraeni

Abstract Composing English academic writing in a Higher Education (HE) English as a Foreign Language (EFL) context can be a student's writing challenge. One solution to address this challenge is to utilize Self-Regulated learning (SRL) strategies. Many studies focus on uncovering SRL in students' independent writing, while a few studies examine SRL in students' collaborative writing. To fill the lacuna, this study aims to explore SRL strategies in students' collaborative academic writing in the EFL context. Informed by a qualitative case study, data were obtained through semi-structured interviews and learning artifacts. The data were analyzed using thematic analysis. The findings showed that students optimized forethought, performance, and self-reflection phases of SRL strategies in their collaborative writing, and students identified the challenges and potential solutions. The challenges include poor group coordination (in terms of time and tasks), unequal participation due to varying motivation levels, over-reliance on artificial intelligence (AI) tools, and interpersonal conflicts within the group dynamic. The suggested solutions, such as structuring project management, fostering positive interdependence, promoting AI use, and building resilient teams, provide practical pathways for educators and researchers to improve collaborative writing outcomes. This study contributes to the pedagogical implementation of SRL strategies in collaborative academic writing.

Keywords Academic writing · Activity system · Collaborative writing · English as foreign language students · Self- regulated learning strategies

Abbreviations

AI	Artificial Intelligence
EFL	English as a Foreign Language

C. W. Anggraeni (✉)
English Education Department, Universitas Tidar, Magelang, Indonesia
e-mail: candradewi@untidar.ac.id

A. Peña-Ayala (ed.), *Self-Regulated Learning*, Cognitive Technologies,
https://doi.org/10.1007/978-981-92-0658-2_8

HE Higher Education
RQ Research Question
SRL Self-Regulated Learning

8.1 Introduction

In an English as Foreign Language context, crafting English academic writing can create hurdles for many EFL students because they must follow rigid writing convention, experience detail writing processes, and produce well-structured academic writing. Highlighting these solutions can inspire educators and students to believe that overcoming these challenges is achievable. Prior studies on academic writing challenges exposed that students faced the writing problems, including idea development, structure, grammar, vocabulary (Asnas & Hidayanti, 2024), plagiarism and originality (Toprak & Yücel, 2020), the writing process and linguistic aspects (Bulqiyah et al., 2021). In addressing the issues, SRL strategies and collaborative writing can be a solution to cope with the students' academic writing problems. SRL has been widely studied in an educational context for many years because of its benefits. In writing instructions, SRL contributes to students' writing (Anggraeni et al., 2025; Fitriati et al., 2023; Pionera et al., 2020; Suhandoko & Hsu, 2020; Wijaya, 2021).

Many studies focus on the implementation of SRL in students' individual writing performance (Eslami & Sahragard, 2021; Mahmud & German, 2021; Şeker & Inan Karagül, 2022; Woottipong, 2020; Xu, 2021), and a few studies are concerned with SRL use in a collaborative writing context (Stell & Iwashita, 2024; Qiu & Lee, 2020). To fill this gap, this study aims to investigate the utilization of SRL strategies among Indonesian EFL students during collaborative academic writing in HE. In the Indonesian HE context, the use of collaborative and participatory classrooms is strongly recommended to fulfill the key performance indicator number seven, which emphasizes the importance of collaborative and participatory learning environments. Therefore, the use of collaborative learning is implemented in response to the curriculum's demands. In writing instructions, collaborative writing provides substantial pedagogical benefits. It significantly enhances students' writing performance, refines organizational structure, content development, and lexical choice, and simultaneously strengthens writing skills while alleviating writing anxiety (Aldossary, 2025; Chu, 2025; Pardede, 2024).

Before conducting the study, preliminary research is led to capturing the complex phenomenon of SRL utilization in a collaborative writing context. The preliminary research revealed that students face challenges in collaborative writing due to communication issues among group members, including unequal participation, scheduling conflicts, differing writing styles, and a lack of accountability. Highlighting these issues underscores their importance and encourages the student to consider solutions. Therefore, it is essential to implement structured strategies that can effectively support students in managing collaboration and enhancing their Self-Regulated learning. Addressing these challenges is expected to foster more equitable participation, improve coordination among group members, and ultimately enhance the overall quality of collaborative writing outcomes.

To conquer writing challenges and enhance writing proficiency, an activity system is used as a framework for understanding the multifaceted interaction among domains that profoundly influence EFL students' writing proficiency. Engeström (2015) underscored six domains of activity system, including subject, rules, tools, object, community, and division of labor. This study aims to explore how SRL strategies can support students' collaborative academic writing, fostering a shared purpose and a sense of community. This study is guided by three research questions (RQ) as follows.

1. RQ1: How do EFL students employ SRL strategies in collaborative academic writing?
2. RQ2: What challenges do EFL students encounter when applying SRL strategies in collaborative academic writing?
3. RQ3: What potential strategies can be implemented to address these challenges?

Following the Introduction, this chapter is organized into several sections. The theoretical framework discusses Self-Regulated learning (SRL) strategies, collaborative academic writing, and their integration. The Materials and Methods section outline the instruments and procedures used in the study. The Data Analysis section presents the analysis of interview data, including coding and theme development. The Results section reports and interprets the findings, followed by the Discussion and Conclusion, which highlights their implications. Finally, two appendices are included: the collaborative writing commitment form and the semi-structured interview protocol.

8.2 Theory

This section reviews prior studies related to SRL strategies, collaborative academic writing, and SRL in collaborative academic writing. For each section, it begins with an explanation of a previous study, followed by a highlighting of the research gap addressed in the current study. Each subsection begins by outlining major contributions from previous studies, including SRL strategies, collaborative academic writing, and SRL in collaborative academic writing. By systematically mapping existing knowledge and delineating these gaps, this section positions the current study within the broader academic discourse and clarifies its unique contribution to advancing research in SRL and collaborative academic writing.

Self-Regulated Learning Strategies

In the development of SRL strategies, various SRL models have been proposed by SRL experts, which are crucial for inspiring educators and researchers to explore effective teaching methods. Panadero (2017) summarized six SRL models, including the cyclical phase model by Zimmerman and Moylan (2009), the dual processing self-regulation model by Boekaerts (2011), Winne's SRL model by Winne and Hadwin (1998), Pintrich's SRL model by Pintrich (2000), the metacognitive and affective model of SRL model by Efklides (2011), and the socially shared regulated learning model by Järvelä and Hadwin (2013).

Although many SRL models exist, this study adopted the cyclical phase model by Zimmerman and Moylan (2009) because it best addressed the students' needs, learning objectives, learning outcomes, and classroom ecology. Järvelä and Hadwin's (2013) SRL model was indeed a prominent model for conducting collaborative writing studies. However, this study adopted Zimmerman and Moylan's (2009) model of SRL because the study focused on understanding the individual regulatory processes that students engaged in during a collaborative academic writing task. Zimmerman and Moylan (2009) proposed a cyclical phase model of SRL comprising three pivotal phases: forethought, performance, and self-reflection. Table 8.1 outlines the phases of the SRL model. Table 8.1 presents the SRL model adapted from Zimmerman and Moylan (2009), which consists of three phases: forethought, performance, and self-reflection. These phases encompass key processes related to task analysis, self-control, self-observation, self-judgment, and self-reaction, providing a framework for understanding learners' regulation of learning processes.

Notwithstanding these benefits, the utilization of SRL strategies is not without challenges. Students often struggle with time management, procrastination, conflicting deadlines, and sustaining motivation in implementing SRL strategies throughout the writing process (Anggraeni et al., 2025; Zhang & Zhang, 2025). Furthermore, students' differences influence the implementation and efficacy of SRL strategies (Zhang & Zhang, 2025). In the development of AI, AI-assisted writing tools have reshaped the landscape of SRL strategies in writing. Amani and Bisriyah (2025) found that students used AI tools as beneficial for enhancing vocabulary, grammar, and receiving feedback; however, they experienced an over-reliance on AI that can hinder writing skill development and proficiency. It is noted that the importance of balancing the integration between AI and human feedback, as well as personalized learning experiences, is crucial.

Current literature highlights the benefits of SRL strategies in enhancing writing achievement, learner autonomy, motivation, and self-efficacy (Anggraeni et al., 2025; Sun & Wang, 2020; Teng & Zhang, 2016). Significant findings encompass the benefits and challenges of implementing SRL strategies, the role of individual differences, and the impact of technology on these strategies. However, existing studies have primarily focused on individual writing performance rather than collaborative contexts. To date, a notable gap exists regarding the implementation of SRL strategies within

Table 8.1 SRL model (Adapted from Zimmerman & Moylan, 2009)

Phase	Category	Key processes
Forethought phase	Task analysis	1. Goal setting
		2. Strategic planning
	Self-motivation beliefs	1. Self-efficacy
		2. Outcome expectations
		3. Task interest/value
		4. Goal orientation
Performance phase	Self-control	1. Task strategies
		2. Self-instruction
		3. Imagery
		4. Time management
		5. Environmental structuring
		6. Help-seeking
		7. Interest incentives
		8. Self-consequences
	Self-observation	1. Metacognitive monitoring
		2. Self-recording
Self-reflection phase	Self-judgment	1. Self-evaluation
		2. Causal attribution
	Self-reaction	1. Self-satisfaction/affect
		2. Adaptive/defensive responses

a collaborative EFL academic writing context. Addressing this gap is pivotal for grasping and supporting effective and meaningful collaborative academic writing practices.

Collaborative Academic Writing

Collaborative academic writing is defined as a collective knowledge-building process that refines ideas and composes academic writing. Studies on collaborative writing had been extensively conducted since they provided new opportunities for language learners to learn (Alsahil, 2024). Collaborative writing enhanced students' writing skills and helped them to share ideas and assist one another (Wonglakorn & Deerajviset, 2023). Writing lecturers were required to create a supportive learning atmosphere and offered clear guidelines for collaborative writing in EFL classes to ensure its effective implementation (Pardede, 2024). Collaborative writing had a significant effect on writing fluency (Pham, 2021). Collaborative writing interventions and metacognitive instruction helped students improve their writing accuracy, fluency, and lexical variation (Wang et al., 2025). In short, collaborative academic writing fosters the development of writing skills and encourages meaningful interaction among students in an EFL context.

Recent studies have broadened knowledge on collaborative writing by exploring students' interaction patterns, strategies, motivation, and writing outcomes. Alsahil (2024) underscored that collaborative writing is a multi-layered and dynamic process shaped by the complex interrelation of interaction types and task demands. Similarly, Chen and Chen (2025) found that the assessment had an impact on students' motivation, particularly in terms of their engagement in collaborative writing. Aldossary (2025) further demonstrated that collaborative writing enhanced organization, word choice, and content development, however reinforcement on grammatical accuracy and mechanics was needed. The previously reviewed studies primarily focused on the implementation and benefits of collaborative writing, utilizing various research designs. To fully capture the advantages of collaborative writing, it is necessary to explore the challenges associated with its implementation. To address this gap, the present study examines the challenges encountered in the collaborative academic writing context, aiming to contribute to a more comprehensive understanding of the field.

Self-Regulated Learning in Collaborative Academic Writing

The notion of academic writing involves articulating ideas clearly through logical sequencing, elaboration, well-supported arguments, rigorous reasoning, and cohesive integration (Fang, 2021). Fang (2021) highlighted six academic writing genres, including a reading response, a book review, a literature review, an argumentative essay, an empirical research article, and a grant proposal. In this current study, the explored academic writing genre was an argumentative essay. In composing academic writing, writers need to consider academic writing skills. In the context of academic writing, it is pivotal to master sixteen academic writing skills, such as contextualizing, summarizing, and sourcing, to help students feel capable and valued in their academic development (Fang, 2021). In the context of SRL in collaborative academic writing, Peeters et al. (2023) found that strategies such as planning, monitoring, and reflecting are interrelated with students' cognitive roles, identity, and motivation, thereby fostering a sense of achievement and purpose.

Prior studies on academic writing highlight the importance of understanding the improvement of writing skills through interventions or teaching methods (Adhami & Taghizadeh, 2022; Anggraeni et al., 2025), which can reassure researchers, educators, and students of the field's ongoing development. The exploration of AI-assisted writing tools (Anani et al., 2025; Cheung & Crosthwaite, 2025; Nhi & Phuong, 2025; Oubibi et al., 2025; Ozfidan et al., 2024; Shen & Chen, 2025; Zhang et al., 2025) demonstrates the innovative potential that can inspire confidence in AI's role.

Additionally, examining challenges and strategies (Asnas & Hidayanti, 2024; Prapobratanakul, 2024; Yunus & Bachtiar, 2025) reassures the readers of the field's ongoing efforts to address the complexities of academic writing.

Another previous study on SRL in academic writing underscores that foreign language learners use interconnected SRL strategies to manage writing, boost performance, and support collaborative learning design (Peeters et al., 2020). These previous studies enriched the body of knowledge of academic writing, and they provided novel insights into the field of academic writing. While the prior studies on EFL academic writing, as reviewed previously, provide valuable insights into pedagogical interventions, the affordances of AI tools, and overarching challenges, a critical gap remains concerning the internal regulatory processes through SRL strategies that students employ during collaborative academic writing tasks, which limits understanding of how internal regulation influences collaborative outcomes, highlighting the need for further investigation in this area.

8.3 Material and Methods

This section delineates the uses of research instruments and methodological procedures conducted in the current study. It explicates the use of semi-structured interviews designed to elicit in-depth insights into participants' experiences, perceptions, and SRL practices within collaborative academic writing contexts. Additionally, students' learning artifacts are discovered to capture observable evidence of SRL processes and collaborative knowledge construction. The section further details the overall research design, including participant selection, data collection procedures, and analytic techniques adopted to ensure methodological rigor and trustworthiness. Accordingly, this section is organized into two main subsections: materials, which describe the research instruments and data sources, and methods, which outline the procedural and analytical frameworks guiding the conduct of the study.

Material

To inform readers about how data was gathered and analyzed, this study conducted semi-structured interviews and analyzed students' learning artifacts. In semi-structured interview sessions, five questions explored SRL strategies, challenges, and potential solutions related to collaborative academic writing.

The semi-structured interviews were conducted face-to-face for each group, lasting 15–20 minutes, and recorded using a smartphone. Both questions and responses were in English. Additionally, students' learning artifacts, including essays, photos of collaborative activities, and AI detector results, were observed and analyzed to support the interview responses. Detailed explanations of the data collection techniques are provided in the method section.

Method

Grounded in a qualitative case study within the interpretivist framework, this study explored the application of SRL strategies in EFL students' collaborative academic writing. A case study was chosen because it captured the real-world conditions of applying SRL strategies in a natural collaborative writing environment. This study was conducted in an essay writing class of the English Education Department at a public University in Indonesia, spanning fourteen meetings from September to December 2024. The current study did not disclose the university's name due to research ethics considerations. The students in the essay writing class were 41 students. The students made a group of three to four students to do collaborative academic writing. The total number of collaborative groups was thirteen. The participants in the implementation of SRL studies were the students in those thirteen groups. However, the participants who voluntarily joined the interview session were five out of thirteen groups. Therefore, there were fifteen students in the interview session and the learning artifacts analysis.

In the first stage of conducting this study, participants were asked to sign a written informed consent form, indicating their voluntary agreement to participate. It was pivotal to collect written informed consent due to research ethics. Based on the written informed consent, all participants agreed to participate in the study. The participants' names were pseudonyms. All participants SRL strategies in their collaborative academic writing activities. Thirteen collaborative writing groups composed comparison and contrast, cause and effect, and argumentative essays. Each group consisted of 3 to 4 students. During the fourteen meetings, the students received writing materials and collaborative assignments explained by their lecturer. The activities aimed to recognize students' efforts and progress, fostering a sense of achievement and motivation. In the teaching materials, the lecturer guided the students to be aware of the learning goals for each meeting. In the collaborative assignments, the students engaged in collaborative academic writing. All activities helped students to optimize their SRL strategies, covering forethought, performance, and self-reflection.

Before implementing SRL strategies, the lecturer clearly explained the concept of these strategies, making students feel reassured and motivated to apply them. The session introduced key concepts, including all strategies in forethought, performance, and self-reflection, to help students understand how to manage their own learning during collaborative academic writing tasks. Therefore, they were able to implement effectively in the collaborative academic writing activities.

In the collaborative academic writing activity, all group members wrote and agreed to the collaborative writing commitment form, as it helped students take more responsibility in their group (see Appendix 8.1). The activities used Google Drive for real-time and asynchronous collaboration, demonstrating effective use of digital tools that could inspire confidence in the process. The writing processes were also done by using the classroom Google Drive. They submitted collaborative writing commitments and all assignments to the classroom Google Drive. In their Google Drive folder, the students actively harnessed the power of Google Docs for collaborative academic writing, engaging in real-time collaboration during class and extending their efforts beyond the classroom through asynchronous work.

Synchronous activities, such as live brainstorming and discussions, along with collaborative outlining and role assignment, are designed to foster engagement and a sense of contribution. While asynchronous activities such as commenting, reviewing, editing, and reflection support individual growth, they also highlight the value of each student's input. Recognizing these activities can help the student appreciate the collaborative effort involved in the classroom. In doing synchronous and asynchronous activities, each student used a laptop or smartphone.

Figure 8.1 presents a well-organized Google Drive workspace containing 13 subfolders, labeled Group 1 through Group 13, each representing different student or project groups, with partially redacted names for privacy. The structure suggests a collaborative academic setup, likely used for collecting, reviewing, and managing essay writing assignments across multiple groups in an HE context.

Within this collaborative academic writing in a digital environment, multiple data sources were gathered. The first data collection instrument was a semi-structured

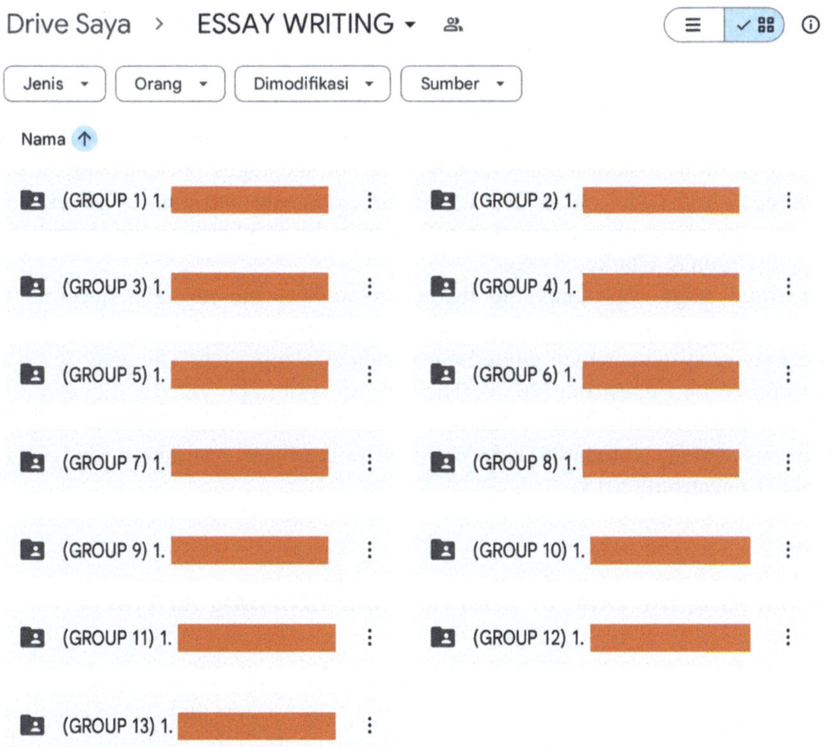

Fig. 8.1 Classroom Google Drive of essay writing class

interview. Five of the thirteen groups were purposively chosen to respond to the interview questions. The groups were selected based on their willingness to participate in interviews. Therefore, the interview involved a total of 15 participants, distributed across five groups: Group 2 (3 participants), Group 5 (3 participants), Group 6 (3 participants), Group 7 (3 participants), and Group 10 (3 participants).

Interview sessions were conducted in groups, yet the students needed to answer the questions individually, highlighting the importance of each participant's responses. Furthermore, the semi-structured interview consisted of five questions in English (see Appendix 8.2). The participants used English in responding to the interview questions. Furthermore, the second data collection instrument was students' learning artifacts. The learning artifacts analysis was used to strengthen the participants' responses in the interview session. The author observed 15 participants' learning artifacts, including students' essays, photos of their collaborative activities, and AI detector results for their essays.

8.4 Dataset Analysis

In this section, the author addresses the research questions by applying thematic analysis to the responses of semi-structured interviews and students' learning artefacts. In analyzing the data, thematic analysis was employed to explain the utilization of SRL strategies, the challenges faced by EFL students in collaborative writing, and potential solutions to address these challenges. The six stages-familiarizing the data, generating initial codes, searching for themes, defining and naming themes, and producing the report were conducted collaboratively, emphasizing the shared effort involved (Braun & Clarke, 2006).

The final stage was analyzing themes to answer the research question and producing the report. Additionally, this study employed the analysis framework of the activity system, which guided our systematic approach. The activity system was proposed by Engeström (2015). The activity system provided a framework for analyzing and understanding human activity, particularly in an educational setting, which consisted of six domains: subject, rules, tools, object, community, and division of labor (Engeström, 2015).

Familiarizing the Data of Interview and Learning Artefacts

During the data familiarization, this study used a data immersion technique through repeated readings of the semi-structured interview transcripts and systematic examination of students' learning artefacts. This process enabled the author to gain a deep understanding of how EFL students engaged in SRL strategies during collaborative academic writing (RQ1), the challenges they encountered in applying these strategies (RQ2), and the strategies proposed or enacted to address the challenges (RQ3).

Generating Initial Codes

After becoming familiar with the interview and learning artefacts dataset, initial codes were generated using thematic coding to identify the data segments related to the research questions. Inductive and deductive coding technique was conducted to categorize codes related to SRL strategies in collaborative academic writing addressed RQ1, codes capturing challenges reflected RQ2, and codes representing students' potential solutions informed RQ3. Coding was implemented across the entire dataset to ensure comprehensive coverage of students' learning experiences.

Each transcript and artefact was examined line-by-line to capture nuanced expressions of strategy use, obstacles, and adaptive responses. Codes were continuously compared, refined, and grouped into preliminary categories to enhance analytical rigor and internal consistency. To enhance trustworthiness, the coding process involved iterative review and constant comparison across data sources. Overlapping or redundant codes were merged, while ambiguous segments were revisited to ensure conceptual clarity. This recursive procedure enabled the development of a well-defined coding scheme that served as the foundation for subsequent theme construction.

Searching for Themes

In this stage, the initial codes were organized into broader thematic patterns by identifying relationships among the codes. Codes related to students' forethought, performance, and self-reflection phases were grouped to address RQ1, while codes reflecting recurring challenges in SRL implementation clustered to address RQ2. Furthermore, codes related how students coped with obstacles in SRL utilization in the collaborative academic writing context were reflected to inform RQ3. This process enabled the themes identification that captured patterns across the dataset.

The development of themes involved an iterative comparison between codes, categories, and the original data extracts to ensure conceptual alignment and analytical depth. Themes were not only formed based on frequency but also on their explanatory power in illuminating students' regulatory processes, constraints, and adaptive responses. During this phase, provisional theme labels were generated and continuously refined to accurately represent the underlying data. To enhance analytical rigor, thematic boundaries were carefully reviewed to minimize. Data excerpts that did not fit within the preliminary thematic structure were re-examined and either reassigned or used to refine theme definitions. This recursive analytical process strengthened the credibility and coherence of the thematic framework prior to advancing to the theme review and definition stage.

Defining Themes

After the potential themes were identified, each theme was refined to ensure clear relevance to the research questions. The theme addressing RQ1 was scrutinized to reflect that they reflected students' SRL practices in collaborative academic writing. The theme related to RQ2 was refined to clearly reflect the sources of students' challenges in implementing SRL strategies in collaborative academic writing. The theme addressing RQ3 was defined to ensure that it portrayed feasible strategies for overcoming the identified pitfalls.

The refinement process involved reviewing the coherence of data extracts within each theme and evaluating the distinctiveness between themes. Theme definitions were revised to ensure conceptual clarity, analytic depth, and non-redundancy. At this stage, detailed theme descriptions were developed, specifying the scope, focus, and interpretive boundaries of each theme in relation to the overall analytic narrative. In addition, thematic naming was carefully calibrated to reflect both the essence of participants' experiences and the theoretical lens underpinning the study. This process required returning to the original dataset to verify that the themes authentically represented participants' voices while remaining analytically meaningful. The finalized themes therefore constituted a coherent thematic structure that directly informed the presentation of findings and discussion.

Naming Themes

In the stage of naming themes, concise names were assigned to each theme to convey their relevance to the research questions. The theme name related to RQ1 highlighted the implementation of SRL strategies in collaborative academic writing. The theme addressing RQ2 emphasized the challenges of the implementation of SRL strategies in collaborative academic writing. The theme addressing RQ3 was named to reflect potential solutions to the challenges of SRL utilization.

The naming process aimed to ensure that each theme encapsulated the central organizing concept underlying the clustered data. Rather than summarizing content, the theme names were constructed to signal analytical interpretation and theoretical alignment with the SRL framework. Care was taken to use a terminology consistent, precise, and reflective of the study's conceptual lens. In addition, theme names were reviewed to maintain parallel structure and conceptual balance across RQ1, RQ2, and RQ3. This consistency enhanced the coherence of the findings section and facilitated a logical progression from strategy implementation to encountered challenges, and finally to adaptive solutions. As a result, the finalized theme names provided a clear roadmap for presenting and interpreting the study's findings.

Producing the Report

The last stage involved producing or presenting the defined themes in systematic ways to answer the research questions. The results were reported by intertwining the interview representative excerpts and evidence from students' learning artefacts to support themes. The analysis is interpreted using the framework of the activity system to explain how the implementation of SRL strategies, associated obstacles, and potential solutions interact within a collaborative academic writing context, therefore providing comprehensive answers to RQ1, RQ2, and RQ3.

The analysis was interpreted through the lens of the activity system framework to elucidate how the implementation of SRL strategies, the obstacles encountered, and the proposed solutions dynamically interacted within the collaborative academic writing context. By situating the findings within this theoretical framework, the study demonstrated how individual regulatory processes were shaped by mediating tools, social interactions, and contextual constraints. This interpretive approach enabled comprehensive and theoretically informed responses to RQ1, RQ2, and RQ3. In presenting the report, careful attention was given to maintaining analytical coherence across themes while preserving participants' authentic voices. Each theme was introduced with a clear analytic narrative, followed by illustrative excerpts and interpretive commentary to clarify its significance. This structured presentation ensured that the findings moved beyond descriptive reporting toward a deeper explanation of patterns and relationships within the dataset.

8.5 Results

This section presents the study's findings on the implementation of SRL strategies in collaborative academic writing. Drawing on the thematic analysis outlined in the previous section, the results illuminate how students enacted regulatory processes across the forethought, performance, and self-reflection phases while engaging in collaborative writing tasks. The analysis also captures the multifaceted challenges students encountered in regulating their learning within group writing dynamics. In addition, the findings highlight students' adaptive responses and proposed solutions for overcoming obstacles in SRL strategy utilization. These insights are derived from the integration of interview data and learning artefacts, enabling a portrayal of students' regulatory experiences. The themes are presented systematically in alignment with the research questions, moving from strategy implementation (RQ1) to experienced challenges (RQ2), and finally to potential coping strategies and solutions (RQ3). Together, these results provide an in-depth understanding of how SRL operates within collaborative academic writing contexts, offering both empirical and pedagogical implications for supporting students' self-regulated learning in HE.

Outcomes

The outcomes of this study summarized the raw data related to the research questions. The first research question related to the utilization of SRL strategies in EFL students' collaborative academic writing. All group members reported using some strategies during the forethought, performance, and self-reflection phases.

Table 8.2 presents the distribution of SRL phases across the collaborative writing groups. As shown, all groups employed forethought strategies, including goal setting and outcome expectations. In the performance phase, strategies varied, with some groups emphasizing environmental structuring and help-seeking, while others incorporated imagery and metacognitive monitoring. Finally, in the self-reflection phase, self-evaluation was consistently employed, with member O in Group 10 also reporting a sense of self-satisfaction.

Table 8.3 outlines samples of participants' responses toward the implementation of SRL strategies. Participants in collaborative writing reported a structured strategy in three phases: forethought, performance, and self-reflection. In the forethought phase, participants set clear learning goals to focus their efforts, which inspired confidence in their ability to succeed. During performance, they managed time effectively, engaged in discussions, and utilized various tools such as laptops and grammar checkers. Finally, in the self-reflection phase, they evaluated teamwork and individual contributions to enhance future performance. Standard tools mentioned include Grammarly, ChatGPT, and Turnitin, underscoring their commitment to quality and collaborative success through goal-setting and mutual support.

The study's second research question dealt with the challenges of SRL strategies in EFL students' collaborative writing. Based on the interview data, four key challenges emerged, including difficulties in managing time and task coordination among group members, varying levels of motivation and engagement, reliance on AI-assisted writing tools, and group dynamics. The challenges suggest that addressing time management, motivation, appropriate use of technology, and group collaboration can help participants work more effectively and achieve better results in composing academic writing. Below is the tabulation of students' responses to the challenges.

Table 8.4 displays the challenges of the implementation of SRL strategies in collaborative academic writing activities. Challenges faced by participants include difficulties in managing time and task coordination (B, E, J, O, G), varying levels of motivation and engagement (A, D, I, M, L), reliance on AI-assisted writing tools (C, H, K), and group dynamics (F, N).

The study's third research question addressed the potential solution to the challenges. Table 8.5 presents the challenges in group work and corresponding potential solutions. Challenges include difficulties in time management and task coordination, varied motivation levels, reliance on AI writing tools, and issues with group dynamics. Challenges include difficulties in time management and task coordination, varied motivation levels, reliance on AI writing tools, and issues with group dynamics.

Table 8.2 Recap of the implementation of SRL strategies

Groups	Members	SRL phases		
		Forethought (task analysis and self-motivation beliefs)	Performance (self-control and self-observation)	Self-reflection (self-judgement and self-reaction)
(a)				
2	A	Goal setting self-efficacy	Help-seeking, time management, environmental structuring	Self-evaluation
	B	Goal setting self-efficacy	Help-seeking time management Environmental structuring Imagery Metacognitive monitoring	Self-evaluation
	C	Goal setting self-efficacy	Help-seeking time management Environmental structuring	Self-evaluation self-satisfaction
5	D	Goal setting self-efficacy	Task-strategies, environmental structuring, time management	Self-evaluation
	E	Goal setting, self-efficacy task interest/value	Help-seeking, time management Environmental structuring Imagery	Self-evaluation
	F	Goal setting self-efficacy	Help-seeking time management Environmental structuring	Self-evaluation
(b)				
6	G	Goal setting self-efficacy	Imagery Environmental structuring	Self-evaluation
	H	Goal setting self-efficacy outcome expectation	Help-seeking time management Environmental structuring Self-recording	Self-evaluation
	I	Goal setting self-efficacy	Help-seeking time management, Environmental structuring Imagery Metacognitive monitoring	Self-evaluation
7	J	Goal setting	Self-instruction, self-consequences Help-seeking Environmental structuring	Self-evaluation
	K	Goal setting task interest/value	Self-instruction self-consequences Help-seeking Environmental structuring	Self-evaluation

(continued)

Table 8.2 (continued)

Groups	Members	SRL phases		
		Forethought (task analysis and self-motivation beliefs)	Performance (self-control and self-observation)	Self-reflection (self-judgement and self-reaction)
	L	Goal setting, outcome expectation	Task-strategies help-seeking Environmental structuring Imagery Metacognitive monitoring	Self-evaluation
(c)				
10	M	Goal setting, outcome expectation	Environmental structuring Self-consequences	Self-evaluation
	N	Goal setting, outcome expectation	Environmental structuring Self-consequences Imagery	Self-evaluation
	O	Goal setting, outcome expectation	Environmental structuring Self-consequences	Self-evaluation self-satisfaction

To foster trust and engagement, peer accountability can be emphasized as a key solution. Suggested solutions for effective time management include setting shared deadlines, breaking tasks into manageable subtasks, and utilizing project management tools. To address motivation disparities, solutions include peer accountability, open communication, and aligning tasks with individual strengths. For AI reliance, it is recommended to set usage guidelines and encourage critical thinking. Lastly, improving group dynamics can be achieved by fostering team bonding, establishing norms, and addressing conflicts early.

Challenges include difficulties in time management and task coordination, varied motivation levels, reliance on AI writing tools, and issues with group dynamics. To foster trust and engagement, peer accountability can be emphasized as a key solution. Suggested solutions for effective time management include setting shared deadlines, breaking tasks into manageable subtasks, and utilizing project management tools. To address motivation disparities, solutions include peer accountability, open communication, and aligning tasks with individual strengths. For AI reliance, it is recommended to set usage guidelines and encourage critical thinking. Lastly, improving group dynamics can be achieved by fostering team bonding, establishing norms, and addressing conflicts early.

Analysis of Results

In analyzing the results, this study employed the framework of activity theory to capture the complex interaction among elements in the utilization of SRL strategies

Table 8.3 Participants' responses samples on the implementation of SRL strategies

Groups	Participants	Responses
(a)		
2	A	In forethought phase, I set my learning goal to help me to be focused on learning process. I also have a belief that I can do and finish a collaborative writing task. In performance phase, I discuss with my friends, and I try to manage my learning time wisely. I also use supported writing tools, laptop, handphone, paper. In self-reflection phase, I can evaluate my collaborative writing so that I must keep a good teamwork and communication with another member
5	D	I know my learning goal because my lecturer always shares each meeting learning goal. Then, I have a motivation to finish my writing. In writing collaboratively, my group uses writing process start from making writing outline, first drafting, revising, editing, writing final draft. My friends and I use ChatGPT to brainstorm ideas, Grammarly to check our grammar, online dictionary, essay writing module, and research articles. We also make commitment to finish the task before the deadline. We also have group reflection to evaluate our group writing
(b)		
6	G	My group has a goal to finish the collaborative writing task. We believe that we can do it. In writing the outline, first, my group draw a mind map or concept web to ease us in sharing writing ideas. My group also uses supported tools such as Grammarly for grammar checking, Turnitin to check similarity result. At the end, we discuss the strengths and weaknesses of our group and our essay
7	J	I know my learning goal for each meeting because it is stated clearly in semester lesson plan. I also encourage my group not to give up in finishing the essays. My group gives rewards for the members who could finish the task on time. I consult with my friends and lecturer. I use laptop, online dictionary, Grammarly, module, etc. we often evaluate group writing performance to check whether we have achieved our goal or not yet
10	M	I set my learning goal with my friends as guidance to produce well-structured essays. My friends and I have the same goal that we must get good scores for this class. We try to do our best in this collaborative writing. We use many tools and sources to help us in writing essays, for example module, laptop, Quillbot, journal articles, Grammarly, etc. In my group, we make a reward or punishment if we can or cannot finish the assignment on time. For the group evaluation, we do reflection on the ways we communicate to write and finish the task

Table 8.4 The challenges of SRL strategies in collaborative academic writing

No	Challenges	Participants
1	Difficulties in managing time and task coordination among group members	B, E, J, O, G
2	Having different levels of motivation and engagement	A, D, I, M, L
3	Reliance on the use of AI-assisted writing tools	C, H, K
4	Group dynamic	F, N

Table 8.5 The potential solutions to the challenges

No	Challenges	Potential Solutions
1	Difficulties in managing time and task coordination among group members	a. Setting shared deadlines b. Breaking tasks into smaller subtasks c. Using project management tools d. Scheduling regular check-ins
2	Having different levels of motivation and engagement	a. Using peer accountability b. Encouraging open communication c. Recognizing contributions d. Clarifying roles e. Aligning task with individual strengths and interests
3	Reliance on the use of AI-assisted writing tools	a. Setting guidelines on AI use b. Encouraging critical thinking c. Discussing the effects of overreliance in using AI
4	Group dynamic	a. Fostering team bonding b. Establishing group norms c. Addressing conflict early d. Encouraging feedback loops

in an EFL collaborative writing context, involving 15 participants who participated in a semi-structured interview session. Figure 8.2 presents six important domains in the activity system, including subjects, rules, tools or mediating artifacts, objects, community, and division of labor. Each domain is interrelated to support the learning ecosystem in achieving the learning goals.

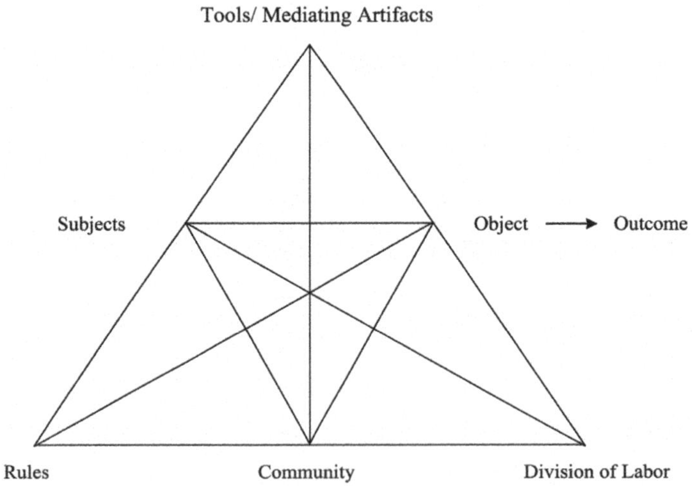

Fig. 8.2 Activity system (Adopted from Engeström, 2015)

In implementing SRL strategies in a collaborative writing setting, the ideal activity system can be considered a framework for analyzing the results of this study. Table 8.6 outlines an activity system framework for SRL strategies in collaborative academic writing, detailing six interconnected domains. The subject involves students in an essay writing class, while the rules encompass collaborative commitments, SRL strategies, writing conventions, and assessment criteria.

Tools include digital aids like Turnitin and Grammarly, alongside academic resources. The object focuses on producing well-structured academic essays. The community is comprised of students and the lecturer, forming the social and instructional framework. The division of labor allocates the roles of active peers to students and a facilitator to the lecturer, who provides guidance and feedback. The ideal activity system plays a crucial role in the success of the implementation of SRL strategies, encouraging the student to appreciate its importance in fostering effective learning processes. However, the participants shared their challenges in the process of implementing SRL strategies in collaborative academic writing. It can be inferred that a contradiction exists between domains in the activity system.

Engeström (2001) highlighted that contradictions are pivotal for development and change within and among activity systems, as they can lead to conflict that drives transformative change and generates innovative solutions. After analyzing the contradiction, a potential solution was derived. The potential solution can be used as a reflection and evaluation of the application of SRL strategies in collaborative writing. Table 8.7 outlines the sources of contradictions in implementing SRL strategies in collaborative writing, showing how challenges arise from tensions among the subject, tools, rules, community, and division of labor within the activity system.

Table 8.6 Activity system in SRL strategies in collaborative academic writing

No	Domains	Explanation
1	Subject	All members in collaborative writing group (students in the essay writing class)
2	Rules	Collaborative writing commitment, SRL strategies, essay writing rules, essay scoring rubric
3	Tools	Essay writing module, Laptop, Turnitin, Grammarly, Quillbot, ChatGPT, Journal articles
4	Object	Writing academic essays. The object relates to the outcome. The outcome is that students can write well-structured essays collaboratively
5	Community	Students (group members) and lecturer
6	Division of Labor	Students as the group members are active peers and are responsible for their tasks. The students must also become active learners Lecturer is a facilitator and a feedback provider

Table 8.7 Contradiction in the implementation of SRL strategies in collaborative writing

No	Challenges	Contradiction
1	Difficulties in managing time and task coordination among group members	Subject—rules—community—division of labor
2	Having different levels of motivation and engagement	Subject—community
3	Reliance on the use of AI-assisted writing tools	Subject—tools
4	Group dynamic	Subject—rules—community

Interpretation

The analysis of results for the first question highlighted that EFL students had already applied the forethought, performance, and self-reflection phases. Although the students did not implement all strategies in each phase, they had experienced regulating their collaborative academic writing by using some of the strategies in each phase of SRL. All students managed their group interaction and shared the same goals in collaborative writing.

Hadwin et al. (2018) highlighted the notion of socially shared regulation of learning, focusing on the management and monitoring processes of group behavior that share the same goals in collaborative learning. Additionally, the activity system of SRL strategies in collaborative writing reinforced the finding that students shared common goals and that there was an interconnection among elements within the activity system.

The results for the second research question revealed the challenges of SRL implementation viewed from the perspective of contradictions in activity systems. The identified challenges arose from specific domains within the activity system that were unable to function effectively under the given conditions. All challenges referred to contradictions that involved the subject of the activity system as the central aspect. By exploring the contradictions, a potential solution can be found. Therefore, a more profound understanding of conflicting elements could reveal innovative pathways to solutions that lead to more balanced, effective, and sustainable outcomes. Furthermore, the results for the third research question provide an overview that every challenge has its potential solution.

Findings

The findings of this study reveal how students employed SRL strategies during collaborative academic writing, as well as the difficulties they encountered in applying these strategies. The analysis highlights the ways students managed their learning processes, interacted with peers, and utilized available resources while completing collaborative writing tasks. Based on the thematic analysis of the data, the findings are organized into three major themes: (1) the implementation of SRL strategies in collaborative academic writing, (2) the challenges encountered in utilizing SRL strategies during collaborative writing activities, and (3) potential solutions that may support the more effective application of SRL strategies in collaborative academic writing contexts.

These themes provide insights into how learners regulate their cognitive, motivational, and collaborative processes while engaging in joint academic writing tasks. The findings illustrate the dynamic nature of SRL in collaborative environments, where individual regulation interacts with group negotiation and shared decision-making. By examining both the successful practices and the obstacles faced by students, this section offers a comprehensive understanding of how SRL strategies operate within collaborative academic writing and how these strategies may be strengthened to enhance students' writing performance and learning experiences.

SRL Strategies Deployment in Collaborative Academic Writing

Findings from the interview reveal that each student employs individual SRL strategies, even when engaging in collaborative academic writing activities. It can be inferred from the findings that students were aware of the importance of regulating their learning. In the forethought phase, the students set their learning goal, which was to compose well-structured essays collaboratively. They shared their individual learning goals with their group's members. The following interview excerpts present-the student's voice in the SRL application.

Excerpt 1. Student A in Group 2

In forethought phase, I set my learning goal to help me to be focused on learning process. I also have a belief that I can do and finish a collaborative writing task. In performance phase, I discuss with my friends, and I try to manage my learning time wisely. I also use supported writing tools, laptop, handphone, paper. In self-reflection phase, I can evaluate my collaborative writing so that I must keep a good teamwork and communication with another member.

Excerpt 2. Student G in Group 6

My group has a goal to finish the collaborative writing task. We believe that we can do it. In writing the outline, first, my group draw a mind map or concept web to ease us in sharing writing ideas. My group also uses supported tools such as Grammarly for grammar checking, Turnitin to check similarity result. At the end, we discuss the strengths and weaknesses of our group and our essay.

Excerpt 3. Student M in Group 10

I set my learning goal with my friends as guidance to produce well-structured essays. My friends and I have the same goal that we must get good scores for this class. We try to do our best in this collaborative writing. We use many tools and sources to help us in writing essays, for example module, laptop, Quillbot, journal articles, Grammarly, etc. *In my group, we make a reward or punishment if we can or cannot finish the assignment on time. For the group evaluation, we do reflection on the ways we communicate to write and finish the task.*

Figure 8.3 validates the students' interview excerpts. The students' faces were covered with smiley emoticons due to research ethics that protect students' identities. Figure 8.3 illustrates the implementation of the forethought and performance phases. It was evident that the students sat with their group members and set their learning goals and self-motivation beliefs in writing an argumentative essay collaboratively.

During the performance phase, students primarily optimize their strategies for environmental structuring, help-seeking, and time management. For environmental structuring, the students use tools or sources that support their collaborative writing. Figure 8.3 shows that they use laptops, smartphones, and paper to facilitate their collaborative writing process. The students also implemented the help-seeking strategy, which they discussed with their friends.

In utilizing SRL strategies in a collaborative academic writing context, the lecturer needs to facilitate and monitor students' writing progress. Based on students' learning artifacts, the lecturer checked students' writing progress by using Brisk Teaching. Brisk Teaching is an AI-driven platform that features a tool to inspect students' writing, particularly in Google Docs. Therefore, students' writing could be inspected

Fig. 8.3 The students did forethought and performance phases

for when they started and ended their writing, the number of times they copied and pasted, the number of times they edited their writing, and the times they wrote in Google Docs.

Figure 8.4 is a sample of students' writing process inspected by the lecturer. Figure 8.4 is the compilation of screenshots for the students' introduction, body, conclusion, and final essay. It is seen that the students finished writing their argumentative essay's introduction on Sunday, 24 November 2024, at 06:53 a.m., with one paste of writing and one edit. However, the writing process in Google Docs was 0 min, which meant that they might have completed their writing process in Microsoft Word first, then copied and pasted their writing into Google Docs.

In the publishing session of the writing process, students were asked to submit the similarity result of their essay. This process highlights the role educators play in upholding academic standards and helps ensure students understand the importance of original work. The purpose of this rule was to ensure that the students maintained academic integrity by submitting original work and avoiding plagiarism. This activity also validated the student's interview response, which indicated that she used

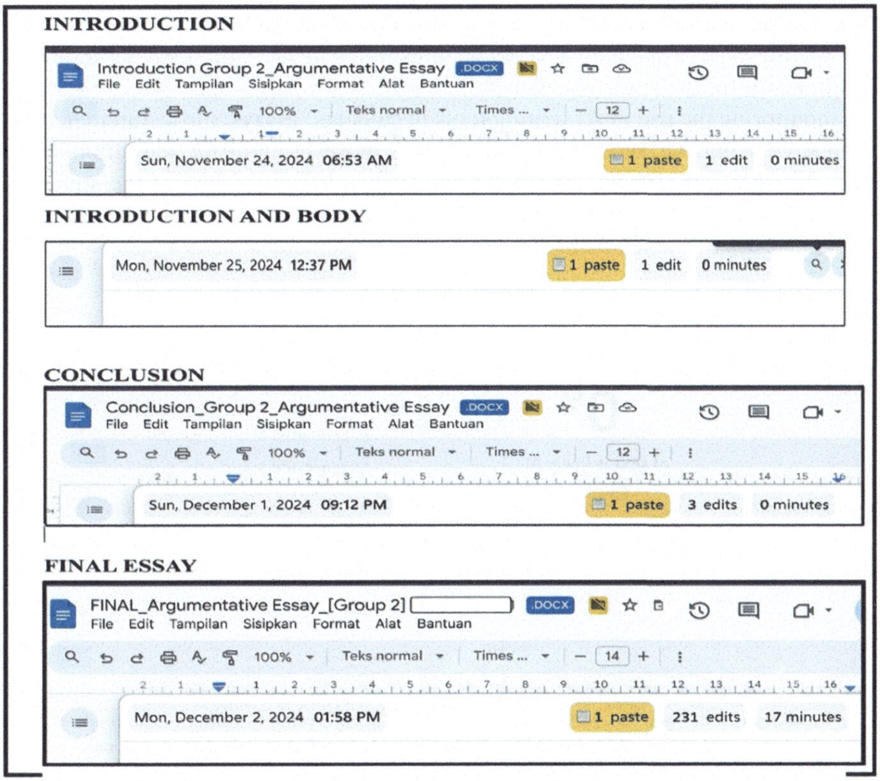

Fig. 8.4 The inspection of students' writing progress

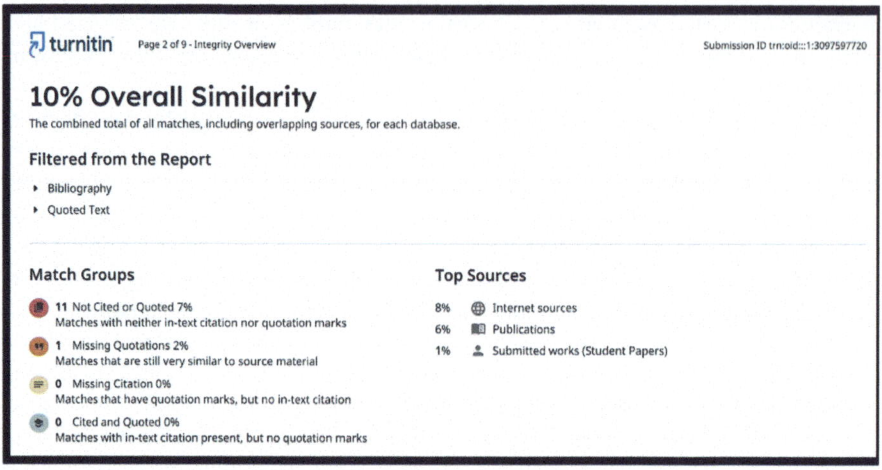

Fig. 8.5 Turnitin similarity result of student's essay

Turnitin as her environmental structuring tool. Based on the learning contract of the essay writing class, a standard acceptable threshold was 15%. Figure 8.5 is a sample Turnitin result for the student's essay.

In monitoring the use of AI writing tools in students' essays, the lecturer checked their essays using AI detector tools, including those in QuillBot and Grammarly. Figure 8.6 shows the results of the AI detector QuillBot for one of the student's essays. The students used 100% human-written content, so there was no AI-generated writing, and 0% of the text is likely AI.

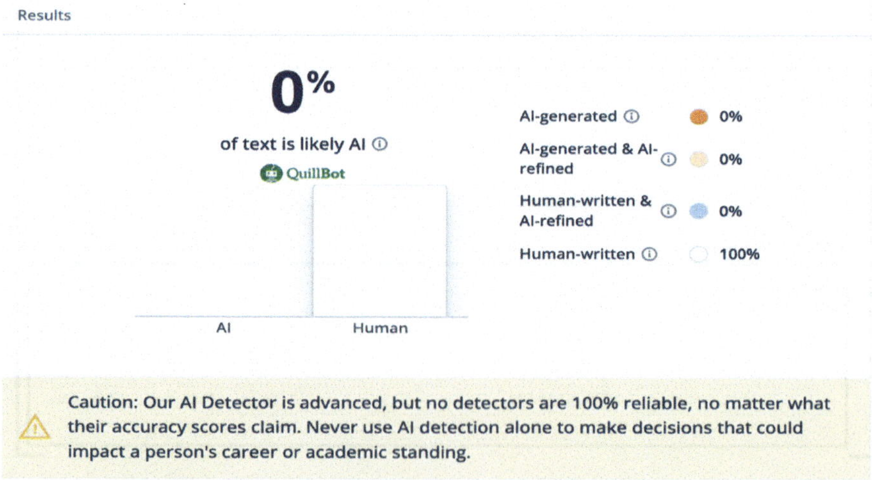

Fig. 8.6 The result of AI detector in QuillBot

To enhance the trustworthiness of AI usage in students' essays, the lecturer also checked the use of AI by utilizing Grammarly's 'Check for AI text & plagiarism' feature. Figure 8.7 presents the result of Grammarly AI detectors for one of the students' essays. Another function of Grammarly in the essay writing class was to check grammar. In Grammarly, the lecturer obtained information about general metrics, which included the number of characters, words, sentences, reading time, speaking time, score, writing issues, and plagiarism percentage, as presented in Fig. 8.8. Additionally, the lecturer used Grammarly to identify writing issues in students' essays. The issues includ correctness, clarity, and engagement, see Fig. 8.9.

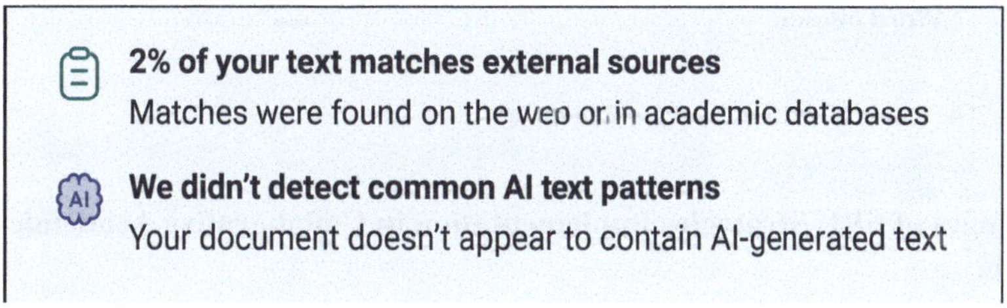

Fig. 8.7 The result of AI detector in Grammarly

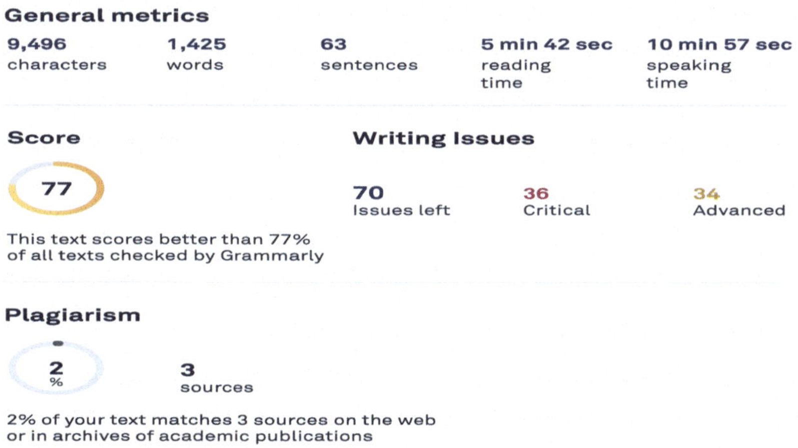

Fig. 8.8 Grammarly results

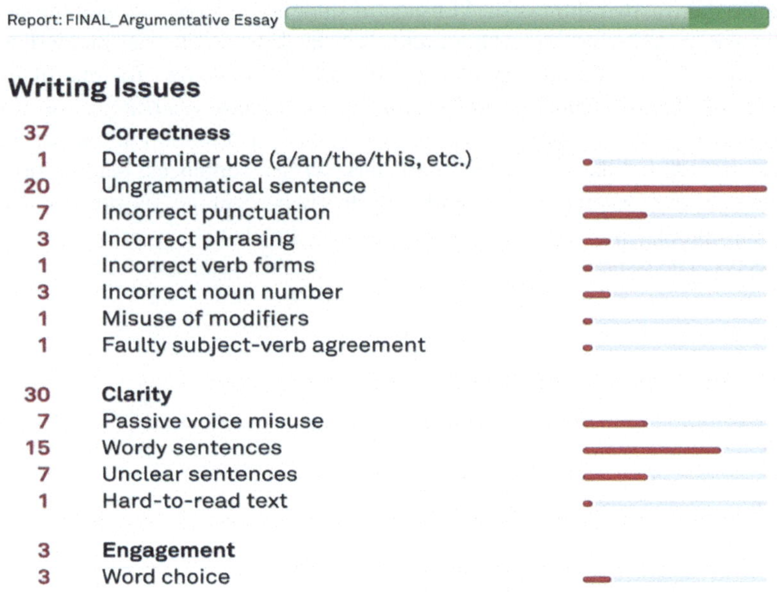

Fig. 8.9 The result of writing issues in Grammarly

Challenges of SRL Strategies Implementation in Collaborative Academic Writing

In implementing SRL strategies in collaborative writing in an EFL setting, it was found that there were four challenges that hindered the implementation of SRL strategies. The first challenge was students' difficulties in managing time and task coordination among group members. Although they had already signed a group writing commitment form, they still experienced time management problems because they also had many assignments. Thus, they sometimes felt exhausted and tired with many assignments. The time management problem also influenced the task coordination among group members, as was stated in one of the interview responses below.

Excerpt 4. The challenge faced by Student E

Personally, I have problems with my time management because this semester I have many assignments in all courses. I feel exhausted. I also had problems with my coordination with my friends in doing the writing task.

The second challenge was students' different levels of motivation and engagement. High motivation students should support their peers, fostering a sense of community and shared effort. In the context of this current study, the essay writing class, the students had different levels of motivation and engagement. It could be seen from their performance in each group. Therefore, the lecturer needed to be aware of this issue because it influenced students' success in writing essays collaboratively. The students who had high motivation and engagement levels should help the students who were in low motivation and engagement levels because they were in the same group and had the same learning goals and outcomes. The following excerpt is a student's response to the issue.

Excerpt 5. The challenge faced by Student M

I think the challenge in my collaborative writing is when I have different levels of motivation compared to my friends.

The third challenge was students' reliance on the use of AI-assisted writing tools. It was found in an essay that indicated that they used AI to compose more than 10% of their essay. When the lecturer confirmed with the students, they provided honest answers because they could not develop their writing ideas and could not manage their time wisely. Then, they apologized to the lecturer for committing academic dishonesty, and promised not to do it again. Nevertheless, the lecturer deducted points from their academic integrity score for the essay. Below is the excerpt of the interview response.

Excerpt 6. The challenge faced by Student H

My group used AI because we lack time to do it. We can't manage our time well. We are sorry about this. We promise we will not do it in the future.

The fourth challenge was the students' group dynamic. The realm of group dynamics refers to interpersonal issues that arise when students work collaboratively. The group dynamic covered unequal participation, conflict, communication barriers, and power imbalances. These issues hindered the development of collaborative skills and impacted learning quality. The following excerpt presents the interview response to this issue.

Excerpt 7. The challenge faced by Student F

I have a problem with my group members, one of them does not have unequal participation that usually makes miscommunication in my group.

After knowing the challenges, it was essential for the lecturer and students to find solutions to cope with them. Many strategies could be considered by analyzing the elements of the activity system that were explained in the previous section, by exploring the right path of the interaction among domains in the activity system, including the subject, the object related to the outcome, the tools, the rules, the community, and the division of labor. The most important point was the synergy between the subject and community to achieve the objective, in this case, to reach the learning goals and outcomes.

Potential Solutions

After analyzing the components in the activity system, it was found that each challenge has its own solutions. The solution for students' difficulties in managing time and task coordination among group members covered setting shared deadlines, breaking tasks into smaller subtasks, using project management tools, and scheduling regular check-ins. The solution for students' different levels of motivation and engagement included using peer accountability, encouraging open communication, recognizing contributions, clarifying roles, and aligning tasks with individual strengths and interests.

Another solution for reducing students' reliance on AI-assisted writing tools was setting guidelines on AI use, encouraging critical thinking, and discussing the effects of overreliance on AI. Dealing with the group dynamic challenge, the solutions were fostering team bonding, establishing group norms, addressing conflict early, and encouraging feedback loops. The following excerpts feature the students' voices on the proposed solution to address the challenges.

Excerpt 8. The solution from Student E

In my opinion, the solution for my challenge in managing my time is I need to set the deadline and divide the tasks into subtasks.

Excerpt 9. The solution from Student M

I have high motivation, but my friend is low in motivation, so I usually highlight her contribution in our collaborative writing and assure her that she also has strengths in our collaborative writing.

Excerpt 10. The solution from Student H

I think over reliance in AI is not good, so my friends and I should not use AI for doing the task, it is our fault. I think it is important to develop my critical thinking, so I will fully rely on my own writing ideas.

Excerpt 11. The solution from Student F

I learned a lot from my challenges. I realize that I must foster my team bonding and address the conflict earlier to avoid miscommunication that impacts my group writing performance.

The solution offered needs to be considered to create a meaningful implementation of SRL strategies in a collaborative writing environment. It was not only the lecturer's role but also the students' role to implement all the solutions provided. By applying the solutions, students could promote a collaborative learning atmosphere that assisted them in achieving their learning goals.

8.6 Discussions

Grounded in SRL, collaborative academic writing, and activity theory, this study provides explanations for the implementation of SRL strategies in a collaborative writing context. Based on the findings, the students implement all stages of SRL, including the forethought, performance, and self-reflection phases. In the forethought phase, all students demonstrate goal orientation and motivational beliefs, either individually or collectively. This reflects strong forethought strategies in SRL. During the performance phase, students actively employ cognitive and metacognitive strategies, including time management, tool utilization, and peer collaboration, to enhance their learning.

In implementing SRL strategies, particularly in the self-reflection phase, students recognize the importance of evaluating group collaboration as part of their learning process. Based on the first finding, they utilize all phases due to the benefits of SRL in writing instructions. SRL assists students in fostering their higher-order thinking through the practice of motivational factors, metacognitive skills, and behavioral aspects in regulating their learning (Cárdenas-Robledo & Peña-Ayala, 2019). In addition, SRL contributes to students' writing performances (Anggraeni et al., 2025; Fitriati et al., 2023; Pionera et al., 2020; Suhandoko & Hsu, 2020; Wijaya, 2021).

The primary study aim is in the realm of collaborative academic writing. Many prior studies highlight the virtues of utilizing collaborative writing, including improvements in the student's writing performance (Chu, 2025), improving the organizational structure, content development, and effective lexical choices (Aldossary, 2025), enhancing student's writing skills and overcoming writing anxiety (Pardede, 2024).

Dealing with the second set of findings on the challenges of implementing SRL strategies, the findings highlight that students face challenges in the process, including loss of focus in collaborative writing, social loafing, reliance on AI-mediated composition, and difficulties with group dynamics. This aligns with Roxas (2023), who emphasized that the challenge in collaborative writing arises when group performance suffers from a lack of participation, a passive member, or inadequate engagement. Addressing both logistical and interpersonal challenges holistically leads to more effective and meaningful group outcomes.

In addressing the challenges of utilizing SRL strategies in a collaborative writing context, the students voice several potential solutions, covering the implementation of collaborative time and task management strategies, socially shared regulation strategies, critical AI literacy strategies, and collaborative writing group maintenance strategies. To mitigate time and task coordination challenges, students employ collaborative time and task management strategies, including setting shared deadlines, breaking tasks into smaller subtasks, utilizing project management tools, and scheduling regular progress checks.

Furthermore, students implement socially shared regulation strategies, including peer accountability, open communication encouragement, recognition of contributions, role clarification, and tasks that align with individual strengths and interests to address motivational and interpersonal barriers. Additionally, students activate their critical AI literacy strategies by using guidelines on AI use, encouraging critical thinking, and discussing the effects of overreliance on AI to combat overreliance on AI tools.

Students should use AI selectively, skeptically, and ethically to avoid overdependence while enhancing learning. Moreover, students employed collaborative writing group maintenance strategies, including fostering team bonding, establishing group norms, addressing conflicts early, and encouraging feedback loops to mitigate challenges in group dynamics. Roxas (2023) highlights that the identified coping strategies include developing a positive outlook, seeking support from others, fostering clear communication, engaging in spiritual practices, and taking breaks to manage stress effectively.

8.7 Conclusions

This study aims to investigate the use of SRL strategies in students' collaborative writing. Although this study explores SRL utilization, it also focuses on the challenges of strategies in EFL students' collaborative writing and their potential solutions. The findings of this study highlight that students must be aware of both the challenges and potential solutions in implementing SRL strategies. In addition, the students and lecturers should analyze the elements of the activity system, including subject, tools, rules, object, community, and division of labor, to get a better understanding of the dynamics of SRL in a collaborative writing environment.

The limitations of this study include the study context and the instruments used for data collection, as well as the limited sample size and participant diversity, which may affect the representativeness of the findings. The study was conducted in one of four essay writing classes in the English Education Department in Indonesia. Therefore, the findings of this current study cannot be generalized due to the nature of this study being a case study. The following limitation is that the semi-structured interviews and learning artifacts cannot fully capture the students' regulation and collaborative skills. To address the limitations, this study recommends that future researchers conduct research in diverse contexts by employing different research designs and multiple data collection instruments to enrich the research findings and contribute to the body of knowledge in SRL-based instruction in collaborative writing.

Furthermore, the study's findings provide practical guidance for implementing SRL strategies in EFL collaborative academic writing. Therefore, it assists writing lecturers in creating meaningful collaborative writing activities, and students develop their self-regulatory and collaborative writing skills. Integrating technology into the use of SRL strategies is pivotal to fostering metacognition, autonomy, and adaptive learning. Theoretically, this study enriches the understanding of SRL by highlighting how students navigate collaborative academic writing through goal setting, time management, tool use, and group reflection. It extends SRL theory by integrating the social and technological dimensions of collaborative writing. Practically, the findings offer actionable insights for students and lecturers to support SRL in group writing tasks, such as fostering peer accountability, managing time effectively, and using AI tools critically. These strategies can help improve both individual regulation and group coordination. Pedagogically, the study informs instructional design by identifying key challenges (e.g., uneven motivation, overreliance on AI tools, and group dynamics) and proposing targeted interventions, such as structured planning, role clarification, and reflective evaluation, to enhance collaborative writing outcomes.

Based on these findings, several recommendations are proposed for future research. First, it is recommended that future studies be conducted in more diverse and multi-sited contexts to examine the transferability of SRL practices across different institutional, cultural, and proficiency settings. Second, the use of longitudinal and mixed-methods designs is strongly recommended to capture the developmental trajectories and evolving nature of students' self-regulation and collaboration over time. Third, further recommendation is directed toward exploring the role of emerging technologies, including AI-assisted writing tools, in mediating SRL processes, particularly in terms of how such tools can be integrated pedagogically to support, not replace, students' cognitive and collaborative engagement. Finally, it is recommended that future research investigate instructional interventions that explicitly scaffold SRL within collaborative writing tasks to develop more effective and context-sensitive pedagogical models.

Acknowledgements I extend my deepest gratitude to John Geoffrey Funk for his meticulous proofreading and linguistic refinement, which significantly enhanced the clarity and professional quality of this article. I also express my special thanks to Alejandro Peña-Ayala for his constructive feedback on the early version of this article and for his generous financial support in facilitating the professional proofreading process.

Appendix 8.1

A sample of Signed Collaborative Writing Commitment

COLLABORATIVE WRITING COMMITMENT FORM

Course : **Essay Writing**
Class : **2**
Lecturer : [redacted]

Assignment: [Argumentative Essay]
Group Members:

- **Student A:** [redacted]
- **Student B:** [redacted]
- **Student C:** [redacted]

We, the undersigned, commit to fulfilling the following roles and responsibilities in the completion of this collaborative writing assignment:

Pre-Writing Phase:

- **All members:** Collaboratively analyze the assignment, choose the writing topic, brainstorm ideas, and organize them into an outline.

Drafting Phase:

- **Student A:** Write the Title and Introduction.
- **Student B:** Write the Body.
- **Student C:** Write the Conclusion and compile the References.

Revision and Editing Phase:

- **All members:** Participate actively in rewriting and revising the first draft, providing constructive feedback and ensuring clarity, coherence, and adherence to the assignment requirements.

Finalization and Submission:

- **All members:** Collaborate on crafting the final draft, incorporating all revisions and edits.
- **All members:** Review and approve the final draft before submission.
- **Designated member:** Submit the final draft on behalf of the group.

We further commit to:

- **Open Communication:** Maintaining open and respectful communication throughout the writing process.
- **Active Participation:** Contributing actively and meaningfully to all stages of the project.
- **Time Management:** Adherence to agreed-upon deadlines and completing tasks in a timely manner.
- **Mutual Respect:** Respecting each other's ideas, opinions, and contributions.
- **Academic Integrity:** Upholding the principles of academic honesty and ensuring that all work is original and properly cited.

Signatures:

- Student A: [redacted]
- Student B: [redacted]
- Student C: [redacted]

Date: 13 September 2024

Appendix 8.2

Semi-structured interview questions

1. How do you use SRL strategies during collaborative academic writing tasks?
2. What SRL strategies do you find most helpful when working with peers on writing assignments?
3. What difficulties do you face when trying to manage your own learning in collaborative academic writing activities?
4. How do group dynamics or technology tools affect your ability to self-regulate during collaborative academic writing?
5. What support or changes would help you use SRL strategies more effectively in collaborative academic writing?

References

Adhami, N., & Taghizadeh, M. (2022). Integrating inquiry-based learning and computer supported collaborative learning into flipped classroom: Effects on academic writing performance and perceptions of students of railway engineering. *Computer Assisted Language Learning, 37*(3), 521–557. https://doi.org/10.1080/09588221.2022.2046107

Aldossary, K. (2025). Unlocking potential: Exploring the enduring impact of collaborative writing on lower proficiency EFL learners. *Educational Process: International Journal, 15*(e2025184), 1–14. https://doi.org/10.22521/edupij.2025.15.184

Alsahil, A. (2024). Behind the scenes: Exploring learners' collaborative writing interactions and strategies. *Computer Assisted Language Learning, 37*(7), 2224–2253. https://doi.org/10.1080/09588221.2022.2157444

Amani, N., & Bisriyah, M. (2025). University students' perceptions of AI-assisted writing tools in supporting self-regulated writing practices. *Indonesian Journal of English Language Teaching and Applied Linguistics, 10*(1), 91–107. https://doi.org/10.21093/ijeltal.v10i1.1942

Anani, G. E., Nyamekye, E., & Bafour-Koduah, D. (2025). Using artificial intelligence for academic writing in higher education: The perspectives of university students in Ghana. *Discover Education, 4*(46). https://doi.org/10.1007/s44217-025-00434-5

Anggraeni, C. W., Mujiyanto, J., Rustipa, K., & Widhiyanto, (2025). Effects of utilizing self-regulated learning-based instruction on EFL students' academic writing skills: A mixed-method investigation. *Asian-Pacific Journal of Second and Foreign Language Education, 10*(15), 1–26. https://doi.org/10.1186/s40862-024-00317-6

Asnas, S. A. M, & Hidayanti, I. (2024). Uncovering EFL students' frequent difficulties in academic writing and the coping strategies: The case of a college in Indonesia. *Journal on English as a Foreign Language, 4*(1), 124–151. https://doi.org/10.23971/jefl.v14i1.7472

Boekaerts, M. (2011). Emotions, emotion regulation, and self-regulation of learning. In B. J. Zimmerman & D. H. Schunk (Eds.), *Handbook of self-regulation of learning and performance.* Routledge.

Braun, V., & Clarke, V. (2006). Using thematic analysis in psychology. *Qualitative Research in Psychology, 3*(2), 77–101. https://doi.org/10.1191/1478088706qp063oa

Bulqiyah, S., Mahbub, M. A., & Nugraheni, D. A. (2021). Investigating writing difficulties in essay writing: Tertiary students' perspectives. *English Language Teaching Educational Journal, 4*(1), 61–73. https://doi.org/10.12928/eltej.v4i1.2371

Cárdenas-Robledo, L. A., & Peña-Ayala, A. (2019). A holistic self-regulated learning model: A proposal and application in ubiquitous-learning. *Expert Systems with Applications, 123*, 299–314. https://doi.org/10.1016/j.eswa.2019.01.007

Chen, W., & Chen, M. (2025). "I became self-motivated": Investigating Chinese students' motivation in assessed collaborative writing tasks. *SAGE Open, 15*(1), 1–15. https://doi.org/10.1177/21582440251322617

Cheung, L., & Crosthwaite, P. (2025). CorpusChat: Integrating corpus linguistics and generative AI for academic writing development. *Computer Assisted Language Learning*, 1–27. https://doi.org/10.1080/09588221.2025.2506480

Chu, P. Q. (2025). Collaborative writing factors affecting English as a foreign language student writing performance. *International Journal of Virtual and Personal Learning Environments, 15*(1), 1–27. https://doi.org/10.4018/IJVPLE.368035

Efklides, A. (2011). Interactions of metacognition with motivation and affect in self-regulated learning: The MASRL model. *Educational Psychologist, 46*, 6–25. https://doi.org/10.1080/00461520.2011.538645

Engeström, Y. (2001). Expansive learning at work: Toward an activity theoretical reconceptualization. *Journal of Education and Work, 14*(1), 133–156. https://doi.org/10.1080/13639080020028747

Engeström, Y. (2015). *Learning by expanding: An activity-theoretical approach to developmental research* (2nd ed.). Cambridge University Press.

Eslami, M., & Sahragard, R. (2021). Investigating the effect of self-regulatory strategy development on Iranian EFL learners' metadiscoursal writing skill. *Language Teaching Research Quarterly, 21*, 54–65. https://doi.org/10.32038/ltrq.2021.21.04

Fang, Z. (2021). *Demystifying academic writing: Genres, moves, skills, and strategies*. Routledge.

Fitriati, S. W., Wijayatiningsih, T. D., Farida, A. N., & Hapsari, C. T. (2023). *Model of self-regulated strategies in a project-based blended synchronous learning in writing class for English language students at a university level*. Unnes Press.

Hadwin, A. F., Järvelä, S., & Miller, M. (2018). Self-regulation, co-regulation, and shared regulation in collaborative learning environments. In D. H. Schunk & J. A. Greene (Eds.), *Handbook of self-regulation of learning and performance* (pp. 83–106). Routledge.

Järvelä, S., & Hadwin, A. F. (2013). New frontiers: Regulating learning in CSCL. *Education Psychologist, 48*, 25–39. https://doi.org/10.1080/00461520.2012.748006

Mahmud, Y. S., & German, E. (2021). Online self-regulated learning strategies amid a global pandemic: Insights from Indonesian university students. *Malaysian Journal of Learning and Instruction, 18*(2), 45–68. https://doi.org/10.32890/mjli2021.18.2.2

Nhi, H. Y., & Phuong, H. (2025) EFL postgraduate students' perceptions on the use of Grammarly and peer feedback to improve their academic writing skills. *International Journal of TESOL & Education, 5*(1), 25–49. https://doi.org/10.54855/ijte.25512

Oubibi, M., Hryshayeva, K., & Huang, R. (2025). Enhancing postgraduate digital academic writing proficiency: The interplay of artificial intelligence tools and ChatGPT. *Interactive Learning Environments*, 1–19. https://doi.org/10.1080/10494820.2025.2454445

Ozfidan, B., El-Dakhs, D. A. S., & Alsalim, L. A. (2024). The use of AI tools in English academic writing by Saudi undergraduates. *Contemporary Educational Technology, 16*(4), 13. https://doi.org/10.30935/cedtech/15013

Panadero, E. (2017). A review of self-regulated learning: Six models and four directions for research. *Frontiers in Psychology, 8*(422), 1–28. https://doi.org/10.3389/fpsyg.2017.00422

Pardede, P. (2024). Collaborative writing in EFL settings: A review. *Journal of English Teaching, 10*(1), 92–109. https://doi.org/10.33541/jet.v10i1.5631

Peeters, W., Saqr, M., & Viberg, O. (2020). *Applying learning analytics to map students' self-regulated learning tactics in an academic writing course*. In H. J. So, A. Mitrovic, M. M. T. Rodrigo, & J. Mason (Eds.), *Proceedings of the 28th International Conference on Computers in Education (ICCE 2020)*. Asia-Pacific Society for Computers in Education. https://library.apsce.net/index.php/ICCE/article/view/3926

Peeters, W., Viberg, O., & Spikol, D. (2023). Self-regulation in foreign language students' collaborative discourse for academic writing: An explorative study on epistemic network analysis. In C. Damşa & A. Barany (Eds.), *Advances in Quantitative Ethnography. ICQE 2022. Communications in Computer and Information Science* (Vol. 1785). Springer. https://doi.org/10.1007/978-3-031-31726-2_18

Pham, V. P. H. (2021). The effects of collaborative writing on students' writing fluency: An efficient framework for collaborative writing. *SAGE Open, 11*(1), 1–11. https://doi.org/10.1177/2158244021998363

Pintrich, P. R. (2000). The role of goal orientation in self-regulated learning. In M. Boekaerts, P. R. Pintrich, & M. Zeidner (Eds.), *Handbook of self-regulation*. Academic Press.

Pionera, M., Degeng, I. N. S., Widiati, U., & Setyosari, P. (2020). Instructional methods and self-regulated learning in writing. *International Journal of Instruction, 13*(3), 43–60. https://doi.org/10.29333/iji.2020.1334a

Prapobratanakul, C. (2024). Thai EFL undergraduate engineering students' perspectives on academic writing: Challenges and strategies. *PASAA, 68*, 1–31. https://www.culi.chula.ac.th/Images/asset/pasaa_journal/file-73-927-t4xf21517303.pdf

Qiu, X., & Lee, M. (2020). Regulated learning and self-efficacy beliefs in peer collaborative writing: An exploratory study of L2 learners' written products, task discussions, and self-reports. *System, 93*, 1–15. https://doi.org/10.1016/j.system.2020.102312

Roxas, M. J. (2023). Collaborative research writing in the new normal: Students' views, challenges, coping strategies, and takeaways. *Journal of Learning for Development, 10*(2), 297–311. https://doi.org/10.56059/jl4d.v10i2.829

Şeker, M., & İnan Karagül, B. (2022). Assisting higher education learners online to acquire self-regulated writing strategies during COVID-19. *Journal of Learning and Teaching in Digital Age, 7*(1), 64–75. https://doi.org/10.53850/joltida.989005

Shen, Y., & Chen, L. (2025). 'Critical chatting' or 'casual cheating': How graduate EFL students utilize ChatGPT for academic writing. *Computer Assisted Language Learning*, 1–29. https://doi.org/10.1080/09588221.2025.2479141

Stell, A., & Iwashita, N. (2024). Enhancing collaboration: Exploring regulated learning strategies in the co-regulatory processes of collaborative L2 writing. *System, 125*, 1–16. https://doi.org/10.1016/j.system.2024.103410

Suhandoko, A. D. J., & Hsu, C. S. (2020). Applying self-regulated learning intervention to enhance students' learning: A quasi-experimental approach. *International Journal of Instruction, 13*(3), 649–664. https://doi.org/10.29333/iji.2020.13344a

Sun, T., & Wang, C. (2020). College students' writing self-efficacy and writing self-regulated learning strategies in learning English as a foreign language. *System, 90*, 1–17. https://doi.org/10.1016/j.system.2020.102221

Teng, L. S., & Zhang, L. J. (2016). A questionnaire-based validation of multidimensional models of self-regulated learning strategies. *The Modern Language Journal, 100*, 674–701. https://doi.org/10.1111/modl.12339

Toprak, Z., & Yücel, V. (2020). A peculiar practice of academic writing: Epidemic writing in the Turkish graduate education. *Cogent Education, 7*(1). https://doi.org/10.1080/2331186X.2020.1774098

Wang, K., Zhang, L. J., & Cooper, M. (2025). Metacognitive instruction for improving the effectiveness of collaborative writing for EFL learners' writing development. *The Asia-Pacific Education Researcher, 34*, 661–673. https://doi.org/10.1007/s40299-024-00886-7

Wijaya, K. F. (2021). English education master students' self-regulated learning strategies in academic writing. *JET (Journal of English Teaching), 7*(1), 15–29. https://doi.org/10.33541/jet.v7i1.2313

Winne, P. H., & Hadwin, A. F. (1998). Studying as self-regulated engagement in learning. In D. J. Hacker, J. Dunlosky, & A. C. Graesser (Eds.), *Metacognition in educational theory and practice*. Erlbaum.

Wonglakorn, P., & Deerajviset, P. (2023). The effects of collaborative process writing approach on Thai EFL secondary school students' writing skills. *LEARN Journal: Language Education and Acquisition Research Network, 16*(1), 495–522. https://so04.tcithaijo.org/index.php/LEARN/article/view/263454

Woottipong, K. (2020). Investigation into Thai high school learners' self-regulated learning skills, self-efficacy and writing performance. *Research in Pedagogy, 10*(1), 32–49. https://doi.org/10.5937/istrped2001032w

Xu, J. (2021). Chinese university students' l2 writing feedback orientation and self-regulated learning writing strategies in online teaching during COVID-19. *Asia-Pacific Education Researcher, 30*(6), 563–574. https://doi.org/10.1007/s40299-021-00586-6

Yunus, M., & Bachtiar, B. (2025). Exploring the complexities of thesis writing in the distance mode: Postgraduate students' perspectives, challenges and strategies. *Asian Association of Open Universities Journal, 20*(1), 68–81. https://doi.org/10.1108/AAOUJ-07-2024-0099

Zhang, J., & Zhang, L. (2025). Exploring the profiles of foreign language learners' writing self-regulation: Focusing on individual differences. *Reading and Writing, 38*, 1533–1559. https://doi.org/10.1007/s11145-024-10568-x

Zhang, Z., Aubrey, S., Huang, X., & Chiu, T. K. F. (2025). The role of generative AI and hybrid feedback in improving L2 writing skills: A comparative study. *Innovation in Language Learning and Teaching*, 1–19. https://doi.org/10.1080/17501229.2025.2503890

Zimmerman, B. J., & Moylan, R. (2009). Where metacognition and motivation intersect. In D. J. Hacker, J. Dunlosky, & A. C. Graesser (Eds.), *Handbook of metacognition in education*. Routledge.

Author Index

A. Peña-Ayala (ed.), *Self-Regulated Learning*, Cognitive Technologies,
https://doi.org/10.1007/978-981-92-0658-2